# CORR

| Symbol | Explanation | Page |
|---|---|---|
| ⊙ | colon needed/used incorrectly | 350 |
| ⊙ | comma needed/used incorrectly | 347–50 |
| ⊖ | dash needed/used incorrectly | 351 |
| ⊙ | exclamation mark needed/used incorrectly | 353 |
| ⊙ | period needed/used incorrectly | |
| ⑦ | question mark needed/used incorrectly | 353 |
| ; | semicolon needed/used incorrectly | 350 |
| // | make sentence parallel | 346 |
| Pred | illogical predication | 346 |
| PV | shift in point of view | 343–44 |
| Q | quotation marks needed/used incorrectly | 351–53 |
| Ref | faulty pronoun reference | 342–43 |
| Rep | unnecessary repetition | |
| R-O | run-on (fused) sentence; find a correct way to join these independent clauses | 339–40 |
| Sp | spelling error | 356–57 |
| SqM | squinting modifier | 345 |
| S/V Agr | subject and verb do not agree | 340–42 |
| T | wrong verb tense | 343–44 |
| Trans | transition needed | 74–75 |
| Vague | find a more precise word or expression | 251–52 |
| Var | sentences lack variety | 269–70 |
| Wdy | wordy; express your idea more concisely | 246 |
| WW | wrong word; check a dictionary | |
| ∧ | caret—something has been left out | |
| ℮ | delete (leave out) | |
| ◡ | close up (base ball) | |
| / | separate; leave a space (alot) | |
| X | obvious error | |

# DISCOVERY

## An Inductive Approach
## to College Writing

# DISCOVERY
## An Inductive Approach
## to College Writing

### Bonnie Klomp Stevens
The College of Wooster

**Holt, Rinehart and Winston**

New York   Chicago   San Francisco   Philadelphia
Montreal   Toronto   London   Sydney
Tokyo   Mexico City   Rio de Janeiro   Madrid

*In memory of my father,*

HENRY DEWITT KLOMP

Cover Design: Gloria Gentile
Book Design: Gloria Moyer

Acknowledgments of copyrighted materials appear on p. 359.

**Library of Congress Cataloging in Publication Data**

Stevens, Bonnie Klomp.
  Discovery, an inductive approach to college writing.

  Includes index.
  1. English language—Rhetoric.  2. English language—
Grammar—1950-     .  3. College readers.  I. Title.
PE1408.S747 1983       808'.042       82-9329
ISBN 0-03-059216-X       AACR2

CBS COLLEGE PUBLISHING
Holt, Rinehart and Winston
The Dryden Press
Saunders College Publishing

# PREFACE

**D**iscovery attempts to draw on the strengths of the traditional college composition course while offering students a new approach to learning about writing. I think that there is much that is sound and valuable in most composition courses and textbooks: I think we are right to ask our students to examine the writing process, to give them practice in writing the various kinds of essays that will be required of them during their college years, to encourage them to develop clearer and more graceful styles, and to help them eliminate from their writing the technical errors that undermine their confidence and distract their readers. Still, although we may be giving our students excellent advice, we may be frustrated by their seeming inability to follow it. Too often, students see their role in the composition class as largely passive. The textbook and the teacher do most of the work; it is the students' job to memorize the rules printed in the textbook and to absorb the principles the teacher discusses in class—whether or not the rules seem logical or the principles seem convincing. When it is time to write a paper and students must suddenly become active, they may well grow confused, finding it difficult to apply principles that they had accepted passively but never fully understood. Their confusion is probably inevitable unless we can find a way to get students actively involved in the process of discovering the rules and principles they will be asked to apply in their papers.

This textbook attempts to give students a more active role in the composition classroom by taking an inductive approach to learning about writing. That is, instead of asking students to memorize rules and principles, the text presents students with evidence—stronger and weaker essays, groups of paragraphs or sentences—and asks them to discover principles and rules of good writing for themselves. The first chapter, for example, asks students to contrast several pairs of essays and paragraphs and then to draw conclusions about audience, topic selection, and thesis statements; Chapter 15 asks students to examine groups of correctly punctuated sentences, to discover the patterns of punctuation in each, and to infer and express rules for themselves.

During the last four years, I have experimented with the inductive approach in my composition classes and have found that it offers both students and teachers a number of advantages. Students understand and remember concepts they discover for themselves more clearly and fully than they do concepts they absorb from a textbook. Further, while working on inducing the principles or rules in any chapter, students practice various skills fundamental to writing and to logical thinking. For example, while attempting to discover the principle governing the punctuation in a group of sentences, students must observe, notice similarities and differences, and generalize about particulars—skills that will serve them well in almost any kind of writing. In addition, the approach requires students to write about what they discover, expressing sometimes subtle and complex ideas about writing in their own words. When these inductive exercises are done in class (as they should be), students get a sense of writing for an audience that is present, responsive, and demanding—their classmates. When one student discovers a principle and tries to express it, other students are likely to respond with criticisms and suggestions: "I still don't understand—say it a different way," or "That doesn't make sense to me," or "It would be clearer if you said it this way. . . . " Thus, students constantly remind each other of the need to make their statements clear and logical. Classes become livelier as students argue about why one essay is stronger than another and draw their own conclusions about how essays should be written; even classes on such seemingly mundane subjects as grammar and mechanics become more interesting, for attempting to spot the pattern in a group of sentences has something of the fascination of a puzzle. The inductive approach also reminds both teachers and students of the tentative nature of all the principles and rules we can devise about writing: there is always the possibility that we will discover new evidence, always the possibility that we will have to modify the conclusions we have just reached.

The inductive approach also offers the teacher a more active and satisfying role in the classroom. Most textbooks are designed to be read rather than taught: they present the ideas, leaving the teacher with little to do aside from summarizing what the students read about the night before. The teacher who wishes to take a more active role must devote much time and ingenuity to devising classroom activities. The inductive approach encourages the teacher to direct the students' discoveries by helping them to examine the evidence. The teacher's ability to guide discussions and to ask questions that will draw students out is thus crucial to the success of every exercise. The teacher does not, however, have to devote a great deal of time to class preparation: there is no need to think of a way to approach a discussion of paragraphing or of subject/verb agreement, for the text provides an approach.

The text is divided into four parts. Each of the chapters in the first two parts, "The Process of Writing a Paper" and "Varieties of Essays," is divided into three sections: Introductory Readings, Advice, and Application. The Introductory Readings sections contain inductive exercises, which generally ask students to compare sample student essays or paragraphs, to comment on their strengths and weaknesses, and then to draw general conclusions about the characteristics of a well-developed paragraph, of a strong comparison-and-contrast essay, of a logical argument, and so forth. I have found that it is best to work with pairs of student essays rather than with single essays, because students are more likely to be truly critical when they are asked to make comparisons. When I tried presenting my students with just one good student essay, they would admire it dutifully but often could not explain why they liked it; when I paired the good essay with a similar but weaker one, the students were usually able to identify the qualities that made one essay superior. The teacher can use these Introductory Readings to get students thinking and talking about a stage in the writing process or about a particular kind of essay, helping them to arrive at generalizations about the kinds of paragraphs and essays they find effective. After the students have discussed the Introductory Readings thoroughly in class, the teacher can assign the Advice section. The Advice sections, which take a more deductive approach, stress the process of writing: for example, after using the Introductory Readings in Chapter 5 to discover the characteristics of a strong descriptive essay, the student can turn to the Advice section to find suggestions about the processes of observation, reflection, and organization. The Application sections contain exercises designed to help students remember and apply ideas brought out in class discussions and in the Advice sections. Some exercises are designed for classes or small groups, and some would work best as individual assignments; some exercises give students sample sentences, paragraphs, or essays to analyze, and some ask them to work with their own writing.

In deciding which kinds of essays to discuss in "Varieties of Essays," I have been guided by Mina Shaughnessy's argument that students need to master seven kinds of writing in order to be prepared for the sorts of writing assignments they will be given outside the composition classroom—from lab reports (narration) to research papers (among others, comparison and contrast, causal analysis, summary, and interpretation). I find Shaughnessy's classification clearer and more practical than the usual classifications of topics or modes of development and have therefore devoted one chapter to each kind of writing she discusses, moving from the generally less difficult, more "personal" ones (narration and description) to the more difficult and "objective" ones (argumentation, summary, interpretation). Since many composition teachers like to assign a definition essay, I have also included a chapter on definition.

The third part of the text, "Some Principles of Style," contains two chapters that discuss such principles as economy, precision, and variety. Students discover these principles through inductive exercises and then apply them in more conventional exercises. I suggest combining the discussion of these stylistic principles with the discussion of various kinds of essays, rather than covering all the style exercises as a group. The Instructor's Manual suggests some ways of making connections.

"Discovering Principles of Grammar and Mechanics," the fourth part of the text, contains four chapters designed to help students identify and avoid some common grammatical and mechanical problems. The exercises in these chapters ask students to infer principles of grammar and mechanics through examining groups of correct sentences or through contrasting correct and incorrect sentences. The first few pages of Chapter 14 ("Sentence Vocabulary, Structure, and Form") acquaint students with the few terms they will need to know in order to do the exercises in this part of the text. One of the advantages of using the inductive approach to study grammar and mechanics is that when students write their own rules, they avoid such technical terms as the perpetually confusing "nonrestrictive clause" and instead suggest more concrete, helpful descriptions such as "clauses that interrupt the sentence but don't affect its meaning." Some teachers may prefer to make the exercises in these chapters a regular part of the course, perhaps reserving one day a week for discussing grammar and mechanics; some teachers may prefer to use these chapters on an *ad hoc* basis, discussing these problems in class or in conference only when they appear in student papers; and some teachers may find that some or all of the exercises in these chapters are too elementary for their students.

The Appendix is a brief list of grammatical and mechanical conventions, designed to help students correct technical errors in their essays. The detailed correction chart at the end of the book is keyed to this appendix; teachers who prefer to use the correction symbols in the front of the book will find that many of the page numbers listed there also refer to this appendix.

In addition to giving answers to exercises and suggesting paper topics for each chapter in Parts I and II, the Instructor's Manual contains several sections that may be particularly helpful to new composition teachers. The sample syllabi illustrate ways to adapt the text for one-semester and two-semester courses and for "regular" and developmental courses. Analyses of sample essays suggest ways of commenting on student writing. The manual also contains some guidelines for student groups that meet to exchange and criticize rough drafts. A copy of the manual may be obtained from your local Holt representative or by writing to the English Editor, College Department, Holt, Rinehart and Winston, 383 Madison Avenue, New York, New York 10017.

Like many other composition teachers, I am greatly indebted to Mina Shaughnessy's *Errors and Expectations*. Shaughnessy's advocacy of an inductive approach first gave me the idea for this textbook, and her remarkable insights into the teaching of writing have been my frequent guide as I prepared the manuscript. I have also received valuable guidance from the following reviewers, who pointed out many weaknesses in the original manuscript and gave me practical suggestions for overcoming those weaknesses: Joseph Cosenza, St. John's University; Dorothy Guinn, Arizona State University; Rosalie Hewitt, Northern Illinois University; Andrea Lunsford, University of British Columbia; Walter E. Meyers, North Carolina State University; Robert S. Rudolph, The University of Toledo; Christopher J. Thaiss, George Mason University; and Joseph Trimmer, Ball State University. Further, I am grateful to several people at Holt, Rinehart and Winston: to Kyle Schmalz for her interest and encouragement when the text was in the earliest stages, to Susan Katz for her confidence in my work, to Anne Boynton-Trigg and Emily Barrosse for their assistance, and, especially, to Nedah Abbott for her patience and good advice.

Many people at the College of Wooster also contributed to this book. I am grateful to my colleagues in the English Department for their interest in my work and for creating a stimulating, congenial atmosphere that makes work possible. I am particularly grateful to Marlene Gast, formerly at Wooster and now at Boston College, who tested much of the material in this textbook in her own classes and suggested many improvements. A number of other people, both students and staff members, have contributed by offering ideas, reviewing portions of the manuscript, or helping with the typing: Susannah Bowne, Isabel Clark, Mary Edson, David Martin, Douglas Ohm, Sharon Patrick, Carol Roose, Carolyn Selby, S. J. Stevens, and Carol White. I owe a special debt to the hundreds of composition students I have had over the past four years, who suffered patiently and cheerfully as I tested early versions of the material in this text. Their cooperation and suggestions have been invaluable.

In this, as in everything else I have attempted during the last twelve years, my greatest debt is to my husband, Dennis Stevens. He has read and proofread every page of this manuscript and has consistently been my most perceptive and helpful critic. His generosity with his time, his encouragement, and his wisdom have made my job much easier and more enjoyable; they have also made this textbook much better than it could otherwise have been.

Wooster, Ohio                                                     **B.K.S.**
February, 1982

# Student Contributors

I am grateful to the students who gave me permission to print their essays and paragraphs in *Discovery*.

Linda Atkinson
Penelope J. Babcock
Katharine L. Blood
Susannah Bowne
Amy Brockett
Duncan Cameron
Laura Chambers
Annette Cooper
Addison Davis
Michelle Day
Valerie DeBonis
Roya Dehdashti
Phillip E. Donaldson
William Duke
Joshua L. Edwards
Melissa G. Fearon
Stephen Ferguson
Cynthia Force
Patricia A. Galster
John Gilbert
Melvin Graves, Jr.
Scott Hanna

Chip E. Hanson
Mark Janezic
Simone Jowett
Kim Kanney
Anthony Krajcik
James Lawless
Sarah Lynn
Maria Margevicius
Douglas B. McGillivray
Robert Merrill
Teresa Monteleone
Sue Pyecroft
Donna Roach
William St. John
John Schmidt
Sally Schultz
Chris Thomas
Miguel Valencia
Bruce Wiebusch
Lorraine Wilkin
Courtney Wilson

# Contents

# Introduction:
# The Inductive Approach

How do we form our ideas and opinions about writing? In one of my composition classes, I asked the students to identify some of the characteristics of good writing. We soon had a long list on the board: good writing, the students said, is clear, orderly, interesting, informative, moving, humorous, to-the-point, flowing, honest. I then asked the students how they had arrived at their ideas—why did they believe that these were indeed the characteristics of good writing? Some of the ideas we had listed, it turned out, came from teachers or textbooks. Most of the ideas, however, came from the students' own experiences as readers and writers. The students enjoyed reading informative essays and therefore concluded that good writing is informative; since they were most pleased with their own work when it struck them as clear, they concluded that clarity is a characteristic of good writing.

We could say that these students had arrived at most of their ideas about writing *inductively*. Inductive thinking is rooted in our experiences and observations: we make a number of observations, detect a pattern in what we have observed, and then draw a general conclusion. For example, we might examine the syllabi for several history courses, notice that all have long reading lists, and conclude that history courses generally require a great deal of reading. Inductive thinking thus moves from the particular to the general. Deductive thinking, by contrast, moves from the general to the particular: we start with a general statement that we accept as true and then draw out its specific implications. For example, if we believe that history courses generally require a great deal of reading, we might conclude that a particular history course that will be offered next term will probably have a long reading list.

Logicians agree that both inductive and deductive thinking are valid. Further, both can be used in the study of writing. Most composition textbooks take a primarily deductive approach. The authors begin by giving you general principles about writing—"Paragraphs should have topic sentences," for example, or "Use a semicolon to separate two independent clauses not connected by a conjunction." It is then your job to apply these general principles to particular cases, either in textbook exercises or in your own writing: "This paragraph is weak because it doesn't have a topic sentence," or "This sentence is incorrectly punctuated because it has a comma, not a semicolon, separating two independent clauses not connected by a conjunction."

This textbook, by contrast, takes a primarily inductive approach to the study of writing. Instead of giving you general rules and principles to apply, it gives you samples of writing to study so that you can draw your own conclusions. Some chapters ask you to make comparisons: for example, you might be asked to read several descriptive essays, analyze their strengths and weaknesses, identify the various techniques the authors use, and then draw your own conclusions about what makes a descriptive essay good. Other chapters ask you to study groups of paragraphs or sentences, notice what they have in common, and then draw your own conclusions about paragraph structure, style, or punctuation. All of these exercises ask you to think inductively, to move from particular observations to general conclusions.

The deductive approach certainly has a place in the composition course—I use it from time to time in this textbook, for the sake of clarity and efficiency. On the whole, however, I prefer the inductive approach, and the students I have had over the last several years have tended to agree. The inductive approach makes learning about writing more active and enjoyable: discovering something for ourselves is more challenging and satisfying than absorbing generalizations that someone else provides. We are also more likely to understand concepts fully and remember them clearly if we can see that they are firmly based in our own observations. The inductive approach also reminds us of the tentative nature of our ideas about writing: there is always the possibility that we will observe something new and will consequently have to modify the conclusions we have just reached. The inductive approach seems to me to offer a natural, flexible, and effective way of learning about writing. Accordingly, although this textbook does offer you some direct advice about writing, most of its pages are devoted to providing you with evidence to examine—essays, paragraphs, and sentences, almost all written by college students. It is up to you to use this evidence well—to observe closely, to detect patterns, and to draw careful and perceptive conclusions.

# PART 1

# THE PROCESS OF WRITING A PAPER

**N**ovelist Joseph Conrad once described the writer's lot as "hard labor for life." His remark is both discouraging and reassuring— discouraging because it warns us that no amount of study and practice will make writing easy, reassuring because it reminds us that college students are not the only ones who find it difficult to develop, organize, and express their ideas. Still, although all writers face the same difficulties, experienced and inexperienced writers generally do not approach these difficulties in the same way. Experienced writers are less likely to find writing agonizing and intimidating because they have come to enjoy its frustrations as challenges, confident that by the end of their struggles they will have produced something worth writing. Unlike inexperienced writers, they usually do not try to go straight from an initial idea to a finished essay and conse- quently do not spend so many hours staring at a blank sheet of paper, waiting for the right words to appear. Instead, experienced writers usually have found some process that they can follow as they write, a process that helps them to see writing as a manageable task by reminding them to work on one problem at a time.

It is useful, then, to begin a composition course by looking at the process of writing, by examining the steps writers follow as they strive to find just what they want to say and just how they want to say it. The process may not be exactly the same every time a writer works, and not all writers follow exactly the same process. Writing would be neither as demanding nor as rewarding as it is if the pro- cess could be reduced to a series of distinct, predetermined steps that would always lead to the desired destination. You will probably find that only some of the techniques discussed in the following chapters will work for you, that you will have to reject some and modify others. The important thing is that you discover *some* process, so that you will not be overwhelmed by the impossible task of trying to do everything at once. The process you devise will be in some ways unique to you, but it will almost certainly include ways of planning, organizing, and revising: you must find some way to decide what you want to say, some way to order your ideas, and some way to evaluate and polish what you have written.

In the following three chapters, the Introductory Readings are designed to help you set your goals, to determine where you want to be at the end of your writing process: What kinds of essays and paragraphs would you like to be writing? The Advice sections of these chapters suggest ways of reaching the goals you have set. Finally, the Application sections ask you to use what you have learned by commenting on other students' writing and by experimenting with your own.

# 1.
# Defining Your Topic:
## From Idea to Thesis

## INTRODUCTORY READINGS AND EXERCISES

**A.** Both the following essays were written in response to the same assignment in a college composition course: "Suppose that the college newspaper asked you to write a guest editorial about a political, social, or academic problem about which you feel strongly. Your goal is to convince your readers that the problem you are describing is real and important." Two students decided to write about poor conditions in this country's prisons and jails. Read both essays and compare them carefully.

### The Culbert County Jail

Most have heard stories about the conditions in our country's prisons and jails. These range from horror stories about intolerable and dehumanizing conditions to complaints that our jails are merely "country clubs" supported by the taxpayer. Some jails may have adequate facilities; the only jail I have seen, however, did not. Throughout my junior year I was a member of a group of students who made weekly visits to the inmates of the Culbert County Jail. The jail is only a twenty-minute walk from the campus, but in that twenty-minute period one is transferred from the idealistic world of college life to the harsh reality of a jail cell.

Upon my first visit to the jail, I was in for a surprise. An old two-story, red-brick building served as the jail. Ironically, the old building had originally been a school. Inside, there were two main cells, one on the first floor for those awaiting trial, and one on the second floor for those who had already been sentenced. The men on the second floor were crowded in a dimly lit room that provided no means of recreation for the inmates. Only after talking with the men who had been in the jail for nearly a year did I begin to get a sense of the loneliness and boredom that characterize prison life. Apathy is also a problem. Crowded away in a dark room, it is easy to imagine that the whole world has cast you off. Thus, apathy and poor morale are among the most serious problems in a jail.

As lonely as these men were, some refused to talk with us. I could not help feeling that these men viewed us as part of the "establishment" that put them in there. Many of the men, however, did choose to talk with us. As they crowded up against the iron bars, each member of our group would begin a conversation with one of the men. It was during these times that I learned that many of the inmates could not be considered hard-core criminals. Some were in for violations such as driving without a license. Since they could not afford to pay the fine, they had no choice but to serve their sentences. Others had wives and children whom they told us about. Although the men's desire to see them again was a real source of strength and comfort, it was also a source of torment since they could not see them now.

While it was tough for those with families, it was even harder for those who were alone. One man in his seventies, Mr. Peterson, had been rejected by his family. They would not even provide him with enough money for a private lawyer—which they could afford—when it came time for his trial. Then there was Randy. He was young, about college age, and alone. I remember the day we read in the paper that he had killed himself in his jail cell.

Near the end of the year, the inmates were moved from the jail into the newly constructed Justice Center. The jail, now abandoned, stands as a monument to the lives of the men it touched. For a while we visited the men in their new accommodations. Here we were able to sit face-to-face with the men as we talked. Surprisingly, we discovered that they had many of the same problems here as in the old jail. While this center was built to provide recreation for the men there, it had failed to do so. After the expense of building the new Justice Center, the county found that it could not afford the expense of hiring someone to direct the program. Loneliness was still a problem; it only took on a new form. There was more room in this jail, but the men were forced to spend more time in their individual cells, as if in solitary. The fact that the new Justice Center had promised so much and yielded so little became a new cause of apathy for the men.

The transition to the Justice Center was to provide additional problems. It would mean the end of our group. Upon our arrival at the jail one evening, we discovered that, because of the complex setup, we would no longer be able to visit the men unless there were three guards on duty. Since there were only two guards on duty at a time, it became impossible for us to visit until further notice. As we were leaving, we glanced toward the upper floor where the men were kept. All was quiet.

## Prisons

You have probably heard one of those occasional news reports about parents who have locked their retarded children in an attic for several years. In these rare incidents, the parents do not understand retardation and go to extremes to avoid dealing with it. This method of avoiding a problem by locking it away from you does little toward solving the problem. The same method of avoiding problems exists on a much larger scale as the United States prison system. Clearly, the prison system's main purpose is to lock up the deviants who threaten society. What is even clearer is that the system does little in the way of rehabilitation.

The prison system is supposed to protect the public and both rehabilitate and punish criminals. The system does protect the public from known criminals by caging them up away from society. The system does not rehabilitate prisoners, however. The large percentage of inmates who return to prison repeatedly is evidence of this lack of rehabilitation. The rehabilitation procedures presently used are ineffective. For example, in any sort of group or individual therapy, the prisoner is caught in a predicament. The prisoner could risk getting a longer sentence by revealing his true inner thoughts, or he could tell the therapists what they want to hear in hopes of getting out sooner. Finally, the prison life does punish criminals, often in unintended ways. Social deviants are not only isolated from society; they are also forced to abstain from heterosexual activity, meaningful work, and any sense of responsibility. This denial of heterosexual activity leads to the widespread occurrence of homosexual rape. It seems that when someone is being sentenced to prison, he is also being sentenced to homosexual attack. The work that prison systems give to inmates has not gone above making license plates. In short, if you feel that the prison system's main purpose is to punish criminals, then you are probably happy with the way it is being run. If you believe that prisons should rehabilitate criminals, then you are probably unsatisfied with the existing system.

Prisons have often been called "schools of crime." The belief is that the prison environment reinforces and instills more deviant behavior. The result is that in addition to not rehabilitating, prisons further corrupt individuals. What is the cost of more fully corrupting criminals? More than twelve billion dollars a year. It costs us thousands of dollars a year to lock up one of society's thousands of criminals. In other words, it is costing society twelve billion dollars a year to avoid dealing with deviant individuals. In view of the extreme expense, the lack of rehabilitation, and the waste of human potential created by prisons, why not eliminate them? Unless there is a revolutionary change in the methods used for treating deviant individuals, the twelve billion dollars a year would be better spent in researching the energy problem. Our current system is undoubtedly a waste of money and effort. We must find a better way to rehabilitate deviant individuals.

## DISCUSSION QUESTIONS

1. Which essay held your interest more? Why?
2. The assignment asks the students to imagine that they are writing editorials for their college newspaper. Presumably, then, the editorials would be read by students, faculty, and administrators, and perhaps by alumni and trustees as well. How would you expect such readers to respond to "The Culbert County Jail"? How would you expect them to respond to "Prisons"?
3. Which author seems to know more about the subject? How can you tell?
4. Compare the introductory and concluding paragraphs of both essays. Does each essay begin and end well? Does the first paragraph of each give you a clear idea of what the essay will be about?
5. Notice the specific examples cited in paragraphs 3 and 4 of "The Culbert County Jail." What effect might these examples have on the reader? Why doesn't the author tell us what crimes Randy and Mr. Peterson committed? What is the effect of referring to these men by name? Compare these paragraphs with paragraph 2 of "Prisons." What important differences do you notice?
6. Both authors occasionally use the terms "inmates" and "prisoners" to refer to the people in prisons, but each author uses other terms as well. What terms does each author use most frequently? Does this difference in language reflect a difference in the authors' attitudes toward prisons and prisoners? Explain.
7. Do you notice any other differences between the language of "The Culbert County Jail" and the language of "Prisons"? How might these differences in language influence a reader's reactions to the essays?
8. If the authors planned to revise their essays, what advice would you give them? List some ways of improving both essays.

**B.** Following are two essays written by the same student. The first is an in-class essay describing why this student decided to attend a particular college; the second is a revision written at the end of the semester. In both cases, the student was free to choose and define her own topic. Compare the original and the revision carefully.

### Original Essay

College has become an essential piece in the puzzle of education. If I do not get any college experience, I will not be able to go
into the field that I enjoy. I chose Edson College because it will
give me the courses I need, because it has modern facilities, and
because it will provide me with an atmosphere in which I can
grow. Edson College has all of the essential ingredients needed to
make me into a part of society.

The college has a program of almost unlimited fields, including
a strong department in my field, business management. Because
Edson has a good course selection, it will broaden my knowledge
and help me to become a well-rounded individual. It will also give
me a solid background in business, so that I can get a good job
when I graduate.

Edson also offers good facilities. The science buildings are especially impressive. Also, the dormitories are comfortable, and the
student center offers lots of extras. The athletic complex is a
large one and offers facilities for many sports. Since I love tennis,
I was especially happy to see that there are so many tennis courts
on campus.

However, courses are not the only requirement for a good college, and neither are facilities. The students are what any college
is made of, and that's why I have chosen Edson. There are lots of
interesting students here, from all kinds of places including over-
seas. The students are friendly and kindhearted, considerate and
helping, but most of all they are serious about what they are
doing here and why they are doing it. College is a place to grow
up and realize that you have a purpose and that college is going
to help you realize your full potential.

I will grow up at Edson College and become a person in society
who functions as a helper for all others when they come to this
point. College will be a place to have fun, but it will also be a
place to learn how to live with others and with myself. This college will make me look at myself during my four-year stay, and I
hope I will heed the advice so that I can become happy within
myself. There are lots of good courses here, and the facilities are
modern and well kept. It makes things pleasant for me to be
around such an enjoyable place. My mind and body should be able
to function here with the quiet and modern surroundings. This
college sums up what I will need in the next four years, and that
along with the people who live here will make me a person who
can be lived with and needed throughout my entire life.

### Revision

When I came to Edson College for an interview last spring, a
sophomore named Ellen took me on a tour of the campus. As we
approached the student center, she noticed a large piece of broken

glass lying in the parking lot. "Someone could puncture a tire on this," Ellen said, almost to herself, and she picked up the piece of glass and casually tossed it into a trash barrel. I think it was then that I seriously began to consider coming to Edson, for I was really struck by Ellen's instinctive concern for the college and the people connected with it. During my day on campus, I met several other students who obviously shared Ellen's concern for the college and were proud of themselves and of the work they were doing. Other colleges I visited had wide course selections and modern facilities, but Edson began to seem special to me because of its students.

Ellen took me to see some of the academic buildings during the morning, and I noticed how busy and serious most of the students seemed. As we walked slowly through the halls of Bradford, I could hear all sorts of voices coming from the rooms we passed: not just professors lecturing, but students asking questions, making arguments, and laughing at jokes. We sat in on a history class later in the morning, and I noticed that almost half of the twenty students in the class asked a question or made a comment at some point. Most of those who didn't talk were taking notes and seemed to be paying attention. When the period ended, many of the students, of course, charged out of the room immediately. Several other students lingered to ask the professor questions, however, and a few others, as they left the room, continued talking about the subject that had been discussed. I had never seen so much student interest at my high school, so I was really impressed. I began to think that maybe Edson was a place where a student could be serious about his studies and not have to feel embarrassed about it all the time.

Ellen announced that we were going to the main dining hall for lunch, and I began to feel nervous about being the only high-school student in a room full of hundreds of college students. I should not have felt nervous at all, for the people I met were friendly. We sat down at a table with five of Ellen's friends; she introduced me, and everyone said "hello." Right away, they got me involved in the conversation by asking me where I was from, why I wanted to come to Edson, what I might major in—not terribly original questions, but I was grateful to them for trying to make me feel comfortable. When I had visited other campuses, most of the students had ignored me when they found out I was still in high school, so I was surprised and pleased by the friendliness I found here.

After lunch, Ellen took me to see several dormitories. The one I liked best was Beumler Hall, where foreign students and American students can live together and put on programs such as international dinners, slide shows, foreign dances, and so forth.

Ellen told me that about 100 international students go to Edson, from about fifty different countries. I was excited by this news because I've always wanted to travel outside the United States but have never been able to do so. I figured that going to a college with lots of international students and maybe living in Beumler would help me to find out about other countries, so that I could decide which ones I most wanted to visit whenever I finally get a chance to travel. I also thought that it would be stimulating to have students from other countries in my classes, especially political science or history classes: for example, I think it's interesting to hear what a student from Taiwan has to say about our foreign policy, or what a Japanese student has to say about World War II.

Toward the end of the afternoon, I asked Ellen what she liked best about Edson. She didn't even have to think about it for a moment: "The people," she said. Although I had only spent one day at Edson, I already agreed. I liked the diversity of Edson's student body, and I also liked the people I had met. I thought that being around people who studied hard and cared about their work would encourage me to do my best, and I knew that I would need all of their friendship during my first time away from home. By the time I boarded the plane for home that night, I knew that I would tell my parents that Edson was now my first choice.


## DISCUSSION QUESTIONS

1. If you were director of admissions at Edson College and wanted to send copies of one of these essays to prospective students, which essay would you decide to send? Why? Which essay makes Edson College seem more attractive?

2. The revised essay is based upon ideas discussed in paragraph 4 of the original. Suppose that the author had instead decided to base her revision on paragraph 3 of the original—the paragraph about the college's facilities. Underline all the vague expressions in this paragraph. How could the author replace these vague phrases with information that would make her description of the facilities more concrete and convincing?

3. Make suggestions for improving paragraph 2 of the original essay. What does the author mean by such phrases as "a good course selection," "broaden my knowledge," "a well-rounded individual," "a solid background," and "a good job"? How could the author clarify the ideas in this paragraph—for the reader and for herself?

4. Compare the introductory paragraphs of the original and the revision. How do the two paragraphs differ? Which did you find more interesting?

5. Notice how often the author repeats ideas in the original version.

Why do you think she repeats herself so often, especially toward the end of the essay?

6. If the author were to revise the essay again, what advice would you give her? List some ways of improving the revision.

C. In an advanced composition course, the professor asked the students to write papers describing and commenting on the education they received before coming to college. The professor told the students that they could approach this topic in any way they liked. Read the following two essays, both written in response to that assignment, and compare them carefully.

## My Education up to Date

On January 31, 1960, at 7:35 A.M., I was given my life. Surprised but pleased, I was of the female gender, and my proud parents named me Mary Lou James. From that day forward my life was one learning experience after another.

Being brought up with older brothers was a big part of my education. I was always warned about what to expect in things ahead. I was always anxious to do better and learn more so that I could be as good (and as old!) as my brothers. Sometimes it was an advantage having older members in the family, but at times I was very afraid, knowing what might lie ahead.

Upon entering kindergarten and my grade-school years, I had many of those fears. I often wondered if I would ever be able to learn. Somehow, I overcame those fears and began my process of learning. In grade school, I learned the usual things like how to read, write, spell, basic math, science, and social studies. I had many pleasant and painful experiences during those years, and these played an important role in my education.

Junior high school had a lasting effect on me. This was the time when school became a whole new experience. The classes were different and harder than those in grade school, and it even offered some elective courses. I learned a lot during those years, not only academically but socially. I began to experience new situations with friends, both girls and boys. Those years I began to grow up. That was the school that prepared me for high school.

High school was an exciting adventure. It was a new surrounding, had new people, and introduced me to different classes. It was a whole new system. Classes were elected, not assigned. There was just so much more to do. There were clubs to join, teams to compete on, and many friendships to make. High school taught me so much about people and self-confidence. My life began to take shape in high school. That was when I decided to go to college.

It would be wrong at this point to say that this brings my education up to date. Schooling and academic achievements were not my only education. The most significant part of my education came from my home and my family. My parents helped me to relate my education to my life by teaching me to try to put things into perspective. They gave me their trust and support when I needed it. They allowed me to develop my own thoughts and ideas and gave me the responsibility for making my own mistakes and learning from them. Most of all, they gave me their love. My brothers, too, were always very helpful and supportive in many ways.

After eighteen years of schooling and education, I've realized that the learning process never ends. One can never learn enough.

## It's Time to Play

Open any newspaper or magazine and you are bound to find an article written by a deeply concerned English fanatic describing the decline of students' writing skills in today's high schools and colleges. I can't disagree with these authors, but their essays don't help me—they just make me chew harder at the end of my pencil and pull a few more hairs out of my head. These analysts, after all, are not the ones with the problem—we students are! The ironic thing is that our inadequate writing skills often prevent us from expressing our own ideas about the issue. Frankly, I would love to take several of my C− papers back to my high-school and grade-school teachers to show them a product of their teaching skills. These teachers all said that they loved children and wanted to make education "fun"; however, they often neglected to teach us about such details as reading and writing.

I cannot remember when my last spelling test took place. I believe it was somewhere in the sixth grade when we were still having spelling bees. Yes, spelling bees, the all-American school game! If you can spell, that's terrific! You get the prize at the end while everyone else stares at you, green with envy. If you cannot spell, the quiz games do nothing more than to seat you back at your desk as the team continues without you. In my case, I worried more about not being the last one chosen for a team than I did about learning how to spell the words. Of course, spelling bees are only one example of the games played. Teachers can think of anything from various versions of *Jeopardy* to a form of *Hollywood Squares*. If you don't have any knowledge to begin with, you never learn anything extra. This, need I say, is not educational.

Games are only one form of fun. Recreational learning has become the next exciting exercise. The three R's today are becoming recreational imagination, recreational objectivity, and recreational thought. All put together, this is the recreational process. Instead of making education fun, education teaches us how to have fun. Must I recollect the many projects we had to make for social studies, math, and science? My grade-school projects consisted of many messy clay structures, numerous attempts at posters and collages, layouts of Indian villages, and my favorite attempt at artistry—my papier-mâché starfish. Naturally, children need to be creative, but not at the expense of learning. Creativity also lies in the education of the mind. No doubt, my starfish was creative—I did receive an A for my creativity. I remember the excitement of getting that A. To this day, though, I am sorry to say that I don't know the first thing about starfish. Almost everyone else in my sixth-grade science class suffered the same lack of learning. For weeks the room was flooded with everything from papier-mâché starfishes to moon craters. I have no hang-up about starfish or moon craters, except that about 90 percent of the class traded writing a paper for making a project. Those who chose to write papers benefitted in the long run, while I got stuck with a decrepit red starfish made out of newspapers and dried peas.

So much for fun and games. Soon we were too old for that and had to learn to develop our minds. In about the seventh grade I began to write for the teachers. Most of them said the same thing: I had a creative mind. That was obvious—I had a starfish to prove it. My A's were for the ideas behind the work, not for the work itself. I still hear that sentence over and over in my mind: "You have the potential to be a good writer if only you would work on your vocabulary." I got the A but never the help on vocabulary, grammar, or any type of constructive English skills. Grammar, like math, is learned from your mistakes. But in math we saw our mistakes, and were corrected for them. We started all over again before going on to the next level. Grammar and sentence structure need to be the same way. I was allowed to slip by with bad grammar because I had "creativity." I kept continuing on to other levels without stopping to correct errors. With this problem, I entered high school.

High school was basically the same. Even though I often got C's for my work, my "skills" slipped by because I was neither a poor nor an excellent student, only "average." Again, when I got A's it was because of my original ideas. (Incidentally, "original" was a word I learned in second-grade vocabulary. Many thanks to that teacher for starting me off on the right track, even though later I never surpassed that level.) My original, imaginative ideas got shuffled up somewhere in high school because I didn't have the necessary structure and organization to express them properly. High schools play the game of senior "mini-courses." The titles were so inviting that I dropped Academic English to take some courses called Science Fiction, Film and Society, and The

Literature of Crime and Detection. Little did I suspect that I was
no longer considered an Academic English student. What I was, I
don't know, but I blew my final chance to try seriously to educate
myself. Luckily the courses I chose were some of the better ones,
but I cannot say I benefitted as much as I could have. I continued
to get A's on my papers and in my classes despite the fact that
my below-average SAT scores put me down a few notches. Even
with my shaky writing background, I managed to get into a good
college.

Well, here I am at college, still trying to make my writing re-
spectable so that I can finally begin to learn how to write. Sadly
enough, there are many who have a worse writing problem than I
do. And there are many like us out there somewhere who have
their names on admissions records for colleges throughout the
United States. They are in for a surprise! They will soon find out
that they cannot write at all. I am sorry to say that I can be of no
assistance. If the games would cease and the educating begin,
then students might learn to write better. Educating the mind is
a game in itself, but you need to play it right. Students first need
to learn some basic skills, and then the games can be enjoyable. If
things continue as they are, more and more students will know
more about constructing a papier-mâché starfish than they do
about constructing a sentence.

## DISCUSSION QUESTIONS

1.  Which author seems more interested in her topic? How can you
    tell? Which essay was more interesting to *you?* Why?
2.  The two authors seem to be writing on the same topic—each de-
    scribes her education from grade school to college. This seems a
    very broad topic. Has either author managed to limit her topic in
    any way? How?
3.  Look at paragraph 2 of "My Education up to Date." What did the
    author learn from her brothers? If the author wanted to revise this
    paragraph, what advice would you give her?
4.  Which paragraph in "My Education up to Date" did you find most
    interesting? Could the author build an entire essay around this
    paragraph? How?
5.  In "It's Time to Play," the author refers several times to a papier-
    mâché starfish she made in elementary school. Why do you think
    she refers to it so often?
6.  Compare the last sentence in paragraph 1 of "It's Time to Play"
    with these possible revisions:

    *Original:* These teachers all said that they loved children and
    wanted to make education "fun"; however, they often ne-
    glected to teach us about such details as reading and writing.

*Revision A:* My elementary and secondary school education was inadequate in several ways.

*Revision B:* My teachers didn't put much emphasis on teaching us how to read and write. Most of their energy was devoted to trying to make education "fun" for us. These teachers all said that they loved children very much.

*Revision C:* In this paper, I will discuss (1) the ways in which my teachers tried to make education "fun," (2) their neglect of subjects such as reading and writing, and (3) my dissatisfaction with the education I received.

Explain why each of the revisions is inferior to the original sentence.

7. On the whole, which essay do you think is stronger? Why?

8. If the authors planned to revise their essays, what advice would you give them? List some ways of improving both essays.

**D.** On the first day of class in a freshman composition course, the teacher asked the students to write paragraphs about their approaches to writing papers. The students could approach this topic in any way they liked, she said: they could talk about the ideal approach to writing a paper, the approach they actually used, or an approach they had used in the past but meant to change. The following two paragraphs were written in response to that assignment.

It is extremely important to develop the habit of writing a good paper following certain steps, which can produce a well-organized and meaningful paper. Before a paper can be written, one must limit the topic. Later, the outline can be written from the notes. The subject is first introduced by a general statement and is followed by a thesis statement, which summarizes the theme of the paper. The other paragraphs should have topic sentences which support the thesis statement. Moreover, the paragraphs must have facts to support the ideas. The last part of the paper is the conclusion, which includes one's personal ideas and summarizes the paper. A good paper needs to follow the above-mentioned steps. In addition, one needs to apply a great deal of effort and concentration to his work.

Lots of students are delighted when the teacher says "write an essay about anything you like," but these open topic assignments always used to terrify me because I never had any ideas. However, when I took an expository writing course during my senior year in high school, I discovered that there are always lots of good topics around, if we know where to look for them. One time, for example, I had to write a comparison and contrast essay. I got a good idea for that paper when I remembered talking to my mother about the strict dress code she had to follow when she was in high school. I wrote a paper contrasting high-school discipline thirty years ago and today. When the class had to write persuasive essays, I remembered how mad I was the year before when my chemistry teacher dropped my grade in the course from about an A− to a C+ just because I blew the final exam. I wrote a paper arguing that final exams should be abolished or at least not counted so heavily. Lots of teachers think that TV isn't good for anything, but I've gotten some good ideas for papers from TV shows. For example, I got my idea for a research paper about an endangered species from watching an episode of *Wild Kingdom*. I also got ideas from remembering places I'd visited, people I'd met, and books I'd read. That expository writing course taught me lots of useful things, but one of the best things it did for me was to make me realize that I have lots of ideas that people would like to read about.

## DISCUSSION QUESTIONS

1. As someone who is beginning a study of writing, how did you respond to the first paragraph? What ideas did you find most helpful? Did you want the author to explain any ideas in more detail? Did you challenge any of the author's statements?
2. As someone who is beginning a study of writing, how did you respond to the second paragraph? Again, consider what ideas were most useful, what points need to be explained in more detail, and what statements might be challenged.
3. On the whole, which paragraph seems more likely to interest and help a beginning writer? Why?
4. How might a more experienced writer respond to the first paragraph? Your professor might suggest some responses to this question.
5. How might a more experienced writer respond to the second paragraph? Again, ask your professor for suggestions.
6. On the whole, which paragraph seems more likely to interest and help an experienced writer? Why?

## GENERAL CONCLUSIONS

Draw together all the observations and comments you have made about the introductory readings in this chapter. List some general conclusions about the differences between an excellent essay and a mediocre one. You might also try summarizing your conclusions in a paragraph that would be helpful to a beginning composition student: for example, what advice would you give to a student looking for a good topic for a short essay?

## ADVICE

During a conversation, your listeners help you to make what you say coherent and interesting. Listeners can guide you with a nod of the head that lets you know you have expressed an idea clearly, a puzzled look that tells you to explain further, a question that prompts you to reexamine a statement. If your listeners look interested, you know that the conversation is going well; if you see them yawning or glancing at their watches, you know that you are doing something wrong. Imagine how much more difficult and frightening speaking would be if you had no idea who your listeners were and could not see their expressions—and if, further, you had to speak for ten or fifteen minutes straight and knew that what you said would be graded.

Writing sometimes seems like trying to talk to someone who is unknown, unresponsive, or, worse yet, nonexistent; it is no wonder that most of us are far less confident as writers than we are as speakers. You may well feel isolated when you are writing. If you are sitting alone in your room at three o'clock in the morning, desperately trying to finish a paper, it is easy to forget that someone will eventually read what you write. But although remembering your readers is often extremely difficult, it is always extremely important. Just as paying attention to your listeners can help you to speak well, thinking about your readers can help you to keep your writing original, purposeful, honest, and clear.

### Identifying Your Readers

Identifying your readers is one of the first steps in the writing process. Sometimes you know a great deal about your readers—when you are writing a letter to a friend, for example, or writing a report for someone who has been your employer for years. At other times you may have to do some research to find out more about your readers. If you are writing a letter to the editor of a newspaper, it often helps to find out as much as you can about the people who read that newspaper; if you are writing a letter of application to a business firm, it makes sense to think about the qualities that particular firm might like to see in a potential employee.

Your most immediate concern, however, is probably with the readers for the papers you write in college. Professors sometimes identify your readers for you: for example, a professor might ask you to imagine that you are explaining a concept to a less experienced student or that you are writing for an audience of scholars. The most perplexing problems arise when your professor says nothing about your readers or tells you to write for a "general audience." In these situations, you will have to use your imagination to create an appropriate audience. If you do not think about your readers at all, you may end up writing something that does not communicate well with anyone; you may also become frustrated, lost, or inhibited because you feel as if you are writing in a vacuum.

It might help to exercise your imagination by thinking about what you would do in the following situations:

1. Suppose that your college has a Teaching Staff and Tenure Committee that makes all decisions about hiring, retaining, and promoting professors. You belong to a student group that would like to have the committee enlarged to include several voting student members. The other students ask you to write four letters explaining your group's goals:
   —a letter to be sent to all untenured professors
   —a letter to be sent to the tenured professor who chairs the Teaching Staff and Tenure Committee
   —a letter to be sent to all students, asking them to join your group (you know that most students support your aims)
   —a letter to the editor of your college newspaper
   What approach will you take in each of these letters? What ideas will you stress in each, and how will you make sure that each letter suits its readers?
2. In your composition class, you belong to a writing group in which students exchange papers and offer each other suggestions for revision. You know the other students in your group slightly: one seems very bright and tends to dominate class discussions, one disagrees with everything you say in class, and one always sits in the back of the room and seems bored with everything that goes on. Your next assignment asks you to argue for or against liberal abortion laws. Will knowing that these three students will read your essay influence you at all as you write?
3. On the first day of a music appreciation course, the professor assigns a paper asking you to explain and defend your tastes in music. As far as you know, the professor will be the only one to read the paper, and you know nothing about the professor. Can you come up with any idea of your audience that will help you as you write?

Discovering or imagining as much as you can about your audience, in addition to being a stimulating challenge in itself, can help you to prepare for the other challenges you will encounter later in the writing process.

## Finding a Topic

When a professor invites you to choose your own topic or assigns a broad topic and asks you to limit it, consider both your audience's needs and your own. Start by assuming that your audience includes intelligent and critical readers who demand some degree of depth in what they read: a superficial paper will not hold their attention or win their respect. As a writer, you should not be content with saying things that your readers probably already know, with asserting that "proper exercise is very important" or that "pollution is a very serious problem." When you are evaluating a topic for a paper, try to imagine how various readers—for example, the students in the previously mentioned writing group—might respond to it. Doing so should help you to avoid trite topics and to look for fresher ideas. You should also, of course, think of yourself and your own interests when you look for a topic. It makes sense to write about a topic you know well, one that truly interests you and has touched your life in some way. You are far more likely to interest your readers if you are informed and enthusiastic about your topic yourself.

Many students despair too quickly when faced with the task of limiting a general topic, convinced that the topic is hopelessly dull or that they will not be able to find anything original to say about it. With ingenuity and determination, however, you can shape almost any general topic to suit your knowledge and interests. Suppose, for example, that your composition professor asks you to write a 500-word essay on the general topic of "entertainment," cautioning you to limit the topic appropriately. You might start by asking yourself a series of questions and seeing which questions lead to the most promising responses:

- *Can I focus on one person?*
  My favorite entertainer: Barbra Streisand
- *Can I focus on one place?*
  The aging movie theater in my hometown
- *Can I focus on one experience?*
  Trying out for the senior play
- *Can I focus on one type (of entertainment)?*
  Music
- *Can I contrast one type with another?*
  Contrast movies and books

This method of limiting a topic can give you a number of ideas for papers in just a few minutes. Most of the ideas, however, would have to be limited further: you could not go into any detail at all if you tried to discuss all of "music" in 500 words. Look back over the list: which of the topics seem appropriate for a 500-word essay, and which would have to be limited further?

You might now pick the most promising idea on your list and narrow it gradually until you reach a topic that seems manageable:

music
  rock music
    rock concerts
      the Wings' concert last summer
        people who attended the Wings' concert last summer
*Topic:* describe the people in their thirties who attended the Wings' concert last summer, trying to recapture the "magic" of the Beatles' days

Such a process of gradually limiting a topic could lead to an amusing, detailed description of five or six people you met at the concert, who came with high expectations, sat murmuring "this isn't like the old days" throughout, and finally left, feeling disappointed and suddenly old. Such a paper would certainly be more interesting than one that begins, "There are many different kinds of entertainment. In this paper, I will discuss music, movies, and sports."

This advice on limiting topics applies most directly to composition courses, where professors sometimes assign general topics such as "entertainment" and ask you to narrow them; sociology and political science professors are seldom so obliging, although they may ask you to "write a term paper on any topic related to one of the themes of the course." When they do, look for ways to apply the advice in this chapter. Suppose, for example, that you are taking an English history course and that the professor assigns a research paper on King Richard III. Even if you find Richard III boring, you may still be able to adapt the assignment to your interests. If you are interested in theater, for example, you could write a paper on various actors' portrayals of Shakespeare's Richard III. Or, if you are interested in politics, you could research some of the political reforms introduced during his reign. If you're interested in military history, you might write a detailed account of the battle of Bosworth Field; if you're interested in the development of technology, you might write about Caxton and the first printing press in England. Of course, you should check with your professor to make sure that your topic fits the assignment before you begin to write. And if the professor insists that you write on a topic you find uninteresting, be consoled by the thought that your interests may be broadened by the experience of writing the paper.

You can also apply these methods of limiting a topic to papers assigned in other courses—provided, of course, that the professor does not set the limits for you by asking you to cover a certain number of points. For example, if you are taking a psychology course and the professor asks you to write a paper about behaviorism, you can limit the topic by asking yourself some preliminary questions and then narrowing your topic gradually:

*Can I focus on one person?*
B. F. Skinner
    Skinner's *Beyond Freedom and Dignity*
        his critique of "freedom"
            scientific determinism
*Topic:* implications of Skinner's determinism for behaviorism itself:
Is the scientist free to investigate others' behavior objectively?

Again, it is wise to check your final topic with your professor before you begin to write.

## Exploring Your Topic

Few things are more intimidating than a blank sheet of paper and the knowledge that that sheet—and perhaps several others as well—must eventually be filled with stimulating, original ideas. Once you get started, however, you may well be surprised at just how much you have to say and, in fact, frustrated because you have to make some cuts. As William Stafford, a contemporary American poet, has said, "A writer is not so much someone who has something to say as he is someone who has found a process that will bring about new things he would not have thought of if he had not started to say them." For Stafford, the first step in writing is "just plain receptivity": the writer starts by being open to all ideas and only later worries about whether or not they will really be used. Your first task, then, is to get past that blank sheet. Most writers find that it's best to start by accumulating several pages of notes. Once you have these notes, you'll feel surer of your direction and more confident of your ability to discuss your ideas fully, meeting whatever length requirement your professor has set.

*Making a list of ideas* is probably the simplest way of getting started. Write your topic at the top of the page—you'll feel better the moment you get something on that blank sheet. Then simply list any ideas that come to mind. Write quickly, and don't reject any possibilities yet; later, you can look over your ideas critically and decide which ones really belong in your paper. For now, just try to get down as many ideas as you can. Here is a list one student wrote:

*Topic:* describe how rock concerts make people in the audience feel comfortable and relaxed

- people's attire reflects group and the music being played
- laughing; getting intoxicated by drugs and alcohol
- no feeling of inferiority during a concert
- consideration and sincerity toward strangers

- if group is rowdy and loud, audience will be rowdy and loud
- many people from different backgrounds are united together to share at least one thing in common, a musical experience
- everyone leaves anxieties and problems outside auditorium
- the Grateful Dead concert
- 18,000 people in an outdoor stadium
- hot, sunny day; everyone sitting in the sun getting burned

The list is clearly disorganized and somewhat repetitious, but the writer now knows that he has a great deal to say about his topic. Looking over the list, we can see how some ideas led to others, to examples and clarifictions. The list has served its purpose. As a reader, what advice could you give this writer about exploring his ideas further? Which ideas seem most interesting to you, and which would you like to see explained in more detail?

*Freewriting* is also an excellent way of generating ideas. Peter Elbow describes this process in his *Writing Without Teachers:*

> The idea is simply to write for ten minutes (later on, perhaps fifteen or twenty). Don't stop for anything. Go quickly without rushing. Never stop to look back, to cross something out, to wonder how to spell something, to wonder what word or thought to use, or to think about what you are doing. If you can't think of a word or a spelling, just use a squiggle or else write "I can't think of it." Just put down something. The easiest thing is just to put down whatever is in your mind. If you get stuck it's fine to write "I can't think what to say, I can't think what to say" as many times as you want; or repeat the last word you wrote over and over again; or anything else. The only requirement is that you *never* stop.

One woman who wanted to write a paper on the values of taking a Black studies course generated the following ideas in just a few moments of freewriting:

*Topic:* advantages of taking a Black studies course

I really think this is an important course to take. Why is it so important? Most of us don't take Bl studies courses in high school. Only 4 Bl students in my h.s. back home; when I came to college, I was really ignorant and close-minded about Bl people. Not really racist, I don't think, but ignorant—maybe it's the same thing. Anyway, I needed to learn more and signed up for the course. Most other students in the course were Black; felt funny walking into class the first day. Realize how Bl students must feel walking into a room with mostly white students. Afraid the Bl prof would be prejudiced against me—again, realize how Blacks feel. Sometimes afraid to speak up, didn't want to sound stupid or bigoted. Good learning experience. This isn't what I meant to say; should talk about course itself. Maybe both. Anyway, learned a lot about Bl history, culture, some lit. Need a good example. Never knew about slave revolts before. Slave journals, myths about slavery. Jim Crow laws—never even heard term before. Helps whites to understand Bls' impatience, frustration. So easy for *us* to be smug, say "wait." Experiences Bl students had in h.s. Some of *them* didn't know much about Bl culture either. Good for us all to learn.

This student had originally planned to write only about the importance of the subject matter covered in Black studies courses. What other possibilities did her freewriting open up for her? Did her freewriting indeed "free" her from the limits of her first ideas by suggesting a new direction that might prove rewarding? What would you advise this student to do as her next step?

*Putting yourself in your reader's place* can also help you to find things to say. If you know your topic well, you may feel that everything you have to say about it is commonplace and obvious. Try to put yourself in the position of a reader who knows nothing about the topic: What questions would such a reader have? One woman wanted to write a paper on needlepoint but feared the topic would be dull. Part of the problem was that her topic was too broad and she had only a vague idea of her audience. When she tried to imagine what questions someone who knew nothing about needlepoint might ask, she discovered a new focus for her paper:

*Topic:* why needlepoint is an enjoyable hobby

- Is it hard to learn? Do you need to take classes?
- What are some basic stitches?
- Why is needlepoint popular? What kinds of people enjoy it?
- Is needlepoint relaxing? Challenging? Creative?
- Are needlepoint kits expensive?
- Is it better to make your own designs?
- What kinds of supplies are needed?
- Do you have to be very artistic to make your own designs?
- Where can you get ideas for original designs?
- Can you use your creations as gifts?

This woman had originally feared that she wouldn't have enough to say. After listing all these questions, she realized that she had so much to say that she would need to redefine her audience and narrow her topic. If she decides to write for readers who already know how to do needlepoint, what might her new focus be?

If you find it difficult to imagine what sorts of questions a reader might have, *talking to friends* might help you to get started. What sorts of questions do they have about your topic? What are their opinions? What parts of your topic do they find particularly interesting? Take notes during these conversations—again, get something down on paper—and then examine your notes critically to see which ideas and questions you can use.

If you use one or more of these techniques, you will find that that intimidating blank sheet of paper is no longer blank; it is filled with sentences, phrases, underlinings, and arrows; and it is probably sitting on top of a stack of other sheets covered with similar scribblings. Will you be able to use all these ideas in your paper? Probably not. You may be able to save some ideas for another paper; the woman who wanted to write about needlepoint, for example, could have written two separate papers for two different audiences. But some of your ideas will probably end up in the wastebasket. Generating ideas only to discard them later is also part of the writing process. At first, you have to suspend your critical judgment while you concentrate on starting the flow of ideas; then, once you have all the notes you need, it's time to let your judgment become dominant again as you define the focus and purpose of your paper more precisely.

## Guiding Your Readers: The Thesis Statement

Once you have narrowed your topic and explored some ideas, think carefully about your reasons for writing your paper. Do you want to share some information with your readers, to help them to visualize a person or scene, or to persuade them to take certain actions? When you are sure of your purpose for writing, express that purpose in a *thesis statement*. A thesis statement lets your readers know what to expect in your paper by revealing both the precise limits of your topic and your purpose in writing about it.

A thesis statement will be most helpful to your readers if it is *unified,* if it clearly identifies the one central idea on which you will concentrate. Consider, for example, the following thesis statement:

> Parties are very popular, especially among college students, and there are several things you can do to make sure that the parties you give will be successful.

This thesis statement seems to promise that the author will do three things: prove that parties are popular, prove that they are especially popular among college students, and give advice for throwing successful parties. It may be, in fact, that the author plans to cover only one of these topics; if so, the thesis statement is misleading. Make sure that any secondary ideas in your thesis statement are clearly subordinated to your central point: "Although everyone enjoys parties, they are especially popular among college students."

In addition to being unified, a thesis statement should be *precise*. Suppose that the author of the thesis statement first quoted decided to concentrate on giving advice for throwing successful parties:

> There are several things you can do to make sure that the parties you give will be successful.

The thesis statement is now unified, but it is too imprecise to give the reader much guidance. A phrase such as "several things" is annoyingly vague: what sorts of "things" does the author have in mind, and how many is "several"? Moreover, the author simply speaks of "parties"; will the advice in this paper apply to all parties, from a spur-of-the-moment pizza party in a dormitory room to a formal dinner given in honor of an ambassador? The thesis statement will be much more helpful if these vague expressions are replaced by ones that reveal the paper's precise focus:

> When you are planning the menu for a small dinner party, be sure to ask your guests about the foods they like and dislike and to select recipes you know well and can prepare in advance.

This thesis statement lets us know that the author will discuss only one kind of party: if we are looking for advice on how to give a fraternity rush party, we know that we should find a different essay. Moreover, the thesis statement lets us know that the author will discuss only menu—not guests, music, or decorations. The thesis statement is so precise, in fact, that it gives us some clues about how the paper will be organized. What plan of organization can you infer from the thesis statement?

One word of caution is needed here, however: do not be so eager to make your thesis statement precise that you make it overly stiff and mechanical. Readers groan when they see such a thesis statement:

> In this paper, I will discuss three important points to remember when planning a small dinner party: (1) ask your guests about the foods they like and dislike; (2) select recipes you have tried before; and (3) select recipes you can prepare in advance.

Formulas such as "In this paper, I will discuss" are overly formal in a short paper and so overused that they are boring in any paper. Similarly, there is no need to number your points if you will be covering only a few—trust your readers to count for themselves. Thesis statements are most inviting when they are relaxed and somewhat subtle:

After giving a disastrous dinner party for five friends last week, I discovered that it is best to ask your guests about food allergies and religious restrictions before you plan your menu and to avoid untried gourmet recipes that will keep you sweating in the kitchen long after your guests have arrived.

This thesis statement gives us all the guidance we need as readers; it also lets us know that we will be reading an essay written by a human being, not one cranked out by a paper-writing machine.

A thesis statement need not be expressed in a single sentence, but it will be most helpful to both you and your readers if you keep it fairly short—two or three sentences at the most. And since the thesis statement is designed to guide the reader, it should come fairly early in the paper. You do not, however, have to make it your very first sentence: you may decide that you want to build up to it by giving the reader some background information first. Many writers like to put their thesis statements at the end of the first paragraph or at the beginning of the second. In longer papers that need an extensive introduction, the thesis statement may come even later. In general, however, do not make your readers wait more than a paragraph before you reveal your topic and purpose.

In any discussion of thesis statements, one question almost inevitably arises: "Does every good paper need a thesis statement?" The answer is no. Certainly, a narrative essay that attempts to build suspense might be spoiled by a thesis statement in the first paragraph: "An experience I had while babysitting taught me not to become alarmed easily, for every strange noise I heard that night turned out to have a completely innocent explanation." Furthermore, many—perhaps most—professional expository and argumentative essays do not have thesis statements. When you are still learning to write well, however, a thesis statement can be a very useful way of disciplining yourself and keeping your papers unified. Writing a precise thesis statement forces you to define your topic clearly and then to keep within the limits you have set for yourself. When you finish writing a paper, you can look back to your thesis statement and ask yourself whether or not you have done all that you said you would do: did you, for example, promise to discuss three points and in fact discuss only two? A thesis statement thus guides the writer as well as the reader.

Before you begin to write the paper itself, then, you have some careful planning to do. You need to identify your audience, to limit and explore your topic, and to compose a thesis statement that will tell your readers how you will approach that topic. All of this may seem like a great deal of preparation, and many students are tempted to skip some of these steps. The task of completing a paper and handing it in on time is so pressing that it may seem foolish to delay long enough to think seriously about audience, topic, and thesis; it seems far more sensible to start work on the first paragraph right away. Many student papers fail, however, precisely because the author began writing that first paragraph too soon. Taking an hour or so to follow the advice in this chapter can save you a great deal of time and frustration later on. If you do a careful job of planning, you will find your task much easier when you go on to organize your ideas.

## APPLICATION

**1.** In a paragraph or short essay, describe your own writing process. What is the first thing you usually do when you start to work on an essay? How do you proceed? Are you satisfied with your writing process, or would you like to change it in any way? For this exercise, think of your professor and the other students in your composition class as your audience.

**2.** Comment on this one-paragraph essay:

> In football, points are scored through touchdowns, field goals, and safeties. There are eleven players on each team. Each player has specific duties, and all contribute to the success of the team. The quarterback may be the most important person on the team, but the best quarterback in the world cannot win games without the support of a strong, united team.

What sort of audience does the author of this paragraph have in mind? How would a reader who knows a great deal about football respond to this paragraph? How would a reader who knows little or nothing about football respond? What advice would you give to the author?

**3.** This exercise requires working in a group with three or four other students. Suppose that your composition professor has asked you to write a short essay on any subject that interests you. After you have picked a general subject, question the other members of your group to see how they respond to it. If you have decided to write about professional boxing, for example, you might find that one of the other students shares your enthusiasm for boxing, another finds it boring, another thinks it is too violent, and another has never seen a professional boxing match. Write a paragraph describing how your knowledge of your audience will influence you as you write. Can you write an essay about boxing that will interest and inform all your readers? The other members of your group might be able to offer you suggestions about ways to approach your topic. If you actually do write on this topic, read your finished essay to the same group of students and ask them for comments.

**4.** Write a profile of the audience for your essays. Describe as fully as you can the range of their opinions, interests, and expectations. How can you make your essays suit this audience? For this exercise, you might think of your audience as consisting of your teacher, your fellow students, and your parents.

**5.** Choose two or three topics from the list below:

| | | |
|---|---|---|
| sports | health | the environment |
| crime | civil rights | poverty |
| feminism | education | politics |

Limit the topics you have chosen by asking yourself the following questions:

Can I focus on one person? _____
Can I focus on one place? _____
Can I focus on one experience? _____
Can I focus on one type? _____
Can I contrast one type with another? _____

Would any of the topics you have just created be appropriate for a 500-word essay? Would any need to be limited further?

**6.** Look over the topics you created in response to the last exercise and pick two or three that seem promising but are still too broad for a 500-word essay. Limit these topics gradually, using the method described on pages 20–22.

**7.** Using the topic for the next paper you plan to write, experiment with these three methods of exploring a topic:

a. *Make a list of ideas* relating to this topic.
b. *Freewrite* on this topic for ten minutes.
c. *Put yourself in your reader's place* and develop a list of questions about this topic.

Now compare the notes you generated with each method of development. Which method seems to work best for you?

**8.** The members of a composition class were asked to write papers on the broad subject of "entertainment." They were asked to limit that subject and then to write thesis statements expressing their topic and purpose. Following are some of the thesis statements they submitted. Which ones are unified and precise? How can the others be improved?

a. I enjoy watching tennis and rugby because of the contrast between brain and brawn.
b. A great downfall in public morale took place when John
   Wayne died because he had made a great impression on the
   lives of Americans and died with honor, and because his
   movies entertained millions of people.
c. Sex on television affects viewers.
d. Supernatural phenomena on the screen incite a curiosity and
   thrill that people in a modern society such as America need in
   order to escape the monotony of everyday life.
e. Watching the Pittsburgh Steelers at Three Rivers Stadium is
   more than just watching a powerhouse football team: it's seeing the people who come to cheer on their favorite players.
f. My experience with a famous actor at home as a family man
   and at work as a professional actor.
g. The American people of today idolize the qualities of certain
   entertainers.
h. The tranquility and independence one encounters while skiing
   become the principal reasons for one's feeling of freedom.
i. There are many interesting and exciting aspects of sailing,
   but the things I enjoy most about sailing are the adventures
   involved.
j. The pregame show prior to most football games is informative
   and interesting.
k. Young children enjoy cartoons because cartoons allow them to
   have a world of their own.
l. The hours of workmanship a friend and I put into building a
   small sailboat of mahogany were rewarding in three ways: (1)
   we had a valuable learning experience; (2) we enjoyed the
   work itself very much; and (3) we produced a work of art to
   last a lifetime.
m. My first day at the races was an amusing and fun time.

**9.**   Write a thesis statement for your next essay. Try to make it as unified and precise as possible. Then ask your fellow students for their
opinions of your thesis statement. Does it give them a clear idea of your
topic and purpose? Do they have any suggestions for improving it?

**10.**   In a freshman composition class, two students decided to write
about football coaches. Both students decided to describe the qualities
that are most necessary in a good football coach; however, they chose
different approaches to the topic. Read both essays, compare them
carefully, and then answer these questions:

a. Which author has done a better job of limiting his topic?
b. Which author seems more interested in his topic? How can you
   tell? Does either essay strike you as forced or insincere?

c. Both authors attempt to support their general statements with specific examples. Which author has done a better job?
d. Does each essay have a thesis statement? If so, identify and evaluate it.
e. On the whole, which essay seems stronger to you? Why?
f. How could each author improve his essay?

### A Good Football Coach

A good football coach must have interest in the players, real knowledge of the sport, and dedication to both the players and the game.

A coach must have an interest in his players. He must be concerned that they're not getting into trouble and should try to help them if they do, because if the players think that the coach doesn't care, they won't try to perform for the coach. I have a friend who was arrested twice and headed in the wrong direction, but when the coach showed that he cared, my friend worked hard at straightening up so the coach could be proud of him.

A coach must also have a good knowledge of football. He must know the rules and techniques involved in the sport, because if he doesn't he won't be able to instruct his players about them. My roommate had a coach who had no knowledge of the sport, so the coach wasn't able to develop his athletes to their greatest potential.

Finally, dedication to both players and the sport is important to a good coach. The coach must be willing to sacrifice things in the interest of his players, because then the athletes will be more willing to sacrifice things for the sport. My coach passed up a lot of parties so that he could spend more time learning about the sport, and his example made us voluntarily sacrifice things ourselves.

If a football coach has these three qualities of interest, knowledge, and dedication, then it usually happens that his team is successful. Because of these three characteristics, many other characteristics of a good coach are developed.

### The Coach

When you first meet this man, he appears to be calm, quiet, and humble. He is in his thirties, with thinning blond hair and black-framed glasses. He is about six feet tall and weighs about 190 pounds: there is a slight formation of a bulge around his stomach, and his voice gives one the impression that he is slow and dumb. He also slurs some of his words, which adds to the impression his voice gives. While talking to him during the off-season, one would get the idea that he doesn't put an emphasis on winning, but on his players' academic achievements. He seems to be an unemotional man coaching football as best as he can.

In the locker room or on the field with Coach Brown, these first impressions soon vanish. His voice becomes loud and commanding as he barks out orders about what is to be done, and your impressions of him as slow and dumb are erased as he points out intricate plays and patterns to be performed on the field. His football knowledge seems to be unlimited as he solves every problem that could possibly arise. He has a set pattern of exactly what must be done that day on the playing field, and before the day is done, all of his objectives will be met.

Before the game starts, you can steadily see the emotions building inside of him. He starts by going over specific assignments and things he wants done on the field. He then tells us how important this game is to us and what we should expect from the opponents. He fills our team with fear by telling us that we must knock them on their behinds before they put us on ours. He paces back and forth preaching, his tone of voice rising constantly. Soon, he is yelling, and all eyes are fixed on him. He scares us into fearing our opponents, and soon we're all fired up as we head for the field.

Once the game begins, he is constantly shouting and yelling instructions. He paces up and down the sidelines like an expectant father. There is fire in his eyes as he explodes at the official for a bad call, and everyone seems to stay back and out of his way. At halftime he repeats his pregame buildup. He convinces us that we are a better team and that we should blow the other team off the field. We head for the field once again, fired up by his words.

The game is won, and there is a smile on Coach Brown's face. The quiet humbleness returns; his second self will not be seen again until Monday's practice.

# 2.
# Organizing Your Ideas:
## From Thesis to Rough Draft

## INTRODUCTORY READINGS

**A.** Examine the following student paragraphs and develop a list of the characteristics of good paragraphs.

1. I decided to come to Edson College because it has a strong varsity athletic program. Both the football and the baseball teams win a high percentage of their games. I participated in both sports in high school and hope to do the same at Edson, but if I don't have time for both I will choose baseball because it really is "the all-American sport." Not only does the college have a good record, but it also has good athletic facilities. If I get hurt, I know that I will have the best training help available. Edson also has much more modern treatment machines than the other colleges I visited do. The intramural program gives everyone a chance to compete. Athletic competition has been around since the beginning of the existence of man. Daily, people play sports of all different kinds. Everybody should get involved in at least one sport. I've always enjoyed competition, and wanting a chance to compete in intercollegiate sports was one of my reasons for deciding to come to college. If you like competitiveness as much as I do, you should seriously consider coming to Edson College.

2. In America today, more and more people are participating in sports. As I realized from talking to three of my friends, people's reasons for valuing physical fitness vary greatly: some play sports for fun, and others really train. Don Howard chose tennis for his sport because he enjoys it. As he says, "I'm sure that there are better forms of exercise, but I want to do some-

thing that's fun." Sam Levin, on the other hand, runs for his health and stresses the importance of a healthy circulatory system, good lungs, and a slower heart rate. He says he doesn't really enjoy the running, but he does enjoy the good feeling in his body and the satisfaction of good health. John Needham is the kind who likes to do everything. He is serious about running and lifting weights to stay physically fit, but he will gladly give up a day of running to waterski, play tennis, or swim. John summed up the various benefits of athletics well when he said, "I want to live a long life and have fun living it."

Comment on the differences between paragraphs 1 and 2.

3. Playing field hockey last fall helped me to become more responsible. I had always been the kind of person who was late for everything, never planned ahead, and did as little work as possible—just enough to "get by." Being on the hockey team soon cured me of being late for things. After being late for practice twice, I realized that I was inconveniencing the whole team, and my embarrassment motivated me to get into the habit of being on time. I also learned to plan ahead: practices and games took up so much time that if I didn't plan out a weekly study schedule, I would get so far behind in my schoolwork that I couldn't catch up. Finally, for the first time I worked as hard as I could at something, both for my own sake and so that I wouldn't disappoint the team. By the end of fall quarter, I was a much better hockey player and also a much more responsible person.

4. Sports is the best form of entertainment in the world. This is due to three main factors. First, one possesses the natural emotion of competition. The feeling of victory gives one a great amount of self-recognition and confidence. Second, the fans and the people competing are able to enjoy themselves. Finally, the single most important factor involving sports is that we as a whole learn about equality, leadership, and good sportsmanship toward people of many diverse backgrounds.

Comment on the differences between paragraphs 3 and 4.

5. There are many superstitions related to every sport, and track is no exception. The warm-up ritual has a tremendous influence on the athlete's peace of mind: most runners always follow exactly the same routine when they warm up, even when there is no logical reason for doing so. Head rotations always

follow jumping jacks. Arm circles always follow head rotations. Trunk rotations always follow arm circles. This same ritual goes on until the runner feels completely relaxed. After the stretching, the runner jogs exactly once around the track. The track shoes go on next. The placement of the spikes in the runner's shoes is not of major importance; still, in order to have the confidence to perform, the athlete must have the same spike in the same hole in every race. Finally, the runner is ready to compete. The runner naturally has to carry the blue baton because the blue baton wins blue ribbons—any other baton can send a perfectly mature athlete into a frenzy. With all these rituals, it is a wonder that the runner has any time to concentrate on the race.

6. Athletes often do irrational things. For example, in races many runners prefer to carry the blue baton because the blue baton wins blue ribbons—any other baton can send a perfectly mature athlete into a frenzy. When getting track shoes ready for the race, the runner must always put the same spike in the same hole in every race, even though the placement of the spikes is really not of major importance. Even the warm-up ritual has a tremendous influence on the runner's peace of mind: most runners always follow exactly the same routine when they warm up—even when there is no logical reason for doing so. Head rotations always follow jumping jacks. Arm circles always follow head rotations. Trunk rotations always follow arm circles. This same ritual goes on until the runner feels completely relaxed. After the stretching, the runner jogs exactly once around the track. With all these rituals, it is a wonder the runner has any time left to concentrate on the race.

Comment on the differences between paragraphs 5 and 6.

Now list some characteristics of good paragraphs. You might also try describing these characteristics in a paragraph of your own.

**B.**  Following are two versions of a paper about soap operas. One is the version the student actually wrote; in the other version, the paragraphs have been jumbled. Compare the two versions carefully.

### In Defense of Soaps

#### Version A

Soap operas have borne the brunt of criticism over the years; they've been accused of being overly melodramatic while catering to a small minority of housewives. I'd like to come to the defense of soaps and show that although they can be corny, they prove amusing to growing numbers of people, including myself.

Critics of soaps claim the writing is hackneyed and stereotyped. I agree that the scripts are at times predictable; after all, there are only so many human tragedies to write about. Although it has been known to happen, the scripts aren't usually Emmy material. I don't often find myself perched on the edge of the couch chewing off nail after nail, but there is that element of suspense that keeps me coming back to see if the villains will be caught or the lovelorn forsaken. Some people complain that the plots in soap operas move too slowly, but I consider this leisurely pace a virtue. I can leave one for five minutes to go get a load out of the dryer and probably not miss a heck of a lot. For that matter, I could leave one for five days or even five months and be able to catch up in one or two episodes.

Other critics charge that the acting in soap operas is too melodramatic and transparent. But all this melodrama is what I find so amusing; it's where the soaps' charm lies. The soaps remind me of vaudeville and silent movies when the acting was exaggerated (rolling eyes, wringing hands, etc.), yet at that time melodrama was taken at face value and was very popular. That's the way I look at the soaps. They are earnest. They're not trying to make any earth-shattering social statements. The soaps are there to just entertain, and we viewers should take it at that.

We viewers—who *are* the viewers who enjoy soap operas? That image of the soap watcher as being a hair-curlered, quilt-robed, bon-bon-eating housewife should be dispelled. Judging by the number of soap columns in newspapers and the fact that Channel Five has its own resident soap expert, I would say that soaps are big business. Naturally, housewives aren't the only ones responsible for this boom. It appears that many students and more and more men, as well as many others, have become fans, including myself—and I don't own curlers and I wouldn't know a bon-bon if I was choking on one.

If soap operas can attract so many viewers, they must have something to offer; at any rate, I certainly find that they do. I enjoy the soaps because they allow me to release some "unacceptable" feelings in the very acceptable environment of my own living room. I often find myself desiring to do physical harm to some characters, or else shouting unheeded advice at others, such as, "For Christ's sake, Monica, tell him it's not his baby!" Soap operas are definitely an inexpensive way to give yourself an ego boost. No matter how low an ebb your life may seem to be at, it's bound to be better than Laura's, who has fallen in love with her rapist; or Karen's, the ex-hooker who is constantly in the process of being either divorced or beaten.

My point of view can be summed up by asking all nonwatchers if soaps are worse than other TV programs. Soaps don't have the insulting canned laughter of sitcoms, nor do they have a fraction of the violence found on "family hour" detective shows. When it comes right down to it, if you had a choice between a soap featuring love, sickness, jealousy, greed, and infidelity, and a game show featuring a toupeed emcee telling a perspiring contestant that he blew the five-thousand-dollar prize package by incorrectly naming Sioux City as the capital of Iowa, which would you choose?

### In Defense of Soaps

#### Version B

Soap operas have born the brunt of criticism over the years; they've been accused of being overly melodramatic while catering to a small minority of housewives. I'd like to come to the defense of soaps and show that although they can be somewhat corny, they prove amusing to growing numbers of people, including myself.

I enjoy the soaps because they allow me to release some "unacceptable" feelings in the very acceptable environment of my own living room. I often find myself desiring to do physical harm to some characters, or else shouting unheeded advice at others, such as "For Christ's sake, Monica, tell him it's not his baby!"

Critics of soaps claim the writing is hackneyed and stereotyped. I agree that the scripts are at times predictable; after all, there are only so many human tragedies to write about. Although it has been known to happen, the scripts aren't usually Emmy material. I don't often find myself perched on the edge of the couch chewing off nail after nail, but there is that element of suspense that keeps me coming back to see if the villains will be caught or the lovelorn forsaken. Other critics charge that the acting in soap operas is too melodramatic and transparent. But all this melodrama is what I find so amusing; it's where the soaps' charm lies. The soaps remind me of vaudeville and silent movies when the acting was exaggerated (rolling eyes, wringing hands, etc.), yet at that time melodrama was taken at face value and was very popular. That's the way I look at the soaps. They are earnest. They're not trying to make any earth-shattering social statements. The soaps are there to just entertain, and we viewers should take it at that.

We viewers—who *are* the viewers who enjoy soap operas? That image of the soap watcher as being a hair-curlered, quilt-robed, bon-bon-eating housewife should be dispelled. Judging by the number of soap columns in newspapers and the fact that Channel

Five has its own resident soap expert, I would say that soaps are big business. Naturally, housewives aren't the only ones responsible for this boom. It appears that many students and more and more men, as well as many others, have become fans, including myself—and I don't own curlers and I wouldn't know a bon-bon if I was choking on one.

Soap operas are definitely an inexpensive way to give yourself an ego boost. No matter how low an ebb your life may seem to be at, it's bound to be better than Laura's, who has fallen in love with her rapist; or Karen's, the ex-hooker who is constantly in the process of being either divorced or beaten.

Some people complain that the plots in soap operas move too slowly, but I find this leisurely pace a virtue. I can leave one for five minutes to go get a load out of the dryer and probably not miss a heck of a lot. For that matter, I could leave one for five days or even five months and be able to catch up in one or two episodes.

My point of view can be summed up by asking all nonwatchers if soaps are worse than other TV programs. Soaps don't have the insulting canned laughter of sitcoms, nor do they have a fraction of the violence found on a "family hour" detective shows. When it comes right down to it, if you had a choice between a soap featuring love, sickness, jealousy, greed, and infidelity, and a game show featuring a toupeed emcee telling a perspiring contestant that he blew the five-thousand-dollar prize package by incorrectly naming Sioux City as the capital of Iowa, which would you choose?

## DISCUSSION QUESTIONS

1. Draw up a brief outline for each version of the essay by identifying the subject of each paragraph in a few words. For example, your outline for version A might begin like this:

    paragragh 1—soaps are amusing

    paragraph 2—plots: predictable, leisurely, some suspense

2. Look over the outlines you have just drawn up and comment on the paragraphing in each version of the essay. Do all the paragraphs in both versions meet the criteria you set in response to exercise A (pp. 33–35)? Which paragraphs seem weak?

3. Paragraph 4 is the same in both versions. What purposes does the first sentence of this paragraph serve?

4. Look at your outlines again and comment on the way the paragraphs in each version are ordered. Can you see some sort of logic behind the ordering of the paragraphs in each version?

5. On the whole, in which version of the essay is organization stronger? Can you suggest any ways of further improving the organization?

**C.** Study the following essay carefully, paying special attention to the ways the author organizes her ideas, both in individual paragraphs and in the paper as a whole.

### Why Do We Run?

There seemed to be no reasonable answer to the questions. Did they really expect us to be able to figure these out? I could tell I was getting impatient and frustrated by the way I jiggled my knees and continually ran my hand through my hair. Patience is not one of my more notable virtues, and on this particular day, I did not feel like testing it. Therefore, before I was about to violently tear my organic lab book into pieces, I decided to go running and forget all about chemistry.

As I walked to the physical education building, I was already beginning to relax and enjoy the beautiful day. Although it was mid-January, it felt like a warm spring day. The sun was shining, and there was a slight breeze. Everywhere I looked, I saw people outside enjoying the weather.

When I reached the track, I saw there were about ten other people jogging. I completely forgot about my chemistry lab and studied the people around me. There was quite a variety of people —young, old, male, and female, each one jogging for his or her own reason. It reminded me of an article I had read in *Harper's Magazine*. It was entitled, "Why People Run"; in it, the author gave all these deep, meaningful reasons explaining why people run. For example, he wrote that people run because every day they destroy their environment with automobiles, litter, and chemicals. Running is a plea of the people trying to return to nature. I say this is untrue, for I do not believe that most people run for this reason.

Completely absorbed in my fellow runners, I wondered why these people run. I passed an older man about sixty, probably running for health reasons—perhaps he wanted to better his cardiovascular system. I do not think it had anything to do with a desire to return to nature. Just in front of me was a heavy-set woman who looked about thirty years old. I thought she was probably running to lose excess weight. Ten meters ahead, I saw a tall, muscular young man, and I assumed he was running to keep in shape for some sport. The point is that none of these people was here because of guilt feelings about ruining our environment.

Not especially anxious to return to chemistry, I sat down on the grass and wondered why I run. I knew it was not to get back to nature or for any health reasons. Running is a painful activity for me, and I really could not figure out why I run. The question began to haunt me: Why didn't I know why I run?

Tired and somewhat frustrated, I decided to return to my

chemistry assignment. I felt a kind of pulling force tugging me back to the chemistry library. I must have actually wanted to go there because I did not even stop to change my sweaty running clothes. Sitting down with my lab book again, I worked diligently on my lab questions. To my surprise, I could do all my questions, and I finished in an hour. I was so happy that I decided to go back to my room and take a break.

Whenever I decide to waste time, I usually end up doing something constructive like cleaning my room or washing clothes. On this day, I wrote in my journal. At first I could not think of anything to write; then I remembered my chemistry lab, and how easy it was to finish after I had gone running. Soon, I remembered numerous times when I had felt frustrated with chemistry. In these situations, I often felt an urge to run and forget all about it. Suddenly, I realized why I run; and in the future, I learned to use this experience to help me do my chemistry homework.

## DISCUSSION QUESTIONS

1.  Analyze paragraph 4 carefully:
    a.  What does the first sentence contribute to the paragraph?
    b.  How are the details in this paragraph ordered?
    c.  What does the last sentence contribute to the paragraph?
2.  Compare paragraph 6 to paragraph 4:
    a.  How is the first sentence of paragraph 6 similar to the first sentence of paragraph 4? How is it different?
    b.  How are the details in this paragraph ordered?
    c.  Paragraph 6 may not seem as tightly structured as paragraph 4. Is it therefore a weaker paragraph?
3.  Paragraphs 2 and 5 are comparatively short. Are they *too* short, or do they serve a useful purpose? Would the paper be improved if the author combined paragraphs 2 and 3 or paragraphs 5 and 6?
4.  This essay does not have a thesis statement. Why do you think the author decided against including one? Would the paper be stronger if she had included a thesis statement?
5.  How would you describe the overall organization of the paragraphs? Can you identify a principle guiding this organization?

## GENERAL CONCLUSIONS

Drawing on all the observations and comments you have made about the introductory readings in this chapter, write a paragraph summarizing any conclusions you have come to about organizing paragraphs and essays. What advice would you give to a less experienced student about writing good paragraphs and essays? Be sure that the paragraph you write follows the advice you are giving.

## ADVICE

It is useful to think of writing as a process, but the various steps in that process are not always easy to distinguish or separate. As you move from thesis statement to rough draft, you will find that the steps in the writing process often overlap or occur simultaneously. If you follow the advice in this chapter, for example, you will try to develop your ideas as fully as possible before you start to organize them into paragraphs; but once you have settled on a plan of organization—and, indeed, perhaps after you have written a rough draft—you may well discover that some ideas need to be developed and supported further. And when you are at last ready to type the final copy of your paper, you may suddenly realize that the thesis statement you composed so carefully no longer fits the paper you have actually written. Marlene Gast, who teaches English at Boston College, offers this description of the frustrations of developing and organizing ideas:

> Paradox and risk lie at the heart of writing: the writer doesn't know where he or she is going unless the end is visible, the end can't be known until the perilous journey of discovery has been undertaken, the introduction can't be written unless the conclusion is in mind, yet the conclusion must always follow a developing idea that emanates from the introduction. Though these apparently contradictory constraints of writing can frustrate and restrain, writing's risky, paradoxical course can also surprise us with rewards. In setting out to write, we act on a kind of faith that we will find along the unknown way something—an expression, an idea, an understanding—we hadn't expected or planned to seek.

Writing is often described as a skill, similar to swimming or driving a car: if you follow the proper steps in the proper order, you will arrive at the desired end. Writing is also an art, however, and the steps in the process do not always follow the predetermined order. Developing, organizing, and revising go on constantly at every stage in the writing process. Erasers, scissors, and a sharp eye for spotting the problems with yesterday's solutions remain the writer's indispensable tools.

## Organizing Your Ideas—Three Basic Principles

Clearly, the pattern of organization you use will depend on the type of essay you are writing. Certain basic principles of organization, however, apply to all types of essays, and to the smaller units that make up the essay—sentences and paragraphs:

1. Keep together ideas that belong together, and keep apart those that should be separated.

2. Give each idea adequate development.
3. Arrange all your ideas in a logical and satisfying order.

The importance of these principles is clearest when we consider them in relation to the smallest unit of communication: the word. Readers would find it difficult to read a se nte nce wh e re wor ds we re ch opp ed up lik e thi s, orontheotherhandallruntogetherlikethis; readers would also find it confusing if we left out essenial etters or did not pay enough attention to oderign letters properly. Mistakes like these are obvious; similar mistakes in organizing sentences, paragraphs, and essays are often more subtle, but they can do just as much to thwart communication. Let's look at each of these principles in more detail, paying special attention to their importance in organizing good paragraphs.

1. *Keep together ideas that belong together, and keep apart those that should be separated.*

You use this principle every time you use coordination and subordination to combine sentences: only sentences that are closely related in thought should be joined together. If you are writing a description of your older brother, for example, you would only confuse your reader by writing, "Sam is over six feet tall. He has curly brown hair, and he is very intelligent." This misleads the reader by seeming to suggest a relationship between curly brown hair and intelligence; it would be far better to join the two clauses that relate to appearance and to leave the clause about intelligence by itself. George Orwell combines clauses skillfully in the opening sentences of his essay "Politics and the English Language":

> Most people who bother with the matter at all would admit that the English language is in a bad way, but it is generally assumed that we cannot by conscious effort do anything about it. Our civilization is decadent and our language—so the argument runs— must inevitably share the general collapse.

These sentences would have been far less effective if Orwell had combined the clauses differently:

> Most people who bother with the matter at all would admit that the English language is in a bad way. It is generally assumed that we cannot by conscious effort do anything about it and that our civilization is decadent. Our language—so the argument runs —must inevitably share the general collapse.

How does this revision obscure the relationships among Orwell's ideas?

In writing effective sentences, then, you constantly make decisions about which ideas belong together and which do not. You make similar decisions when you choose a subject for an essay and narrow it down to a manageable topic. You decide, for example, to write about the advantages of having a roommate during freshman year. Thus you may decide to include in your essay discussions of the importance of making friends and learning to get along with people, since these ideas clearly "belong" to your topic; you will not include a discussion of how noisy the dormitory gets during the evening since this idea does not "belong." After making these preliminary decisions about what belongs in your essay and what does not, you are faced with the various other decisions involved in organizing an essay: you have to divide your essay into paragraphs.

We can understand a great deal about the function of the paragraph by considering its comparative length. Like the sentence, the paragraph expresses a complete idea; since the paragraph is longer than the sentence, however, it does more than this. Like the essay, the paragraph not only states an idea but also explains and supports it; since the paragraph is shorter than the complete essay, however, it cannot give full treatment to an idea as complex as one that even a shorter essay discusses. When organizing your essay into paragraphs, then, look for topics within topics: ideas which, although too narrow to serve as the topic for an essay, need more than one sentence of explanation and support.

Also look for similar ideas that can be grouped together to form paragraphs. One student, for example, decided to write about how much the students who serve as resident assistants contribute to dormitory life. She accumulated the following notes, numbering them so that she could refer to them more easily:

*Thesis statement:* A good resident assistant can help to make dormitory life easier and more enjoyable.

1. lets you in when roommate locks you out of room
2. cheers you up when you get homesick
3. some r.a.'s are never around
4. creates good atmosphere on hall
5. keeps hall quiet—discipline
6. tells janitor when repairs are needed
7. in fall, organizes get-acquainted parties
8. lots of people apply to be r.a.'s
9. helps in emergencies
10. organizes hall meetings to talk over problems
11. puts up decorations for Christmas, Easter, etc.
12. meets with other r.a.'s in building once a week
13. keeps bulletin board: information about campus events
14. helps when roommates have a quarrel
15. friend to those who are lonely—stops by to visit
16. cheers you up when you're discouraged about academics

Look over this list and think about how the student might organize her essay into paragraphs. Are there any ideas that could be developed into paragraphs by themselves? Any that could be grouped together to form unified paragraphs? Any that should be cut because they are not directly related to the topic?

Once you have a general idea of how your thoughts can be grouped into paragraphs, it's time to think about *topic sentences.* Just as a thesis statement indicates the content of an essay, a good topic sentence reveals the purpose of a paragraph, imposes limits on what will be discussed, and may indicate a plan of organization. It is broad enough to cover the entire paragraph but narrow enough to give a sharp, detailed picture of what the paragraph contains. A precise topic sentence helps the writer to check the unity of the paragraph: any sentence that does not directly explain or support the topic sentence does not belong in the paragraph. The writer can also check the unity of the entire essay by making sure that every topic sentence directly explains or supports the thesis statement.

Topic sentences also help the readers by directing their attention to the main idea in each paragraph. Thus, although a topic sentence may be placed anywhere in a paragraph, the reader will usually find it most helpful if you place it near the beginning. The first sentence of this paragraph from Charles Dickens' *Great Expectations,* for example, sets up the comparison that will govern the entire paragraph. The narrator is describing the way an escaped convict eats:

> I had often watched a large dog of ours eating his food; and I now noticed a decided similarity between the dog's way of eating and the man's. The man took strong sharp sudden bites, just like the dog. He swallowed, or rather snapped up, every mouthful, too soon and too fast, and he looked sideways here and there as he ate, as if he thought there was danger in every direction of somebody's coming to take the pie away. He was altogether too unsettled in his mind over it to appreciate it comfortably, I thought, or to have anybody dine with him, without making a chop with his jaws at the visitor. In all of which particulars he was very like the dog.

The topic sentence in this paragraph focuses our attention on the central point the narrator wishes to make: we read everything that follows in the light of this sentence, and so are able to appreciate the significance of each detail more fully and easily.

Students are often tempted not to bother with topic sentences, complaining that they are too troublesome and not really necessary, and it is true that many professional writers do not use a topic sentence in every paragraph. Even when a paragraph does not have an explicit topic sentence, however, it should have one central idea that controls and limits. Moreover, even if you do not see the need for a topic sentence, consider your readers: they might very well appreciate the extra guidance it gives, particularly if you are discussing complicated ideas or presenting a long argument. Beginning writers are wise to use topic sentences consistently, especially if they have trouble writing unified paragraphs: a topic sentence is one of the simplest, surest way to help yourself decide what belongs in a paragraph and what does not.

2. *Give each idea adequate development.*

A sentence must be grammatically and logically complete, and an essay must fulfill all the expectations established in its thesis statement; similarly, each paragraph must fulfill the expectations established in its topic sentence by completely developing its central idea. The paragraphs in your essay are all parts of the whole, but they are also units in themselves: each should have a unifying idea and purpose; each should accomplish something; and each should be fully developed. After you have decided which ideas belong together in a paragraph, therefore, you need to work on developing that paragraph into a complete whole.

A paragraph is complete when all its ideas and assertions are fully explained and supported. If it has a good topic sentence, you can test a paragraph's completeness by seeing whether or not everything in that topic sentence is explained and supported. To recall an example used earlier, if your paragraph begins with the topic sentence "A resident assistant provides encouragement and emotional support to students who have problems adjusting to life away from home," you will need to explain what sorts of problems students often have and support your assertion that a resident assistant can help; only then will your paragraph be complete. If your paragraph has an implied topic sentence, you will have to identify the main idea of that paragraph carefully and make sure it is fully developed. In either case, you will need to make sure that no other sentence in the paragraph introduces a new idea or assertion that needs several sentences of development itself. If you slip into the middle of your paragraph an assertion that "Since resident assistants provide so much help, they should receive higher salaries," you will not only destroy the unity of your paragraph but also make that paragraph incomplete by introducing an idea that you do not defend or develop.

The following paragraph, for example, is not adequately developed:

Soccer, the sport of Europe, is gaining great popularity in the United States. It began this feat back in 1974 when a great Brazilian player named Pele was signed by the New York Cosmos. Further evidence of this was shown just this last year when a total of 77,000 people went to watch one playoff game. I think that some day the sport of soccer will be more popular than baseball in the United States. The figures above show very clearly that soccer is quickly gaining popularity in the United States.

What information should the author add to support and develop the assertions this paragraph makes?

3. *Arrange all your ideas in a logical and satisfying order.*

So far, we have concentrated on the parts of an essay, on sorting and developing ideas so that each part will be unified and complete. The next task involved in organization is arranging these parts in the best possible order—whether this means ordering the words in a sentence, the sentences in a paragraph, or the paragraphs in an essay. This should be a conscious process, not an automatic one. The order in which ideas first occur to you probably will not be the most effective order to use in your essay: it may make sense to you, but will it make sense to your readers? You need to find an order which the readers will be able to follow and which will help convince them that your ideas are important and valid. Before making a final decision, consider several different ways of ordering your ideas; you may be surprised to find that an order which seemed unlikely at first can give your ideas added clarity, coherence, and force. Among the methods you should consider are the order of time, the order of space, and the order of importance.

The *order of time* (chronological order) is a natural choice for narrative paragraphs and essays; the writer simply arranges events in the order in which they occurred. If you have written essays about your own experience, essays that trace the development of your ideas and attitudes, or essays that describe a process, you have probably already used the order of time. You may also find that you can use the order of time to give structure and coherence to essays that do not, at first, seem to fit the narrative pattern. For example, look back to the list of ideas for the paper about the resident assistant. Could the author use the order of time to organize her ideas into an essay?

The *order of space* (spatial order) is often used in descriptive paragraphs and essays. Imagine yourself standing in a particular spot, and describe the things you see in the order in which you see them from that perspective. You may choose to direct your readers' view around a room—from right to left or left to right, from near to far or far to near, and so forth; just be sure that you are consistent and that your directions are so clear that the readers can follow your description easily. You may decide to use the order of space to give your readers a clear idea of what a scene, object, or person looks like. The order of space is not useful only in descriptive paragraphs and essays, however. Experiment with the list of ideas about the resident assistant again, this time seeing if the author could use the order of space to organize her ideas.

*The order of importance* (climax order) can be used in many sorts of essays. Don't let your sentences, paragraphs, and essays trail off into relative insignificance; remember that the last thing people read is most likely to stay with them and may will determine their overall impression of your work. Reserve the important final position in sentences, paragraphs, and essays for your most telling detail, your most striking fact, your most convincing argument. Return to the example of the essay about the resident assistant one last time and see if the author could use the order of importance as the organizing principle for her essay.

## The Effortless Outline

Teachers and the authors of composition textbooks traditionally lecture students about the virtues of outlining; students traditionally ignore them. Outlines seem too mechanical; moreover, drawing up a formal outline seems to take too much time, time that could be better spent doing some of the actual writing. And, indeed, we have all at some time been required to write a formal outline that we never used. If you follow the advice given in this chapter, however, you will find that you have created an informal outline almost without meaning to. You have written topic sentences for each paragraph: these can be the major headings in your outline. You have grouped your various ideas under these topic sentences: these are your subheadings. And, since you have arranged your main ideas in a logical order, you don't need to worry about which to label "I" and which to label "II."

Take just a few moments to recopy your now-orderly notes onto one sheet of paper so that you can check the unity, development, and order of your paragraphs. Here, for example, is a sample outline for a student's essay about a college course.

*Thesis Statement:* Medieval History was an excellent course because the teacher was well organized, congenial, and knew his subject so well that he made it really come alive for the students.

I. The course was always a model of organization.
- A. Detailed syllabus told us dates for papers and tests, assignments for each day
- B. Lectures always clear and orderly—helped us understand textbook assignments
- C. Willing to make changes in schedule when we said we couldn't handle reading
- D. At end of every class, told us what we would discuss next day

II. Professor Best was very congenial
- A. Likes students
- B. Welcomes questions, different opinions

III. Most important, Professor Best knew his subject thoroughly

A. Ph.D. in Medieval History
B. Wrote book on War of the Roses
C. Has taught this course for over ten years
D. Knew all about events and personalities of period
E. Broad view of the period—discussed literature, religion as well as kings, battles
F. Covered some unusual topics—e.g., women in Middle Ages

Evaluate this outline. Are all the paragraphs unified? Do any need further development? Is the order of the paragraphs appropriate?

Drawing up an informal outline such as this one can help you to spot and solve problems with development and organization before you begin to write your rough draft. It's well worth the short time it takes.

## Writing the First Draft

Finally, you are ready to write the first draft of your paper. There are almost as many approaches to writing rough drafts as there are writers. I know one writer who begins by spending several hours perfecting his introductory paragraph: once that is in final form, the rest of his paper seems to flow onto the page almost effortlessly—and amazingly quickly. When one of my college roommates worked on her rough drafts, she could not stand to cross anything out; if she had to change a sentence, she would begin on a new sheet of paper even if it meant recopying several paragraphs. Watching her copy pages over and over again used to drive me crazy, but for her this method was almost a psychological necessity. Writing the rough draft is an idiosyncratic process. You will have to experiment with various approaches to writing rough drafts and discover which one works best for you.

Many writers find it easiest to start by writing the first paragraph of the body of the paper. Introductions and conclusions are especially difficult, so you may not want to think about them until you're ready to revise. In fact, you may not want to write your paragraphs in order at all. Many writers find it much easier to get started if they begin by writing the paragraph they find most interesting or exciting, even if it will eventually be the seventh paragraph in a ten-paragraph paper. Other writers would find such a disorderly process hopelessly confusing and must always start with their first paragraph. Again, experiment and see what works for you. If you encounter a "block" when writing a particular paragraph, however, it may be best to put that paragraph aside for a while, write the rest of your paper, and then return to the problem paragraph. If you get at least some parts of your paper written, you are less likely to become utterly discouraged and frustrated.

The pace at which a rough draft is written varies from writer to writer. Some crash through the rough draft very quickly, never pausing to reconsider a phrase or decide whether or not a sentence really belongs in a particular paragraph; such writers may have to write four or five drafts, but they can write them in the same amount of time other writers devote to just two or three. Some writers, on the other hand, work quite slowly, continually erasing or rewriting. These writers can't stand to go on to the next sentence until they are satisfied with the previous one. Perhaps the majority of writers strike a compromise between the crash-through draft and the laboriously crafted one. They write fairly quickly but pause occasionally to underline or put parentheses around a sentence or phrase that may need to be rewritten, to write alternative word choices in brackets or in the margin, or to write "revise this" or "ugh" next to a paragrah that seems weak. Such writers do not make major revisions until they have finished the first draft, but they constantly leave themselves reminders of the changes that must eventually be made. Almost everyone agrees that this is not the time to look up spellings in a dictionary or to worry about punctuation.

The tools used in writing rough drafts also vary greatly. Many writers use lined paper and skip every other line so that it will be easier to write in additions and changes later. For obvious reasons, many writers use a pencil when working on rough drafts. Some are surprised to find that it's easier for them to write rough drafts on typewriters. If you get stuck while writing a rough draft, it sometimes helps to switch from pen to pencil or from pencil to typewriter; I don't know why this works, but it sometimes does. The best single piece of advice I can give you is to write on just one side of a piece of paper. Later, when it's time to revise your rough draft, you can perform surgery on it by cutting out paragraphs you want to discard or revise and simply taping the sections you want to save into your second draft. Many writers find that scissors are their most useful tools in doing revisions.

More important than any techniques or tools, however, are your attitudes toward your first draft and your timing. Many of us wait until the last possible moment before starting on a first draft, confident that we can go straight from writing the last word of the draft to typing the first word of the final copy. It is much wiser to write your first draft as far in advance as possible, so that if you are dissatisfied with it—and you almost certainly will be—you will have plenty of time to revise. Your first draft is almost never your best work. Reconcile yourself to the fact that it is indeed your *first* draft, the first among several, and will need extensive rewriting and polishing before you are ready to type. Such an attitude toward your first draft will make writing much easier and more enjoyable: you are less likely to be overcome by anxiety about whether a word, phrase, or paragraph is perfect if you know that you will have many chances to reevaluate and rewrite. Writing a paper is indeed a long and involved process; even when you have finally finished your first draft, a third and crucial stage of that process still lies ahead of you—revision.

## *APPLICATION*

**A.** Evaluate and revise this two-paragraph essay, paying special attention to paragraph unity. Make sure that the new paragraphs you create have precise, comprehensive topic sentences. Will the author need to add any further information in order to develop both topic sentences adequately?

(1) The course in Ethnic Dance keeps you constantly learning new dances from around the world. (2) You have no choice but to stay active the whole class period. (3) There is never any time to watch the clock, because before you know it, the class is over. (4) Before I took this course, I had never realized how many varieties of ethnic dance there are.

(5) This class is ideal for those who are trying to lose weight. (6) It really keeps you in good physical shape. (7) Most of the dances are lots of fun and easy to learn. (8) Although each of the dances is unique, they all have certain basic things in common. (9) Even outsiders would occasionally join in our class. (10) The music made you want to dance. (11) Your whole educational outlook on other people's way of life was broadened right in Ethnic Dance. (12) I would recommend this course to anyone who would like to enjoy getting a grade.

**B.** Both of the following paragraphs were written in response to an assignment asking the students to describe what they and their families would do if they had only twenty-four hours to live. Which student does a better job of developing and organizing ideas? How could the paragraphs be improved?

1. If I had only twenty-four hours to live, I would spend those last hours with the people that I love. My family are the people with whom I would spend the last hours of my life. My family are the ones that helped me when I was having hard times. They shared my problems and made life easier for me. My family helped me to accept the idea of death. They would also help to make death itself easier for me.

2. Many people wonder how their last hours of life would be spent. What would the members of my family do if they had only twenty-four hours to live? My mother, who has never been able to travel, would want to spend her last hours on a cruise around the world. My father would simply go to church and devote his last hours to the Lord. My sister would try to beat me in Monopoly, which is something she has never done. My brother, who has about eight different girlfriends, would most

likely spend his last day with them personally; that would be one tired man. As for me, I would just spend my last hours with all my loved ones. I suspect that not all of our last-hour wishes would come true, but it sure is interesting to think about them while time is still left.

**C.** The following paragraph discusses paragraph length. Revise the paragraph, paying special attention to the way the sentences are ordered. You might find it helpful to work with a small group of other students.

(1) If you find that one of your paragraphs is too long, try to find a logical way to divide it: perhaps there are two separate ideas hidden in your topic sentence. (2) The length of your paragraphs should reflect the importance and complexity of the central ideas that guide them. (3) A series of short, choppy paragraphs, like a series of short, choppy sentences, might break your readers' attention by interrupting them too often. (4) Don't fall into the trap of simply repeating ideas instead of developing them. (5) You should just be sure that your paragraphing is never arbitrary, that each paragraph does have a substantial idea to develop. (6) Some ideas need only a few sentences of explanation or support, whereas others need much more. (7) A very long paragraph, even if it is well unified, might make your readers lose track of your central idea before they reach the end. (8) You cannot test a paragraph's development by counting the number of sentences it contains, any more than you can test a sentence's completeness by counting its words. (9) In general, the paragraphs in a short essay should be between six and twelve sentences long. (10) Remember that an occasional short paragraph can be effective if used to give emphasis to a particularly important point. (11) If you have several paragraphs that are only a few sentences long, try to find a way to combine two of them under a more comprehensive topic sentence; this is much better than trying to "pad" a paragraph by adding unnecessary or irrelevant sentences. (12) Also, consider your readers when you decide how long your paragraphs should be.

**D.** A student developed the following list of ideas in support of her thesis statement:

*Thesis statement:* Children can be either strengthened or defeated by the challenges they face when their parents get divorced.

1. may develop negative feelings about marriage, be afraid to get married yourself

2. special closeness to the parent you live with
3. have to become more independent
4. feel left out, different—e.g., at father-daughter banquet in Girl Scouts
5. feel guilty: could you have prevented divorce?
6. tempted to take sides, get angry with one parent
7. mixed feelings when parents start to date other people
8. get more realistic view of marriage, choose very carefully yourself
9. parents may try to bribe you with gifts, trips, etc.
10. embarrassed to tell friends
11. may miss out on advice from parent of opposite sex—hard when dating
12. partly depends on how old children are when parents get divorced
13. learn to see parents as individuals, people with special, separate needs
14. parents may tell you horrible things about each other
15. may try to get your parents back together—frustrating
16. may wonder if parent who left doesn't love you

How can the student organize these ideas? Which ideas belong together in paragraphs? Will any of the paragraphs need further development? What would be the most effective way to order these paragraphs? Write an informal outline that could be used for an essay on this topic. Again, you may find it helpful to work in a group with several other students.

**E.** Select a local or campus issue and carefully articulate your stand on it in a thesis statement. Next, using any method of generating ideas, develop a list of at least a dozen points which support your position. Now try to organize all these ideas into paragraphs: How can these ideas be grouped? Will any of the paragraphs need further development? What is the most effective way to arrange your paragraph? Write an informal outline that could be used in a paper on this topic. You might find it helpful to work with a small group of other students.

**F.** The following paper is based on information a student gathered from interviewing several other students about their reasons for attending a particular college. As you will see, she had some problems developing and organizing her ideas. How could she organize her paragraphs more effectively? What further information will she need to obtain in order to develop her ideas more adequately?

I talked to a few upperclassmen and asked them a few questions about Edson College. Most of them came here not knowing what they wanted to major in. They knew that a liberal arts college would give them a wide variety of courses and also a lot of personal attention from the teachers, seeing that the student-teacher ratio here is very good—about thirteen to one.

Many of the students liked the personal atmosphere and the reputation the school had with many graduate schools. They all agreed that they were influenced to go here by the high school they had attended. They were all looking for something much different from high school, which unanimously was seen as a great waste of time. One girl I interviewed said she like Edson because it had no physical education requirement, which in high school prevented her from being number one in the graduating class.

I found all the people that I interviewed thought the professors to be very good and very ready to help, although one boy found them to be experts in their field but thought they really didn't know how to teach the courses. He also felt he would have liked a little bit more attention from his professors.

Another boy found Edson all he had expected, although he was disappointed in how the school puts down fraternities and sororities and puts so much emphasis on academics. He strongly feels that socializing and getting to know people other than in a classroom is an important part of a college education.

I talked to one international student who was looking for a small school. She spoke English, and she wanted to study the culture and the differences between her culture and ours. She had to work very hard but found her professors to be very helpful. She also found the other students to be very sophisticated or from "a good family background." The one bad thing she did not like was that she found the students to be very competitive, which she found could be a drawback, always competing in sports and school work.

All the people I talked with have enjoyed Edson and believe it has helped them pick a major, find their independence, and send them in some direction in life.

**G.** In a paragraph or short essay, describe the process you followed while organizing an essay you just completed or one you are currently writing. Answer some or all of these questions: How did you organize your ideas into unified paragraphs? What were your reasons for deciding whether or not all your paragraphs needed topic sentences? How did you check to make sure that all your paragraphs were adequately developed? What alternatives did you consider before deciding on the best way to order your paragraphs? Did you make an outline, or did you find some other way to check your organization?

Your professor may ask you to hand in this analysis along with your essay.

**H.**  Both of the following essays were written in response to an assignment asking students to explore some topic related to reading. Read both essays and compare them carefully, paying special attention to the development and organization of ideas.

### An Appetite for Words

I really don't know how or when it happened. And my parents aren't sure they can remember a time that it didn't exist. They only know that one day, long before they were ready, I was reading. Since it seemed perfectly natural to me, they made a few minor adjustments and resigned themselves to a daughter whose childhood was spent with book in hand. My mother raided the adult side of the library and signed out books for me, my father skeptically shared his "handyman" books with me, and my brothers tried their best to explain their freak sister who never watched television. Years out of childhood and now with a family of my own, I haven't changed all that much. Accommodations and adjustments are made, but the need remains the same. Even as I must eat and sleep and breathe, so must I read. In fact, there are times when I gladly give up the first two in favor of the last.

I must confess that I am not a gourmet reader. My tastes run more to gluttony. If it's put in front of me, I read it! I read the ingredients list on cake mixes, canned goods, and multiple vitamins. I read my son's *Hardy Boys* mystery books when I should be cleaning his room. I even read, repeatedly and without thinking, things that aren't particularly interesting to me. Is there anyone but a compulsive reader who knows the American Dental Association's toothpaste pledge by heart? But before you think that I'm totally off-balance, let me assure you that even gluttons have their standards. I personally draw the line at income tax forms, letters from the bank, and my husband's economics texts. They don't even elicit a nibble of interest from me.

Gluttons do need variety, however, and I am no exception. Labels and lists only fulfill a small part of my craving. The remainder must be satisfied with tons of newspapers, magazines, and books. The *New York Times, National Geographic, Nursing '80,* and numerous others are all gobbled up soon after their arrival. Very little escapes! It takes an act of sheer willpower when it comes to my book club. Money spent on books is not budgeted as a luxury; it is regarded, rather, as a necessity. So each month there is only the consideration of which book to buy and which to wait for at the public library. There is, of course, never any attempt to resist the library—I gladly plunge in and enjoy its feast.

Now I'm sure that this must seem a rather time-consuming and odd characteristic for a person to have. And you may be right. I've probably passed through a great deal of life with very little appreciation, because my eyes were glued to a printed page. There are no regrets, however, no apologies, and no plans to alter the present course. For reading is an absolutely essential part of my life. With its memories of the past and its promises of the future, my table overflows with a rich repast.

## The Importance of Reading

Reading is very important throughout life, for enjoyment as well as for practical reasons. But children of this day and age do not read enough during their free time. This is not necessarily the fault of the children, but the fault of television.

As technology develops, society grows further and further away from old and simple ways of pleasure, mainly reading. To become a good reader, like most things, one must practice reading often. In the age of technology, kids can simply turn on the television when they wish to be entertained. Why should a child read when he can actually have the audio and visual effects of television? What is worse, society has permitted prime-time air play for trashy and uneducational television shows. However, it is the responsibility of the parents to use their discretion regarding the types of television shows watched by their children. They should realize, for example, that violent shows can have a very harmful effect on children, as a number of studies have shown. It is also the parents' responsibility to provide children with good reading material.

There is a very wide range of reading material for children, and many of the books and stories are very good. *The Call of the Wild* is just one example. But children must be pushed to read when they're at a youthful stage in life. As stated before, children would prefer to watch television as opposed to reading. Yet, reading is so very important in life and should be studied early. As children grow up, their reading skills must also improve to live a normal live in our language-oriented culture. For example, if a person wishes to buy a home, he must know and understand how to read a contract or he could be swindled.

Reading has one substantial quality that television does not have—the development of the mind. When reading, one must use his imagination to visualize his interpretation of the material he is reading. For instance, if a person is reading about a beautiful meadow, he must try to visualize in his mind what the author is trying to say. On television, the scene is already set, and the mind cannot use its originality to portray a beautiful meadow.

People who spend too much time watching television may become mentally lazy and unable to make the effort required for reading. They may also become physically lazy and unfit because they would rather spend the time in front of a television set than outdoors getting fresh air and exercise.

With the cooperation of both parent and child, it may be possible to set a little time out of the day for reading. When I was ten years old, my father told me I was not reading often enough. He decided to remedy that by having me read a half hour a day before I could watch television. At the time I did not like the new proposition, but as time went by I started to enjoy reading. After about one year I did not even need pressure from my parents to read because I was so interested in reading. Today, I am glad that my parents had helped me along, for now I must read a great deal at college. This reading would have been a chore if I were not already used to reading and to enjoying it. Thus, if children can find a little time out of the day to read, it will help them in the long run to become proficient readers.

## DISCUSSION QUESTIONS

1. Did both students limit the topic adequately?
2. Does each essay have a thesis statement? If so, identify and evaluate it.
3. Do both students stick to their topics throughout their essays?
4. Are the paragraphs in both essays unified? Have both authors kept together ideas that belong together and kept apart those that should be separated?
5. In each essay, are all the paragraphs developed adequately? Which paragraphs need further development?
6. Are the paragraphs in each assay arranged in a logical and satisfying order?
7. What other suggestions for improvements would you give to the author of each essay?

# 3.
# Polishing Your Essay:
# From Rough Draft to Final Copy

## INTRODUCTORY READINGS

**A.** Following are two versions of a student essay, the original and a revision. Read both versions of the essay and compare them carefully.

### *Version A*

Upon first sight, people usually receive an inaccurate impression of me. My facial expressions and my sometimes vague attitude confuse others as to the person I really am. Not too many people have made up their minds about whether or not they like me. It's not that I don't want to be friendly; it's just that I find it difficult to immediately warm up to people. I feel uneasy and awkward. Others can sense this awkwardness in the air; however, they mistake it for snobbishness, which is a problem for me.

I have been told by people whom I know well now that when they met me, they found it hard to like me. Surprisingly enough, I don't find it unbelievable. Their first reaction is to comment on my aloofness. This aloofness they talk about is not that at all; I was just plain shy. Meeting new people and making friends is something I look forward to, but when faced with the challenge of doing so, I become extremely nervous and anxious. Being outgoing was and is not one of my strongest points.

I know a lot of people suffer from this same dilemma. Recently, I have been trying to conquer my problem. My nervousness overwhelms me when I know I have to meet people. I become panicky. I seem to have a complex that maybe these people won't like me, or I won't fit in. So, instead of being more determined, I retreat behind an attitude that I'm better than they are. It's a childish way of behaving, and I'm not giving these people a chance to know me or me to know them. But by realizing this, I think I am gradually beginning to grow out of it.

Sometimes I wonder, even though this problem is so distinguishable to me, will I ever rid myself of my fear of meeting people? I would like to be able to confront these situations with a positive attitude and not have people question the authenticity of my feelings toward them and myself. I become so frightened that I cannot think of anyone else, least of all trying to overcome my feelings.

Maybe I do walk with my head and nose up in the air, which indicates a definite snobby attitude. Also the flip of my head, nervous laughter, and stubborn look upon my face might mislead people to misunderstand the real me. I could try to set the blame on others, that they judge me too soon, and I have in many cases; however, I would be backing away from the problem again. I know I can solve my shyness with a little endurance; nonetheless, I will not use people as my testing ground in the future; I want people to like me as I am the first time around and not have to prove myself. If I don't get along with them, maybe it's because we just can't. I hope that the next time I feel insecure and doubtful, I'll remain firm and not surrender to foolish emotions.

### Version B

Upon first sight, people usually receive an inaccurate impression of me. My facial expressions and my sometimes vague attitude confuse others as to the person I really am. Not too many people have made up their minds about whether or not they like me. It's not that I don't want to be friendly; it's just that I find it difficult to warm up to people immediately. Others can sense this awkwardness in the air; however, they mistake it for snobbishness, which is a problem for me.

Meeting new people and making friends is something I look forward to, but when faced with the challenge of doing so, I become extremely nervous. A few summers ago I was a waitress in Florida. I obtained the job easily and did not figure on having trouble adjusting to my co-workers. I can still recall the horrible feeling that was in my stomach when I saw everyone sitting together at one table. Naturally, I stayed alone most of the day because I was scared. I waited until someone came to talk to me. He was so friendly that I couldn't help but feel at ease. I can't help wishing that I could have been the one to start the conversation.

Now that I am older I realize that it was and still is a childish way of behaving. But I think I know why I am so overwhelmed by the shyness. I seem to have a complex that maybe these people won't like me or I won't fit in. So instead of being more determined to prove myself, I retreat behind an attitude that I'm better than they are.

When I walk with my head and nose in the air, I can't blame people for thinking that I'm a snob. Also, the flip of my head, nervous laughter, and stubborn look on my face might mislead people to misunderstand the real me. They only help me to hide my nervousness while imparting a negative impression of me.

Recently, I have been trying to conquer this dilemma, and I think I can because I understand myself better. I hope that next time I feel insecure and doubtful, I'll remain firm with myself and not surrender to foolish emotions.

## DISCUSSION QUESTIONS

1. List the changes the author made in her revision.
2. Look over the list of specific changes and generalize about the *kinds* of changes the author made. For example, what kinds of material did she add? What kinds of material did she leave out? Why do you think she made these changes?
3. Evaluate the paragraphing in each version of the essay. Are all the paragraphs unified and well developed?
4. How are the paragraphs in each version of the essay ordered?
5. If the author planned to revise her essay again, what advice would you give her for further improvements?

**B.** Following are two versions of a student paragraph, the original and a revision. Read the two versions and compare them carefully.

### *Original*

On my street, summer evenings are very interesting. The Salvation Army yard is generally filled with people playing basketball on the courts or people playing tennis against the walls of the building. Children are found climbing up the sides of the building or doing cartwheels and flips in front of it. Old people and some parents are sitting on their porches gossiping with each other or scolding one of the kids playing kickball or tossing baseballs. Everyone on the block will stop and watch Virginia, the neighborhood drunk, boisterously embarrass her guest. Everyone returns to his or her own activity. Everyone except the young lovers and the noisy neighbors slowly goes back home.

### *Revision*

Summer evenings are the times when everyone on my street is usually outside and active. The Salvation Army yard, located at the end of the street, is generally filled with people playing basketball on the courts or people playing tennis against the walls of the building. Commonly, children are found climbing up the sides of this building or doing cartwheels and flips in front of it. Down the street, old people and some parents are sitting on their porches gossiping with each other or scolding one of the kids playing kickball or tossing baseballs in the middle of the street. Occasionally, everyone on the block will stop and watch Virginia, the neighborhood drunk, boisterously embarrass her guest. After her performance, everyone returns to his or her own activity until night falls. Then everyone except the young lovers and the noisy neighbors slowly goes back home.

### DISCUSSION QUESTIONS

1. List the differences between the original paragraph and the revision.
2. How do the changes the student made contribute to the effectiveness of the paragraph?

**C.** Following are two versions of a student essay, the original and a revision. Read both versions and compare them carefully.

### The Virtues of "the Freshman Crazies"

#### *Original*

What is the meaning of the word "entropy"? Entropy is the measure of the degree of disorder of molecules. I am not concerned with molecular entropy levels. Today, I will discuss the entropy of the mind—the mental entropy of college freshmen. Collegiate mental entropy (CME) has several more common names: among them are "the freshman crazies," "not having your act together," and, of course, "going nuts." Collegiate mental entropy is a chaotic state of frustrating disorganization and confusion with which many college freshmen must cope. Collegiate mental entropy is probably also one of the most beneficial lessons that can be learned from a college experience.

When you go trotting off to college, most of you will have doubts; some people are even fearful. Some of you may become more outgoing. For other people, growing introversion is a problem. College will change people in some way—either there's an improvement, or they get worse. Some of you will become confused, scared, suffer from depression, and grow disorganized—you will be suffering severe collegiate mental entropy. You will find yourself asking, "What am I doing here?" or "Is this really worth it?" You will begin to be unsure of your relationship with yourself and with others. You may become slightly disorganized or completely lost. You may suddenly find yourself dazed and confused after attempting to reassess all the values you once believed so firm and sure. Millions of other people have gone to college and were at one time freshmen with the same hang-ups.

Some people manage to just "float" and remain unaffected by any sort of confusion. Some students become so nonproductive that they drop out of school for a while in order to make some sense of the disorder which surrounds them. The same is true in high school: some people find the adjustment from grade school hard, while for others this transition is made quite easily.

The causes of the "freshman crazies" are reasonably obvious. The most important factor in freshman frustration is environmental adjustment. When the average freshman goes to college, he is transferring himself into a new and generally less secure environment than that to which he is accustomed. He finds himself in what is often a highly pressured situation in which he must make rather weighty decisions for himself and bear the consequences for the wrong course of action. The adjustment freshmen must make to their newfound freedom in academic matters can be quite difficult. Many freshmen come to college and realize for the first time how unenlightened they really are. When one considers all the factors involved in adjusting to college, one begins to understand why the freshman year can be the most traumatic.

Collegiate mental entropy is less than enjoyable. Freshman frustration is indeed bitter medicine. Emotional chaos is probably one of the most beneficial aspects and profitable experiences of a college career. Collegiate entropy builds character in a disquieting way. Following a period of "the freshman crazies," a person can begin to understand himself and the elements that make him what he is. A person can also begin to better understand those around him. Building character through frustration is rather painful. No one ever said it was going to be pleasant. It must be remembered that the ability to adjust is one of the most important abilities one can possess. Acute mental distress caused by forced adjustment can often create a more patient, open-minded, adaptive, and flexible individual. Emotional anguish teaches one to cope—the most important lesson of all. Life is coping with the millions of different situations that present variety. It is an introductory course in coping and dealing with the world around you. There is no advanced placement.

If you go to college and fall into the entropy rut, do not worry. It will pass. Bear in mind that every other freshman is going through the same turmoil. Smile when you remember that college is the only place on earth where a person can "lose his cookies" and still be considered sane by everyone around him.

## The Virtues of "the Freshman Crazies"

### *Revision*

What is the meaning of the word "entropy"? In simplest terms, entropy is the measure of the degree of the disorder of molecules. However, I am not concerned with molecular entropy levels. Today, I will discuss the entropy of mind—specifically, the mental entropy of college freshmen. Collegiate mental entropy (CME) has several more common names: among them are "the freshman crazies," "not having your act together," and, of course, "going nuts." By any name, collegiate mental entropy is a chaotic state of frustrating disorganization and confusion with which many college freshmen must cope. Oddly enough, however, collegiate mental entropy is probably one of the most beneficial lessons that can be learned in a college experience.

When you go trotting off to college, most of you will have doubts, and some of you may even have fears. Some of you may become more outgoing; others might become more introverted. Inevitably, college will change people in one way or another—some for better, some for worse. In any event, some of you will become confused, scared, depressed, and disorganized—you will be suffering severe collegiate mental entropy. You will find yourself asking, "What am I doing here?" or "Is this really worth it?" You will begin to be unsure of your relationship with yourself and with others. Eventually you may become slightly disorganized or, even worse, completely lost. You may suddenly find yourself dazed and confused after attempting to reassess all the values you once believed so firm and sure. None of it is new. Millions of people have gone to college, and those millions were at one time freshmen with the same hang-ups.

Of course, some people have more trouble than others with freshman mental chaos. Some people just manage to "float" and remain unaffected by any sort of confusion. On the other hand, some students become so nonproductive that they drop out of school for a while in order to make some sense of the disorder which surrounds them. CME has an incredible way of manifesting itself in varying degrees in different people.

The causes of the "freshman crazies" are, like its symptoms, reasonably obvious. The most important factor in freshman frustration is environmental adjustment. When the average freshman goes to college, he is transferring himself into a new and generally less secure environment than that to which he is accustomed. He finds himself in what is often a highly pressured situation in which he must make independent decisions about everything from course selections to sex and bear the consequences for the wrong course of action. As if relying on one's own judgment for the first time were not difficult enough, the adjustment freshmen must make to their newfound freedom in academic matters can also be quite difficult. Many freshmen come to college and realize for the first time how unenlightened they really are; many who were always at the top of their high school classes now must struggle to get passing grades. All this forces them to reexamine their opinions. When one considers all the factors involved in adjusting to college, one begins to understand why the freshman year can be the most traumatic.

As you may have guessed, collegiate mental entropy is less than enjoyable. Freshman frustration is indeed bitter medicine. However, emotional chaos is probably one of the most beneficial aspects and profitable experiences of a college career. Collegiate entropy builds character in a disquieting way. Following a period of the "freshman crazies," a person can begin to understand himself and the elements that make him what he is. In the process, a person can also begin to better understand those around him. Granted, building character through frustration is rather painful, but no one ever said it was going to be pleasant. It must also be remembered that the ability to adjust is one of the most important abilities one can possess. Acute mental distress caused by forced adjustment can often create a more patient, open-minded, adaptive, and flexible individual. Of course, emotional anguish teaches one to cope—the most important lesson of all. Face it, life is coping with the millions of different situations that present themselves in the course of one's existence. Collegiate distress, especially the freshman variety, is an introductory course in coping and dealing with the world around you. It is a course in which there is no advanced placement.

If you go to college and fall into the entropy rut, do not worry. It will pass. Bear in mind that every other freshman is going through the same turmoil, and smile when you remember that college is the only place on earth where a person can "lose his cookies" and still be considered sane by everyone around him.

## DISCUSSION QUESTIONS

1. Compare the two versions of the first paragraph carefully. The revised version of this paragraph contains several words and phrases that are missing from the original. Underline these words and phrases and explain what they contribute to the paragraph.
2. Compare the two versions of the second paragraph carefully.
   a. Compare sentences 1–4 in the revision with sentences 1–5 in

the original. In which version is the author's point made more clearly? Why?

b. The sentence "None of it is new" appears in the revision but not in the original. What does this sentence contribute to the paragraph?

3. Compare the two versions of the third paragraph carefully.

   a. What did the author cut from this paragraph when he revised? Why do you think he made this change?

   b. Underline any words, phrases, or sentences that appear in the revision but not in the original. Explain what these additions contribute to the paragraph.

4. Compare the two versions of the fourth paragraph carefully.

   a. In the revision, why is the phrase "like its symptoms" important?

   b. Compare sentence 5 in the revision with sentences 5 and 6 in the original and explain the significance of the differences you notice.

5. Compare the remaining paragraphs in the essay carefully, identifying differences and explaining their significance.

6. Generalize about the differences between the two versions of the essay. What kinds of changes did the author make most frequently when he revised? In what ways is the revision stronger than the original?

## GENERAL CONCLUSIONS ABOUT ROUGH DRAFTS AND REVISIONS

Look over your comments about all the rough drafts and revisions you have just examined. List some of the tasks involved in revision, or write a short paragraph giving advice to someone beginning a revision of a paragraph or essay.

## Introductory and Concluding Paragraphs

Comment on the following introductory and concluding paragraphs. What techniques do these paragraphs use? When you notice that two paragraphs use similar techniques, comment on which one uses the technique more effectively. As you study the individual paragraphs, be thinking of any generalizations you can draw about what introductory and concluding paragraphs should accomplish.

1. *Introductory paragraph from a political science paper criticizing one of Khrushchev's speeches:*

In "The Crimes of the Stalin Era," Khrushchev attempts to discredit Stalin as a leader of the Soviet Union and as a Marxist. The validity of his charges against Stalin as a military leader can best be affirmed or denied by historians. His critique of Stalin as a Marxist, however, can be evaluated by seeing how well these criticisms coincide with the theories and traditions of important Communist works. In many instances, Khrushchev does not attack Stalin on a Marxist basis at all; in others, his criticism reveals an apparent lack of understanding of several important Marxist concepts. Khrushchev's speech itself contains serious flaws if examined as a work in the Marxist-Leninist tradition.

*COMMENTS* (*techniques this paragraph uses, purposes it serves, effectiveness as an introductory paragraph*):

**2.** *Introductory paragraph from a paper written for a literature course, discussing narrative technique in Defoe's* Moll Flanders:

Defoe has captured an effect in his famous novel *Moll Flanders* that I have never seen before. It is truly unique in that it is unlike anything found in any other novel. Defoe has cast before his readers the story of a woman telling a story. By this I mean that Defoe portrays a woman narrator revealing the story of her own life in a unique way. And away she went from the truth. In *Moll Flanders* we see a woman's life told the way she would tell it. Interestingly enough, Moll's story (the one she is telling in this novel) is filled with inconsistencies, as facts are jumbled, and important bits of information are left out.

*COMMENTS:*

**3.** *Introductory paragraph from a political science paper on judicial review:*

Perhaps the most serious argument against the validity of judicial review is that it is undemocratic. In his article on "Judicial Review and Democracy," Henry S. Commager presents this view with impressive vehemence. He points out that "every act adjudicated by the court has not only been ratified by a majority, but it has . . . been subjected to the most anxious scrutiny as to its conformity with the Constitution." When the court concludes that an act is contrary to the Constitution and declares it to be void, Commager asserts that it is opposing the thoughtfully expressed will of the people. His criticisms are important because judicial review is an integral part of American politics, and if Commager is correct, it will be necessary for us, as students and citizens, to revise our opinion of the courts and their place in the regime. However, Commager's arguments point to even more important issues that ultimately force us to try to understand what kind of regime we live in.

*COMMENTS:*

**4.** *Introductory paragraph from a history paper on King Richard III:*

Popular histories portray Richard III as a spiteful, bitter, and self-seeking monster whose actions were guided by his overriding ambition for power. Richard's relentless march to the throne is marked by murder, deceit, and villainy. Central to these acts of villainy is his responsibility for the murder of two young boys, the Prince of Wales and the Duke of York. By killing them, Richard secured his own claim to the throne. How accurate is this standard rendition in the light of historical facts? Is Richard the murderer of two young innocents?

*COMMENTS:*

**5.** *Introductory paragraph from a psychology paper on the nature of aggression:*

Why is mankind eternally plagued by war? Why does the rate of violent crime in the United States rise every year? Why, in short, are men so aggressive? Psychologists' answers to these questions vary greatly. Is aggression learned behavior, something that the ideal society could eliminate? Or is aggression innate in man, something that no society can escape? We will probably never find certain answers to these questions. Still, it is interesting to examine the various theories that psychologists offer to explain the nature and origin of aggression.

*COMMENTS (compare with the fourth introductory paragraph):*

**6.** *Introductory paragraph for a research paper on men's involvement in the feminist movement, written for an interdisciplinary women's studies course:*

"Since society's rules and systems are made by men . . . women are oppressed by men. And men must, then, be somehow forced to change their aggressive, domineering, selfish ways so that women can be free." Many men today would agree with Margaret Mead's statement, at least in part: they would agree that men have traditionally oppressed women and must change their attitudes and their actions. Recently, many men have proudly begun to call themselves feminists and to support the cause of women's rights. These male feminists, however, would argue that they do not have to be "forced" to change. Believing that both men and women need to be liberated from sexist roles and traditions, male feminists are taking the initiative by forming their own consciousness-raising groups, joining organizations such as the National Organization for Women, and actively campaigning for the ratification of the Equal Rights Amendment.

*COMMENTS:*

**7.** *Introductory paragraph from a paper on inflation, written for an introductory economics course:*

As Ben Franklin said, "A penny saved is a penny earned." But many people are finding it hard to save in these inflationary times. Prices are going up all the time, too, and people are finding that a dollar just doesn't buy as much as it used to. Everyone agrees that the United States must find a way to fight inflation, but economists are far from agreeing about what the best course of action is. Examining the views of three leading American economists shows us what a complex problem inflation is and how difficult it will be to solve.

*COMMENTS (compare with the sixth introductory paragraph):*

**8.** *Introductory paragraph for an essay comparing Socrates's and Antigone's views of law, written for an interdisciplinary freshman seminar:*

What is law? Webster defines it as "all the rules of conduct established and enforced by the authority, legislation, or custom of a given community or group." Both Socrates and Antigone come into conflict with the laws in their respective cities. However, they view the law very differently. It is interesting to compare and contrast their views of law.

*COMMENTS (compare with the first paragraph in "The Freshman Crazies," p. 62):*

**9.** *Introductory paragraph from an essay on the role that impulse can play in one's life, written for a composition course:*

It was a long, hot, difficult summer, and it was filled with apprehension about my future. My day at the factory was monotonous and boring because I had to stand in the same spot and count metal parts all day. It was on one of these days that I let my mind drift and search for what was really important in my life. While standing in front of my metal lathe, I asked myself if this is what I would like to be doing all my life. I silently answered myself with a quick "no." Upon saying "no," I suddenly realized that I should find some vocation that would make me content and happy. Within a few hours, I had resigned from my job and enrolled in a community college. This experience made me realize how often our decisions are based on impulse rather than on careful, time-consuming deliberation.

*COMMENTS:*

**10.** *Concluding paragraph from the essay on impulse (see last introductory paragraph):*

Impulsive decisions can thus help us by forcing us out of routines that might otherwise become paralyzing. Gazing around the factory on that hot midsummer day, I suddenly realized that everyone around me looked old and that I didn't want to look and feel that way for the rest of my life. I ran from that factory as if I were running for my life, and I have never regretted running. If I had stopped to think about what I was doing, I would have probably lost my nerve—and my chance to improve my life. We all take pride in our rationality, but we should realize that we often act on impulse and that our impulses sometimes help us more than our most careful, reasonable decisions can.

*COMMENTS:*

**11.** *Concluding paragraph from the paper about Richard III (see fourth introductory paragraph):*

An impartial investigation of the facts proves that the popular view of Richard III does not have a solid historical basis. Richard did not stand to benefit from killing the boys; his kingship was secure. It is not even certain that there was a murder, for there are no contemporary records claiming the princes were dead. The Bill of Attainder makes no mention of the murders. Finally, there is another suspect with a better motive than Richard's: Henry VII. No just court anywhere in the world would convict Richard on the basis of such scanty and inconclusive evidence.

*COMMENTS:*

**12.** *Concluding paragraph from a paper on* The Rime of the Ancient Mariner, *written for a literature course:*

In conclusion, as I have shown, the albatross in *The Rime of the Ancient Mariner* might represent God. Of course, Coleridge may or may not have intended this. I am sure there are many critics that disagree with me, and their views may be just as valid as mine, or even more valid. I would certainly defer to the opinions of more experienced and qualified critics. I have not read enough of Coleridge's other works to know whether or not it's likely that the albatross represents God, but it seems possible. The evidence is inconclusive, however.

*COMMENTS:*

### GENERAL CONCLUSIONS ABOUT INTRODUCTORY AND CONCLUDING PARAGRAPHS

1. What did the introductory paragraphs you found effective have in common? What did all these paragraphs accomplish? List some of the characteristics and purposes of a strong introductory paragraph.
2. What did the concluding paragraphs you found effective have in common? What did these paragraphs accomplish? List some of the characteristics and purposes of a strong concluding paragraph.
3. Comment briefly on the introductory and concluding paragraphs you found ineffective. Did these paragraphs have any common weaknesses?

## ADVICE

Ben Jonson was one of the greatest of Shakespeare's contemporaries. In "To the Memory of My Beloved Master William Shakespeare," Jonson praises Shakespeare as a poet gifted with great genius, a poet of whom "Nature herself was proud." But Jonson then goes on to praise Shakespeare for a quality that he does *not* owe to Nature:

> *Yet must I not give Nature all; thy Art,*
> *My gentle Shakespeare, must enjoy a part.*
> *For though the poet's matter Nature be,*
> *His Art doth give the fashion; and that he*
> *Who casts to write a living line must sweat*
> *(Such as thine are) and strike the second heat*
> *Upon the muses' anvil; turn the same,*
> *And himself with it, that he thinks to frame,*
> *Or for the laurel he may gain a scorn;*
> *For a good poet's made as well as born.*

What does Jonson mean when he says that even Shakespeare had to "strike the second heat"? The line alludes to the blacksmith's art: after heating and hammering a metal object once, the careful blacksmith

will heat it and hammer it again—"strike the second heat"—to make
the shape more perfect. Blacksmiths, then, must revise their work; according to Jonson, even a natural genius such as Shakespeare also had
to revise—and even to "sweat"—in order to make his works as good as
they are.

Frequently, we tend to neglect revision. It seems the least glamorous and least exciting part of writing a paper, and it is also in many
ways the most painful: since we all tend to fall in love with our own
words, we hate to change them. Also, many of us suffer from the illu-
sion that really good writing "just flows"; if we really have to work at
writing an essay, it will be "forced," "artificial," and probably not
worth much. Jonson's poem tells us just how mistaken this idea is: all
writers have to revise.

The first step toward successful revision, then, is realizing that revision is an essential stage in the writing process. Revision often makes
the difference between a poor paper and a good one, between a good
paper and an excellent one. Hemingway says that he revised the last
page of *A Farewell to Arms* thirty-eight times; the first version probably wasn't half bad, but the thirty-eighth one was almost certainly
better. In the college world of packed schedules and inflexible dead-
lines, you will rarely have the time to be as exacting as Hemingway
was, but you can realistically hope to allow yourself time for at least
three revisions. Each revision should begin with a critical rereading of
your paper or a part of your paper, involve a rethinking of your ideas
and of the words you use to express them, and end in careful rewriting.
Revision does not, however, have to involve a great deal of recopying;
avoid recopying whenever possible by crossing out, making insertions,
and cutting and pasting. Some paragraphs will have to be rewritten,
but others remain essentially intact through several revisions.

Five questions can guide you at various stages of your revision:

1. Is the *purpose* of my paper clear and consistent?
2. Should I *add or cut* any material?
3. Is the material *arranged* logically?
4. Do I show the *relationships* among my ideas?
5. Do my *words* express my ideas clearly, emphatically, and correctly?

If you follow the procedure suggested in this chapter, you will ask
yourself the first question during your first revision; the second, third,
and fourth questions during your second revision; and the fifth question during your third revision. You may, of course, decide to modify
this procedure depending on your own preferences and on the amount
of time you have given yourself to revise, but you should be sure to ask
yourself all five questions at some point in the revising process.

## First Revision: Making Your Purpose Clear

Try to complete your rough draft at least two or three nights before your paper is due. It is crucial that you put your paper aside for a while so that you can get some distance from it. Your goal, after all, is *revision:* before you can rewrite, you need to get a fresh look at your paper, to see it as if for the first time so that you can spot the problems that might trouble your readers. It's always difficult to detach yourself from what you've written, but letting some time go by between writing and rereading helps. Putting your paper aside for even a few hours can help, but a day or two would be much better.

When you return to your paper, put yourself in a critical frame of mind by trying to see yourself as an editor—or as your professor. Try to forget that you wrote the paper and approach it as a critical reader seeing it for the first time. You might try reading it aloud to give yourself a little more distance from it; you may be surprised to realize how unfamiliar your paper can seem when you hear it for the first time. Read slowly and carefully, making checks or notes in the margin whenever you spot a possible problem.

If you are revising a paper you have written for a course, *check the assignment again* after you finish this first rereading. Rambling away from a topic while writing is a common problem, and you may be horrified to discover that although your professor asked you to discuss the causes of the Franco-Prussian war, you ended up discussing its effects.

If you have indeed fulfilled the assignment, it's time to look critically at your thesis statement. Does it express your purpose clearly? Does it give the reader an adequate idea of the scope and direction of your paper? And does your paper indeed live up to your thesis statement? Again, watch for such problems as promising to discuss three causes of the Franco-Prussian war and in fact discussing only two. If there is a discrepancy of this sort between your thesis statement and your paper, you will have to revise one or the other.

Now is also the time to give careful thought to your introduction and conclusion. If you are like many writers, you may have only a functional introduction so far—something like "In this paper, I will discuss . . ."; if so, you probably have "awful—change this" scrawled in the margin. Writing an introductory paragraph is excruciatingly difficult for many writers, but there's no way to avoid it any longer.

An introductory paragraph has two purposes: to announce your topic and to capture the reader's attention. The second purpose is definitely subordinate to the first. Although a dull introductory paragraph can make your readers lose interest before they have given your ideas a fair chance, an overly elaborate or cute one can waste valuable time and make your paper seem contrived and silly. So exercise moderation and good sense while writing your introductory paragraph; don't be so intent on "catching the reader's eye" that you neglect your principal goal of announcing your topic and intentions. The Introductory Readings section of this chapter showed you several techniques you can use in introductory paragraphs.

When you have finished working on your introductory paragraph, start working on your conclusion. In a short paper, a separate concluding paragraph may not be necessary; often, a sentence or two will do. You do, however, need to find some way to warn your reader that the end is coming and to bring your paper to a smooth, satisfying finish. If you leave your readers wondering if they somehow misplaced the last page of your paper, you have a problem.

Ideally, a conclusion should do exactly what its name implies—it should draw a conclusion by bringing together all the parts of your paper and helping the reader to interpret everything you have said. It often seems temptingly easy to end with a summary, but simple summaries make effective conclusions only in long, complex papers; if your paper is only a few pages long, your readers will be bored by a repetition of ideas they read about only a few minutes before. Look for subtler ways to direct your readers' attention to the main point you wish to make. For example, you might decide to make your conclusion echo your introduction: if you asked a question in your introduction, repeat the question and then answer it in your conclusion; if you used a quotation in your introduction, repeat all or part of it in your conclusion and comment again on its significance; if you used an anecdote in your introduction, refer to it again in your conclusion. Echoing your introduction in your conclusion can give the readers a satisfying sense of completeness, a sense that all of the promises made at the beginning of the paper have been fulfilled at the end. After reading the paper, they have a chance to reexamine the question, the quotation, or the anecdote and to understand its implications more fully. Such a conclusion is much more artful and more satisfying than a simple summary.

When you have finished working on your thesis statement, introduction, and conclusion and are satisfied that all three help to make your purpose clear to the reader, you have completed your first revision. You might want to take a short break; being away from your paper will once again help you to become more detached from it. After an hour or so, you can begin your second revision while your paper's purpose is still firm and clear in your mind.

## Second Revision: Cutting, Adding, and Reorganizing

Your second revision is likely to be even more painstaking and painful than your first. Having made sure that your paper's purpose is clear, you must now make sure that every part of your paper is consistent with that purpose and that your paper fulfills its promises as completely and clearly as possible. The second stage of revising involves four related but at times contradictory tasks: cutting, adding, reordering, and making transitions. You may find it helpful to devote a separate rereading to each of these tasks, or you may find yourself doing all of them at once. Just be sure that you don't neglect any of the four.

As you reread your paper critically, cut or cross out anything that is repetitious or irrelevant. This process can hurt as you realize that whole paragraphs over which you labored will have to go because they don't directly support your thesis. These paragraphs may be excellent in themselves, but they will harm your paper by obscuring its purpose. No matter how much you like them, cut them out. Be firm and merciless. Also watch for repetitions of ideas, for these too can weaken your paper by annoying your reader.

Even as you are cutting some sentences and paragraphs, you may need to be adding others. Do any of your statements have to be clarified by concrete examples? Do any of your assertions need further support? Are any steps missing in your argument? For example, do you move from an assertion that a Black studies course will help white students learn about Black history to an assertion that the course will help eliminate racism without explaining how knowledge of history combats racism? Do you use any unfamiliar terms that should be defined? Put yourself in your readers' place and try to think of any additional information they might need in order to understand and be persuaded by your ideas.

Also check the order in which you have arranged your ideas. If you followed the procedure suggested in this textbook, you decided on your basic pattern of organization long ago. Now, check to make sure that you follow that pattern consistently. Some students find it helpful to make an extremely quick outline of their papers at this time—just a word or two capturing the point of each paragraph. Such an outline allows you to see the shape of your paper at one glance and may help you to spot any gaps or inconsistencies in your organization. For example, an after-the-fact outline of "The Freshman Crazies" might look like this:

Paragraph 1—define collegiate mental entropy
          2—symptoms of CME
          3—degrees of CME
          4—causes of CME
          5—benefits of CME
          6—reassurance

It may seem bizarre to make even a short outline after writing a paper, but the few minutes it requires can be very helpful. If the author of "The Freshman Crazies" had drawn up such an outline after completing his paper, he would have been reassured to see that his organization is indeed sound: each paragraph does have a distinct unifying purpose, each does help to develop the topic, and all are arranged in a logical order. If making a post-mortem outline does not appeal to you, look for another method of checking the organization of your paper.

When you are sure that your paper contains all the ideas needed to develop your thesis and that those ideas are arranged in the best possible order, make sure that the *relationships* among your ideas are clear to the reader. Even if your ideas are arranged in a perfectly logical order, your reader may not be able to follow your paper unless you make that order apparent. As you read, pay attention to transitions within paragraphs as well as to transitions between paragraphs.

One of the easiest ways of showing relationships among ideas is by using *transitional words and phrases*. Such words and phrases can help your reader follow your train of thought by pointing out such relationships as cause and effect, time sequence, contrasts, and additions. Notice how transitional words and phrases indicate relationships among ideas in the following paragraph. In previous paragraphs, the student has discussed several techniques novelist Daniel Defoe uses to create sympathy for one of his heroines, Moll Flanders.

| | |
|---|---|
| *In addition,* the episodic nature of the novel *also* helps to distract us from Moll's unprincipled | *(addition)* |
| conduct. *After* the death of Robin, Moll confesses that she was "not suitably affected with the | *(time sequence)* |
| loss" *and also* says that her two children were "taken happily off [her] hands." One might | *(addition)* |
| question Moll's indifference toward Robin, who was "really a very good husband" *and also* | *(addition)* |
| "a tender, kind, good-humored man as any woman could desire." *Even more significant* is | *(emphasis)* |
| her casual remark about her children, *for* it | *(cause and effect)* |
| reveals her insensitivity. The reader, *however,* | *(contrast)* |
| barely has time to think twice about Moll's lack of compassion, *for* it is only a matter of two | *(cause and effect)* |
| paragraphs *before* she begins to court "several | *(time sequence)* |
| very considerable tradesmen." The transition is made complete *on the next page.* Defoe plunges | *(time sequence)* |
| into the next stage of Moll's life, taking care to remind the reader that Moll was "tricked once | |
| by that cheat called love," *but* failing to mention | *(contrast)* |
| the honest, sincere love of husband Robin. | |

Useful as transitional words and phrases are, they can be overdone. If every sentence begins with *consequently, however,* or *moreover,* your style will quickly become monotonous and overwrought. It is therefore wise to use other methods of showing relationships among ideas as well: using parallel sentence structure, repeating important words or phrases, referring to previous paragraphs or ideas, and making occasional summary statements to prepare the reader when you are about to draw a conclusion. All these techniques are illustrated in "The Freshman Crazies." Using a variety of such techniques will help make your paper smooth and easy to follow.

When you are satisfied that you have made all the relationships among your ideas clear, you have finished your second revision. If possible, put your paper aside again for at least a few hours.

## Third Revision: Working on Words

Your main task in the final stage of revision is to look carefully at the words you have chosen to express your ideas—are they as clear, emphatic, and correct as you can make them? This is a good time to read your paper aloud to yourself slowly: your ear may catch disharmonies that your eye has missed.

Several years ago, I drew up a checklist for my students to use in the final stage of revision. The checklist reminded them to evaluate their level of diction, tone, sentence length, and sentence variety; it also reminded them to beware of such problems as wordiness, vagueness, euphemisms, and clichés. Under the heading of "Grammar and Mechanics," I listed every technical problem I could think of, from sentence fragments to misspellings. The checklist was logically organized and admirably complete. The only problem was that it was utterly useless. No one could possibly check for so many problems all at once, and no one would be insane enough to attempt a separate rereading for each of the problems listed. My students accepted the checklist politely, but I doubt that any of them ever used it.

In recent years, I have stopped using a printed checklist and have instead encouraged students to make up their own individual checklists. This approach is much more practical, and all it requires is some introspection. Begin by trying to identify the stylistic and technical problems you have most often had in previous papers; if you have a number of your corrected papers available, get them out and notice your teachers' comments and corrections. See if you can find a pattern in your errors and weaknesses. You may notice, for example, that your most frequent errors are using clichés, forgetting the commas in compound sentences, and misspelling words that end in -ance or -ence. Note these problems on your checklist—perhaps a large index card that you can keep on your desk. Make your checklist as specific as possible: "remember commas in compound sentences" will be more helpful than "be careful about commas." Add to your checklist when a new kind of error crops up in your writing. Remember, however, that if your checklist contains more than about ten items, it will be too long to be of any use to you. Limit yourself to listing your most frequent errors.

Once you have developed your checklist, you can use it whenever you reach the final stage of revision. Before you reread your paper, study the checklist for a few minutes to remind yourself of the kinds of problems for which you should be watching. If you are very ambitious, you might decide to devote one or two rereadings to looking just for your most frequent or most serious kind of error. If you know that you often write sentence fragments, for example, you might want to reread your paper once with the sole purpose of testing the completeness of every sentence. Refer to your dictionary and to the Appendix often during this final stage of revision; it's a shame to let minor errors in grammar, punctuation, or spelling distract your reader from your ideas. When you are sure that your words are clear and correct, it is finally time to type your paper. Even when the paper is typed, however, you will not quite be through with it.

## Proofreading

Proofread your paper more than once. Most of us proofread a page before taking it out of the typewriter so that we can make corrections without going through the annoying business of reinserting the page and trying to line it up again. This proofreading is not enough, however. When you have finished typing your paper, put it aside again—overnight, if possible. If you are now too close to your deadline for such luxuries, putting the paper aside for even an hour or so will help.

The most important part of proofreading is to keep yourself from simply reading your paper. If you become interested in your ideas or caught up in admiring your style, you will read too quickly and fail to spot typographical errors. Look for ways to slow yourself down and to force yourself to look at just one small portion of the paper at a time. I find it useful to place an envelope under the line I am proofreading: by blocking out everything but that line, the envelope slows me down and reminds me that at this point I should be paying attention to words, not ideas. Some students say that it helps to proofread your paper backwards so that it's impossible to pay attention to anything but words. If this technique doesn't drive you insane, it could work. A compromise method is to proofread your paragraphs in reverse order so that you at least can't get caught up in your ideas for very long. If you proofread your paper several times, go slowly, and refer to your dictionary whenever you're in doubt, you should catch most or all of your typographical errors.

## Getting Help

Outside help is valuable at several points in the revising process. During your first revision, you might ask some friends to read your paper and then question them to see if they understood your purpose; if they didn't, you have some rewriting to do. When you are doing your second revision, ask your friends if they can follow your paper without trouble and if they think that any statements need further clarification or support. Friends who are willing to help you check for mechanical and stylistic problems and to help you proofread your final draft are invaluable. Many of us tend to be shy and secretive about our writing and are particularly reluctant about showing others our papers before they are in final form. This tendency is understandable, but we should fight it if it keeps us from getting the help we need.

A few cautions are needed, however. First, check with your professor before you ask anyone for help with your papers. Some professors think that students should be completely independent when they write papers; others may not object if you get help with proofreading but say that you may not allow your friends to help with content or organization. Make sure that you know your professor's policy on receiving outside help. All professors agree that you should never let another person write any portion of your paper for you. If a friend suggests an excellent idea or phrase during a conversation and you can't resist using it, acknowledge the contribution in a footnote; you may feel silly, but it's the honest thing to do.

If your professor approves of outside help, you still need to be cautious about accepting it. After all, you are the writer and are ultimately responsible for the paper. Don't accept suggestions automatically, for your friends may have very good intentions but still steer you in the wrong direction. If your friend points out what seems to be a technical error, check your dictionary or the Appendix before you make the change. If your school has a writing center staffed by professionals, you can be more confident that their advice is sound, but even so you should think carefully about making changes. Even professionals are human beings who sometimes make mistakes.

All this talk about continual rereading, rewriting, checking, and changing may make revising sound like hard work. It *is* hard work— hard, and time-consuming, and often painful. As Ben Jonson says, we have to "sweat" when we revise, and we may find it a wrenching process continually to cut or change words, sentences, and paragraphs that had pleased us just a short time before. A poet like Shakespeare, Jonson says, must "turn" a line, "And himself with it," when revising. We may often feel that we are indeed turning ourselves, as well as our papers, upside down during the constant reevaluation of our ideas and words that revision requires. Even so, revision can be an exciting process. Few experiences are more satisfying than watching your paper grow with each revision as you gradually hammer what was once a vague, uncertain idea into the final shape that you will present to your readers.

## APPLICATION

**A.**  1.  Suppose that you have only a few hours to revise a paper. How would you adapt the revising process described in this chapter so that you can do an adequate job in a limited time?
     2.  Suppose that you are writing an in-class essay and will have only fifteen minutes for revision. How could you adapt the revising process to fit this situation?

**B.**  Take another look at four or five of the sample student essays in Chapters 1 and 2; your professor may tell you which essays to select. Analyze and evaluate the introductory and concluding paragraphs in these essays, commenting on the techniques the authors use and on the effectiveness of these techniques. You may find it helpful to refer to your lists of the characteristics and purposes of strong introductory and concluding paragraphs (see questions 1 and 2, p. 69).

**C.**  As an experiment, write three different versions of an introductory paragraph for the next paper you plan to write, using three of the following techniques:

- begin simply by stating your topic
- begin by asking a question
- begin by proving the importance of your topic
- begin by suggesting the inadequacy of widely held opinions
- begin with a definition
- begin with a quotation
- begin with an anecdote

Which version of your introductory paragraph do you prefer? Why?

**D.**  Following is the rough draft of a student essay on getting along with a roommate. What sorts of changes should the author make at each stage of the revision process?

- *First revision—Making Your Purpose Clear*
  Check thesis statement, introduction, and conclusion
- *Second revision—Cutting, Adding, and Reorganizing*
  Check to see if any material should be cut or added, if material is

presented in the best possible order, and if the relationships
among ideas are made clear
- *Third revision—Working on Words*
  Check for problems with style, grammar, and mechanics (Do you
  notice any kinds of errors that the author makes frequently and
  should add to her checklist?)

Meeting your new roommate for the first time can be a traumatic experience—probably one which you will never forget. It is
natural to have the precollege paranoia concerning roommates.
Most of this paranoia may stem from those horrible tales you
hear about your parent's old roommates at college and experiences your brothers and sisters may have had. Granted, there
may be some truth in those tales but keep in mind that they may
have been exaggerated also. Your roommate may turn out to be a
good friend of yours. They can be sources of great information
concerning all aspects of life. As many upperclassmen have
learned from experience there are certain tricks of the trade
which it behooves you to know if you are going to peacebly survive your college years.

The first and most important lesson is the easiest one to learn.
Talk to your roomate. Talk to him/her as an individual and carefully listen to what he/she has to say. The majority of the problems which arise between roommates can be easily solved if you
simply talk to one another. It may not be easy to do this at first
when you don't know each other well, but it is something that
each individual must work for and make an honest effort. Talking
about common interests such as sports, music, families, and
hometowns at first make it easy to lead into other conversations
and begin to understand one another. If your roommate is per-
turbed for some reason, take the time to try to find out the reason
for this behavior. Perhaps it is acadamics, problems with a boyfriend, personal conflicts with people on the hall or there may be
no rational reason for this hostility, but it is vitally important to
make the effort.

Another guideline and point of interest is to be assertive. If
something your roomate does bothers you then it is up to you to
approach the subject and solve the problem. For example, it is not
advisable for anyone to lend clothes, money or anything of senti-
mental value to other people unless you know them well enough
to trust them. If your roommate borrows something of yours without permission it is your responsibility to tell your roommate this
and to make yourself clear. Do not complain to the other people
on the hall but solve the problem yourself. Nevertheless, remember to be careful to use a considerable amouunt of tact and sensitivity. The best results can be obtained when you face your

roommate with a problem if you remain calm, fair and non-judg-mental.

Always be considerate of your roommate. You will find it easier to live together if you make the effort to get along with one another. This can be as easy as you wish or as difficult. If you are considerate of your roommate life will be less complicated. Some hints are: (a) establish study habits which are benefitial to both of you, (b) set aside certain hours of the day for sleep, (c) give your roommate time during the day when he/she can be alone in the room to have some privacy, (d) be careful about bringing boy-friends and girlfriends to your room—you don't want to monopo-lize the room, (e) plan to spend some weekends away from the room to give your roommate some privacy and space, (f) be care-ful of the stereo and respect each other's tastes in music. Living with a roommate requires you to give up some of your old habits and form new ones; it is a give and take situation.

There are some things which you can do in advance to get to know your roommate before you meet them at college. When you receive their address it is smart to write a brief letter about your-self before school starts—or call them. Also find out if you will be having one roommate or more than one. Avoid being in a triple, that is having two other roommates beside yourself. Three is a bad combination. Decide in advance what person is going to bring the stereo and other things so that you will not need to duplicate items. This will save traveling space and space in the room. De-cide upon the decoration of the room so each one is satisfied. If these things are done in advance then it will put you on a more informal level when you meet each other formally for the first time.

Getting to know your roommate will take time, but what better way to get to know someone than if you live with them. If you talk to each other be considerate yet assertive on issues then you should have a good start on what may turn out to be a longlast-ing friendship. It should be rememebered that not everyone can get along with all types of people. If you are having roommate problems and can not work them out, then discuss them with your Resident Assistant (RA) or the dormatory directors. If life is unbearable, then you can always change roommates. You will find yourself making friends throughout the year so you and your roommate can still remain independant from each other. As the time goes on you will settle in and you will learn to recognize your roommates moods and learn how to get along with him/her. When this happens you will loose your nervousness and begin to relax with one another. Like anything else which takes time, learning to live with your roommate will take time also.

**E.** Make up a checklist you can use when proofreading your paper to eliminate problems in style, grammar, or mechanics. If you have some of your corrected papers available, read them over and notice what sorts of errors you make most frequently. Make the items on your checklist as precise as possible, and don't include more than ten items.

**F.** Following is a paper in need of careful proofreading. Proofread the paper using one or more of the techniques suggested in this chapter. Do you have any other techniques that you use when proofreading a paper?

### College Life

College life is supposedly one of the best times of our lifes. Presently, I find that concept just a little hard to except. Although I can see some fun tyring to break through the pressure and all the work. As a freshman, my view of college life, is still very limited.

Everyday of the term is usually based on intencive studing. Most of the day revolves around attendence at your classes and various appointments, at night you franticly try to finish the assinged work and to comprehend as much as possible. In the meantime there is usually housecleaning to be done. The bigest outside task is is learning to cope with a roomate.

When you were younger and had not yet learned any better, you always wished you could live with one of your best friends. Well, you learn to stop wishing once you do get a roomate. There are certain common curtousies and personel right which should not be violated by anyone. When they do happen to be violated, suddenly that right was never defined. Roomates also play a very major role in ones survival, happiness, and success at school, one of the main reasons for this are that roomates spend so much time together.

College life is also noted for being the right time in most peoples lifes. The right time for love, marriage, fun, and acedemic work. But most people cannot find a good balence between work and pleasure.

Making it through classes is often more difficult then the homework assignments. Eight o'clock classes are renowned for being the most difficult. An eight o'clock calss that requires any amount of thought or concentration should not be taken. The bigest battle of the early morning class is staying awake, however this battle is shared by both the faculty and the student. Its hard to develope an intrest in a subject when your falling asleep.

Before anyone takes a course, they always ask what the proffeser is like and what the course is about. The proffesers to be avoided are the ones who are armed with chalk in one hand and the erasor in the other. Note-taking tends to be difficult when the instructer writes and erases simultanously. Any proffeser with a monotone voice can be guarenteed that his courses are amoung the last to be chosen. Even if his course contains the most intresting material, in class no one enjoys the embarassment of being found in a deep sleep.

With all of these problems, it is hard for a student to find the courses you can really enjoy; let alone to have fun. It may be that college life will get easier to handle as the years go by. At this point, however; I find it hard to belief that this is the best time of my life.

**G.**  Following are three versions of a student essay—two drafts and the final copy. Study the evolution of the paper, paying particular attention to these questions:

1. What changes has the author made in her thesis statement? Were these changes improvements? Why or why not?
2. What changes did the author make in her introduction and conclusion? Why do you think she decided to make these changes?
3. Did the author make any significant cuts or additions? Did she reorder any of her material? Did she make the relationships
   •  among her ideas clearer?
4. What changes did the author make in style, grammar, and mechanics? Are all the stylistic changes improvements? Why or why not?
5. What can you infer about the process this author followed while writing and revising her paper? For example, what did she try to accomplish in her first draft? What tasks did she concentrate on in her first revision? How does the author's revising process compare to your own?

### Draft 1
Never before in my life have I spent so much time studying; never have I continually had to share every inch of my living space with almost no chance for total privacy; and never have I been my own boss (the only one?) with nobody else around to tell me that I must brush my teeth and then to enforce the order. These are all major changes experienced in the transition from high school to college, but the largest (greatest) alterations in my life have been in my daily habits. At home I had many ways (did many things) not considered "sensible" by my parents which have

been amended here; other newly acquired habits are unwise but convenient.

At home I made a fairly successful attempt to go to bed each night at 11:00, and I usually filled (obtained, got) my 8-hour quota of sleep. I slept in my own room in my own house, not in a dormitory room shared with a roommate. At college ~~I consider m~~ my bedtime ranges from about midnight on a good night to 3 a.m.on a particularly bad night or a weekend. Often, my homework keeps me up even later; if I get 7 hours of sleep, I am pleased. Here I am jarred awake by a blaring alarm, & must further prepare myself to face the cruel world reluctantly. Seldom was I compelled to use an alarm at home, for my mother was good about waking me early enough so that I had time to come to full consciousness gradually. One distinct advantage of the ~~low level~~ small quantity of sleep is that I never suffer from insomnia; in fact, I always fall asleep in a few seconds.

My eating follows a much more regimented schedule at school than it did ~~in high~~ at home. Whereas I frequently skipped meals and snacked & nibbled heavily at home, here I regularly eat lunch and dinner, w/few snacks between. Now that I have to pay for the food I eat between meals, I think twice before I have a snack. Breakfast is a treat received for going to bed early so that I can rise early. Here I live on salads, fruit, and vegetables; the desserts and snacks are still tempting, but I partake of them in smaller quantities. Therefore, my school diet is also more nutritious than my diet at home was. At home I baked frequently & kept the kitchen well-stocked w/ sweets, which therefore comprised an overly large portion of my diet.

You would think that this change in diet would help me lose weight, but so far I have been unsuccessful. One reason may be that I get less exercise here, except for walking around campus. At home I participated in intramurals. I hope this changes when I take tennis next quarter.

College life may bear some resemblances to high school life, but, of necessity, it is characterized (marked) by radical changes. The changes I have described here are only a few among many.

### Draft 2

My lifestyle ~~has~~ <sup>has</sup> changed radically ~~in~~ the ~~past two~~ <sup>w/</sup> transition from high school to college: <sup>suddenly have little</sup> I study more than I ever had, I ~~have very few square~~ <sup>space</sup> ~~inches~~ to truly call my own, & I am around other people more than before. However, the greatest alteration in my lifestyle ~~have~~ <sup>has</sup>

been in my daily habits. In some ways my life here is more rigid, in some ways more flexible. At home I had many practices, not considered "sensible" by my parents, which have been amended here; other newly acquired habits are unwise but convenient. Most of these new patterns have been developed as a defense for situations in which I am at the mercy of others.

The first aspect of my day-to-day life in which I have made <sub>a</sub> radical changes is my sleeping pattern. At home I made a fairly successful attempt to go to bed each night at 11:00, & I usually got attained my 8-hr quota of sleep. At college my bedtime ranges from about midnight on a good night to 3a.m. on a bad night or weekend; if I get 7hrs. of sleep I am pleased. Seldom was I compelled to use an alarm at home, for my mother was good about waking me early enough to come to consciousness gradually. Here I am jarred awake by a blaring alarm, & must & lukewarm use shock therapy, in the form of hot shower coffee, to prepare myself to face the world. One distinct advantage of the small quantity of sleep is that I never suffer from insomnia as I occasionally did at home; infact, I rarely feel my bed.

Although my sleeping habits have become irregular, my eating established follows a much more regimented schedule at school. Whereas I frequently skipped meals & snacked & nibbled heavily at home, here I regularly eat lunch and dinner, w/ few snacks between.

(Breakfast is a treat received for going to bed early so I can rise early). My school diet is also more nutritious. At home I baked frequently & kept the kitchen well-stocked w/ sweets, which
              constituted
therefore ~~comprised~~ an overly large portion of my diet. Here I live on salads, fruit, & vegetables; the desserts I partake of in smaller quantities.
                                 Homework keeps me up late, and
Many of my habit changes are beyond my control.∧I can do nothing for the fact that the hall does not settle down early in the evening, thereby keeping me awake late; I have no control over the cafeteria menu. College life may bear some resemblances to high school life, but, of necessity, it is characterized by radical changes.

## The Transition

My lifestyle has changed radically with the transition from high school to college: I study more than I ever had, I suddenly have little space to truly call my own, and I am around other people more than before. However, the greatest alteration in my lifestyle has been in my sleeping and eating habits. In some ways my life here is more rigid; in some ways more flexible. At home I had many practices, not considered "sensible" by my parents, which have been amended here; other newly acquired habits are unwise but convenient. Most of these new patterns have been developed as a defense for situations in which I am at the mercy of others.

The first aspect of my day-to-day life in which I have made a radical change is my sleeping pattern. At home I made a fairly successful attempt to go to bed each night at 11:00, and I usually got my eight-hour quota of sleep. At college my bedtime ranges from about midnight on a good night to three in the morning on a bad night or weekend; if I get seven hours of sleep I am pleased. Seldom was I compelled to use an alarm at home, for my mother was good about waking me early enough to come to consciousness gradually. Here I am jarred awake by a blaring alarm, and must use shock therapy, in the form of a hot shower and lukewarm coffee, to prepare myself to face the world. One distinct advantage of the small quantity of sleep is that I never suffer from insomnia as I occasionally did at home; in fact, I rarely feel my bed.

Although my sleeping habits have become irregular, my eating follows a much more established schedule at school. Whereas I frequently skipped meals and snacked and nibbled heavily at home, here I regularly eat lunch and dinner, with few snacks between. (Breakfast is a treat received for going to bed early so I can rise early.) My school diet is also more nutritious. At home I baked frequently and kept the kitchen well stocked with sweets, which therefore constituted an overly large portion of my diet. Here I live on salads, fruit, and vegetables, indulging in desserts in smaller quantities.

Many of my habit changes are beyond my control. When my professors do not give me assignments that keep me up half the night, the other people on my hall keep me awake with their noise; I have no control over the cafeteria menu, and I cannot afford to buy the snacks that tempt me. Most of the radical changes in my life result not from choice but from the necessity of adapting to the realities of college.

# PART 2

# VARIETIES OF ESSAYS

**A** college writing course may be said to have two purposes. The first, broader purpose is to help the student become a better writer, with all that becoming a better writer implies. A writing course thus encourages the student to observe carefully, to think logically, to organize material coherently, and to express ideas clearly and gracefully. Writing is, in itself, an exciting and intellectually challenging subject that deserves to be studied for its own sake.

A college writing course also has a second, more immediately practical purpose: to prepare students for the various kinds of writing they will probably do during their college years. In this sense, a college writing course is not only valuable in itself; it is also a valuable preparation for other courses. Building on some observations Mina Shaughnessy makes in *Errors and Expectations,* we can identify eight kinds of statements students are frequently asked to make in college papers:

- *This is what happened.* (narration)
- *This is the look (sound, smell, or feel) of something.* (description)
- *This is like (or unlike) this.* (comparison and contrast)
- *This (may have, probably, certainly) caused this.* (causal analysis)
- *This is what this is.* (definition)
- *This is my opinion about this.* (argumentation)
- *This is what someone said.* (summary)
- *This is my interpretation of what someone said.* (interpretation)*

Think, for example, of a writing assignment that may at first seem far removed from the essays you write in a composition class—a

---

* Mina Shaughnessy, *Errors and Expectations* (New York: Oxford University Press, 1977), pp. 257–272.

laboratory report about a chemistry experiment. The report will probably involve a clear narration of just what you did in the experiment and a precise description of everything you observed: a change in the color of a chemical, the pungent smell produced, the texture of a product. You may compare the properties of one chemical with those of another; you may speculate about what caused a mixture to react as it did; you may define a technical term. You may have to use your observations as the basis for an argument about the best way to proceed. In an extended report that involves research, you may have to summarize the findings of several scientists and to interpret their conclusions in the light of your own experiments. In many other college writing assignments, from history term papers to essay questions on economics examinations, you will also need to narrate, to describe, to compare and contrast, to analyze causes and effects, to define, to argue, to summarize, and to interpret.

The following chapters explore ways of making and supporting the eight kinds of statements previously listed. These chapters thus attempt to prepare you for the various sorts of writing you will probably be called upon to do in college; they simultaneously introduce you to eight varieties of thought and expression that are worthy of study for their own sake.

# 4.
# Narration

## INTRODUCTORY READINGS

**A.** Read the following two essays, compare them carefully, and discuss the questions that follow.

### Cape May

That Friday night in August was not unlike several other Friday nights that summer of 1965. I sat on the arm of the yellow overstuffed chair, leaning my elbows on the fresh white-painted windowsill. A twilight breeze came in with the passing of each car on the road. I heard my mother and father whispering in the dining room. Immediately my heart leapt and my fingertips tingled. I knew what it meant when my parents whispered in the dining room on Friday nights in August. It meant one thing: a trip to the shore the next day. Now I can see that they were probably discussing if they could afford it and where we would stay, but when I was ten I saw no reason as to why we couldn't go to Cape May every weekend. I leaned my head toward the dining room to try and catch their words, but the whooshing of the cars outside blocked their already quiet voices. Soon curiosity got the best of me, and I slipped off the chair's arm and crept into the dining room. There I saw my mother and father, their heads bent together under the warm light of the Tiffany lamp. It is a picture I will never forget.

So we were off to the shore that Saturday in August. I don't recall that trip in particular, but I'm sure it was like all the other bumpy, sticky, unbearably long rides to Cape May that we had made before. We slouched in the wagon, all mopey and wilted,

until we reached the drawbridge that led to the town. Then we
came alive; we leaned our heads as far out the window as my
mother would allow us, and we ogled at the passing signs for salt-
water taffy and rafts for rent. We then turned up that road that
led right straight to the ocean. Cool salty breezes crossed my face
and coated my lips. The anticipation always seemed more than I
could bear.

We always stayed at older hotels and guest homes. They stood
out so—white clapboard buildings on warm pebble lawns. They
were always the same: pastel metal lawn chairs out back, cool
sandy carpeting in shadowed hallways, a not-unwelcome smell of
must and damp, fresh sea breezes drifting through sheer white
curtains. Once in our room, we wasted no time shedding our
shorts and wriggling into our swimsuits before tearing off to the
beach.

I remember that Saturday. My father and I walked up to Charlie's to get everyone burgers for lunch. We walked quickly, picking up our feet in short jerky motions to keep from burning them
on the roasted sand. We waited in line at Charlie's, the sand
gritty on the wood planks beneath our feet. The smells of grease
and catsup and Noxema mingled around us. Then the walk back,
just as quickly but a little more carefully—nothing is worse than
a sandy burger. We ate hungrily, stuffing and gulping, but something seemed to be missing that Saturday. There weren't as many
jokes, and my father was not as eager to toss us around in the
breakers as he usually was, and he complained that his arm and
shoulder ached—probably from surf fishing he said—and he
scolded me for getting catsup on my swimsuit (he never scolded).

Later my mother asked us to forget about that weekend, that
my father wasn't himself, that we shouldn't remember him that
way, that we should remember only the happier visits to the
shore. But, of course, I have never been able to forget it, nor have
I wanted to. My father's ways that weekend were just another
part of the scene like Charlie's burgers, the lost beach ball, the
collected shells. My mother wouldn't understand. She wanted us
to keep forever a shiny bright image of my father, untainted and
unblemished. But I knew that people were not that way, that
flaws are essential and cannot be dissected from the whole just
because one wished it. And I knew that my love was an unshak-
able thing quite able to pass the tests of imperfections and time.

We returned late Sunday afternoon. There was so much confusion that night: the ambulance arriving, the thumping of that
machine, my mother's short shriek, my neighbor telling my little
sister and me to kneel by our beds and pray. I couldn't breathe;
my chest felt closed and small. I kept shutting my eyes tightly

and wishing that I could sleep through it all as my older sister
was doing.

The first thing that struck me when I awoke the following
morning was that it was sunny. Sunlight streamed through my
white tie-backs. Why did I suppose it would be otherwise? Down
in the kitchen, someone had brought doughnuts. That was odd;
doughnuts were for special days like Sunday after church. Were
we expected to eat them? Maybe I should just reach in the box
and grab one, but then I might get one I don't like. Although I
thought it was wrong and somehow bad, I looked through the
dozen for the chocolate-covered one just as I always had. My
grandmother set a cup of tea in front of me. I felt stunned, not
sadness or a sense of loss, just kind of stunned and confused. How
was I supposed to act? What was I supposed to feel and do?

The morning went on. People from up the street brought flowers and cakes and meatloaves. I thought that was strange, to
bring food. Someone had brought something made with miniature
marshmallows, and we started giggling trying to figure out what
it was. Even my mother giggled with us; it must have been a nice
relieving surprise to find something so silly that Monday.

The next few days were a blurry series of people coming and
going, arms hugging and patting, eyes moist and staring deep
into mine. Old aunts would say, "Life goes on," and I soon came
to realize they were right. As I sat in the quiet living room, I
could hear my friends playing in the park, and when five o'clock
rolled around, we sat down to eat. I saw that by next week the
lawn would have to be mowed and by next month the leaves
would have to be raked. I thought of those waves in Cape May
breaking and breaking over my father's footsteps in the sand and
carrying them off to somewhere else.

And it occurred to me that all would not end when I died either. Children would still have parties, Christmas trees would
still be put up, the snow would melt, the tulips bloom, and the
ocean waves would keep pounding the jetty hour after hour.

### Brian's Death

My older brother, Brian, died when he was just nineteen years
old. I was only eleven at the time, but I remember the incident
very clearly. I had been playing in a baseball game—it was a
Saturday afternoon in May—and came home, all upset because I
had struck out twice. My parents were crying, and before I could
ask what was wrong, Mr. Ellis, who lived down the street, took
me aside and told me that Brian had been killed in a car accident. Of course, I started crying, too—I just couldn't believe he

was dead. Later on, I thought about what had happened and realized that I had learned several things: about the dangers of reck-
less driving, about the importance of appreciating the people we
love while we still can, and about what's really most important in
life.

Brian had always loved to drive fast. He had gotten two tickets
for speeding and my father had yelled at him both times and
threatened to take his driver's license away, but he never had.
After the accident, my father blamed himself for not being firmer,
but I don't think he was really responsible: he was just trying to
be a good father and always wanted to be kind to his kids and
give them another chance. He was always nice to me, too—he
used to threaten to ground me when I would stay out too late at
night and not get my homework done, but he always gave in
when I promised I would be better in the future. Brian made
promises, too: both times he said he had learned his lesson and
wouldn't speed again, and my father believed him. Brian got a
real charge out of driving fast. He was a good driver and said he
loved the feel of total control that fast driving gave him. I can remember going out with him a couple of times and watching the
speedometer climb and climb—it was fun, but it always made me
nervous. Now, whenever I'm tempted to speed up, I think about
what happened to Brian and slow down. He had just lost control
of his car, I guess, and gone right through the guard rail on the
overpass. The car had flipped over twice, witnesses said, and
Brian and his girlfriend, Nancy, were killed instantly. When you
drive recklessly, you endanger other people's lives as well as your
own. The excitement just isn't worth taking the risk.

When I got home that afternoon and saw my parents crying, I
realized just how much I had always loved Brian. During the days
that followed, when we were trying to get over the shock as my
parents made arrangements for the funeral, I thought about him
a lot and about all the good times we had had together. My Aunt
Amy and Uncle Joe (he's my father's brother) came to help with
the arrangements, and at one point Aunt Amy said, "I never
really got to know Brian that well. I wish I had, but it's too late
now." That remark really struck me as true. I had known Brian
pretty well, of course, even though he was eight years older than
I was, but I wished I had talked to him more. Maybe I could have
warned him about how dangerous it is to drive fast. He probably
wouldn't have listened to me, but at least I would have tried, and
I would have gotten to know him more. A couple of weeks after
the funeral, I was helping my mother go through the stuff in
Brian's room—we both kept breaking down and crying—and I
found a couple of overdue library books about making movies during the 1940's. I had never even known Brian was interested in

old movies. It made me feel like I didn't even know my own
brother that well. This experience taught me that we should try
to really know and appreciate the people we love, for we never
know how long they'll be around.

The day of the funeral was really hard. I can hardly remember
the service at the church because we were all crying so hard: my
parents, me, my fifteen-year-old sister Liz, Aunt Amy and Uncle
Joe, and all the other relatives and neighbors. A lot of Brian's
friends were there, too, crying and looking stunned. Nancy's parents didn't come because they blamed Brian for their daughter's
death, and even now they won't speak to my parents because they
think they didn't discipline Brian enough. I think it's really horrible to hold a grudge against a dead person, but I can understand
how they feel. After the funeral we went back to the house and a
lot of neighbors and Brian's friends came over. It was hard to
make conversation: we tried talking about Brian and all the good
things about him—doing well in school, being captain of the
swim team—but we kept on breaking down all over again. I
knew that people were coming over to be nice and see if they
could help us with anything, but I kept wishing they would go
away and leave us alone.

As time went on, I got over the shock and thought about what
the whole experience has taught me. I guess the most important
lesson was about what really matters most in life. On the day
Brian was killed, I had been playing baseball and had struck out
twice. It was no big deal—it was just a game between two neighborhood teams, so I shouldn't have been so worked up about it.
The disappointing part was that I had worked on my batting the
whole summer before and had really improved, and now here I
was striking out twice. Some of the guys on the other team made
insulting remarks, too—just joking around, but it made me mad.
So as I was walking home, all I could think about was how mad
and frustrated I was and how maybe I should just forget the
whole thing and give up baseball. It seemed really important.
Then I got home and heard Brian was dead, and the whole baseball game seemed so silly. There I was worrying about my batting
average and meanwhile my older brother had died and I didn't
even know it. I felt really ashamed. It's not that I think baseball
is stupid; I'm on the college team now. It's just that we should
have more of a perspective on life and not let ourselves get all
upset about less important things when it's the big things that
matter so much more.

When Brian died, it was the first death in my family. Two of
my grandparents and one of my uncles (not Uncle Joe) have died
since then, but Brian's death made the biggest impression on me.
We should try to learn from all our experiences, even when they

hurt us a lot. From Brian's death, I learned not to drive recklessly, to appreciate the people I love, and not to let little things
bother me too much because it's the big things that really matter.

## DISCUSSION QUESTIONS

1.  Describe the authors' apparent purposes in writing about these ex-
    periences. What ideas or impressions does each author want to
    communicate to the readers?
2.  Comment on each author's use of detail. For example, you might
    focus on the details in the fourth paragraph of "Cape May" and in
    the third paragraph of "Brian's Death." How are the details in
    these paragraphs related to the authors' purposes? Does either
    essay contain details that should be omitted?
3.  Describe the way each essay is organized. How is the organization
    of "Cape May" similar to that of "Brian's Death"? How is it dif-
    ferent?
4.  Examine the introductory and concluding paragraphs of each
    essay. What does each author attempt to accomplish in these para-
    graphs? Do you consider these paragraphs effective and appro-
    priate?
5.  When did you first realize that "Cape May" was about the death of
    the author's father? Why do you think the author withheld this in-
    formation for so long? Was it a wise decision?
6.  Describe the way each essay affected you as you read it. Which
    essay drew a stronger response from you? Why?
7.  If the authors planned to revise their essays, what advice would
    you give them?

**B.**   Read the following two essays, compare them carefully, and then
discuss the questions that follow.

### A Day at the County Fair

Last summer, my boyfriend Pete and I decided to take his little
brother Mike to the Culbert County Fair. We thought it would be
fun to watch Mike having a good time because he's only ten years
old and still gets excited about things like roller coasters and fun-
houses. It *was* fun watching Mike enjoy himself, but I'll have to
admit that Pete and I enjoyed ourselves just as much. I guess
you're never too old for something like a county fair, because we
all had an exciting day.

We got up early that morning and climbed into Pete's old Mustang at 9:00 because we wanted to have a full day at the fair. It

takes almost an hour to get from my house to the fairgrounds, and the traffic was really heavy that day; I guess a lot of people wanted to go to the fair. Sure enough, the Mustang started giving us trouble about halfway there: it got overheated and we had to pull over to the side of the road for a while. We worried all day that the car would give us trouble on the way home too, but luckily it didn't.

When we finally arrived at the fair, we parked the car and got out. We walked right past the agricultural exhibits—I'm sure that some people find them interesting, but we don't know how to tell a prize cow from a sick one. So we walked over to the rides. We had a lot of fun with the bumper cars. I told Pete that all of the bumper cars were more reliable than his beat-up old Mustang. Mike suggested that we take one home with us and leave the Mustang behind, and we all laughed. We went on the whip, the ferris wheel, and many other rides too—I can't even remember them all now, but we enjoyed every one. Then we got to the roller coaster. I've always been afraid of roller coasters and thought I would just watch Pete and Mike, but Pete insisted that I get on with him, so I finally gave in. It was a huge, fast roller coaster with all kinds of dips and loops; it was extremely scary. I screamed the whole way, but I had fun, too. As soon as we got off, I said, "I want to go on again!" Pete and Mike laughed at me about that one, and I still haven't lived it down.

We had hot dogs for lunch—somehow, they always taste better at a fair than they do when you make them in your own kitchen. After lunch, we went on some more rides and then went to the funhouse. We all had a great time. When we were in the room with all the mirrors that distort your image, Pete said I looked better in the mirror that makes you look skinny than I do in real life. I punched him in the arm, but I knew he was only kidding. By now we were all getting pretty tired, but we wanted to stay for the show at night, so we just took a long time over dinner—hot dogs again—and rested up.

The show was fabulous. There were some local performers who were all good, but the highlight was a big star—Johnny Cash! I don't know how they can afford to pay someone so famous at a county fair, but I sure am glad they did. He was really great: he sang "A Boy Named Sue" and the one about the prison, and he joked around with the audience a lot. I've watched him on TV many times, but I liked him even better in person. Getting the chance to see him was very special.

It was after 10:00 when we finally started for home. Mike was really tired and fell asleep in the back seat. Pete and I were exhausted too, and we kept praying that the car wouldn't act up. As I said before, it didn't, and Pete dropped me off at my house at

about 11:30. I was so tired that I just stumbled upstairs and fell
right into bed, promising my parents that I would tell them all
about my day in the morning. It was an exhausting day, but so
much fun that I can hardly wait to go to the Culbert Country
Fair again next year.

### Flowers I'll Never See

My brother and I were looking at the exhibitions at the annual
Culbert County Fair. At the very end of one of the rows of exhibitions was a small tent. In front of the tent was a long, thin table.
On it was a box with a stencilled sign that read, "Flowers You
Will Never See." My brother looked in, laughed, and as he ran
away said it was the "old oak." I looked in and saw a model of a
coffin surrounded by flowers, and I knew it was time for me to get
out of the area. But I'll never be known for my quickness, and before I could make any move, I felt this hand clasp me firmly on
the shoulder. I knew him without his having to introduce himself:
a traveling preacher.

I was dragged into the tent and was asked by the man if I was
going to Heaven or Hell. I wasn't any dummy, or so I thought. I
quickly realized he would go beserk and scream at my hypocrisy
or tell me to elaborate if I said I was going to heaven. And I
couldn't imagine what would have happened if I admitted that I
was a shoo-in for the hot rocks of Hell. Sitting down and thinking
I was real smart, I told him I was going to purgatory. That was as
neutral of an answer as I could muster. He sort of stared at me,
not knowing exactly what to say, then reached down and picked
up his Bible. Sliding it across the cardboard table that separated
us, he told me in a low voice to find the word "purgatory" in the
Bible. He kept on talking, and the more he talked, the faster his
words came out.

There I was, sitting in a fold-up chair, leafing through the
Bible for the meaning of purgatory. By this time, the man was
getting really excited. He grabbed the Bible and told me again
there was no such place as I had claimed. Well, I hadn't taken
any classes in any seminaries, so I wasn't in any sort of shape to
get into deep theological arguments with him. I knew I wasn't
going to get anywhere if I insisted I knew what I was talking
about. I realized that what I was saying was purely the doctrine
of my church.

He had been sitting on the other side of the table staring
across at me like a judge that was going to hand down the final
verdict. Looking at him, I could guess that the verdict was guilty.
But guilty of what? Here I was, only a runny-nosed twelve-year-

old and about to be condemned. The preacher picked up his chair, giving me a sweet smile that showed his gold fillings, moved over, and sat beside me.

Since he hadn't yet told me I was a completely hopeless case, I tried some plea bargaining. After mumbling and squeaking for a few minutes, I decided to stop when I got to the part about stealing my brother's multicolored marbles. Unlike the priest in confession, he would, I knew, use anything I said against me.

When he started talking to me, I must have mentally blocked out his words, because for the life of me I can't remember what he talked about. All I knew was that the sun was shining and my brother was outside having a good time, and this man in his three-piece earth-toned suit with a wilted weed of a flower was telling me that the savior was coming.

And of all the wonders this earth has ever seen, the savior did arrive in that very tent. The flaps of the tent parted, and in he walked. Taking me by the hand, my father delivered me into freedom.

## DISCUSSION QUESTIONS

1. Comment on each author's choice of a topic. Did each author do a good job of selecting and limiting a topic?
2. Describe the authors' apparent purposes in writing about these experiences. What ideas or impressions does each author want to communicate to the readers?
3. Comment on each author's use of detail. For example, you might focus on the details in the third paragraph of "A Day at the County Fair" and in the fourth paragraph of "Flowers I'll Never See." How are the details in these paragraphs related to the authors' purposes? Does either paragraph contain details that should be omitted?
4. Describe the way each essay is organized. Are the paragraphs in each essay unified and well developed?
5. Examine the introductory and concluding paragraphs of each essay. What does each author attempt to accomplish in these paragraphs? Do you consider these paragraphs effective and appropriate?
6. If the authors planned to revise their essays, what advice would you give them?

C.   Read the following two essays, compare them carefully, and then discuss the questions that follow.

## Chairness

The Church of the Good Shepherd held discussion groups every Sunday night. This story is about my first time in an adult class.

Reverend Baker paraded into the crowded room, ignored the lectern, and sat on the table. He set down the books he had been carrying and went right to business.

"Plato had wondered," said Rev. Baker, "about chairs."

We looked at each other.

"Plato had pondered," continued Rev. Baker, "what made a chair a chair. He would look at a chair and see that it had arms, legs, back, and all the things that had fit the description of a chair; but Plato felt that the chair had something else. Whatever this 'something' was, it permeated all chairs. Plato had felt that there was more of this 'something' in a king's throne than in a simple armchair and that there was more of this 'something' in a simple armchair than in a common stool. He gave this something a name. Plato named it 'Chairness.'

"Plato then came to the conclusion that all chairs in the real world possess Chairness; but some chairs possess more Chairness than others. He also concluded that outside of the real world (out there, somewhere) existed a perfect, pure, and ideal example of a chair that all terrestrial chairs have an image of.

"Plato didn't stop there. He applied the same thoughts to humans. 'Does each of us possess Humanness?' asked Plato. 'Does each of us possess an image of the perfect and pure example of a human that is not in our world? Does such a being exist?' As you can see, the parallels are beginning to form between—"

"Hold on," I said.

"Yes?"

"I don't think I get this Chairness stuff. Is Chairness qualitative or quantitative?"

"What do you mean?"

"Can you measure it? Is there a unit of Chairness?"

"I suppose it's possible."

"Does a chair's Chairness remain constant? If I took an axe to one of those wooden folding chairs and demolished it, would the net Chairness of the debris equal the initial Chairness? If I had one piece of chalk, one person could write on the chalkboard. If the piece is broken in half, two people could write. The amount of chalk has not changed, but the Chalkness appears to have doubled. Chairness doesn't seem quantitative to me."

Rev. Baker looked at all the people in the room. He turned to me and said, "Perhaps Chairness is qualitative."

I said, "I don't think so. Can only a chair possess Chairness?"

"If Plato said so—"

"But you're sitting on a table. You must recognize Chairness in that table. That table suits your needs better than these wooden chairs. I prefer the wooden chair. Therefore, you and I have differing ideas as to what Chairness is. Everyone must have a slightly different idea as to what an ideal chair is. A Hindu scholar would see more Chairness in a thorn bush than in a Lazy-Boy recliner. Since there is no single characteristic that is common to all chairs, there can't be any one omnipresent image residing in any chair. Now if you apply this line of thought to the concept of Humanness—"

"And that," said Rev. Baker to the class, "is where we shall begin our discussion."

That was when I was sixteen. For some reason, the vestry announced the following week that from that point on, no one under eighteen years of age would be allowed to participate in the adult classes.

## Just Cause

When I was small, the summer days were long and warm and filled with the staccato sounds of locusts; the nights were blessedly cool with the constant background of chirping crickets and shrill tree frogs. All the world was just and fair: at school if you cheated or threw a spitball, you were sent to Mr. Johnson, the principal; if you lied to your mother or smacked your little brother, you were not allowed out to play. For every punishment there was a just cause. Then, two things happened that shattered my illusions of justice.

There was a cool woods near my home, not a creeping-jungle woods but more like an overgrown-park woods. My best friend Terry and I went there every day. There was one end of the woods that was covered with small green plants that we called "umbrella" plants. We didn't go to that end often becase of an upturned stump that we were told housed a large brown snake. We could see that end from the end we played in, and one day it was lush and green and the next it was scorched and blackened. We were itching to find out what had happened, and we finally did from Terry's little brother. It seems two brothers that we knew only slightly had started the blaze.

It was some time later that I finally saw the younger of the two boys. Half his face and one of his arms were pink and puffed and seemed very painful. Whenever I saw him at the shopping center, I would look down at the pavement or at my reflection in the drugstore window. But that face had become an unforgetable part of my memory. It really gripped me; I knew starting fires was a

terrible thing, but to be deformed for life was certainly different
from being forbidden to attend the church fair. It then occurred to
me that there wasn't a universal system of just punishment for
certain wrongdoings.

It was one or two summers later that my second lesson in unfairness was to happen. I was about to cross the street in front of
my house when a boy unknowingly rode his bike into the path of
a car. I heard that screech that seems to stop your heart, and I
turned and everything seemed to slow way down. I saw the boy
fly over his handlebars as if on a string; I watched the headlight
shatter and appear to float away. That is the last thing I remember. How badly he was hurt or if he was taken away, I cannot recall.

I had now learned that people were punished even when they
had done nothing wrong. I was no longer as content and comfortable with being a good girl. So I would lie awake in my cool
sheets listening to the chirping crickets and piping tree frogs and
thinking that any time or anywhere something terrible could happen to me or my family, and that there was nothing I could do
about it.

## DISCUSSION QUESTIONS

1. Describe the authors' apparent purposes in writing about these experiences. What ideas or impressions does each author want to
   communicate to the readers?
2. The author of "Chairness" does not explain the significance of the
   incident he describes. Why do you think he decided against making his interpretation of the incident explicit? Was it a wise decision?
3. The author of "Just Cause" does explain the significance of the two
   incidents she describes. Why do you think she decided to make her
   interpretation of these incidents explicit? Was it a wise decision?
4. "Chairness" consists almost entirely of dialogue. Did you find this
   technique effective? Explain.
5. "Just Cause" describes two separate incidents. Is the essay nevertheless unified? Explain.
6. Examine the introductory and concluding paragraphs of each
   essay. What does each author attempt to accomplish in these paragraphs? Do you consider these paragraphs effective and appropriate?

## GENERAL CONCLUSIONS

1. The six essays you have just read could be described as *narrative
   essays*. Write a brief definition of the term *narrative essay,* identify-

ing the characteristics that distinguish narrative essays from other sorts of essays.

2. Draw together all the observations and comments you have made about the introductory readings in this chapter. List some of the characteristics of a strong narrative essay, or summarize your conclusions in a paragraph that would be helpful to a beginning composition student. What advice would you give to a student who was writing a narrative essay based on personal experience?

## ADVICE

The first essay assigned in a college composition class is often a narrative essay. "Write a narrative essay based on a personal experience," the professor says. The assignment sounds invitingly easy. What could be simpler or more enjoyable than writing about your trip to California or your first day at college or the swim meet when you came in first in three events? Narrative essays can indeed be enjoyable to write and to read. You always stand a better chance of interesting your reader if you are interested in your topic yourself, and most of us find our own experiences highly interesting. Moreover, narrative essays offer certain practical advantages: you don't have to spend time doing research or gathering information since you already know the material and can concentrate on shaping it into an essay. And, as a fringe benefit, writing about your own experiences can help you to examine those experiences more closely, so you may derive some unexpected insights into them. Unless they are written carefully and thoughtfully, however, narrative essays can strike the reader as dull and pointless. In order to write a successful narrative essay, you will have to pay careful attention to selecting an appropriate experience about which to write, deciding what sorts of details to include, organizing your essay, and guiding your reader's interpretation of the experience.

### Selecting an Experience

When we are asked to write a narrative essay about a personal experience, the experiences that come to mind most readily are likely to be ones that we remember because they were in some way glamorous or exciting—high-school graduation, a sports victory, a trip to Paris. Such experiences, however, may not make the best topics for narrative essays. Your high-school graduation, unless it was truly unusual, was probably similar to the graduations of most of your readers; the emotions you felt, no matter how profound or sincere, were probably very much the same as those of millions of other high-school graduates. Are you likely to find a way to make your essay original and interesting? An essay about a sports victory will probably run into similar problems: most of us have read dozens of essays or articles about athletes facing their greatest challenges, overcoming their fears and doubts, and persisting against discouragement and exhaustion until they finally won. An essay about a trip to Paris is too likely to become a catalogue of museums and restaurants.

When looking for a topic for a narrative essay, then, it is often wisest to reject experiences that appeal to you simply because they seem exciting—"The Day I Hit Ten Home Runs for My Team." Certainly, it is possible to write an excellent essay about a high-school graduation or a sports victory. It is possible to write an excellent essay on any topic, even a topic that has been used by thousands of other writers. E. B. White's great essay "Once More To The Lake" could almost be subtitled "How I Spent My Summer Vacation." The point is that the surface glamor is not enough. The experience must also have a more profound significance that you can identify and communicate to your readers. An essay about a trip to Paris may turn out to be a clichéd description of the usual tourist attractions; an essay about a trip to the corner grocery store may be more truly memorable if it includes a description of the grocer's pathetic attempts to make his little store compete with the large supermarket chains.

Look for experiences you remember not simply because they were exciting at the time but also because they taught you something by giving you fresh insight into a person or a part of life. Don't pick the most obvious topic without giving it careful thought, and don't give up in despair because your life seems too ordinary and devoid of excitement to interest anyone else. Every life contains hundreds of experiences worth writing about if we are alive and sensitive to the implications of every action, word, and gesture. Examine your experiences carefully when you are looking for a topic: some seemingly ordinary incident may be the basis for an excellent essay if you can see past the surface and uncover for your reader the significance hidden within. Look back at the Introductory Readings in this chapter and select the essay that most interested you. How did the author's ability to observe and interpret experience help you to see the significance of the events described?

## Deciding on Details: Supporting a Central Impression

When you recount an experience in a narrative essay, you almost certainly do not want to include every detail you remember about that incident. The essay would become impossibly long—and, probably, intolerably boring—if you describe what everyone you mention was wearing and quote every word that was said. On the other hand, a narrative essay devoid of detail is also not likely to be interesting. How, then, do you decide which details to include and which to leave out?

It's best to begin by determining what sort of *central impression* you wish to create in your essay. This major decision will then guide the later ones about which details belong. Suppose, for example, that you are writing about your first day at a summer job at a factory. If you have decided to write a humorous essay, you will want to include many details about the little things that went wrong, the amusing mistakes you made, and the tricks your more experienced co-workers played on you. If, on the other hand, you want to create the impression that factory work is boring and ultimately deadening, you will want to mention those details that suggest the monotony of the job and to describe the tired, numb expressions on the other workers' faces. In such an essay, it would probably not be a good idea to mention the jokes your co-workers played, unless you see those jokes as a feeble, pitiful attempt to fight the dreariness of the daily routine.

The details a skillful narrative essayist includes may sometimes seem surprising, but they always have a purpose. In "Cape May," for example, why does the author mention her uncertainty about whether or not to look for the chocolate-covered doughnut on the morning after her father died? How does this detail contribute to the impression the author creates throughout her essay? Whenever you have to decide whether or not to include a detail in a narrative essay, ask yourself what it contributes to the overall impression you want to build. If it does not contribute anything, leave it out, no matter how striking or amusing it may seem.

## Organizing a Narrative Essay

Chronological order is the natural choice for a narrative essay: the incidents are described in the order in which they occurred (see Chapter 2, p. 46). Using chronological order is not always as simple as it seems, however, for if you are not careful to give the readers the information they need at every step, you may have to backtrack to fill in crucial details. It is difficult for readers to get caught up in the emotion of the experience if they have trouble following the chain of events.

You may, of course, decide to violate chronological order intentionally on occasion. Sometimes it is good to begin with the climactic event in order to capture the readers' attention and to help them focus on the most significant part of the experience. You can then go back to narrate preceding events. The author of "Brian's Death" attempts to use this technique, but the opening paragraph's effectiveness is muted by unnecessary details. How could the author revise this paragraph to give it greater impact?

## Guiding Your Reader's Interpretation of the Experience

A narrative essay should have a point as well as a plot. We read a newspaper article simply to find out what happened, but we expect something more when we read a story or a narrative essay. We do not necessarily expect shockingly original observations about the nature of life and death, but we do expect that the story or essay will have an interest beyond whatever suspense is created by the incidents themselves; we read not only to learn what happened but also to discover what significance the author sees in the story.

It is, however, dangerous to think every narrative essay needs a "moral" tacked on to the end. Most mature readers will be dissatisfied by an essay that ends with a simplistic statement such as "This experience taught me to count my blessings." Many otherwise promising narrative essays are spoiled by a clumsy conclusion that attempts to force-feed the "moral" to the reader. Do any of the Introductory Readings err in this regard?

Should you make the point of your narrative essay explicit? The only possible answer is "it depends"—on the particular experience you are describing, on the particular impression you wish to create, and on the particular idea you wish to convey. If you have done an excellent job of creating a central impression through a careful selection of details, you may not have to state your point at all; on the other hand, you may be able to weave your interpretation into the essay so skillfully and subtly that the interpretation becomes a part of the story. Whether or not you decide to make the point of your narrative explicit, the essay should have a point, and that point should be clear to an intelligent reader.

## APPLICATION

**A.**   List five or six of your experiences that might be used as topics for narrative essays. Remember that incidents from childhood often make good topics.

Now go through your list and pick out the experiences that seem most promising. Why do these topics seem best to you?

**B.**   Pick one experience from the list you developed in response to the first exercise.

1. What would be the point of a narrative essay you might write about this experience? What sort of central impression would you try to create?
2. Freewrite about this experience for ten or fifteen minutes, writing down all the details you can recall. Then go through what you've written and underline details that would contribute to the central impression you would try to create.
3. If you were to write a narrative essay about this experience, how

might you organize it? What sort of introductory paragraph
would be effective?
4. If you were to write a narrative essay about this experience, do
you think you would make your point explicit? Why or why not?

**C.** Read this short narrative essay and then answer the questions
that follow.


## A Night on the Town

If you find yourself with nothing to do at six o'clock, where
should you go for a change? Go to New York City and watch the
nuts come out.

My friend Dave, my cousin Ed, and I went there last weekend.
We all had a good time riding around and drinking beer. Later
we went to a movie in Times Square. New Yorkers must never go
to bed, because at 12:00 people were still walking around like it
was still afternoon.

At one particular time early in the evening, we had stopped at
a light when all of a sudden we started talking to the people in
the car next to us. We found out that they were from Yonkers. It
felt as though we had known them a long time. As the light
turned green, we waved and beeped the horn. It was a surprising
experience.

There was one funny incident that happened while we were
riding in the car. My friend was telling me that there are twenty-
five murders per week on the average in New York City. All of a
sudden we heard a big bang, and my cousin exclaimed, "There
goes number twenty-six!" We just laughed, but it really is not
funny at all.

1. Comment on the author's choice of a topic. Is the topic appropriate for a short narrative essay?
2. Do all the details in the essay contribute to creating a central
impression? Should any details be omitted? What sorts of details
might be added?
3. How is the essay organized? What do you think of the introduction and conclusion?
4. If the author planned to revise this essay, what suggestions
would you give him?


**D.** Read this narrative essay and then answer the questions that
follow.

### Another Day at the Races

The alarm clock blasts. I roll over in bed, not quite believing it is time to rise. Half asleep, I look at the clock, which reads quarter to seven! For a brief moment, I do not remember why the alarm rang. With a start, I sit up in bed, realizing today is the day of the Regional Track Meet. Hurriedly I jump out of bed to dress and to pack my sweatsuit and spikes in my Andover bag. Quickly I run out the back door to the car. Just as speedily, I rush back inside to pick up the car keys I had forgotten. Finally, after picking up half the track team, I arrive at school. The first person I see is the coach, looking at his watch with a worried expression on his face. After taking one glimpse at his face, the team wastes no time piling the pole vault poles, starting blocks, hurdles, camping equipment, and ourselves onto the bus. Once in the bus, I begin to concentrate on the tactics and the rituals of the Mile Relay. Just the thought of the race makes my heart beat faster and my stomach churn. All too quickly, we arrive at the school where the meet is being held. The team swaggers off the bus ready to face another Saturday at the races. Three other girls and I stroll off the bus ready to start performing the comical charade required to run the Mile Relay.

Like most races, the Mile Relay has its own special rules. Since the Mile Relay is the last event of the day, there is plenty of time to perform this ceremony. First, the Mile Relay team and I jog over to the stands and lie down (as if to sleep) between the spectators. Meanwhile, the rest of the team warms up on the track. Because the team is unusually quiet, it only takes the coach a few minutes to notice that the Mile Relay Team is not warming up with the rest of the team. Soon another runner brings a message over to where we lie. The message usually sounds something like this: "IF you don't warm up this instant, you may never run again." For a brief moment we ponder the options, but the disturbed look on the coach's face brings us back to reality. So we wander down onto the track, yawn, and casually ask our coach if he wanted something. This promotes an angry outburst which entertains the other twenty teams which have come to compete. After warming up, we go back to the stands and this time lie down right beside the coach. This never fails to upset the coach. In less than ten minutes, he assigns the relay team a job that keeps us busy for the rest of the day.

About four o'clock in the afternoon, the last call for the Mile Relay sounds through the stands. At this time, the coach looks down onto the track and realizes his Mile Relay team is nowhere to be found. We usually wait until the head official personally calls Andover's Mile Relay team to the starting line. This distinctive invitation makes us feel special and helps morale. By the time we saunter over to the starting line, the coach is there waiting angrily with the blue baton. The blue baton naturally wins blue ribbons. Standing in order, we receive instructions from the official. Still in order, we walk over to the starting line and wait for the race to begin.

The gun blasts and the race begins. Even during the race, our team continues to perform our ceremonies. Each leg of the mile relay is run the same way. All four of us sprint the first few steps of our prospective legs. This helps us to get ahead of the competition from the start and also to tire us before the end of the race. After gaining position, each of us immediately slacks off to give the other runners a fighting chance. When they pass us, we discover a flaw in our plan and begin running again. At the 220 mark, we look around to watch the other racers and to see the expressions on the coach's face. The expressions make us run a bit faster, and at the 330 mark we "hit a wall." This is when a runner thinks he can not run another step. At this point, we also swear never to run the mile relay again. Finally, the finish line is in sight. We stumble up to the line and in barely a whisper we signal to our teammate to "go" and "reach." As she reaches her hand back, we usually fumble the baton for a few yards. This same procedure goes on for four laps, until the last person crosses the finish line.

Finally the race is over! I stumble back onto the bus and collapse on the seat next to my teammates. We admire the medals we managed to earn. The bus chugs along, but we arrive back at school on schedule. Once at school, we drag ourselves to the car for the final ride home. Half the track team piles into my car, and I proceed to take them home. At last I pull into my driveway. With my last burst of energy I run inside, up the stairs, and back into bed. I close my eyes, relieved the Saturday at the races has come to an end.

1. Is the topic the author chose appropriate for a narrative essay?
2. What is the author's attitude toward the event she describes? How does she convey this attitude to the readers?
3. Do all the details in the essay contribute to creating a central impression? Should any details be omitted or added?
4. How is the essay organized? What do you think of the introduction and conclusion?
5. Why do you think the author chose to use the present tense rather than the past tense in this essay?

# 5.
# Description

## INTRODUCTORY READINGS

**A.** Following are the original and revised versions of a student's short descriptive essay. Read both versions and compare them carefully.

### Lunch at Mom's Coffee Shop

#### *Original Version*

The coffee shop is one of my favorite places to eat. I really like everything about the place, so I always enjoy going there for a meal. Yesterday, the scene was typical of what you'll usually find on a summer day. The bright orange booths against the wall have lamps hanging in the middle of the table, which makes one feel right at home. In one booth are a husband and wife conversing over lunch. They seem to like each other and are having a pleasant conversation. In another booth is a family with a cute little baby who is playing happily while his parents watch. In a corner booth, a couple of guys are arguing about something and look really tense. There is also a booth with three cute girls in it; they are clearly having a good time while eating pork rinds. Up in front of the room is the place where you order your food; a friendly, older woman is working very laboriously at cleaning up the grill area in between waiting on customers. It's interesting to notice that the clock hanging on the wall is off by four hours. The large windows give you a good view of the campus. Past some trees, you can see the large, modern physical education center and the track where some joggers are doing their best to keep going despite the hot summer sun. The jukebox in the middle of

the room is playing a few tunes. Looking up, I see a beautifully
wood-stained ceiling with lots of lights. This really is a nice place
to eat.

### *Revision*

Eating lunch in Mom's Coffee Shop is a peaceful, enjoyable experience for me. I sit down and relax, letting my eyes take in
everything around me. I glance across the room and notice that a
clock hanging on the wall is off by four hours, which seems to
give one the impression that time isn't important here. The bright
orange booths against the wall have lamps dangling down in the
middle of the tables, somehow seeming to make each booth a
world of its own. Straight ahead of me are a man and a woman
conversing easily over lunch. I gather that they are married because of their informal, casual manner toward each other. Neither
one seems compelled to fill up every moment with chatter: the occasional silences seem comfortable, and they don't seem interested
in trying to impress each other. To my left is a family with a six-
month-old baby who is playing with a bag of crackers, experimenting with the sound and feel of cellophane while his parents
smile at him and offer quiet encouragement. To my right is a
booth with three teenaged girls in it; as they whisper and giggle
to each other, they munch on pork rinds, nibbling slowly so that
they can stretch out their time in the air conditioning. Up in
front of the room is the place to order food. A plump, middle-aged
woman is humming to herself as she cleans up the grill area in `
between waiting on customers. Looking out the window, I can see
the birches swaying slightly in the breeze as birds circle lazily in
the cloudless sky. The jukebox in the middle of the room is
quietly playing an old Simon and Garfunkel song. Looking up, I
see a dark wood-stained ceiling with lights placed carefully
throughout the room in diagonal rows. All is peaceful and quiet.

## DISCUSSION QUESTIONS

1.  Compare the original and the revision and list all the differences
    you notice, even if they seem small or insignificant.
2.  Look over your list and generalize about the *kinds* of changes the
    author has made. For example, what kinds of details has he added?
    What kinds of details has he omitted? What kinds of changes has
    he made in word choice? What kinds of changes has he made in
    organization?
3.  Speculate about the author's reasons for making the changes you
    have noticed. For example, why do you think he moved the de-
    tail about the clock toward the beginning of the essay? What has he
    added to the description of the clock, and why?

**B.** The students in a freshman composition class were asked to write descriptive essays about places they knew well. Two students decided to write about houses in which they had lived as children. Read the two essays and compare them carefully.

### A Unique Place to Live

I really love the house where I grew up. It was located on a very pleasant, friendly street that was mostly residential but had an elementary school on one corner and a drugstore on the other. Our house was in the middle of the street, on the opposite side from the elementary school and the drugstore. I'm really glad that I was able to grow up in a nice home in a safe neighborhood —not everyone is so lucky.

Our house was made of brick and had two stories and an attic. On the first floor was a large living room, a dining room, and my brother's bedroom, a kitchen, a family room, and a small bathroom. The living room and dining room had off-white walls and a beige carpet that we tried to keep clean, but it was always getting dirty; my mother says she'll never get a beige carpet again. The living room had a large picture window which gave us a pleasant view of the street. The kitchen was modern and cheerful. I guess my favorite room was always the family room—its decor was unique, and I always thought it was a great place for watching TV or talking to friends.

Upstairs was my bedroom, my parents' bedroom, my other brother's bedroom, and another bathroom. Unlike the bathroom downstairs, this one had a tub and shower. My parents' bedroom was the largest room and had blue walls and a big shag rug. My brother's room was nice enough to start out with, but it was always a mess—my parents constantly had to tell him to clean up his junk. Of course, my favorite room upstairs was my own bedroom. It had yellow walls, several throw rugs, and curtains made of a really interesting printed material. I had decorated the room myself and had picked out a very pretty bedspread and had hung several good prints and photographs on the walls. I always tried to keep my room neat, even my desk and the bookshelves where I displayed a lot of keepsakes and souvenirs I had accumulated for years. I'll admit that the room got messy from time to time, but it was never as bad as my brother's room.

We moved away from that house shortly before I started college—my father got a job in another state—but I will never forget it. The places where we spend our childhoods are always special. I will always be grateful that I was privileged to grow up in such a good environment.

## Thunderstorms and Houses

The nights that were raining were some of the best. I used to love sitting in my dark room watching the thunderstorms move in. Windy nights I could look out my window and see my neighbor's huge oak tree whipping back and forth. When lightning would strike, I could see a huge silhouette of the tree in the sky. The wind would blow and make a whistling sound where the weather stripping had come loose. The thunder would make the windows rattle, and I always used to think that one of them would break. If I had my window cracked open, I could hear the rain falling on the street outside. Sometimes it would rain so hard that the downspout by my window would overflow because of all the oak leaves in it. After the storm had stopped, there would always be some water that would continue to leak down on the front steps below. Then all I could hear was the sound of thunder way off in the distance until it became very still and the only sounds I could hear were those of the house breathing.

That was the house that my dog, two cats, two brothers, four sisters, mother, father, and grandparents lived in. Now my mother and father are living in a new house. We no longer have the dog, my grandparents are dead, and my brothers and sisters and I are living away from home. Once a year we all come together during the summer and have a family reunion. This past summer after everyone had gone back, I stayed up and listened to a storm from the bedroom of my parents' new home. I turned out the light and then sat back in bed.

The wind blew, but it was not as loud as it had been when it rushed through the oak tree. When lightning struck, it was washed out by the street lights and the front-porch lights. The double-layer glass windows were very sturdy and never shook when thunder clapped. The screen on top of the gutters prevented blockage, so they were always clear for the rain to flow through. I could not tell when the rain stopped because the house is well built and keeps noise out. It does not breathe and make sounds like our old house.

I was talking to my neighbor with the oak tree not too long ago. He told me that the new owners of my old house had put on an addition and remodeled it. The paint they put on was an awful color, and the yard was always unkempt. I then realized that part of me was gone forever.

## DISCUSSION QUESTIONS

1. Discuss the authors' apparent purposes in describing these houses. What ideas or impressions does each author want to communicate to the readers? Do the authors make their purposes explicit?

2.  Comment on each author's use of detail. What sorts of details does each author include? How are these details related to the authors' purposes?
3.  Describe the way each essay is organized. Does each plan of organization seem appropriate to the author's purpose? Pay particular attention to introductory and concluding paragraphs.
4.  Pay close attention to the words each author uses. Underline any words or phrases that strike you as vague. How could these words or phrases be made more precise?
5.  On the whole, which essay did you find stronger and more interesting? Why?

**C.** Following are two student essays: a description of a room that had formerly been an auditorium but is now an unused room in a math building, and a description of a supermarket. Read the essays carefully, paying especially close attention to the way the students develop and organize their ideas.

### The Auditorium

The double doors bang behind me with an eerie, hollow sound. My eyes take time to adjust to the dim atmosphere of the defunct auditorium. The archaic wooden floorboards groan in complaint as I creep down the aisle to one of the long-abandoned seats. Along the aisles separating the seats, the floorboards are worn out and bare. In contrast, directly under the seats, the floorboards are well preserved with varnish. As I sit down, dry, musty dust rises from the old, dirty-green cushion; my cramped knees press against the wooden back of the chair before me.

Although many joyful moments may have been spent in this auditorium, all the gaiety is long gone. In a corner, the portrait of a pale, old woman with her frozen pose, her narrow, straight lips, and her lifeless brown eyes portrays the feeling of the room. While sitting before the stage, I suddenly feel small, distant from any life. The constant hiss of the radiators and the occasional bangs from the pipes add to the haunted atmosphere. Creaks from the 1902 auditorium tell me this is not the place to be alone.

Surrounding the obsolete stage are various stage props, perhaps from the last production. The brick backwall is characoal black as if charred by a fire. Looking closely, feeling its surface, I discover it is only a coarse coating of jet-black paint.

Descending stairs to the right of the stage lead me to a large, deserted dressing room. It is divided by two small sections, male and female, and one large area with a series of makeup mirrors along one wall. These mirrors are surrounded by bare light bulbs, blanketed with spider webs. Throwing a switch, I find, to my surprise, that the majority of the bulbs work, disrupting the dimness of the room. On the counter in front of the mirrors is an out-of-style, silky, feminine, red glove that would cover a woman's arm to the elbow.

Walking around the partition to one of the small dressing rooms, I find it barren, except for two sinks, side by side. On one is a dusty drinking glass with a small dead spider in it. Opening a door to the left of the sinks, I find one toilet, and am amused by a crude handwritten sign taped to the wall next to it, saying, "DO NOT FLUSH DURING PERFORMANCE."

Suddenly, the two o'clock bell rings in Laytor Hall; the familiar stomping sound of the math students leaving their classes echoes to the basement.

## The Supermarket

Supermarkets are America's number one necessary evil. When you enter a supermarket, you are entering another world: a world of chaos, continuous motion, and mellow Musak by which to shop.

You are greeted by automatically opening doors, which seem to act as a vacuum, sucking you in past the wide-eyed, screaming child at the gumball machine, into the main shopping area. You are confronted by an array of shopping carts, each with its own squeak or loose wheel; the choice is yours. At first the noise is enough to unnerve you—cash registers being pounded on by a fat woman, clacking away on the gum that she has probably been chewing for the past eight hours, and shopping bags being shaken open by grocery boys who shout conversations at each other across the aisles.

You reach into your pocket to get the shopping list of the day which is, by now, hauntingly echoing in your brain: "Milk, eggs, bread, Pampers . . . milk, eggs, bread, Pampers." As you travel down the first aisle, you are surrounded by shelves of irresistible eatables which seem to scream out at you, "Buy me. . . . No, buy me." The mountains of shelves seem to act as a tunnel, with you, racing through, desperately grabbing any necessity you might sight. You are emptied out at the end of this tunnel, only to find yourself facing a bed of meats: meats of every size and shape, weight and price. As you walk along the meat display, you notice some movement behind the opaque, mirrorlike windows about the meats. As you strain your eyes like a cat into the night, you observe a scene much like one in a horror film. There, hanging from the ceiling, are skinned carcasses of cows, pigs, and chickens, just waiting to be cut, cleaned, inspected, packaged, and priced. As the lifeless meat hangs there, like crucified objects, fat men in white coats and white hard hats—butchers, as they're more commonly

referred to—are busily dismembering their kill for the feisty
little shoppers. As you quickly dart past the meat display, the
thought of becoming a vegetarian does not seem so farfetched
anymore.

You are traveling down the last aisle of this seemingly endless
maze of overly advertised products, when you hear a subtle, or-
chestrated version of "The Way We Were." You stop your par-
tially filled shopping cart in respect to Barbra Streisand, but more
importantly, for the splendor of that moment, only to realize that
this faint, Lawrence Welk type of music has been filling the supermarket since you entered; only you were too busy concentrating on the business of completing your shopping list to notice it.
Your moment of splendor is suddenly interrupted by the screaming of a young child—or monster as I like to think of them—
whose disturbance is being caused simply because he got a gi-
raffe-shaped lollipop rather than a seal-shaped one. You swiftly
continue past this lovely child, restraining yourself from jamming
his lollipop down his throat.

Your journey through the supermarket is nearly at a close. The
only other obstacle to overcome is exiting successfully with a few
dollars remaining in your wallet. Your groceries have been
checked through by the gum-chewing saleslady, and your bill has
been paid. You wish the saleslady a pleasant day—whether you
mean it or not is another matter—and leave. As you exit through
the automatically opening doors, you think back on your thirty-
minute ordeal and wonder, "Was it really all that bad?" After a
brief pause, you emphatically say, "Yep."

## DISCUSSION QUESTIONS

1. Constrast the opening paragraphs of these essays. How are they
   similar? How are they different? Are they both effective ways to
   begin descriptive essays?
2. In each essay, pick the paragraph that seems most striking to you.
   Why do you consider these paragraphs especially good? Comment
   on the techniques the authors use to develop these paragraphs.
3. Comment on the organization of "The Auditorium." Does the author follow the same plan of organization throughout? What transitional devices does he use to help us follow the essay?
4. Comment on the organization of "The Supermarket." How is it
   similar to the organization of "The Auditorium"? How is it different? Which essay seems to move at a faster pace? Why?
5. Notice that while the author of "The Auditorium" uses "I"
   throughout his essay, the author of "The Supermarket" uses "you."
   Can you explain and justify the authors' choices?
6. Contrast the closing paragraphs of these essays. Is each conclusion
   appropriate to the author's purpose?

**D.** Following are a prose paraphrase of a poem and then the poem itself. Read both and then answer the questions that follow.

### *Paraphrase*

She had thought that everything about living with her lover would be pleasant and enjoyable. Instead, the apartment was dingy and untidy, and her lover was often disappointingly unromantic. She still loved him, for the most part, but these things troubled her.

### Living in Sin
#### —ADRIENNE RICH

*She had thought the studio would keep itself;*
*no dust upon the furniture of love.*
*Half heresy, to wish the taps less vocal,*
*the panes relieved of grime. A plate of pears,*
*a piano with a Persian shawl, a cat*                                              5
*stalking the picturesque amusing mouse*
*had risen at his urging.*
*Not that at five each separate stair would writhe*
*under the milkman's tramp; that morning light*
*so coldly would delineate the scraps*                                            10
*of last night's cheese and three sepulchral bottles;*
*that on the kitchen shelf among the saucers*
*a pair of beetle-eyes would fix her own—*
*Envoy from some village in the moldings . . .*

*Meanwhile, he, with a yawn,*                                                     15
*sounded a dozen notes upon the keyboard,*
*declared it out of tune, shrugged at the mirror,*
*rubbed at his beard, went out for cigarettes;*
*while she, jeered by the mirror demons,*
*pulled back the sheets and made the bed and found*                              20
*a towel to dust the table-top,*
*and let the coffee-pot boil over on the stove.*
*By evening she was back in love again,*
*though not so wholly but throughout the nights*
*she woke sometimes to feel the daylight coming*                                 25
*like a relentless milkman up the stairs.*

## DISCUSSION QUESTIONS

1. Adrienne Rich creates two distinct images in her poem: lines 4–7 describe what the woman had thought "living in sin" would be like, and the rest of the poem describes what it actually is like. Contrast these two images. What are the major differences be-

tween them? How does Rich create such vivid images in just a few
lines?

2. Suppose that line 11 read "of last night's meal and several sepulchral bottles." Why would these seemingly minor changes make
   the line less effective?

3. Rich describes the woman's lover in lines 15–18. What can you
   infer about him from these lines? How is he different from the
   woman?

4. Contrast the poem with the paraphrase. Both tell essentially the
   same story; why is the poem so much stronger and more memorable?

5. Write your own prose paraphrase of the poem. Keep it short—just
   four or five sentences—but see if you can capture the vivid impressions conveyed by the poem.

## GENERAL CONCLUSIONS

1. The student essays you have just read could be described as *descriptive essays*. Write a brief definition of the term *descriptive
   essay*, commenting on the characteristics that distinguish descriptive essays from other sorts of essays.

2. Draw together all the observations and comments you have made
   about the introductory readings in this chapter. List some of the
   characteristics of a strong descriptive essay, or summarize your
   conclusions in a paragraph that would be helpful to beginning
   composition students. What advice would you give to a student
   writing a descriptive essay?

## ADVICE

Look again at the poem by Adrienne Rich. Most of it is dominated by
visual images—the grime on the window panes, scraps of food, beetle-
eyes, the dust on the table-top. The poem is enriched, however, by the
poet's references to sounds, such as the dripping faucet, the lover's
yawn, and the out-of-tune notes from the piano; and we can almost feel
the stairs shaking under the milkman's foot. Rich's description of the
lovers' apartment thus appeals to several of our senses. It appeals to
our intellect as well, for Rich also shares her thoughts about the realities of "Living in Sin" with us. The poem thus both describes and inter-
prets a scene.

   In your own descriptive essays, you can use many of the same techniques that Rich does. Like Rich, you should make your description appeal to several of the reader's senses, not only the sense of sight. Develop your powers of observation so that you can notice all significant
details. Imagine how much less interesting Rich's description would
have been if she had said only that the apartment was messy and had
not mentioned the specific details that made it so. Make these details

as concrete and specific as possible. A description should not, however, be simply a list of details. There is little point in minutely describing every object in a room unless you have a worthwhile reason for doing so. Like all other types of writing, a description should have a purpose. Through a vivid description of a rundown nursing home, you can arouse your readers' compassion and indignation; through a detailed description of a vain man who devotes too much attention to his appearance, you can provoke their scorn and laughter. A description is most effective when it succeeds in creating a central impression and in conveying that impression to the reader, when you not only tell what something looks like but also comment on it explicitly or implicitly. Description thus involves both observation and reflection: the writer must first carefully observe the thing to be described and then reflect on its significance.

## Observation: Noticing Details

"Trifles," Charles Dickens says in *David Copperfield,* "make the sum of life." Certainly, details can make the difference between a bland description and a vivid one. When the police question a witness about a crime, they press for specific details. The witness who observed only that the criminal was of medium height, medium weight, and had "longish, brownish" hair is of little help. The witness who noticed that the criminal was 5'10", weighed about 180 pounds, and had chin-length sandy hair, green eyes, a scar on his left cheek, only three fingers on his right hand, and a large mole on his forehead is much more helpful. When you write a description, try to be a careful witness; notice the details that a casual observer might miss.

How can you train yourself to be a careful observer? No trick will transform you into a good observer instantly; nothing can take the place of alertness, intelligence, sensitivity, and close attention. The poet Wordsworth described his practice by saying, "I have at all times endeavoured to look steadily at my subject." Keep this statement in mind when you write a description. If it's possible, go to the place you wish to describe (or stare at the person you wish to describe) and simply notice and write down everything you observe. Don't settle for vague generalizations: search for the details that may reveal the true character of the place or the person. Look back at "The Auditorium" in the Introductory Readings in this chapter. What did the author apparently do while gathering the information for his essay?

## Reflection: Creating a Central Impression

Consider this excerpt from a student's descriptive essay:

> My bedroom is rectangular, about 13' by 11'. The walls are
> painted sky blue, and the ceiling is white. The major articles of

furniture are a twin bed, a desk, a bureau, and an easy chair. The bed has a dark blue corduroy bedspread and two white throw pillows. The desk, which is oak and has three drawers down the left-hand side, has on top of it a brown pencil can containing two black pens and a yellow pencil, a green blotter, and a picture of my girlfriend, Phyllis.

This description is certainly detailed. We know the size and shape of the room, the color scheme, even the number and color of writing instruments in the pencil can. Still, the description falls flat: few readers would be anxious to keep reading to learn the dimensions of the bureau or the color of the easy chair. This description is merely a list of facts, and, as such, has little to hold the interest and attention of the reader.

When writing a descriptive essay, you might start by jotting down just such a list of facts, for it is a good idea to start by noticing as many details as possible. Before you begin to write the essay itself, however, you need to reflect about what you have noticed. Why do you want to describe this room? Perhaps you want to explain how it is an expression of your personality; perhaps you want to explain how you have made it into a peaceful place of refuge away from the noise and clutter of your younger brothers and sisters downstairs. In other words, before you begin to write, decide what *central idea or impression* you want your essay to convey. You can then sort through all the details you have noticed and decide which ones belong in your essay. If you are describing your bedroom as a place of refuge, for example, it might be best to forget about the contents of the pencil can and instead describe in detail the serenity of the sky-blue walls, the harmony of the color scheme, and the print of a Monet landscape hanging over your bed.

You may decide to state the central idea or impression you want to convey in a thesis statement at the beginning of your essay. The thesis statement can then guide your reader's interpretation of all the details that follow. In some essays, you may prefer to present all your details first and reveal your central impression only in the conclusion; in other essays, you may decide it's best to let the details speak for themselves. But whether your thesis is explicit or implicit, presented at the beginning or at the end, be sure that you do have in mind some central idea or impression that will guide your selection of details and make sense of them for the reader.

## Organization: Ordering Details

*Spatial order* is often the most effective method of organization to use in a descriptive essay (see Chapter 2, p. 46). In some essays, you may decide to combine spatial order with chronological order, thus giving your essay a narrative framework; do any of the essays in the Introductory Readings use such a plan of organization?

Also consider your *point of view* in a descriptive essay—the position from which you, as the writer, view the person, scene, or object you are describing. Having a definite point of view will help make your description easier to follow. For example, you might imagine yourself as standing or sitting in one particular spot and describing people and objects as they appear to you from that position; or you might picture yourself as moving from one place to another, describing people and objects as you pass them. A combination of fixed and moving points of view is sometimes effective, but be especially careful to make your directions so clear that the reader can follow you without trouble and share your thoughts and impressions about the scene. Look back at the Introductory Readings and describe the author's point of view in "Lunch at Mom's Coffee Shop," "The Auditorium," and "The Supermarket."

## Capturing Details: Choosing Your Words

One summer, I worked as a secretary in a real estate office run by a shrewd businesswoman. Before I phoned the newspapers with the advertisements her agents had written, I brought the ads to her for final approval. I remember one time when she was particularly critical of an ad for a house in the country. "Look at this lousy ad!" she complained. "It says 'great barn.' What the hell is that supposed to mean, 'great barn'? We'll make it 'sturdy, modern barn.'" "*Is* the barn sturdy and modern?" I asked doubtfully. "Who knows?" she said. "It'll sell the house."

And it did.

We don't have to approve of this woman's ethics in order to admire her sense for which sorts of words are truly descriptive. Words like *great*—or *interesting* or *unique* or *pretty* or *nice*—tell us nothing about the object or person being described except for the writer's opinion of it, an opinion we may or may not share. "My brother is an interesting person" may mean that he knows volumes of baseball trivia or that he can function well on only three hours of sleep a night or that he enjoys doing yoga exercises during dinner. Tell the readers the facts, and let them decide whether or not your brother is interesting. Avoid all-purpose adjectives such as *interesting* and make your language as concrete as possible (see Chapter 12, "Precision").

An incident in *Adventures of Huckleberry Finn* shows us how concrete details can reveal far more than vague generalizations. Huck spends some time living with the Grangerfords, a wealthy, aristocratic family. He is awed by their luxury and seeming refinement, which far surpass anything he has seen before: "It was a mighty nice family, and a mighty nice house, too. I hadn't seen no house in the country before that was so nice and had so much style." When Huck moves beyond the vague terms "nice" and "style," however, and begins describing the house in detail, we see that all is not quite what it seems:

> On a table in the middle of the room was a kind of lovely crockery basket that had apples and oranges and peaches and grapes piled up in it which was much redder and yellower and prettier than real ones is, but they warn't real because you could see where pieces had got chipped off and showed the white chalk or whatever it was, underneath.

When we read this description, we begin to suspect tht the Grangerfords, although they seem so superior to other people, are also somehow deficient "underneath"; at any rate, these chipped pieces of fruit make us realize that the Grangerfords' claims to refinement and "style" are not so clear as Huck believes. A good description does not *tell* us that an object is beautiful or ugly; it *shows* us that the object is beautiful or ugly by describing it in precise detail and concrete language.

Description, like any other kind of writing, is essentially a means of communicating with an audience. Through descriptive essays, you can convey to your readers your ideas and impressions about people, objects, and places; through descriptive paragraphs, you can add to the beauty and forcefulness of narrative, expository, or argumentative essays. As always, holding the reader's attention and interest is one of your first responsibilities as a writer. In a descriptive essay, this means observing details that your readers might miss without your aid, interpreting with insight all that you notice, finding a method of organization that effectively brings out your ideas about whatever you may be describing, and finding the words that will most precisely and vividly re-create your observations and impressions for your readers.

## APPLICATION

**A.** Observe another student in the class closely and write down everything you notice. It would probably be best to pick someone you don't know well; at any rate, don't use any information you've learned about this person outside of class (for example, "French major, comes from New Jersey"). Use the details you observe to infer all you can about the person's personality and interests (for example, "often comes to class with wet hair; probably likes to swim"). Then read your description to the class, not revealing the person's name. Is your description so precise and detailed that the other students can tell which person you're describing? How many of your inferences about the person's personality and interests are correct?

**B.**   Go to a place you know well—your dormitory room, the cafeteria, a classroom—and spend half an hour observing it closely. Write down everything you notice. Did you observe anything about the place that you had never noticed before? Has this close observation changed your impression of the place?

**C.**   Look over the notes you accumulated in response to exercises A and B and pick the list of notes that seems most promising to you. You might find it helpful to work in a group with three or four other students.

1. If you were going to write a descriptive essay about this person or place, what central idea or impression would you want to convey to the reader? Express that idea or impression in a thesis statement.
2. Which of the details on your list would contribute to this central idea or impression and therefore belong in your essay?
3. How might you organize a descriptive essay about this person or place? What would your point of view be?

**D.**   Write a series of short paragraphs, describing the same scene, person, or object from several different points of view, both fixed and moving. For example, you might describe what a building on campus looks like when you first spot it in the distance, when you stand very close to it, or when you walk by it slowly; you might even try describing what it might look like if you flew over it in a helicopter.

**E.**   Following is a student's short descriptive essay. Read it and then consider the questions that follow.

### Silent Night

It was two weeks before the Christmas of my fourteenth year, and my house was filled with the delicious sights and smells of the season: evergreen boughs on the mantle, a log rolling over in the grate, delicately scented bayberry candles, a steaming mug of cocoa heating my palm. My mother and I sat in the living room that evening; I had my needlepoint and my mother had her paper. The TV was on with the usual news about Vietnam, and the screen showed the casualty figures and maps with big X's and sweeping arrows on lands I would never see and, or so I thought then, would soon forget.

It was later that evening that I remember hearing "Silent Night." Suddenly, all the news reports that I had been shutting out came flashing back to me. I thought of all the soldiers that would not be returning home to ham dinners and gayly wrapped presents under the tree. Images raced through my mind: no more colored lights on fragrant, green branches; no more sticky candy canes or Christmas cookies; no more snowball fights; no more "Silent Night." I sat and wept silently till my tears blocked out the white candles on the windowsill and our family crèche, till I could no longer see the bowl of bright rock candy or our cat stretched out before the fireplace. I felt as if I'd been covered in gray velvet; I sat there and cried as I'd never cried before, even when my father had died. I now realized the random brutality of war; more importantly, I had felt death's finality.

My mother put down her paper, turned to me, and asked me what was wrong. I told her and she said nothing, but came over and put her arms around me and waited with me by the crackling fire.

1. What sorts of details does this author include? How do these details help to make her description of the living room vivid?
2. What central impression does the author create in the first paragraph? Does this impression change as the essay progresses?
3. What method of organization does the author use in this essay? Is it effective? Would you consider this essay "purely descriptive," or is it something else as well?
4. Why is the title the author has chosen particularly appropriate for this essay?

# 6.
# Comparison and Contrast

## INTRODUCTORY READINGS

**A.** The students in a freshman composition course were asked to write essays contrasting two courses they had taken in college. Read the following two essays and compare them carefully.

### The Bore and the Challenge

My head was bobbing up and down. I turned around and looked about the class. As I expected, I saw ten out of twenty heads burrowed snugly into folded arms. Our professor must have been teaching out of a beta state of consciousness. He didn't realize his words were traveling endlessly into space.

This had to be the most boring class I had ever conceived possible. If you're into numbers, great; but what if you're not? Every time we would meet, the professor would open with, "Good morning, class." It always reminded me of the television show *The Little House on the Prairie*. Next he would say, "Now let's go over last night's assignment." This guy must have been a whiz with numbers, because he always moved quickly and never seemed to make mistakes. My best guess is that he is an android. He is the type of teacher that used no voice inflection or change in vocal expression. Is it really possible to have a robot for a teacher?

This professor hardly ever paid any attention to the class. He would stand up at the blackboard doing problems and explaining them in a monotone, but he didn't seem to care about whether anyone was paying attention or not. He hardly ever asked for questions or comments. People would cut that class all the time, but he really didn't seem to care. You got the impression that he was just putting in his hours and collecting his paycheck.

My favorite class so far in college has been Management Behavior. This class would tell you all about people in working roles. It would tell you why they behave a certain way in a given situation. It would also tell you how to manage and properly and effectively control the person and the situation. I really considered this a useful class because I plan to be an executive someday, and I'm sure that I'll be able to use what I learned in this class. A good businessman has to understand people and how to work with them.

The professor in this class was highly qualified. He has a Ph.D. from Harvard, which I consider really impressive. He's published a lot in his field, too: he's one of the coauthors of the textbook we used in class, and when I was doing research for my term paper, I kept on running across his name in bibliographies. More important, he has a lot of practical experience in business because he was president of a large firm before he went into teaching. It's really important that a business professor have some background in business so that he can give you insights into what it's like in the real world.

The two classes couldn't have been more different, except that I got the same grade in both—a B. But while I learned a lot in Business Management, I had to force myself to go to math. Most of my college courses have been pretty good, but one bad class like that math class can ruin a whole semester. I think the college should be more careful when it hires professors and gives out tenure.

### Organization Can Make the Difference

One quart of gas can make the difference between arriving safely at your destination and being stranded by the side of the road for hours; one point can make the difference between passing and failing a final exam. Often, success or failure can be determined by something that seems insignificant, something we may not even notice if all goes well. Last semester, I took two courses that were similar in many ways, but one course was an enjoyable and rewarding experience while the other was a constant frustration that ultimately didn't teach me very much. There was one crucial difference between Contemporary American Politics and Introduction to Sociology: organization.

At the beginning of the semester, the two courses seemed similar, and I was looking forward to both of them. The subject matter in both courses interested me, and I was intrigued by the books each professor assigned. Both professors had excellent qualifications: each had a Ph.D., each had been teaching for over ten

years, and each had published articles in his field. Further, each
professor was enthusiastic about the course and showed a good attitude toward students. The political science professor took some
time to try to learn our names and then tried to get us all involved in an opening discussion on current politics; the sociology
professor helped us relax by telling some jokes and inviting us all
to come see him at his office whenever we had questions or problems. I left campus the first day thinking that I had a great semester ahead of me.

Even on that first day, however, I should have seen that while
one course had been carefully planned and organized, the other
had not. The political science professor handed out a printed syllabus that outlined the course. Attendance counted; there would
be a midterm and one paper to write, in addition to the final
exam. During the semester, we would be expected to read current
articles and write summaries of them. Our final grade would be
based on the grades on all these assignments. The syllabus explained the topic for each lecture, when each assignment would be
due, and what would be covered in each test. The sociology professor, however, never made his requirements clear. On that first
day, he was casual and even evasive when students asked questions about requirements, saying that we could "settle all that
later." As the semester went on, it became clear that he had
never really planned the course out. We never knew what was
going to happen to us. We had a midterm that was announced one
week in advance, and we had no idea what would be on it. When
everyone did poorly on the test, he announced that he wouldn't
count it after all; he was trying to be nice, but that meant that
the course grade would be based entirely on the final exam. We
never knew what the topic of the next lecture would be, and he
was often vague about reading assignments: he would just tell us
to "keep moving ahead in your textbooks." When the final exam
came, all we knew was that it would be based on the subjects discussed in class and on the material in two textbooks—that is a
lot to cram for. We always felt lost and anxious.

In individual lectures, too, the difference in organization was
striking. In political science, the professor knew exactly what he
was going to say and wasted no time in saying it. He almost always stuck to the announced lecture topic; when he digressed, he
let us know that he was digressing. He would number the points
he covered and tell us which ones were most important. As a result, I had clear, organized notes, taken down in outline form.
This made everything much easier when it came time to study for
the test. The sociology professor gave lectures that were far from
being organized. He would ramble on without direction, jumping
from slum conditions to the time when he was a soldier in Italy in

World War II and back to sexual stereotyping. Some of the digressions were interesting, but I was often confused about the point of the lecture—if it had a point at all. After fifty minutes, my notes consisted of a full page of funny faces, scribbles, and geometric shapes.

In my political science course, the professor's careful organization helped me to learn the material and to feel prepared and confident; in my sociology course, I was so confused by disorganized lectures and so distracted by worrying about requirements that I learned very little. Not every teacher has to follow exactly the same pattern, and I realize that the highly organized structure of my political science course probably wouldn't be appropriate for some sorts of courses, such as seminars or discussion classes. I can see why some professors want their courses to be more flexible. Still, I think all teachers should at least have an idea of the direction of the course and should make their expectations clear to the students. The student will learn more if the professor is organized.

## DISCUSSION QUESTIONS

1. Compare the two essays' introductory paragraphs. Did each introductory paragraph catch your interest? Did each give you a clear idea of the essay's scope and purpose?
2. In "The Bore and the Challenge," what standards does the author use in evaluating the math professor? In other words, what specific reasons does he give for finding the math professor inadequate? Does he use the same standards in evaluating the business professor?
3. In "Organization Can Make the Difference," what standards does the author use in evaluating the political science professor? Does he use the same standards in evaluating the sociology professor?
4. Comment on the *order* in which each author has arranged his paragraphs. Drawing up a quick outline of each paper may help you to see the organizational patterns. How are the two patterns of organization different? Could each pattern be effective in a comparison and contrast essay?
5. Compare the two essays' concluding paragraphs. Does each conclusion interpret and build on the specific similarities and differences the author has discussed?
6. On the whole, which essay draws a sharper, clearer contrast between two courses? Why?

B. Two students in a composition class wrote essays comparing and contrasting two people. Read both essays and compare them carefully.

## Two Patients

It's three o'clock in the afternoon, and another eight-hour shift is beginning in the Intensive Care Unit. Tonight, I realize, will be at best a tentative success, as I plan to spend my time between two beds. Two patients, one nurse, and a multitude of problems. The physical and clinical assessments of these two women are vastly different, alike only in their complexity. But they share at least two things in common: each is supported by a large, overwhelming piece of equipment, and each has lost her independence because of her illness.

In any Intensive Care Unit, it is very easy to overlook the patient and instead concentrate on his machines, numbers, and procedures. But even a short, superficial personal assessment tells me that both these women need more than an accurate, efficient nurse. First, I turn to May. May has a chronic respiratory problem that has flared into such an acute phase that she has a tracheostomy (a surgical opening in her neck and trachea into which a plastic tube has been placed). This must be connected to a respirator (a machine providing artificial respirations) at all times to enable her to breathe. This is not the first time this has happened to May; but, unlike in previous episodes, this time she has collapsed and succumbed completely—to everything but death. She cannot speak because of her tracheostomy; nevertheless, she communicates forcefully. Her eyes are mirrors of emotion. They follow me around the unit, pleading, cajoling, and harassing me no matter where I am. She refuses to participate in any of her care and, instead, demands more than she knows I can give. When I am near her bed, her hands reach out and grab at my uniform and her fingers entwine around mine with desperate strength. I tell her that I must go to the patient in the next bed, and she becomes instantly agitated and even more insecure. She is, for much of the time, beyond my reach.

So, too, I find, is Kathy, but for completely opposite reasons. She is flat on her back in a special bed, with a very painful fracture. The nurse from the previous shift tells me that she is refusing to drink fluids or cooperate in any way, and that she seems remote. One look into her eyes and I know why. Even though they are dulled by her pain medication, they still convey her disbelief and despair. And her resentment. Without a word, she shouts the unfairness of her situation and the nurses' seemingly impossible demands. Her hands are clenched and her body withdraws from my touch, just as her mind has temporarily withdrawn from reality.

As different and as difficult as each woman is to work with, it is clear that each is coping with her situation in the only way

that she thinks is possible. Separated by only ten feet, they are
miles apart in their defense mechanisms and psychological needs,
but ever so close in their common need to deal with their fear and
frustration. And I, I have eight hours to travel the miles between
them and attempt to reach each of them, if only in some small
way.

## My Sisters

My younger sisters are both still in high school. They are similar in many ways, but in other ways they are as different as night
and day. In appearance, they are very similar. Both do well in
school, but one really enjoys school while the other does not; although they are both athletic, they don't like the same sports.
Also, one is much quieter and shyer than the other.

My sister Sally is eighteen and is a senior in high school. She
is 5'6" tall and is slim and has long sandy-colored hair and blue
eyes. My sister Meg, on the other hand, is sixteen and a sophomore in high school. She looks just like Meg except that she's a
little taller—she's 5'7", slim, and has sandy hair and blue eyes.
Also, her hair is shorter than Meg's is.

Their attitudes toward school are very different. Meg has always received good grades in her classes, but she says she finds
school boring. She could probably be a straight-A student if she
tried, but she's content with the B's she can get without working
much at all. She says she might not even go to college next year,
which has my parents very upset. Sally, however, is a really
hard-working student and is always right at the top of her class—
I wouldn't be surprised if she graduates as valedictorian. Sally
loves school, especially her science classes; she's definitely going
to college and thinks she might want to go on to medical school.
My parents are really excited about that idea and have already
started talking about "my daughter, the doctor."

Meg is much more enthusiastic about sports than she is about
school and is on three different teams: field hockey in the fall,
swimming in the winter, and softball in the spring. In fact, she
says the only reason she would even consider going to college is
that she would like to play college-level sports. You can imagine
what my parents think of that! Sally also likes sports, but not the
team sports that Meg enjoys. Sally likes to swim but has never
been interested in trying out for the team. Her real love is tennis,
and she's very good at it. Last summer, she came in first in her
division in a tournament sponsored by our local newspaper.

Also, my sisters have very different personalities. Meg is very
outgoing and loves to go to parties. She has a lot of friends and
really enjoys being with them. Sally, however, is rather shy and

really doesn't like going to parties. She has a few close friends and enjoys just talking to them or playing tennis or going on walks with them. At a party, you will probably find her sitting in a corner with one friend and having an intense conversation.

Even though my sisters are so different, they are both wonderful people, and I like them both very much. Their differences make each one unique and special to me. I always look forward to vacations because they give me a chance to be with both of my sisters.

## DISCUSSION QUESTIONS

1. What is the purpose of each essay? Clearly, each essay points out similarities and differences between two people, but does either have a further purpose? If the essay does have a further purpose, where is it expressed?

2. What are the grounds of comparison in each essay—the specific points of similarity and difference discussed? In each essay, are the two people discussed similar enough to make a comparison worthwhile? Does the author point out interesting, subtle differences?

3. Comment on the *order* in which each author has arranged her paragraphs. Drawing up a brief outline of each paper may help you to see the organizational patterns. How are the two organizational patterns different? Could each pattern be effective in a comparison and contrast essay?

4. Compare the concluding paragraphs. Does each conclusion interpret and build on the specific similarities and differences the author has discussed?

5. On the whole, which essay did you find more interesting? Why?

C.   Following are two versions of an essay a student wrote to contrast what her family was like before the birth of a younger brother with what it was like after the birth. The content is the same in both essays, but the organization is different. Read both versions and compare them carefully.

### The Births

#### Version 1

The coffeepot was just beginning to rumble. The lights were dim throughout the house, but the moon cast a reassuring glow through the front window. The television held the attention of two young children and their grandmother. Then the telephone rang . . . my brother, handicapped, had just been born. We could not have known then how much this birth would affect everyone in the family.

We, as a family, had never been very close. We seemed to have had our own separate paths, which did not cross very often. My father was always away on business trips. His occupation demanded more time and changes in location than he would have liked, but he had to surrender to its obligations in order to support us. I remember seeing him for a few short days near Christmas-time each year.

My only image of my mother in those days was one of a bustling housekeeper. The greatest amount of time that I saw her remain still was during dinner each night, which lasted about twenty minutes. Then she would scamper downstairs to continue the laundry chores or upstairs to make a dent in her pile of sewing items. I did not see my mother much, but the house was spic and span.

I knew I had an older brother, but I found myself forgetting that he existed. I caught glimpses of his form near the refrigerator when I would use the bathroom very early in the morning. His friends were his life; his home was his restaurant.

I often escaped to the woods with my large golden retriever at my side. I had made a tree house where I lived during the day, playing "house" with my dog and friends. Being bored when at home, I preferred the variety and challenges of the outdoors.

Then my brother, handicapped, was born. My father returned home from his excursions around the world. He realized the insignificance of his insatiable pursuit of material goods and secured a job that allowed him to remain at home, spending time with the people he loved. My mother settled, now ignoring the cookie crumb that had fallen into her shag rug. She suppressed her constant urge to maintain a spotless home, spending happy, warm hours with her children and husband instead of with her vacuum cleaner. Big brother ceased living among his friends at the pizza shop and moved into our house. His values changed dramatically: family gatherings took the place of his peer parties. I suddenly lost interest in my tree fort and found excitement, warmth, and security inside my house. My handicapped brother had transformed a related but fragmented group of people into a unified family. That cool, dark night when the telephone rang in harmony with the rumbling of the coffeepot, the birth of a handicapped child brought the birth of a family.

## The Births

### Version 2

The coffeepot was just beginning to rumble. The lights were dim throughout the house, but the moon cast a reassuring glow through the front window. The television held the attention of two young children and their grandmother. Then the telephone rang . . . my brother, handicapped, had just been born. We could not have known then how much this birth would affect everyone in the family.

We, as a family, had never been very close. We seemed to have had our separate paths, which did not cross very often. My father was always away on business trips. His occupation demanded more time and changes in location than he would have liked, but he had to surrender to its obligations in order to support us. I remember seeing him for a few short days near Christmas-time each year. When my handicapped brother was born, however, my father returned from his excursions around the world. He realized the insignificance of his insatiable pursuit of material goods and secured a job that allowed him to remain at home, spending time with the people he loved.

My mother also changed quite a bit. My only image of her before my brother was born was one of a bustling housekeeper. The greatest amount of time that I saw her remain still was during dinner each night, which lasted about twenty minutes. Then she would scamper downstairs to continue the laundry or upstairs to make a dent in her pile of sewing. I did not see my mother much, but the house was spic and span. But after my handicapped brother was born, my mother settled, now ignoring the cookie crumb that had fallen into her shag rug. She suppressed her constant urge to maintain a spotless home, spending happy, warm hours with her children and her husband instead of with her vacuum cleaner.

I had always known I had an older brother, but I found myself forgetting that he existed. I caught glimpses of his form near the refrigerator when I would use the bathroom very early in the morning. His friends were his life; his home was his restaurant. When my handicapped brother was born, my older brother ceased living among his friends at the pizza shop and moved into our house. His values changed dramatically: family gatherings took the place of his peer parties.

Before my younger brother was born, I often escaped to the woods with my large golden retriever at my side. I had made a tree house where I lived during the day, playing "house" with my dog and friends. Being bored when at home, I preferred the variety and challenges of the outdoors. After the birth, I suddenly lost interest in my tree fort and found excitement, warmth, and security inside my house. My handicapped brother had transformed a related but fragmented group of people into a unified family. That cool, dark night when the telephone rang in harmony with the rumbling of the coffeepot, the birth of a handicapped child brought the birth of a family.

## DISCUSSION QUESTIONS

1. The two versions of "The Births" illustrate two different ways of organizing comparison and contrast papers. Draw up a brief outline for each version of the paper, identifying the main point discussed in each paragraph.
2. Look over each outline and write a few sentences describing the method of organization used. What are the major differences between these two methods?
3. On the whole, which version of the essay do you prefer? Which version draws a sharper, clearer contrast between the way the author's family was before her brother's birth and the way it was afterwards? How does this version's organization contribute to the essay's effectiveness?
4. Do you think that the method of organization used in the version you prefer would be good in all comparison and contrast essays? When might a different method of organization be preferable?

## GENERAL CONCLUSIONS

Draw together all the observations and comments you have made about the introductory readings in this chapter. List some of the characteristics of a strong comparison and contrast essay, or summarize your conclusions in a paragraph that would be helpful to beginning composition students. What advice would you give to a student writing a comparison and contrast essay?

## ADVICE

Comparison and contrast papers are among the most frequently assigned kinds of papers in college courses. Your psychology professor may ask you to compare the theories of Freud and Jung, your political science professor may ask you to compare the views of Madison and Jefferson on the question of political parties, and your English professor may ask you to compare a poem by Shelley with one by Keats. Such essays can be enlightening when they illuminate one or both of the things being compared: by contrasting the views of Madison and Jefferson on political parties, for example, you may come to a better understanding of what is unique about each man's ideas. Unfortunately, however, comparison and contrast papers are among the most difficult kinds of papers to write well. Unless they are planned carefully, these papers can become disorganized, confusing, and worst of all, pointless. The most common weakness in a comparison and contrast paper is an uncertain or insignificant purpose.

## Determining the Objects and Grounds of Comparison

Sometimes your professor will tell you exactly what to compare and what points to consider: "Compare the poetic theories of Wordsworth and Coleridge. Be sure to cover these three points. . . ." Other assignments, however, will be much more open-ended: "Compare two political leaders"; "Compare two styles of architecture." When the professor does not determine the objects and grounds of comparison for you, you have some careful decisions to make.

The first piece of advice is as crucial as it is obvious: make sure that the two things you are comparing really are comparable, that they are fundamentally similar in important ways. If the two things you are comparing are so dissimilar that the differences between them would be readily apparent even to a casual observer, there is little justification for writing a comparison and contrast paper. A comparison of television commercials and magazine advertisements could be interesting; a comparison of television commercials and grand opera almost certainly could not. And even if you pick two basically similar things to compare, you can still run into problems if you are content with pointing out large, obvious differences: "While magazine advertisements must rely on printed words and still pictures, television commercials can use music and moving pictures." Narrowing your topic is often a good way of avoiding the obvious and focusing your attention on subtler, more interesting differences. How could you limit your topic if you were writing an essay on television commercials and magazine advertisements?

Once you have found and limited your topic, start thinking about the *grounds* of your comparison—the specific points of similarity and difference that you will discuss. It's probably best to begin by making a list of all the similarities and differences you can think of, reserving until later your decisions about which ones are significant enough to mention. For example, suppose that your composition professor asks you to write an essay comparing and contrasting two means of communication. Rejecting immediately media that are too dissimilar to warrant comparison—for example, television and CB radio—you decide to write about telephone conversations and letters. Next, you decide to limit your topic by disregarding business letters and calls and focusing on personal communication. It's now time to start working on your list:

### *Personal Telephone Conversations and Letters*

*Similarities*
1. both let you keep in touch with friends
2. both can be used for short- or long-distance communication

*Differences*
1. expense: long-distance calls more expensive
2. phone call takes less time and thought

3. both offer ways of overcoming separations
4. both allow you to accomplish the same tasks, such as transfer of information, taking notice of birthdays, etc.
5. neither lets you see the person you're communicating with; both rely on *words* rather than facial expressions, gestures, etc.

3. getting a letter always seems more "special"
4. on phone, can tell a lot from tone of voice
5. can enclose pictures with letter
6. letters give you record of what was said
7. telephone lets you respond to questions, clarify statements; friend can ask, "What do you mean?" Can clear up misunderstandings immediately
8. on phone, know how friend responds to what you say; friend may offer suggestions, opinions
9. in letter, can take time to think about just what to say—fewer chances for "slips"
10. have more control in letter—can decide what topics will be discussed, make sure everything important is said, avoid things you don't want to talk about
11. friend may have to interpret letter; on phone, can ask *you* to interpret, explain

You can think of further similarities and differences later, but this list provides you with a good start. It's now time to study your list carefully and to start thinking about the direction your essay will eventually take.

## Clarifying Your Purpose

In some comparison and contrast papers, you will have a definite purpose from the outset. You may, for example, decide to contrast the Democratic and Republican platforms to show why one party's platform is stronger. Often, however, you may have only a vague idea of your purpose before you draw up your list of similarities and differences. It is essential that you decide precisely what your purpose will be before you go any further. If your purpose is simply "to show the similarities between X and Y," there's no point in writing the paper: Why should the reader be interested in a list of similarities and differences that goes nowhere and proves nothing? Look back at the Introductory Readings in this chapter and identify any essays that lack a clear, significant purpose.

Comparison and contrast papers can serve a number of interesting, useful purposes. Contrasting two plans for a national health-insurance program, for example, might prove that one plan is less expensive and more practical; contrasting jogging and swimming might prove that although both promote fitness, swimming is preferable because joggers are prone to various injuries. If you were trying to decide on a purpose for the paper about telephone conversations and letters, you might study the list you had prepared and conclude that the similarities are fairly obvious and don't seem to lead anywhere. The list of differences seems more promising. Looking over the list, you might decide that the most interesting items concern the greater amount of control exercised by a person writing a letter. Go through the list and check off the items that relate to this topic. You may also be able to use a few of the other items, but they will not be important to your paper. You are now ready to write a tentative thesis statement revealing your purpose: "Although making a telephone call is an easy way of keeping in touch with friends, writing a letter is preferable because it allows you to decide exactly what will be said, how it will be said, and how much will be said."

The next step is to think of *specific examples* to support the assertions you will make. For the paper on letters and telephone calls, personal experience is probably the best source of examples. You may recall a time when you called a friend to talk about a problem but were frustrated because the friend kept interrupting you and changing the subject. Or you might mention a time when you hurt a friend during a telephone call by making a hasty, inconsiderate remark that you would never have made in a letter. To show the advantages of writing letters, you might mention a time when writing to a friend and struggling to explain a problem helped you to clarify your ideas and find a solution. Once you have a clear sense of your focus and purpose, finding appropriate examples should be much easier.

## Organizing Your Essay

Organizing a comparison and contrast essay is always tricky. Basically, you have two options. If you are contrasting the Democratic and Republican platforms, for example, you may decide to write first everything you have to say about the Democrats and then every-

thing you have to say about the Republicans. Or you may decide on
a point-by-point comparison: a paragraph contrasting the Democratic and Republican stands on the economy, a paragraph contrasting their views on foreign policy, and so forth. Each option offers advantages and disadvantages.

If you choose the first option—several paragraphs devoted just to
the Democrats and then several paragraphs devoted just to the Republicans—you will have a good chance to present a coherent, continuous explanation of each party's views. This method of organization is often best when you are comparing two things that require
extended, complex discussion—two poems, for example. It is also
preferable when you want to create two contrasting moods. Look
back at the Introductory Readings and comment on whether or not
this approach works well in "Two Patients" and the first version of
"The Births."

This approach does have its dangers, however. Too often, comparison and contrast essays using this approach are really two separate
essays hiding under one title. The author discusses the Democratic
party's position on the economy and civil rights and the Republican
party's position on school prayer and foreign policy, then makes a
desperate attempt to yoke the two parts of the paper together in a
concluding paragraph. No real comparisons can be made in such a
paper. And even if you are careful to discuss exactly the same points
in both halves of your paper, you may still run into trouble if you
rely too heavily on your readers' memories and their abilities to see
similarities and differences for themselves. This problem is especially acute in a long paper. If you write a twenty-page paper comparing the Democratic and Republican platforms and discuss the
Democratic stand on foreign policy on page 2, your readers may
have forgotten many of the details by the time they reach your discussion of the Republican stand on foreign policy on page 13. You
can compensate for this problem by referring frequently to the first
half of your paper, briefly reminding your readers of points you
made earlier: "Rejecting the Democratic view that X is the proper
approach to this problem, the Republicans favor Y."

Given all the problems inherent in this first option for organizing
comparison and contrast essays, a point-by-point comparison may
seem preferable. This approach might indeed work well in a paper
comparing the two platforms: each paragraph could make a clear
contrast between the two parties' stands on a particular issue, and
there would be no danger that the readers would forget what you
said about one party before they could read about the other. Still,
the point-by-point approach is not appropriate for all comparison
and contrast essays. Readers sometimes feel yanked back and forth
by this kind of comparison: they have only a few moments to focus
on one thing before you start demanding that they contrast it with

something else. And you may find yourself scrambling for new ways to say "on the other hand," "however," and "in contrast."

Which method of organization is preferable for comparison and contrast essay? The answer seems evasive but is nevertheless unavoidable: it depends on the subject you are discussing and on the kinds of comparisons and contrasts you wish to draw. You may also wish to devise variations on either pattern. You might find some way to combine the two approaches, or you might decide you will first discuss all differences and then discuss all similarities. Almost any method of organization can work if you keep in mind the need to make real comparisons and to help your readers see those comparisons. Draw up a tentative outline for the paper contrasting telephone conversations and letters. What method of organization might work well with this topic?

## Writing Introductions and Conclusions

The introductory paragraph for a comparison and contrast essay should serve some of the same functions that any good introductory paragraph does: it should clearly identify your topic and purpose, and it should capture the reader's attention. Be particularly careful to mention both of the things you will be comparing. A surprising number of writers forget to do so, with the result that the readers do not even realize that they are reading a comparison and contrast essay until they reach the second half of the paper. You may want to use the first few sentences of your introduction to list quickly the less important points of similarity and difference and then, in the next few sentences, lead into your thesis statement by focusing on the specific points on which you will be concentrating. Here, for example, is a possible introductory paragraph for the paper comparing letters and telephone conversations.

If you want to tell a friend about a problem that has been troubling you, should you write a letter or make a telephone call? Letters and telephone calls have some of the same advantages and disadvantages: both can overcome the distance between you and your friend, both allow you to express your ideas and feelings, and neither lets you see the person you're communicating with—whichever you choose, you will have to rely on words rather than gestures or facial expressions to convey your meaning. But there are also important differences between letters and telephone calls. If you are simply in the mood for a pleasant chat and have nothing pressing to discuss, a telephone call may be just what you need. If you have something really important to say, however, it would be wiser to write a letter. Unlike making a tel-

ephone call, writing a letter allows you to decide exactly what
will be said, how it will be said, and how much will be said.

An introductory paragraph such as this one clearly identifies the
two things to be compared and contrasted, focuses the readers' attention on the most important points to be discussed, and indicates both
the purpose of the paper and the eventual conclusion.

Conclude your comparison and contrast essay by reminding the
readers of the purpose of your paper. You may want to review some
of the main points of similarity and difference you have discussed,
but don't let your concluding paragraph become a mere summary:
your purpose is to draw a real *conclusion,* not simply to offer a con-
densed version of your paper. The paper comparing letters and telephone calls might end with a paragraph such as this:

> Writing that letter to Mike convinced me of the real advantages
> of writing about problems rather than talking about them over
> the telephone. Writing gave me the time I needed to express my
> thoughts precisely; trying to put my feelings into words helped
> me to clarify them and to gain more insight into the situation.
> And, since writing put me into complete control of the "conversa-
> tion," I was able to focus sharply on the points I wanted to discuss
> instead of being distracted or annoyed by irrelevant comments or
> questions. One week later, when I received Mike's letter in re-
> sponse, I could see that he too had benefitted from the extra time
> that writing allows and could offer me advice that he had thought
> through carefully and worded tactfully. Telephone conversations
> are wonderful for quick, easy communication when your main
> goal is simply to keep in touch; when it comes to discussing seri-
> ous and complex questions, however, nothing can take the place
> of writing a letter.

Such a paragraph reemphasizes the purpose of a comparison and
contrast essay by focusing on what is learned through the comparison. Your readers may disagree with your conclusions, but they will
not be left wondering why you decided to make the comparison in
the first place.

## APPLICATION

**A.**  Evaluate these thesis statements from comparison and contrast
essays. Have the authors selected workable topics? If not, how might
the topics be improved? Do the thesis statements clearly identify the
authors' topics and purposes? Suggest ways of improving any thesis
statements that seem weak.

1. Rock concerts in Japan are very different from those in America because Japanese audiences are much quieter and less responsive.
2. Although I enjoy playing both football and tennis, the two sports are very different because football requires cooperation with a team while success in tennis depends upon the individual's skill and planning.
3. Democracy and communism are very different forms of government.
4. Although the quarter system appeals to many students because it offers a long winter vacation, the semester system gives us more time to reflect about what we're learning and to explore a subject in depth.
5. Getting a liberal education is better than going to a vocational school.

**B.**　Write a paragraph comparing and contrasting two of the essays in the Introductory Readings. What will the purpose of your comparison be? What specific points of similarity and difference will you discuss? How will you organize your paragraph?

**C.**　Suppose that your composition professor asked you to write a 500-word comparison and contrast essay on one of these general topics:

- compare and contrast two movies
- compare and contrast two people
- compare and contrast two courses you have taken
- compare and contrast two personal experiences
- compare and contrast two places

Your first task would be to limit the topic by choosing the object of your comparison; for example, if you chose the first topic, you might decide to discuss two recent movies directed by the same person. How might you limit some of the other topics? Remember that the two things you are discussing should be similar enough to make a comparison worthwhile.

**D.**　Using one of the topics you developed in response to the last exercise, draw up a list of similarities and differences (see p. 133). Then, go through your list and check off the items that seem least obvious and most interesting. What might your focus be if you wrote a comparison and contrast essay on this topic? What would the purpose of your essay be? Express your focus and purpose in a tentative thesis statement.

**E.**　Refer to the topic and notes you developed in response to exercise 4. How might you organize a comparison and contrast essay on this topic? Do you think you would decide first to say everything you have to say about one of the objects of comparison and then say everything you have to say about the other? Would you use point-by-point comparison? Or would you devise another method of organization? Give the reasons for your choice.

# 7.
# Causal Analysis

## INTRODUCTORY READINGS AND EXERCISE

**A.** The students in an advanced composition class were asked to write essays analyzing the causes of attrition at their college; that is, they were asked to explain why a large number of students left the college before graduating. The professor told them to gather information for their essays by interviewing other students. Read the following two essays and compare them carefully.

### Causes of Attrition at Edson College

If this freshman class is like the freshman classes of the last five years, only about 450 of the nearly 600 students who entered Edson this fall will graduate from the college four years from now. An article in last week's *Edson Record* said that almost one-fourth of the students in every freshman class leave Edson before they graduate. Why is the attrition rate at Edson so high? It could be that Edson turned out to be different than these students had expected. Many students find the academic program here far too difficult and just can't keep up. Also, many students are disappointed by Edson's rather dull and limited social life. Finally, the high cost of attending college here may make many students think about leaving.

One of the major reasons why a person might leave Edson is the tough academic program. Before I came here, I talked to an admissions counselor who bragged about Edson's high academic standards. After being here two quarters, I can say that his bragging was justified. I have papers to write every week for English and usually over 100 pages to read each night for my history course alone. My chemistry class keeps me in the lab two afternoons a week and also requires me to read and study every night. Many other students also find the academic program very challenging. My roommate was put on probation at the end of last quarter and will have to leave the college unless he can bring up his grades; he works past midnight every night but is still afraid that he won't be able to make it. An upperclassman who transferred to Edson from a college in New Jersey told me he's amazed by the academic requirements here. He said that he has done more work in two quarters at Edson than he did in two years at his former college. Academic pressure might be a major reason why some people leave Edson, but it is not the only one.

Whenever you sit down to lunch in the student cafeteria on Friday, someone is bound to start complaining about how boring the weekend ahead looks. The problem stems, in part, from the geographical location of the college. Edson is located in a small town with very few forms of entertainment for the college student: there are just two movie theaters, a few bowling alleys and pool halls, and half a dozen bars—and, of course, students who are under twenty-one can't go to the bars anyway. The closest large city is forty minutes away, which poses an inconvenience for people without cars. The social life on campus offers several possibilities—movies, fraternity parties, the pub, occasional plays, concerts, or dance recitals—but many people get tired of the same activities week after week. Most of the students here are dissatisfied with the social life.

The high cost of attending Edson College is another source of complaints. It costs over $7,000 a year to attend Edson, and next year the tuition may go even higher. When you add in the cost of books, supplies, and travel, you begin to see just how expensive Edson really is. Almost everyone I know has to have some sort of financial aid, but many say that the financial aid office is unfair. I talked to one person on my hall who says that even though both his parents are retired, Edson gives him very little aid. The only reason he is able to attend Edson at all is that he was able to take out a student loan. Many people find the financial commitment here a major problem.

What can Edson do to cut down on attrition? If the professors want to keep their students here, they should consider requiring less work. No one wants to see Edson turn into an "easy" school, but some sort of compromise should be possible. Students, faculty, and administrators should look for ways to improve the social life by encouraging greater diversity in weekend activities. Finally, the administration should try to keep the tuition from going any higher and should also make sure that financial aid is distributed fairly. Edson College has a great deal to offer students, but it

needs to look for ways to solve the problems that make so many
students leave.

## Liberal Education: Too Much of a Challenge?

Last week, an article in the *Edson Record* started a great deal
of discussion about attrition at the college by predicting that almost one-fourth of this year's freshman class would leave the college before graduating. What are the reasons for this high attrition rate? Some students, of course, leave the college because they
have to, because their grades fall below the college's minimum
standards. But why do so many students leave voluntarily? Many
students complain about such matters as the high tuition, the
poor cafeteria food, and the limited social life. These complaints,
however, are made by students who stay at Edson, as well as by
students who leave; those who are basically satisfied with the college somehow find a way to pay the bills, to put up with the food,
and to create their own social lives. The students who leave tend
to have more serious and fundamental reasons for being discon-
tented. I talked to six students who plan to transfer to other colleges next year and discovered that they are leaving because
Edson turned out to be precisely what they had once thought they
wanted—a liberal arts school with high academic standards.

All the students I talked to said that one of their main reasons
for deciding to come to Edson was the college's excellent academic
reputation. These students had thought that they wanted a school
that would challenge them and a diploma that would impress prospective employers. Once they got to Edson, however, they found
that the academic pressure was too much to take. One said that
he had always been an A student in high school and couldn't adjust to being a C student here. Another said that although she is
able to get high grades here, she found that the cost is too high:
she spends too many Saturday nights working on papers or catching up on reading rather than relaxing with her friends. A third
complained of the constant concern about grades among Edson
students and the extreme pressure from professors who make you
feel guilty if you do anything but study. Thus, even some good
students want to leave Edson because they dislike the time demands and the anxiety about grades.

These students also said that they chose Edson because they
wanted to attend a liberal arts school, but four of them now want
to leave so that they can enroll in vocational or preprofessional
programs. "I had wanted to major in art history," one said, "but I
kept wondering what sort of job that major would get me." Several used the word "practical" when they described the kind of
education they now want: one that will lead to a well-paying job

right after graduation. They came here with vague ideas about wanting to be "well-rounded," but they are leaving because they want to be employed. As graduation gets closer, some students become more and more nervous about finding jobs.

Still, many students who find the academic pressure hard to take and who are worried about jobs nevertheless stay at Edson because they find their studies so exciting and valuable that sacrifices are worthwhile. The students I talked to, however, didn't share this sense of excitement or this belief in the value of "impractical" studies. Even those who said they enjoyed most of their classes had never really become involved in the intellectual life of the campus; some hadn't been able to decide on a major because none of the subjects they studied really excited them. "I realized this year that I just don't enjoy studying that much," one said, "so I want to go someplace where academics are stressed less."

Ironically, the very reasons these students gave for wanting to come to Edson in the first place were also their reasons for wanting to leave. They had wanted a school with "high academic standards" but were unhappy when they realized how much time and pressure those standards involve; they had wanted a liberal arts education but then decided this sort of education was too "impractical"; they had wanted a school that would challenge them but never really responded to that challenge. At least for these students, the ultimate cause of attrition was that they didn't think carefully enough when they first decided on a college.

## DISCUSSION QUESTIONS

1. Compare the two introductory paragraphs. What does each author accomplish in his introduction? Did each introductory paragraph catch your interest? Did each clearly identify the essay's scope and purpose?
2. List the causes that each author cites as contributing to attrition. How does each author support his statements about the causes of attrition? Is the evidence each author offers relevant and sufficient? Does each author show a clear relationship between the possible causes discussed and the problem of attrition?
3. Comment on the organization of each essay. How are the paragraphs ordered? Is this order logical and effective? Would you suggest any changes in organization?
4. Compare the concluding paragraphs. What does each author accomplish in his conclusion? Does either author claim more than he has proven?
5. On the whole, which essay did you find more plausible and interesting? Which offers a more convincing, probing analysis of the causes of attrition?

**B.** The students in a freshman competition class were asked to write essays speculating about the ways in which the feminist movement might affect the American family during the next twenty years. Read the following two essays and compare them carefully.

### The Feminist Family in 2001

It is 6:00 on a Friday evening in 2001, and a woman is returning home from her job. She has been invigorated but not exhausted by her time at the office, for she, like her husband, works just four hours a day. She finds her husband in the kitchen, checking on a casserole in the oven; he tells her about his morning on the job and his afternoon at home, and she tells him about her morning at home and her afternoon on the job. They ask their son, who has just finished setting the table, to go tell his sister that it's time to stop mowing the lawn and to come in to dinner. As they enjoy their meal, the family discuss their plans for the weekend: tonight, the mother and father will go to a movie; on Saturday, the mother will take her son to a football game, and the father will take his daughter on a shopping trip.

This description of family life may sound like science fiction, but it may have become a reality by 2001. Women having careers is not just a passing trend; it will continue to grow until women have achieved their equality with men. How might full sexual equality affect American home life—the way responsibilities are shared, the relationship between husband and wife, the way children are brought up? We can expect some serious difficulties at first, but ultimately full equality between the sexes should benefit everyone in the family.

During the next decade, the struggle for sexual equality will probably create some tensions and some practical problems in the family. Some husbands will probably feel that it is somehow disgraceful to have wives who work, that "real men" support their families by themselves. They may feel jealous or inadequate if their wives make more money than they do. Wives may resent their husbands' efforts to keep them at home; wives who insist on the right to work may also feel secretly guilty if they suspect that they are indeed neglecting their homes and families. If women try to overcome these guilt feelings by trying to be the perfect wife and mother as well as the perfect worker, they may suffer from stress and exhaustion. Problems will multiply if the couple has children: friends and relatives may criticize the mother who goes to work instead of staying home with her children, and arranging for good child care may be frustrating, expensive, and perhaps impossible. Even children who do receive excellent care may feel cheated if their mothers are the only ones on the block who are not at home all day.

As time goes on, however, we can reasonably expect that couples will find ways to overcome these problems and will be able to enjoy the benefits of sexual equality. The husband, relieved of the full responsibility of supporting the family, may be more relaxed and less obsessed with work; he may even be less likely to have ulcers and heart attacks caused by tension and overwork. He may also find it a pleasure to come home to a wife who can fully sympathize with the problems he encounters on the job: she, too, knows what it is like to have an unreasonable boss or an irresponsible employee. The wife, in turn, has a more stimulating, satisfying life. She takes pride in her ability to help support the family and is no longer bored and frustrated by a day spent washing windows and watching soap operas. The house may not be spotless, but ring-around-the collar is a small price to pay for equality.

In ten years, it is very likely that couples who want to work and have children will have found new, creative ways to share their responsibilities. They may both work part-time, they may share a job, they may arrange to do part of their work at home, or they may establish cooperative day-care centers where parents make sure that their children receive the best care possible. As working mothers become more and more common, children will be less likely to resent such arrangements. By then, going to a day-care center may seem as normal as going to elementary school does now. Someday, it may even be that the children with stay-at-home mothers will be the ones who feel deprived because they can't go to the center to have fun with their friends.

By 2001, the American family may have changed dramatically for the better. Bad marriages would be more likely to end in divorce, for a woman who can support herself will not feel tied to her husband by financial dependence. Marriages based on love and not on dependence, however, would be more satisfying to both partners. The sharing of responsibilities could make the relationship between husband and wife much closer, for both would understand the problems of both jobs and domestic work. They would respect each other as equal partners in the tasks of supporting and caring for the family. The children might benefit even more. They would get to know each parent equally, which would be good in many ways; for example, a teenaged girl worried about dating problems would feel freer to go to her father for advice. They would not have rigid ideas of male and female roles. They would not think of housework as a woman's job and lawn work as a man's job, and they would know that it's all right for a woman to be strong and intelligent and for a man to be gentle and caring. Also, if both parents work outside the home, they would be more likely to demand that the children share in household chores, so the children may become more responsible at an earlier age; they will no longer be able to rely on Mom as a full-time maid. From their earliest years, these children will have learned to adapt to a variety of adults—mother, father, day-care teachers —and so may well become more flexible and outgoing, far less likely to cling to their mothers' skirts when they encounter new people and situations.

A family bound together by love, respect, understanding, and shared responsibilities—will this be feminism's ultimate effect on the family? It could just be that the feminist movement, which some people see as a threat to marriage and children, will be the very force we need to preserve and revitalize the family.

## Feminism's Effects on the Family

As more and more women decide that they want to keep working after they get married and even after they have children, it is interesting to think about how the family system may be affected by this phenomenon. Will wives be able to handle the pressure of having jobs and taking care of children? Will husbands be willing to let their wives have careers? Will children be harmed or helped by these changes? It's impossible to be sure of what the long-range effects will be, but we had better get used to the idea that things may be very different for the American family twenty years from now. The typical family will no longer consist of a working father, housewife mother, and a few children; instead, it will consist of a working father, a working mother, and a few children.

One good effect could be that children will learn to be more responsible at an earlier age. As women develop jobs or careers, their energies will no longer channel only into the child. Since the child will not be dependent on his or her mother, we might find a more responsible child. The children of the house will be doing the housework so mother and father can keep their careers. With both parents gone during the day, children will find themselves making their own decisions, thus taking responsibility for their own actions. Self-discipline will be taught since the child will have to schedule his or her own time for schoolwork, play, and chores. The child might well grow up to become a more dependable and productive worker, since he or she would have learned to handle responsibilities at an earlier age.

One possible bad effect is that there may be an increase in tension between the father and the mother. Many husbands do not want their wives to work, for they think that wife's proper role is at home doing the housework and taking care of the children. If the wife insists that she wants to work, there might be a lot of fights and arguments in the family. In some cases, the husband might give his wife a flat-out "no," which would probably make her angry. In most cases, however, the husband and wife would be able to work out some sort of compromise that they would both find acceptable.

If they do decide that the wife should also work, they will have to find ways to care for the children. Maybe the wife will be able to work on a night shift so that she can care for the children during the day and then go to work at night. If this happens, the husband will have to agree to spend most of his evenings at home with the children, or they will have to hire a babysitter. If both parents work during the day, then they will have to find some sort of day-care center for the children. One effect of the feminist movement, therefore, will probably be an increase in the number of day-care centers. There will probably be all sorts of day-care centers—some run by churches, some run for a profit, some run by the government for low-income mothers. Some companies may provide day-care centers for their female employees. If the day-care center is very close to the place where the mother works, this could be a real advantage, for the mother would be able to stop in and see her children frequently during the day.

Couples that do not have children may benefit a great deal if both husband and wife work. Since they would have two salaries instead of just one, their standard of living would go up quite a bit. They would still have to find some way to take care of housework, but with two salaries they could afford to hire a housekeeper, or possibly the wife could just work part-time.

There might be other long-range effects as well. For example, wife abuse might decrease. Many sociologists say that many abused wives stay with their husbands because they are afraid they would not be able to support themselves if they left. If a woman works, she would be more likely to leave home if her husband beats her, for she would know that she's capable of supporting herself. So there might be an increase in the divorce rate. On the other hand, the abused wife might leave home temporarily and insist that her husband get treatment. If he really loves his wife, he will do what she asks, and the marriage will be saved.

Women who want to work and have families will change not only the direction of their own lives, but also the lives of their husbands and children. We can't be sure about what all the long-range effects of feminism on the family will be, but probably there will be both good effects and bad effects. Families will have to work together to find solutions to the problems that arise.

## DISCUSSION QUESTIONS

1. Comment on the content of each essay. What possible changes in the American family system does each author foresee? Did you find each author's speculations plausible? Which author's speculations struck you as more interesting and imaginative?
2. Comment on the organization of each essay. How are the paragraphs ordered? Is the order logical and effective? Would you suggest any changes in organization?
3. What techniques does the author of "Feminism's Effects on the Family" use in the introductory paragraph? Are these techniques used well? Would you suggest any changes in the introductory paragraph?
4. "The Feminist Family in 2001" has, in effect, a two-paragraph introduction. Why do you think the author decided to write such a long introduction? Should the author condense the introduction into one paragraph?
5. On the whole, which essay did you find more original and convincing? Why?

**C.** Additional exercise: Suppose that you are a medical researcher looking for a cure for leukemia. You develop an experimental drug and administer it to a patient who has leukemia. The patient recovers, and you hypothesize that the drug caused the recovery. List the steps you might take to test this hypothesis. What sorts of supporting evidence will you need to find in order to prove that the drug really did cause the cure?

## GENERAL CONCLUSIONS

Draw together all the observations and comments you have made about the introductory readings in this chapter. List some of the characteristics of a strong cause-and-effect essay, or summarize your conclusions in a paragraph that would be helpful to beginning composition students. What advice would you give to a student writing a cause-and-effect essay? Did the exercise about medical research give you any additional ideas about ways of proving that a cause-and-effect relationship exists?

## ADVICE

According to some pediatricians, infants begin to understand their world when they first grasp the relationship between causes and effects. The world seems a haphazard place to newborns, full of random events that they can neither predict nor control. Newborns cry not in an attempt to communicate but simply to express their discomfort or frustration. Gradually, however, infants start to realize that events are related, that some events seem to cause others. They realize that their cries and their other actions produce fairly predictable results: if they cry, their parents come running to see what the trouble is; if they overturn their cups, their milk spills to the floor. So as they learn these first lessons in cause and effect, the world begins to make sense to infants, and they begin to learn how they can control it.

In our own attempts to understand and control our world, we constantly ask ourselves questions about cause and effect. What caused a friend to become angry? What will the effects be if I go to this college, accept this job, marry this person? Professors frequently assign papers asking their students to trace causes or to predict or report consequences. What were the causes of World War I? Why did John Kennedy win the 1960 presidential election? How did Jimmy Carter's policies affect the economy? How will a new bill affect the housing industry? Scientific writing also frequently explores cause and effect: what caused a volcano to erupt, a chemical to react, a disease to develop? If you go into business after college, you might be asked to determine the causes of a drop in sales or the probable effects of a new advertising campaign. Cause-and-effect essays concern themselves with two of the most basic but perplexing questions we can ask ourselves—Why did this happen, and what will happen? Although it is doubtful that either question can ever be answered with absolute certainty, our speculations about cause and effect give us some valuable insights into our lives and also some hope of controlling events. If we understand why something happened, we may be able to make it happen again or to prevent it from happening again; if we understand what the consequences of an action might be, we can make a wiser decision about whether or not to take that action.

In causal analysis, we can reason either from effect to cause or from cause to effect. When reasoning *from effect to cause,* we start with something that already exists (the effect) and try to determine what made it happen (the cause): for example, why did Congress decide to eliminate a student loan program? We can also reason *from cause to effect* by starting with something that has happened or may happen (the cause) and trying to determine what effects it has produced or might produce: How will Congress's action affect college enrollments? Whether you work from effect to cause or from cause to effect, one of your first tasks will be to show that the effects you discuss really are the results of the causes you have identified.

## Proving a Cause-and-Effect Relationship Exists

A student in a freshman composition class wrote a one-paragraph essay about a successful crime-prevention program:

When a violent crime is committed, citizens are outraged and want to do something about it. If the police can harness this outrage and energy, the community can benefit greatly. A pilot program in Fountain Valley, California, provides a good example of this. In 1970, after a brutal attack on a small child, the police and a citizen group formed a "Block Watch." Each day, one parent would take responsibility for a block. A special plaque was hung on that neighbor's door all day, so that the children would know that they could go to that house for assistance of any kind. The operation grew and soon encompassed many other kinds of crime prevention. The results were amazing: street crimes declined, fewer houses were burglarized, and to this day no children in the community have been victimized. When you consider that Fountain Valley is a city of over 180,000 people, these results are especially encouraging

At first glance, this description of the program's success seems quite convincing: the Block Watch program was adopted, and the crime rate dropped dramatically. Still, a skeptic might argue that the author has not proven that the block watch was responsible for the decrease in crime. Perhaps the crime rate would have fallen even if Fountain Valley had not adopted the program. Did the city do anything else that might also account for the decrease in crime? Did it, for example, hire ten new police officers and assign them to street patrols? Did the police department adopt new policies that made it easier to apprehend criminals? Did a tough new judge discourage crime by handing out stiffer sentences? Did citizens install burglar alarms in their homes?

We are often much too casual about assuming that a cause-and-effect relationship exists. We notice that one event follows another and assume that the first event caused the second. In making this assumption, we are guilty of the logical fallacy called *post hoc, ergo propter hoc* ("after this, therefore because of this"—see Chapter 9, p. 190). Superstitions often develop because we assume that events are related when they really are not: "I broke a mirror yesterday morning, and last night my fiancée called off our engagement. Breaking a mirror really does cause bad luck." In cause-and-effect essays, *make sure you provide adequate evidence for any statements about cause and effect.* It is difficult to be absolutely sure about causes and effects, even when we are considering our own motives and actions. I think that I became an English teacher because I love writing and literature, but can I be sure that the real cause wasn't a subconscious desire to please my father, also an English teacher? I think that attending a writing conference next week will have good effects on my teaching, but can I really be sure? Still, if we are cautious about making assumptions and careful to provide supporting evidence, we can make a reasonable case for the existence of a cause-and-effect relationship.

Suppose, for example, that you wanted to prove that the Block

Watch program really was the cause of Fountain Valley's reduced crime rate. You could look for several sorts of supporting evidence:

1. *Provide examples to show that the two phenomena are causally related.* Can you give specific examples of times when parents participating in the Block Watch program sheltered children who were being harassed by strangers? Can you give examples of times when these participants noticed suspicious situations, notified the police, and thereby prevented burglaries or street crimes? Such examples would show a direct relationship between the program and crime prevention, and should help to convince your readers that it was not just coincidence that the decreased crime rate followed the initiation of the program.

2. *Eliminate other possible causes.* Try to anticipate other explanations of what might have caused the drop in the crime rate and show that they do not apply. For example, you might argue that Fountain Valley took no other action that could explain the decrease in crime: it hired no new police officers, adopted no other new policies or programs, elected no new judges, and in general, took no other new steps to prevent crime. Such evidence will make your readers more likely to believe that the Block Watch program must have been the cause of the reduction in crimes.

3. *If possible, provide other examples of times when the cause produced the same effect.* In looking for further support for your assertions about the Block Watch program, you might try to find another city that adopted such a program and had a similar drop in crime. Such evidence increases the probability that the program and the decrease in crime are causally related.

4. *If possible, provide a control.* Try to find an example of a city that was similar to Fountain Valley in many respects—population, size of police department, history of unsuccessful attempts to control crime—but did not have a Block Watch program. If this city's crime rate rose or remained constant during the same period that Fountain Valley's rate fell, you will have found further support for your thesis.

Unfortunately, it is not always possible to find all these kinds of support for an assertion about cause and effect. For example, if you want to argue that concern about the economy was the primary cause of Ronald Reagan's election as president, it will be difficult for you to provide a control. Still, remembering the kind and amount of evidence needed to support an assertion about cause and effect should make you more cautious in your assumptions and should also give you some ideas about where to look for the evidence you will need. You may not be able to find all these types of supporting evidence for every cause-and-effect essay you write, but you should not be satisfied until you have found at least some.

## Distinguishing Among Types of Causes and Effects

Seldom does a phenomenon have just one cause. If a person falls down a flight of stairs and breaks a leg, we can be fairly safe in assuming that the fall caused the broken leg. When we are trying to determine the causes of a more complex phenomenon, however, we will probably find that there are several causes. Similarly, when we are reporting or predicting the effects of some action or event, we should look for more than one. There are various types of causes and effects, and learning to distinguish among them is an important step toward writing a clear and accurate cause-and-effect essay.

When we are looking for the causes of a phenomenon, for example, we should distinguish among necessary, sufficient, and contributing causes. A *necessary cause* must always be present before an effect can be produced. A scientist might argue, for example, that only people who have been exposed to a particular kind of bacteria develop a certain disease. If it is impossible for people who have not been exposed to develop the disease, then the bacteria are a necessary cause of the disease. If everybody who is exposed to the bacteria develops the disease, then the bacteria are also a *sufficient cause*—they are all that needs to be present in order for the effect to occur. It may be, however, that many people who are exposed to the bacteria never develop the disease at all. In that case, the bacteria can be only a *contributing cause*— other causes must also be present before the effect is produced. Perhaps only those people who are malnourished develop the disease when they are exposed to the bacteria; if so, malnutrition and the bacteria are both contributing causes. It may be, of course, that there are other contributing causes as well.

Suppose, for example, that you are writing an essay to explain why your college decided to build a new theater. You interview several administrators, who tell you that a wealthy alumna donated a large sum of money to the college, and the administrators decided to use the money for the new theater. If the administrators assure you that the college could not possibly have afforded to build the theater if it had not received the gift, you can conclude that the gift was a necessary cause of the theater's being built. But was the gift a sufficient cause? Probably not, for the college could have decided to use the money in another way. Thus the gift was a contributing cause but not a sufficient one. Your job now is to look for other contributing causes—the administrators' interest in improving the theater program, faculty support, the rundown condition of the old theater, students' demands for better facilities, the college's desire to compete with another college that just built a new theater, and so forth. An essay that discussed nothing but the gift would not be thorough.

It is also important to distinguish between *immediate* and *ultimate* causes and effects. It is easier to recognize immediate causes: John Lang fell down a flight of stairs and broke a leg. The fall is the *immedi-*

*ate cause* of the broken leg—the apparent cause, the one immediately preceding the event, and the one you discover first. But why did John fall down the stairs? Did he trip? If so, did he trip because of poor eyesight, a railing that gave way, or a roller skate at the top of the stairs? Or was John pushed? If so, who pushed him and why? If you investigate further you may find that John's sister pushed him down the stairs, because she was angry about an insulting remark he made. You thus conclude that the insulting remark was the ultimate cause of John's broken leg—unless you want to probe still further and find out why John made the remark. An *ultimate cause,* in other words, is an underlying cause, usually less readily apparent than an immediate cause; it starts a chain of events that ultimately leads to the final effect.

In your essay about your college's new theater, for example, you might decide to go beyond an immediate cause—the alumna's gift— and find out why she decided to donate the money to the college in the first place. You may interview the alumna and ask her why she donated the money. If she replies, "Because I really love the college," you could keep probing and ask her why she loves it. She may tell you that when she was a sophomore and her family was in debt, the college decided to give her a special scholarship so that she could complete her education. She was so moved by this generosity that she vowed she would repay the college some day. You can now start your paper by asserting, "The college will be able to afford a new theater building next year because, in 1927, it helped out a student struggling to stay in school"—a much more interesting thesis statement than "The college will be able to afford a new theater building because an alumna donated some money."

In an essay in which you reason from cause to effect, be equally diligent about looking for ultimate effects as well as immediate ones. If you decided to write not about the causes for the theater's being built but about the effects it will have on the campus, you might decide that the immediate effects will include an increase in the number of experimental plays produced since the new theater offers facilities for theater-in-the-round as well as a traditional stage. Ultimate effects might include an increased interest in theater leading to a greater number of theater majors leading to a demand for more theater professors. Just as you would be careful to identify causes as necessary, sufficient, or contributing, you should be careful to identify effects as *certain, probable,* or *possible.*

It is difficult to know when to stop when you are looking for ultimate causes or effects. If you are writing about the alumna's reasons for donating money to the college, for example, it really is not necessary to find out why her family was in debt in the first place: whatever the reasons were, they are not relevant to her decision to donate the money. Similarly, it is difficult to know when you have identified enough contributing causes; in most cases, it won't be possible for you to find all of them. You will have to use your judgment to decide when your discussion of causes or effects is probing enough to be interesting and reasonably thorough.


## Organizing Your Essay

Use the introductory paragraph of your essay to make the limits of your investigation clear. If you are writing about the causes of the Revolutionary War, for example, will you discuss all the contributing causes or only the major ones? If you are discussing the probable effects of a new energy policy, will you discuss only the effects it will have in this country or also probable effects on the world oil market? Your thesis statement should set the limits of your discussion precisely, or you might be criticized for failing to mention a cause or effect that you never intended to discuss.

You can follow a number of patterns in ordering your paragraphs in a cause-and-effect essay. Here are a few possibilities:

- from immediate to ultimate causes or effects
- from more obvious to less obvious causes or effects
- from less important to more important causes or effects
- from one type of cause or effect to another (for example, in a long essay on the causes of the Revolutionary War, you might discuss first economic causes, then political causes, then philosophical causes)
- from certain effects to probable effects to possible effects
- from necessary causes to contributing causes


Notice that most of these patterns are variations on the *order of importance*. As in almost any paper, you should try to build to a climax. End with your most startling or provocative idea.

Cause-and-effect essays require a writer who is both imaginative and cautious. You must be imaginative enough to see causes or predict effects that less perceptive people might miss, but you must also be cautious enough to require a great deal of evidence before you assert that X must have caused Y or that Y will certainly cause Z. Remember that we can never be absolutely certain about either causes or effects, and don't be ashamed to qualify your statements by saying that X *may* have caused Y or that Y *will probably* cause Z. If your language is properly cautious, your speculations can be much bolder and more imaginative.

## *APPLICATION*

**A.** Each of the following paragraphs asserts that two events are causally related. In each paragraph, has the author proven that a cause-and-effect relationship exists? What further sorts of evidence should the author provide?

1. This company made a serious mistake when it chose Paul Harper as president. Since Harper assumed the office three years ago, our profits have fallen by 20 percent, and we've lost four of our top executives to rival companies.
2. The new back-to-basics writing program that Culbert County initiated in its high schools has been a great success. Since we started the program five years ago, the median verbal SAT score for Culbert County seniors has risen significantly.
3. This college has a poor social life because the administration and faculty think that study is all-important. Their attitudes have prevented an active, varied social life from developing.
4. Making George Nelson a regular on "The Young Executives" has really saved the show. Before Nelson joined the cast, the show was barely making it; now, it consistently rates in the top ten.
5. Feminism has hurt the American family system. Ever since increasing numbers of married women have started going back to work, the divorce rate has gone through the ceiling.

**B.** All the following sentences make statements about cause and effect. Label the causes as necessary, sufficient, or contributing. For some sentences, more than one answer may be possible.

1. Chris got an A in the course because she came to class every day.
2. Becky failed the course because she never came to class.
3. Steve decided to drop out of college because he couldn't find anyone to room with next year.
4. The workers went on strike because they thought their wages were too low.
5. The Geology Department hired Professor Lent because she had a Ph.D.
6. Senator Murphy won the election because he promised to cut taxes.
7. Carrie's chronic eyestrain cleared up because she got new glasses.
8. Phil is overweight because he eats too much.
9. Kevin never learned to read well because he watches five hours of television every day.
10. The Achlands had a car accident because their brakes failed.

**C.** For this exercise, you may want to work in a small group with other students. Suppose you had to write a cause-and-effect essay about the reasons for voter apathy in the United States.

1. List as many causes of voter apathy as you can think of.
2. Label these causes necessary, sufficient, or contributing and immediate or ultimate.
3. Decide which of your ideas about the causes of voter apathy need further support. What kinds of support will you have to find?
4. Pick out the most interesting and plausible causes on your list and find a way to organize them into paragraphs. Draw up a rough outline showing how you might order these paragraphs in your essay.

**D.** For this exercise, you may want to work in a small group with other students. Suppose you had to write a cause-and-effect essay predicting the effects of a recent or proposed change at your college—for example, a proposal to change the number of required courses or to cut back on the number of faculty.

1. List as many effects as you can think of.
2. Label these effects necessary, sufficient, or contributing and immediate or ultimate.
3. Decide which of your ideas about the effects of the change need further support. What kinds of support will you have to find?
4. Pick out the most interesting and plausible effects on your list and find a way to organize them into paragraphs. Draw up a rough outline showing how you might order these paragraphs in a cause-and-effect essay on the topic you have chosen.

**E.** Following is an essay analyzing the effects of making students read aloud in class. Read the essay and answer the questions that follow.

### Reading Out Loud

As I was sitting in my English class in junior high, I was praying my English teacher would not call on me to read out loud. I sat there trying to hide behind the person in front of me. The anguish of waiting to see who was going to be called upon kept building and building inside to the point where I felt nauseated. I had an empty, guilty feeling that there was no escape from being called upon. Then it happened; she called on me, and my heart sank. As I proceeded to read, my pulse rate shot up, the blood was rushing to my head, and beads of sweat started forming on my forehead. Many elementary, junior-high, and high-school English teachers make students read out loud frequently, but I wonder how many teachers have thought about the effects this technique can have on the students. Having to read out loud in class can make students so embarrassed that they fight with each other, resent their teachers, and, worst of all, grow to hate reading itself.

Elementary-school teachers often ask students to read out loud to check up on whether or not the students have mastered the assigned vocabulary words. This technique of checking up on students' progress, however, can actually slow down that progress. If a young student makes a mistake while reading out loud, the class usually laughs at the reader. Therefore, the student feels humiliated and never wants to read out loud again. The teacher responds by saying, "It's not polite to laugh." Any ten- or eleven-year-old student is not going to understand the full meaning of politeness. As the class continues to giggle, the reader becomes more embarrassed and begins to think, "I hate reading."

In the vulnerable years of junior high, reading out loud can have a big effect on a person in two ways. First, the reader who does a good job of reading and is praised by the teacher is going to be called "teacher's pet." Second, there is the reader who just cannot read out loud because of all the pressure he feels. So after class has ended, the reader confronts the person who snickered in the back of the room, telling him never to do it again. Words are exchanged between the two, and the next thing both are on the floor fighting. Instead of helping the students learn to read and to enjoy reading, the teacher has made some students envious, some students insulting, and other students angry.

Finally, when high school rolls around, reading out loud is not considered the "cool" thing to do. When the teacher calls on a student to read, the student will just roll his eyes and say under his breath, "Ah, come on." Reading becomes a joke: it is something no "cool" person would do. When the reader makes a mistake, he will act as though he did it purposely to be funny. Now it is the person who reads well who is looked down upon and perhaps even rejected by his peers. Once again, reading out loud has created divisions among students.

Imagine how differently students at all levels might feel about reading if teachers found another way to check up on how much students have learned. What would happen if the teacher gave the class an assignment to work on and then took the students aside, one by one, to have them read out loud in private? If the students made mistakes, the teacher could correct them, but no one would be there to laugh. Students could improve their reading without ever being embarrassed about what they don't know. Students who read well could enjoy the teacher's praise without being envied and disliked by other students. Wouldn't this approach make students more likely to enjoy reading and to want to do well? Reading out loud in class was the worst thing I ever had to do in school. I hope that teachers find another way to teach reading so that future students won't dread reading class as much as I did.

## DISCUSSION QUESTIONS

1. The author's introductory paragraph is rather unconventional. What techniques does he use in this paragraph? Does the paragraph contain a thesis statement? On the whole, do you find this paragraph effective?
2. How does the author support his assertions that reading aloud causes various problems? Is his support adequate? What other sorts of support could he offer?
3. How is the essay organized? Could the author have used another way of organizing his ideas about the various effects of reading aloud?
4. What does the author accomplish in his concluding paragraph?

# 8.
# Definition

## INTRODUCTORY READINGS

**A.**  Two students in a freshman composition class wrote essays defining *pride*. Read the two essays and compare them carefully.

### What Is Pride?

The *Grosset Webster Dictionary* defines "pride" as "arrogance, loftiness, conceit, self-respect, dignity, and valuing oneself." Pride is something that most people strive for. To have pride means to have self-respect for yourself or something that means a great deal to you. Some people will do just about anything to get this pride. I guess you can say that pride is something you must have to live a satisfying life. Without pride, your life is meaningless. You have nothing that means anything to you or has any importance to you.

Pride can be expressed in many different ways, and there are many different kinds of pride. For instance, I have a great amount of pride in myself. I am proud of the way I have turned out and of all the things I have accomplished thus far in my life. I am also proud of the community where I live. Because of this pride, I do as much as I can to make it a better place. I feel that it is wrong for people to say that they dislike the city they live in unless they do something to improve it. I have another sort of pride, which is pride in my family. I feel that my family is the best family in the world. We are a close family and get along with each other very well. Because of this family pride, I enjoy bringing friends to my home. Without family pride, I think one would begin to lose pride in many other things. I guess you can say that family pride is the basis for all pride.

Another kind of pride is pride for something that means a lot to you—for instance, pride in your school. I remember in high school how people had so much pride in their school that any other high school was simply not as good as their own. These are a few of the ways in which pride can be expressed.

Pride is so important that some people will do just about anything to get it. For instance, some people cheat, steal, lie, and exaggerate. A person who wanted to feel proud about his grades might cheat on an exam, but the only person he's hurting is himself. A person can also lie or exaggerate about something that would make him look better in the eyes of his friends, or he might be too proud to admit it when he makes a mistake. By doing this, the person will soon be locked into a corner with nowhere to go. His lies would have caught up with him at this time. This is why I say people will do just about anything to get pride.

Pride is something a person must achieve by himself. Real pride can't be based on cheating or lying. Pride helps people to feel good about themselves, their communities, their families, and their schools. Pride helps people to live happy and satisfying lives.

## Pride: Sin or Strength?

Our Sunday-school teachers may have told us that pride is a sin and goes before destruction; at the same time, our other teachers, our parents, and our coaches may have encouraged us to take pride in our work, in ourselves, or in our ability. "Pride" is used in a confusing variety of ways, sometimes condemned as the cause of mistakes and unhappiness and sometimes praised as essential to success. What *is* pride? Is it something we should try to overcome or something we should try to develop? By examining the various ways in which "pride" is used, we can get a better understanding of its true nature.

Pride seems to be something between an emotion and an opinion: it is a feeling of dignity and self-respect based on an opinion that something—a country, a family, a person—is good and worthwhile. When we use "pride" in a positive sense, we usually see it as a moderate emotion based on a justified opinion. For example, we probably wouldn't criticize someone who says, "I'm proud of my parents because they're honest and hard-working." There's nothing obnoxious or excessive about this expression of pride, and it's based on a reasonable opinion: we believe that one should be proud of honest, hard-working parents. We also wouldn't criticize an excellent pianist who admitted that he felt proud after performing a piece well or a social worker who said that she was proud that she had spent her life helping people. We aren't offended by quiet assertions of pride when we think that the people have a right to be proud. Furthermore, we tend to believe that this kind of pride can do a lot of good by pushing people to make real efforts and do worthwhile things. The pianist, for example, might work very hard to improve partly because he enjoys the feeling of pride that he gets whenever he does well.

We do criticize pride, however, when it seems excessive and unjustified. For example, we don't like people who continually brag because their parents are rich; bragging is excessive, and wealth is not, in itself, something to be proud of. When pride gets carried to this extreme, it can give people inflated images of themselves, make them overlook other people's accomplishments, and lead them to expect special treatment. A mediocre pianist who is so proud of his talents that he won't admit that anyone else can play better than he can is ridiculous, and a social worker who is so proud of her record that she expects other people to praise her all the time is obnoxious. This kind of pride can make people very unpleasant to be with—no one likes to listen to people who can only talk about themselves and how wonderful they are. Also, because this kind of pride isn't really justified, it can lead people into making mistakes: for example, the mediocre pianist might be so proud of himself that he tries to become a professional even though he doesn't have enough talent to succeed.

It may be that pride is not, in itself, either good or bad. Everything depends on the amount of pride one feels, on the basis of one's pride, and on the way one expresses one's pride. It may be that our Sunday-school teachers warned us about pride not because pride is always bad but because it is always dangerous. Once pride begins to develop, it can grow very quickly and soon become excessive; and since pride can keep us from seeing our own faults, we may not even realize how proud we are until it is too late to change.

## DISCUSSION QUESTIONS

1. Compare the two introductory paragraphs. What does each author accomplish in this paragraph? Did each introductory paragraph catch your interest? Did each clearly identify the essay's scope and purpose?

2. Does each essay contain a thesis statement that sums up the author's definition of *pride*? If so, identify and evaluate this thesis statement.

3. Comment on each author's use of examples. What purposes do the examples in each essay serve? Did you find the examples interesting and helpful? Explain.

4. Both authors, in addition to defining pride, say that some kinds of

pride are good while others are not. Comment on the criteria each
author uses to distinguish between "good pride" and "bad pride."
Do you find these criteria sensible and perceptive? Explain.
5. Comment on the organization of each essay. How are the paragraphs in each essay ordered? Do you find each essay's organization clear and logical?
6. On the whole, which essay offered a clearer and more interesting
definition of pride? How could the other essay be improved?


**B.** The students in a freshman composition class were asked to write
definition essays. One student chose to write an essay defining *assertiveness;* the other chose to write an essay defining *victory.* Read the
two essays and compare them carefully.


### Passivity, Aggressiveness, and Assertiveness

When I came to college last fall, I was looking forward to
taking college courses, joining college organizations, and dating
college men; most of all, however, I was looking forward to meeting my college roommate. I was sure that we would become best
friends—after all, my mother had roomed with the same woman
all through college, and they still keep in touch after over twenty-
five years. Unfortunately, my roommate didn't seem particularly
interested in my friendship, although she was extremely interested in my possessions. Without ever asking my permission,
Kyle would borrow my clothes, lend my albums to her friends,
rummage through my desk in search of any supplies she needed,
and help herself to the food I kept in the room (her own supplies
of food, I discovered later, were safely hidden away under her
bed). Every weekend, Kyle's out-of-town boyfriend came to visit;
every weekend, Kyle told me to go sleep in the lounge. What did I
do? Why, I complimented Kyle on how nice she looked in my
clothes, smiled sweetly when I learned she had lost one of my
albums or used up my last sheet of typing paper, and offered her
another potato chip as I trudged off to the lounge with my pillow
and blankets. I was furious inside, but I never said a word. I
might as well have worn a T-shirt reading "Welcome": I was already the perfect doormat. When I finally worked up the courage
to tell my resident assistant about my frustrations, she used a
word that I wish I had learned about a long time ago: assertiveness.

As my resident assistant explained it, assertiveness is the determination to make sure that one's rights are respected. It is an
attitude based on self-respect and firmness. When I looked the
word up in the *Oxford English Dictionary* later, I learned that it

is derived from a Latin word meaning, among other things, "to claim," "to defend," and "to affirm": assertive people claim and defend what is rightfully theirs, and they aren't afraid to affirm that they deserve to be treated fairly. My resident assistant advised me to develop some assertiveness and stand up to Kyle, rather than keeping all my resentment inside.

Of course, my first reaction was to reject this advice because I was afraid—what else would you expect from a doormat? How could I make friends if I dared to be assertive? Wouldn't people be offended and angry if I became aggressive instead of simply giving in all the time? My resident assistant assured me that being assertive doesn't mean being aggressive: although many dictionaries list "assertiveness" and "aggressiveness" as synonyms, the two words are actually very different. She used an example to make the difference clear. Suppose you went to a restaurant and ordered a medium-rare steak but got a well-done one instead. If you were a passive person, you would choke down the steak without a word of protest. If you were aggressive, you would be hostile and offensive ("aggressive" comes from a Latin word meaning "attack"): you would angrily insult the waiter, demand to see the manager, and make loud complaints about the chef—thereby embarrassing your friends and ruining their evening. On the other hand, if you were assertive, you would politely but firmly ask for another steak without making a scene. But you wouldn't give in until you got the steak you wanted; after all, if you are paying for the meal, you have a right to get what you ordered. It is possible to be assertive without being pushy or unpleasant. Assertiveness began to sound pretty good to me, so I told my resident assistant I would give it a try.

What happened with Kyle? I wish I could say that she developed a new respect for me when I quietly announced that from now on she could not borrow my things without permission and that I would no longer be sleeping in the lounge on weekends. She was puzzled; she tried to laugh it off; when she realized that I was serious and determined, she was angry. After two weeks, when it was clear that I was not going to go back to being conveniently passive, she told me to move out. But now I was actually enjoying being assertive: I told her that she had no right to ask me to give up my room, and that if she was unhappy she was welcome to leave. And that's what she did. So being assertive didn't help me to become friends with Kyle. It did, however, help me to build a good relationship with my new roommate. I've also found that my new attitude has helped me to enjoy other friendships more because I no longer go around feeling abused and miserable. I can't be friends with aggressive people like Kyle—I no longer even want to try—but I can be friends with other assertive people. I think that most people respect me more now that they can see that I respect myself, and self-respect and mutual respect are the only firm foundations for true, satisfying friendships. After all, who wants to be friends with a doormat?

## The Thrill of Victory

Inside every competitor there is the desire for victory. Victory is the glory of competition and the ultimate thrill in any contest or conflict. Whether it be two people or two teams or two countries battling each other, victory is the ultimate goal and desire. To overcome an enemy or to succeed in a struggle against the odds is to know victory.

Victory cannot exist without competition. In every political battle, sporting event, or business situation, there is a definite competition between two parties. Competition is competing against someone else to see who is better and who will achieve victory. Competition is present everywhere. It is not only related to sports or battles, but is present in everyone's everyday life.

To live in the world today, one must be a competitor; to be a successful competitor, one must be victorious. Every culture in the world is built around the desire to compete for a better life and achieve victory. The factory worker competes against other factory workers to get a better job, whereas a business competes against other businesses to produce and sell more products. In every case, competition leads to victory, which produces a better life.

In America today, one area where the desire for competition and victory is especially important is in professional sports. In professional sports, the game is not played for the sake of enjoyment in the playing itself, but for the thrill of victory. This fact is very clear when we think about how much more popular victorious teams are than losing teams: if a team is doing very well during a season, a lot of people will come to their games, but if the team is not doing too well, they will generally have much smaller crowds. A good example of this is the Portland Trailblazers. In 1976 they won the NBA championship. All through that year, they had capacity crowds. People with season tickets were all right, but other people had to buy tickets months in advance. The next year, the Trailblazers were in the playoffs but did not win the championship. During that year they still had capacity crowds, but now it was possible to buy tickets a few weeks in advance. The next year the Trailblazers did not do very well because the starting lineup was injured. All through that season, people could buy tickets at the gate. This example proves that people do not go to sporting events because they enjoy seeing the game played but because they hope that their team will be victorious. In professional sports today, victory is not everything—it's the only thing.

To gain victory, one must be a good competitor. A good competitor must have several important qualities, including determination, dedication, and a desire to win. Most of all, a good competitor must have confidence in his own abilities. A competitor who does not really believe that he is capable of achieving victory will never make the extra effort it takes to win. In every aspect of life, the competitor must put the desire to achieve victory first in order to win.

Victory is the nature of existence. No one can go through life without meeting up with an enemy. When the two parties meet, and the competition begins, victory holds the answer as to which one will receive the gratification of being better. The person or group that achieves victory has met the task, overcome the enemy, and won the struggle against the odds.

## DISCUSSION QUESTIONS

1. Compare the two introductory paragraphs. What does each paragraph accomplish? Did each introductory paragraph catch your interest? Did each clearly identify the essay's scope and purpose?
2. Does each essay contain a thesis statement summing up the author's definition of the word discussed? If so, identify and evaluate this thesis statement.
3. Does each author stick to the task of defining a word? Does either digress or "pad" at any point?
4. List all the techniques each author uses to define the word being discussed. Are all these techniques used well? What do the various techniques contribute to the definitions?
5. Do any of the words in either essay need further definition or clarification? Consider, for example, the definition of *competition* in paragraph 2 of "The Thrill of Victory."
6. Comment on the organization of each essay. How are the paragraphs in each essay ordered? Do you find each essay's organization clear and logical?
7. On the whole, which essay offered a clearer and more interesting definition? How could the other essay be improved?

## GENERAL CONCLUSIONS

Draw together all the observations and comments you have made about the Introductory Readings in this chapter. List some of the characteristics of a strong definition essay, or summarize your conclusions in a paragraph that would be helpful to beginning composition students. What advice would you give to students writing a definition essay?

## ADVICE

Definition is a form of exposition; that is, it is a form of writing that you can use to understand and explain an idea. When you write definitions, you attempt to show what a word means or what a thing is, to capture its essence and thereby distinguish it from all other words and things. Occasionally, you might devote an entire paper to defining a term: an art history paper might attempt to define *Impressionism,* or a religion paper might attempt to define *faith.* More often, you might use part of a paper to explain a word that might be unfamiliar to your readers, to clear up an ambiguity, or to set the terms for an argument. In a political science paper arguing for or against the censorship of obscenity, for example, it would be wise to begin by defining *censorship* and *obscenity.*

When they need a definition, most people automatically turn to the dictionary. But although the dictionary is a good source to check, it is usually not sufficient in itself. A dictionary generally provides the most commonly accepted definition of a word, but it does not necessarily provide the only or the best definition. In a paper discussing democracy, for example, you are not bound to accept a dictionary's definition as final and absolute. You may have new ideas about what a democracy is, or you may find a better way of expressing traditional ideas. Your definition will be more challenging to write and more interesting to read if it is based at least in part on your own reflections.

### Thinking About Words

Your first step in arriving at a definition should be investigating and thinking about the word you plan to define. Unless you devote some time to this first step, your definition is likely to be shallow and conventional. This is the time to consult dictionaries, to use freewriting to explore your own ideas about a word, and to recall your reading and personal experiences that might give you some additional insights and thereby enrich your definition.

At this stage, you might decide to explore a word's *etymology,* to study its derivation and discover how its form and meaning have changed over the years. If you were planning to write a paper defining *politics,* for example, it might help you to know that *political* is derived from the Greek word for *city,* that in the seventeenth century worldly people who were indifferent to religion were called *politickes,* and that *politic* can mean either "sagacious" or "scheming." To do this sort of investigation, you should look for the most authoritative and informative dictionary you can find. An unabridged dictionary will probably be more helpful than the paperbacks most students use for quick reference. An especially good dictionary is *The Oxford English Dictionary,* which traces words to their first known appearance in print, sometimes as long as 700 years ago. Your college library almost certainly has a copy of the *OED* as well as some dictionaries devoted exclusively to etymology, such as Eric Patridge's *Origins: A Short Etymological Dictionary of Modern English.*

Dictionaries are thus an excellent place to start your search for a definition, but your search should not end with somebody else's ideas about what a word means. Use the information you find in dictionaries to stimulate your own thoughts. *Freewriting* can be an excellent way to explore those thoughts. As explained in Chapter 1, freewriting is a technique you can use to generate ideas about a topic; when you freewrite, you write down everything that comes into your head without stopping to worry about whether the ideas make sense, whether you will actually be able to use them in your paper, or whether you are expressing them well. For the time being, you simply concentrate on getting ideas down on paper, knowing that you can come back later to select, add, and revise. In ten or fifteen minutes of freewriting about *politics,* for example, you might explore the implications of what you've learned about the word's origin and history, mention the various ways in which you've heard the word used, and jot down some tentative ideas about what you think the essence of politics is.

Your reading and your experiences can give you further insights into the word you are defining. For example, books you've read in political science classes—from Aristotle's *Politics* to a text on American government—might bring you closer to an understanding of what politics is and how it works. If you have read Robert Penn Warren's novel *All the King's Men* or other literary works about politics and politicians, you should have some additional insights. You might also try to think of public figures who seem to exemplify the quality you are defining: Is there a president, a senator, or a party leader whose actions show a particularly keen understanding of politics? Also look to people and events closer to your own experience—the president of your Student Government Association, who seems the epitome of the campus politician, or your participation in a local election campaign.

At this point, you do not have to be concerned about whether or not you will be able to include in your paper all the information and ideas you gather or whether or not the people and events you recall will eventually be useful examples. For now, your objective is simply to clarify your own ideas about the word you will be defining. The more time and effort you devote to reflecting about this word and all its meanings, the richer and more interesting your paper will be.

## Using Various Methods of Definition

When you think that you have arrived at a clear understanding of the word you wish to define, it is time to start looking for the best ways of communicating that understanding to the reader. You can choose among several useful methods of definition; in a paper devoted exclusively to definition, you may well decide to use a combination of methods.

The most common method of definition is often called *formal definition* or *analysis.* Dictionaries and textbooks often use this sort of definition, first putting the term to be defined in a class and then showing how it differs from everything else in that class. Thus, *The American Heritage Dictionary* defines *semicolon* as "a mark of punctuation indicating a degree of separation intermediate between the comma and the period." We can divide this definition into three parts to show that it conforms to the standard pattern of a formal definition:

| *Term* | *Class* | *Differentiation* |
|---|---|---|
| semicolon | a mark of punctuation | indicating a degree of separation intermediate between the comma and the period (shows how a semicolon differs from other punctuation marks) |

How could you construct a formal definition for *college* or *depression?*

Dictionaries often use a second method of definition as well by listing *synonyms,* words that have meanings very similar to that of the word being defined. In a definition of *joy,* for example, you might decide to mention such synonyms as *happiness, delight,* or *gladness.* A list of synonyms is not sufficient in itself, however. For one thing, a synonym may not give the reader a full understanding of the term: if you defined *joy* simply as *happiness,* the reader might very legitimately wonder, "And what is happiness?" Moreover, you will seldom if ever find two words that have exactly the same meaning and exactly the same emotional associations. Is *happiness* really a synonym for *joy?* Doesn't *joy* suggest a deeper, more intense emotion? If you use synonyms, use them together with other methods of definition; better yet, take the time to explain the subtle differences between the word you are defining and the synonyms you have listed. William Safire uses synonyms and near synonyms cleverly in this entry from *Safire's Political Dictionary:*

*Blooper*—an exploitable mistake; a slip of the tongue, or unthinking comment that can be seized upon by the opposition.

A *blooper* is worse than a *goof,* more adult than a *boo-boo,* not as serious as a *blunder,* equivalent to a *gaffe.* Repeated commission of any results in a description of having *foot-in-mouth disease.*

Notice that Safire does not rely exclusively on synonyms and that he carefully distinguishes *blooper* from similar words. How could you use synonyms to define *college* or *depression?*

*Negative definition* is the reverse of definition by synonyms: you can attempt to define a word by contrasting it with its opposite or, in general, by showing what it is not. In a definition of *courage,* for example, you might explain the true nature of courage by contrasting it with cowardice on the one hand and recklessness on the other. Mark Twain uses a negative to define courage in *Pudd'nhead Wilson's Calendar:* "Courage is resistance to fear, mastery of fear—not absence of fear." Notice that Twain uses positive as well as negative definition, however. Telling your readers what something is not will not be enough; you must also tell them what it is. How could you use negative definition in an essay defining *college* or *depression?*

Also useful as a supplement is *definition by example.* Concrete examples often are more useful than abstract definitions and can help to make your meaning clear. In the preceding paragraphs, for example, I thought it necessary to supplement my definitions of various methods of definition with examples from a dictionary, from Safire, and from Twain. Here is one more example of definition by example: in *A Prosody Handbook,* Karl Shapiro defines *alliteration* as

Correspondence in sound between nearby, especially initial consonants:

It will *f*lame out, like *sh*ining *f*rom *sh*ook *f*oil.

Shapiro's explanation is clearly worded, but even so the example is helpful because it gives a vivid illustration of what alliteration is. Again, examples are best used in combination with other methods of definition. How could you use examples in a definition of *college* or *depression?*

## Writing Your Paper

In a paper in which you will be devoting only a few sentences or a paragraph to defining a term, it makes sense to put the definition near the beginning; for example, in a paper arguing that a particular policy or institution is racist, define *racism* before you go on to make your argument. If you are devoting an entire paper to defining a term and plan to use several methods of definition, you will need to do some careful thinking about the best way to organize all the ideas and information you want to include.

As in most papers, it's a good idea to start by indicating the limits of your topic. Suppose, for example, that you are writing a paper defining *culture*. Do you plan to discuss all the possible meanings of culture, from the cultivation of plants and animals to artistic and intellectual refinement? Will you use *culture* as the biologist uses it or as the anthropologist uses it? It might be possible to write a fascinating essay showing how all the meanings of culture are related, but unless you plan to do so, you should begin by being very clear about which meanings you plan to explore; otherwise, you may confuse and disappoint your readers.

After you have made the limits of your topic clear, you can organize your material in a variety of ways. If you have become very interested in the etymology of the word you are defining, you might decide to follow chronological order in your paper, discussing the origins of the word and then showing how its meaning has changed over the centuries. In a paper using several methods of definition, the order of importance might be a good principle of organization. You could begin by using a negative definition to show what the word does not mean; then you could build to a climax by showing what it does mean, perhaps using synonyms and examples and finally arriving at a formal definition. Or you could begin with a formal definition and then use a series of examples to make its meaning clearer, or use several paragraphs to show how the word you are defining is in fact different from a number of words that are often accepted as synonyms.

Pay very close attention to your style in a definition paper. Since your goal is to help your readers understand a word more fully, the words you use in your explanation must be unambiguous and helpful throughout. Make sure that your definitions do not simply repeat words without defining them: "A tragedy is a literary work about a tragic situation" leaves the reader wondering what *tragic* means. Whenever possible, avoid using unfamiliar words in your definitions. Samuel Johnson's dictionary contains the most famous example of an overly elaborate definition: a "network," Johnson says, is a "reticulated fabric, decussated at regular intervals, with interstices at the intersections." How could someone who does not know what a network is possibly understand this definition? It is probably a more common error to define an abstract term by equating it with other abstract terms: "loyalty is fidelity, trustworthiness, and devotion." Do not leave your readers trapped in a circle of abstractions that themselves need to be defined; search for the precise, concrete words that will help your readers understand the meaning you have discovered in the word you are defining.

## APPLICATION

**A.** Use an unabridged dictionary to discover as much as you can about the origins and histories of these words:

alienation                     liberal
concert                        maturity
education                      politeness
essay                          redemption

How does the information you have found help you to understand these words? How might you use this information in a definition paper?

**B.** Choose one of the words from the previous list and freewrite about it for ten or fifteen minutes. As you freewrite, draw upon the insights you have gained into this word through your reading and your experiences. Then, look over your freewriting and see if it contains any ideas you might use in a definition paper.

**C.** Construct a formal definition for the word you have chosen and then make some rough notes about how you might use other methods of definition in a paper about this word.

**D.** Study the following definitions and identify the methods of definition the authors have used. When you notice a formal definition, show how it can be divided into three parts—term, class, and differentiation.

1. Learning is broadly defined as relatively permanent changes in behavior that result from experience; the extent to which it occurs in humans distinguishes them from all other forms of life.

   —ELEANOR WILLEMSEN, *Understanding Infancy*

2. Let us define a plot. We have defined a story as a narrative of events arranged in time-sequence. A plot is also a narrative of events, the emphasis falling on causality. "The king died and then the queen died," is a story. "The king died, and then the queen died of grief," is a plot.

   —E. M. FORSTER, *Aspects of the Novel*

3. Political parties are the most distinctively political voluntary associations to be found in democratic countries. They are the organizations that form expressly to take over the reins of government by winning electoral contests.

   —MARTIN DIAMOND ET AL., *The Democratic Republic*

4. A hooked or a knotted rug consists of a pile surface attached to a rug base. The primary difference between the two types of rugs is the way that the pile is attached to the base. With a hooked rug, the pile is "threaded" through the rug base; with a knotted rug, the pile is "tied" onto the rug base.

—VIRGINIA COLTON, ED., *Reader's Digest Complete Guide to Needlework*

5. narr
   naar
   Pronounced NAHR, to rhyme with "far." From German: *Narr:* "fool," "buffoon."
   1. Fool.
   2. Clown, buffoon. "He acts like a *narr*." "Don't be a *narr!*"
   Two Israeli spies, caught in Cairo, were put up against the wall. The firing squad marched in. The Egyptian captain asked the first spy, "Do you have any last wish?"
   "A cigarette."
   The captain gave him a cigarette, lighted it, and asked the second spy, "Do you have a last request?"
   Without a word, the second spy spit in the captain's face.
   "Harry!" cried the first spy. "Please! Don't make trouble!"
   He was a real *narr*.

   A *narr* said, "We have a rabbi, he gets paid so little, I don't know how he keeps alive. In fact, he would starve to death except for one thing: every Monday and Thursday—he fasts."

—LEO ROSTEN, *The Joys of Yiddish*

**E.** Evaluate these student definitions. Comment on the methods of definition they use, their strengths, and the ways in which they might be improved.

1. Insecurity is when you feel insecure about yourself or your situation. It is anxiety, nervousness, and a lack of self-confidence. Insecure people are afraid to try new things because they are afraid they will fail, and they often feel uncomfortable when they have to face a challenge. Almost everyone feels insecure sometimes, but some people always feel insecure. We should try to overcome our insecurity, because insecurity can interfere with success.

2. "I love New York," the commercial says. I love my best friend. I also love my parents. My parents love each other, and my neighbor loves my new car. But what is love? It has been described as an emotion, a liking, a fascination, a

devotion; the list is endless. There are also various kinds of love and ways of loving—parental love, platonic love, and romantic love, all resulting from a mutual exchange of feeling. It is this exchange of feeling and sharing of fond emotions that characterize the truest sort of love. We may say that we love Miss Universe in a swimsuit or Robert Redford in snug blue jeans, but our feelings in such cases are infatuation, not love. True love develops only when it is shared by two people who are drawn together by a strong emotional bond.

3. As a literary art, satire brings to light the ridiculous quirks of a particular object or situation. In satire, the writer avoids the extremes of angry fury and comic nonsense and tries to represent the subject in a critically humorous or humorously critical way. It is the nature of satire to find fault, but satire is not satire if the ridicule becomes too abrasive; the subject cannot be made a simple object of wrath or amusement. At its best, satire is subtle and restrained. As John Dryden says in *A Discourse Concerning Satire,* "there is still a vast difference betwixt the slovenly butchering of a man and the fineness of a stroke that separates the head from the body, and leaves it standing in its place." Satire calls for a sure, fine stroke that is delicate but devastating: we might think of Dryden's own portrait of David in *Absalom and Achitophel.*

4. *The Standard College Dictionary* defines "jazz" as "a kind of music, chiefly extemporaneous but sometimes arranged, characterized by melodic, harmonic, and rhythmic variation, syncopation, flatted thirds and sevenths, and a melody played against various chord patterns." Jazz began very early in the history of music and is in a class by itself. You can sit down and listen to jazz, but it is not an easy kind of music to dance to. Many people think that rhythm and blues is similar to jazz, but there are many differences between the two. Rhythm and blues is easier to dance to because it has a regular beat and you know what is going to happen next. Jazz is so unorganized that musicians can put anything into the music, and you will think it belongs there.

# 9.
# Argumentation

## INTRODUCTORY EXERCISES AND READINGS

### A. Identifying Logical Fallacies

Logic helps us to reason correctly by reminding us to examine the relationships among our ideas. We may make true statements and yet fail to make a strong argument because we have not made sure that our ideas are related in the ways that we say or imply they are.

The following groups of sentences are illogical. In each group, all the sentences illustrate the same logical fallacy. After studying the problems with the individual sentences in a group, identify the common fallacy that makes them all illogical and write a brief description of it.

### GROUP A

1. The professors at this college are selfish and lazy. My chemistry professor is never in his office, and my economics professor took two weeks to grade the last set of papers.
2. The professors at this college are dedicated and hard-working. My history professor spent two hours helping me revise my paper, and my geology professor holds extra review sessions for students who are having trouble.
3. Women are much smarter than men. In my graduating class, eight of the top ten students were women.
4. When I got home from Ace Market last week, I found that the milk I had bought was sour and that the head of lettuce was all brown inside. Ace Market is a lousy store and sells rotten food.
5. My next-door neighbor, who is Danish, is always fighting with his wife and hitting his kids. Last week, the police arrested a Dane who had held up a store and shot the owner. And even

Hamlet killed Polonius, Laertes, and Claudius. All Danes are by nature violent and aggressive.

*FALLACY A:*

GROUP B
1. Abortion, like any other form of murder, is morally wrong.
2. Deciding to have an abortion, like any other purely private and individual decision, should not be regulated by the government.
3. Deans should not be allowed to discipline students. Why should innocent students be punished at the whims of uncaring administrators?
4. Of course deans should discipline students. Who is better qualified to deal with student misconduct than concerned, wise administrators?
5. John Smith is the best candidate for the presidency because he has the best qualifications and the most experience.

*FALLACY B:*

GROUP C
1. I urge you to vote against this pollution-control bill. The senator who wrote it cheats on his wife and is a known alcoholic.
2. I urge you to vote for this pollution-control bill. The senator who wrote it is a dedicated, hard-working man who gives half of his annual salary to charity.
3. Why should I take Professor Peabody's course in ethics? What can she know about ethics? She's been divorced twice.
4. Bill deserved a better grade in his chemistry course because he's a wonderful person.
5. I won't vote for Ken for student government president—he's so ugly!

*FALLACY C:*

GROUP D
1. Frank Blair is the most qualified candidate for the Republican nomination because he got the most votes in the last five primaries.
2. John Ashe isn't qualified to be president—he comes out on the bottom in every primary.
3. Professor Black must be the smartest man on campus—every quarter, all his classes are filled.
4. Fords must be better than Chryslers—after all, Ford sales were much higher than Chrysler's last year.

5. State University has over five times as many students as Edson College does. Clearly, State University is the better school.

*FALLACY D:*

GROUP E
1. Just as a plant flourishes when it is given plenty of water and sunlight, so a child flourishes when given plenty of love and affection.
2. You can't teach a dog to obey unless you slap it occasionally; similarly, you can't teach children to behave unless you hit them when they are bad.
3. Every required course at this college is essential to a liberal education. Just as a car cannot function properly if it is missing one of its required parts, so a student cannot function properly if he or she is missing one of the required courses.
4. If a table falls apart, we blame the carpenter; if a student fails, we should blame the teacher.
5. Learning calculus is just like learning to ride a bicycle—once you learn it, you never forget it.

*FALLACY E:*

GROUP F
1. I stayed up all night studying for the final, and I got a 97. Cramming the night before a final obviously makes all the difference.
2. I stayed up all night studying for the final, and I got only a 71. The more you study, the worse you do.
3. Sally ate some mushroom pizza Tuesday night, and she felt sick all day Wednesday. She must be allergic to mushrooms.
4. One day I disagreed with Professor Jones in class; sure enough, I got a D in the course. I think it's unfair that teachers penalize students for disagreeing with them.
5. She was in the room just a few minutes before we discovered that the window was broken. Therefore, she must be the one who broke it.

*FALLACY F:*

GROUP G
1. You ask why the tuition may go up again next year? Can any price be too high for a sound liberal education? Liberal education frees the mind and enables the student to explore a wide variety of fields. Why are you attacking the validity of liberal education?

2. You think that the proposed tuition increase is justified? Why are you always defending the administration's decisions? Are you just too frightened to say what you really think? Don't you believe that it's important for students to learn to think for themselves?
3. The college should not attempt to regulate Hellweek activities. The fraternities make a great contribution to the campus's social life, and they also have community service projects.
4. I'm glad you asked me about my opinion on the new pollution-control bill. I've always loved the outdoors—I was a Boy Scout for six years, and now I take my family on a camping trip every summer. Certainly, we should all protect the environment and take advantage of the great outdoors. Next question?
5. How can you criticize me for plagiarizing my paper? Didn't Shakespeare himself borrow plots from other authors? Haven't you ever cheated on an exam?

*FALLACY G:*

## Argumentative Essays

**B.** Following is a one-paragraph student essay arguing that nursing homes are often unsuitable for elderly people. The second paragraph, not written by a student, makes a similar argument. Read the two paragraphs, compare them carefully, and answer the questions that follow.

Deciding on the best way to help an elderly person is difficult and painful. Concerned family and friends may doubt their own ability to care for an elderly person who has become forgetful and depressed and may therefore think that a nursing home is the best place for him. Before they make a final decision, however, they should remember that elderly people are generally happier and more alert in a stimulating, varied environment. The elderly person's apparent senility may be the result of retirement, which often leads to a decrease in stimulation, or of a physical problem such as arteriosclerosis (hardening of the arteries) that can reduce the oxygen supply to the brain and therefore reduce the elderly person's ability to see, hear, taste, smell, and feel. These gradual changes make contact with the outside world more difficult. The elderly person who moves to a nursing home may have even more severe problems because the atmosphere in most nursing homes is far from stimulating. The floors, walls, and furniture are usually a neutral color; the halls are generally quiet; contact with other people is often limited; food is bland. The elderly person who finds himself in these cold, unfamiliar surroundings may well respond to the outside world even less and may therefore become even more forgetful and depressed.

* * * *

As soon as a senior citizen shows the slightest sign of senility, his relatives and so-called "friends" seize the excuse to pack him off to a nursing home. They don't really care what happens to him, and he is too weak and helpless to resist. Once a senior citizen is shut up in a nursing home, he gets worse and worse and eventually turns into a vegetable. Young people who ship their elders off to nursing homes are selfish and heartless; we can only hope that some day their children will do the same to them.

## DISCUSSION QUESTIONS

1.  Each paragraph argues that elderly people will deteriorate if they are sent to nursing homes. What evidence does each author provide to support this argument?
2.  Comment on the *tones* of these two paragraphs—the authors' apparent attitudes toward their subject, their readers, and themselves. Which author's tone is more appropriate and persuasive? Why?
3.  Does either paragraph contain any of the logical fallacies you identified in response to the first exercise?
4.  What is your impression of the author of each paragraph? How are these impressions conveyed?
5.  Describe the intended audience for these paragrahs—which readers would the authors be most eager to persuade? How might these readers respond to the first paragraph? to the second?

C.   When the students in a freshman composition course were asked to write argumentative essays, two decided to argue that women's sports at their college were treated unfairly. Read the two essays, compare them carefully, and then answer the questions that follow.

### Women's Sports at Edson: Unsupported and Neglected

Just last week, Edson College hosted a conference on the status and future of women's sports. Women athletes and coaches from colleges all over the state attended to discuss the programs at their schools and to make plans for strengthening these programs. Did the *Edson Record* cover this conference? Yes—in one short article on page 6. Had Edson hosted a similar conference on men's sports, you can be sure that the *Record* would have had a front-page article with pictures. The *Record's* failure to report adequately on this conference is a typical example of the neglect of women's sports at Edson. Women's sports deserve but do not receive the full support of the administration and the students.

Over the years, the women's sports program has been trying to catch up to the men's sports program, but to date they have not totally succeeded. The administration is responsible for great inequalities in the number of sports offered and in the facilities made available. Edson's catalogue lists eleven varsity sports for men and only seven for women. The situation is better now than it was a few years ago, when women could participate in only five varsity sports, but real equality still has not been achieved. All the men's outdoor sports have both playing fields and practice fields, but the women's lacrosse and field hockey teams do not have their own practice fields, and the soccer and softball teams have to share one field for both practice and playing. Women swimmers and basketball players complain that the men's teams always get the best hours for the pool and the gym, leaving women only a few hours early in the morning or late in the evening for practice. Many women's teams, such as the soccer and softball teams, are not allowed to use college vehicles when they travel to away games: they are given gas money, but that's all. Often, this means that not all the team members are able to attend the games.

The most serious inequality is that while all the men's varsity teams have professional coaches, several of the women's teams do not. The women's track team is coached by an admissions counselor who had no previous experience as a coach, the women's softball team is coached by an economics professor who happened to play softball in college, and the women's soccer team has a student coach this year. How can women athletes be expected to learn about their sports and improve their skills if the administration doesn't provide them with well-trained coaches?

Students are also guilty of neglecting women's sports. Last year, our women's swim team was ranked third in the state, but even though the all-state meet was held right on campus, fewer than 100 Edson students attended. At a home women's softball game last week, there were only about twenty Edson students watching; according to the women athletes I talked to, this number is pretty typical. It is very discouraging for these athletes when almost nobody shows up to watch them compete.

Students might be more likely to support women's sports if our newspaper gave them adequate coverage, but the *Record* clearly discriminates against them. I looked through all of last quarter's issues and found that six had front-page pictures of men's sports, but only one had a front-page picture about women's sports. The April 17, 1981, issue had seven articles about men's sports and

only four about women's sports; the April 24 issue had eight articles about men's sports and again only four about women's sports.
The number of pictures is also unequal: for example, on April 24
there were three pictures about men's sports and none about
women's sports. If women's sports would be given the same number of articles and pictures in the *Record,* it would be one big step
toward the equality of men's and women's sports.

Of course, some people think that the present inequality is all
right. As the captain of the football team said when I interviewed
him, "Women's sports aren't as exciting to watch as men's sports
are, and the women's teams don't bring in as much money and
recognition to the college." Anyone who has watched a professional women's basketball team compete knows that women's
sports can be very exciting. If some of the women's teams at
Edson aren't very exciting to watch, maybe it's because the athletes haven't been given the coaching and facilities they need in
order to improve their skills. If the college really supported the
women's teams, the players would improve, the games would be
more exciting, and the teams would bring the college more recognition and more money through increased attention and ticket
sales.

Furthermore, some people argue that the college shouldn't be
so concerned about which teams bring in the most money and recognition. When I talked to Wendy Howard, the coach of the
women's basketball team, she made some important points. "Why
do we have an athletic program at Edson?" she asked. "Is it to
make money and make the college famous, or is it to give our students a chance to enjoy competition, to learn new skills, and to
become more physically fit? Should we favor the sports that draw
the biggest crowds, or should we try to give all our students an
equal chance to benefit from participating in athletics?"

I think that the answers to Ms. Howard's questions should be
obvious. The college should stop discriminating against women's
sports. It should expand the women's varsity sports program,
make sure that women's and men's teams share all fields and facilities equally, and provide all women's teams with qualified
coaches, even if it means cutting down on the men's program
somewhat. The students should support the women's teams by attending their games more frequently, and the *Record* should pay
as much attention to women's sports as it does to men's. The
women's athletic program deserves much more attention and support.

## Women's Sports Are Treated Unfairly

Edson women athletes are not treated as equals to the Edson
men athletes. The administration claims that the men recruit

more, have larger teams, and use more equipment; therefore, they need more money. The administration seems to neglect the fact that if women had more money they would recruit more, have larger teams, and need more equipment.

Being on the women's soccer team, I know that women's soccer is not given as much support as the men's soccer team is. We have one playing field, which is also used for intramural sports. The men have a practice field and a playing field. Anyone who dares to step foot on either of these fields will probably be sorry. Another thing men have that women's soccer is deprived of is transportation. The administration will give the women's team gas money, but they are hesitant about lending the vehicles to us. One woman soccer player bought a van so more team members could go to the games. It's not fair when one has to tell a team member that she cannot go to the game because she doesn't play enough and there is not enough room. Some people argue that because women's soccer is relatively small, the transportation situation is fair. However, if other extracurricular activities like trips to Cleveland or a park receive the vehicles, there is no reason why the women's soccer team should not be able to use them. Why did the school buy them, if not for the students' use?

The one thing that would really help develop a strong women's soccer team would be a good coach. Since the women are already at a disadvantage by coming into sports later than the men, I think the administration should hire a good, qualified coach. If the team receives nothing else until they prove themselves, that is fine. It is so hard to get a team started without a coach. There are women who do not know how to play the game and want to learn. How can the women who know the sport teach the women who want to learn when they are trying to get organized enough to work together as a team? I have been out on the field where it gets very frustrating because half the team does not understand the concept of the game. It makes me want to throw in the towel right then and there. I know I cannot because I must support my own sex and all the other women athletes struggling to be equally recognized. If there was a coach, she could help organize and help everyone improve. As a result it would take the team a shorter time to show their interest and enthusiasm. After they have shown this, then the administration can finance equipment, uniforms, and appropriate playing fields. The women's tennis team has improved tremendously since they got a professional coach five years ago; if the women's soccer team got similar help, we would improve just as much.

Other women's teams are treated just as unfairly. The men's teams get everything they want, but the women's teams get practically nothing. The women's intramural program is also very small compared to the men's program. The administration is very

sexist and obviously thinks women's sports are not very important. I'm surprised that they don't tell us to organize sewing circles instead of athletic teams! What they should realize is that
women's sports are as important to Edson as men's sports are because women's sports make an equal contribution to the school.
It's not fair that we are treated so unequally by administrators
who don't know anything about sports and probably never play so
much as a game of Ping-Pong themselves.

The only way this inequality can be ended is for women athletes to become involved, to make people aware, and to fight the
injustice. First the women need the administration to recognize us
so that we can get the proper coaches to help us develop our
skills. We also need to get the support of other students, who
don't seem to care about women's sports at all, and the men athletes, who are very smug and superior. Once we prove that
women are just as good at sports as men are, if not better, then
we can fight for more money, which will lead to more recruiting,
larger teams, and more equipment.

## DISCUSSION QUESTIONS

1. Examine the introductory paragraph of each essay. What techniques does each author use? What does each introductory paragraph accomplish?
2. The author of each essay argues that women athletes are not given
   as much attention and support as men athletes are. What evidence
   does each author provide to support this argument? Which author
   provides more convincing evidence?
3. Examine paragraphs 6 and 7 of "Women's Sports at Edson: Unsupported and Neglected." Why do you think the author included
   them? What do they contribute to the essay?
4. Examine paragraph 4 of "Women's Sports Are Treated Unfairly."
   What logical fallacies does this paragraph contain?
5. Does either essay contain any other logical fallacies?
6. Comment on the *tones* of these two essays—the authors' apparent
   attitudes toward their subject, their readers, and themselves.
   Which author's tone is more appropriate and persuasive? Why?
7. Describe the intended audience for these essays—which readers
   would the authors be most eager to persuade? How might these
   readers respond to the first essay? To the second?

## GENERAL CONCLUSIONS

Draw together all the observations and comments you have made
about the Introductory Exercises and Readings in this chapter. List
some of the characteristics of a strong argumentative essay, or sum-

marize your conclusions in a paragraph that would be helpful to beginning composition students. What advice would you give to a student writing an argumentative essay?

## ADVICE

Many sorts of writing seek to persuade us, to make us change our beliefs or actions. A descriptive essay about a rundown mental hospital might persuade us that the patients are not receiving adequate care; a narrative essay about a frustrating conference with an unsympathetic dean might persuade us that some college administrators are not concerned about the problems students face. Advertisements often try to persuade us to buy a certain product by subtly appealing to our vanity, our fears, or our fantasies.

Argumentation is a form of persuasion that seeks to make us change our beliefs or actions by appealing not to our emotions but to our reason, by using logic and evidence to establish the truth of an assertion. In conversation, we often use *argument* to mean "quarrel": "Bill and Ken had a big argument today. Bill told Ken he was stupid, and Ken called Bill a jerk." If we use terms more strictly, however, this exchange would not qualify as an argument unless Bill and Ken offered evidence to support their assertions. Writing an argumentative essay involves making careful assertions and supporting them with the best evidence we can find.

Since argumentative essays try to make the readers change their beliefs or actions, keeping the readers constantly in mind is crucial. We look for evidence that our readers will accept as accurate, relevant, and sufficient; we try to think of and reply to all the objections our readers might raise; and we keep our tone moderate and respectful so that we won't offend our readers. It would be unreasonable to hope that even the best argumentative essay could persuade every reader—after all, there are still some people who think that the earth is flat and that the Nazis didn't commit mass murder. If your essay is careful and intelligent, however, you can reasonably expect to persuade some readers and to make all open-minded readers consider your ideas seriously. Remember, too, that the readers you most want to reach are those who disagree with you; they are, after all, the ones whose opinions you want to change. Don't insult them by ignoring their point of view or implying that their position is merely stupid.

### Choosing, Limiting, and Defining Your Topic

In many cases, the topic of your argumentative essay will be determined for you. An economics professor, for example, might ask you to argue for or against a particular theory or policy, or a history professor might ask you to argue that a book does or does not offer an accurate picture of the period it discusses. When you are free to pick your own topic, remember the general principles that should always guide your selection: *choose a topic that interests you,* and *choose a topic that you can discuss adequately in the space allowed.*

During the last several years, I have read a number of half-hearted argumentative essays defending my college's composition requirement and have suspected that the authors chose this topic not because it interested them but because they felt sure it would interest me. I have also read many listless and uninformed essays about such topics as nuclear proliferation or solar energy and have suspected that the authors chose topics they considered impressive, not interesting. You cannot expect to write a strong, persuasive essay if your topic bores you. Look for an issue about which you feel strongly, and don't worry about whether or not your professor will be impressed. And by all means take the position you really support, not the one you think your professor supports. It's quite possible that the students who wrote those mediocre essays defending the composition requirement could have written impassioned, enthusiastic essays opposing it.

It is quite possible, of course, that you *are* truly interested in nuclear proliferation or solar energy, but even so you should think twice before writing about these subjects in a short argumentative essay. If you are limited to writing four or five pages, will you have time to do justice to these topics? Will you have time to present your views fully, to support them adequately, and to answer all the objections your readers might raise? Remember, too, that writing about such topics requires a good deal of research. If you don't have enough time to do such research, consider writing about a local or campus issue. If you do decide to write about a national or international issue, limit the topic severely; in a paper about solar energy, for example, you might limit yourself to discussing one particular experiment, arguing that it showed that solar energy is or is not practical in a certain situation. How might you limit your topic if you wanted to write a 500-word essay on nuclear proliferation?

Also, be sure to *choose an issue that really is an issue.* "War causes great suffering" would not be a good thesis statement because no sane person could possibly disagree with it. One *could* disagree with the statement that "A college education is often beneficial," but even so the statement is so close to being a truism that your chances of writing an original essay are slim. Choose a controversial topic, one about which reasonable people can reasonably disagree. You will find the process of writing the paper more challenging and satisfying, and your essay is more likely to interest your readers.

In your thesis statement, be sure to *define your topic precisely.* Establish the limits of your argument clearly so that your readers cannot refute your ideas by asking questions that are not relevant to the issues you really want to discuss. Check to make sure that all the words in your thesis statement are as unambiguous as possible. "The foreign language requirement at this college is impractical"—impractical because the college cannot afford to hire enough teachers to staff the required courses? Or because students will find no practical use for knowing a foreign language? Or because the one semester of required instruction will not teach students enough to let them make any real use of the language?

## Making and Supporting Assertions

Some statements need little or no support. "I took a math course in 1980" is a statement of fact that can stand by itself; "John F. Kennedy was assassinated in 1963" would need, at most, a footnote to support it. Simple statements of preference do not really need to be supported, although they may need to be explained. If you said, "I found my math course worthless," it would be absurd for me to insist, "No, you actually found it worthwhile." When you state your beliefs about a fact or make judgments that go beyond personal preference, you are making statements that need to be supported before they can be convincing: "Oswald acted alone when he assassinated Kennedy"; "All math courses are worthless." An assertion becomes an argument when it is supported by evidence and logic.

Before you start making lists of the assertions you want to make and the evidence you will use to support them, *think about the general form that your argument will take.* You can reason either *deductively* or *inductively*. In *deductive* reasoning, you move *from the general to the particular:* you start by making a general statement, apply it to a particular instance, and then draw your conclusion. A deductive argument sometimes takes the form of a *syllogism:*

1. Courses that prepare you for the challenges you will face after college are good courses. (major premise)
2. "Marriage and Family Life" prepares you for the challenges you will face after college. (minor premise)
3. Therefore, "Marriage and Family Life" is a good course. (conclusion)

In order to make such an argument convincing, you would need to support your major and minor premises. Why is any course that prepares you for challenges you will face after college a good course? Just what do you mean by "good"? How does this course prepare you for those challenges? If you can prove that your major and minor premises are true, you will also have proven that your conclusion is true, for it follows from them inevitably. If either your major or your minor premise is false, your conclusion is probably false as well. Look back at the

Introductory Readings, reexamine the first paragraph about nursing homes, and identify the deductive argument implicit there.

*Inductive reasoning,* which is probably used more often in argumentative essays, moves *from the particular to the general:* you begin with particular facts and then use them to draw a general conclusion. This text uses an inductive method to study writing. In a punctuation exercise, for example, you observe the ways commas are used in a number of particular sentences and then draw a general conclusion about how compound sentences should be punctuated. You might find inductive reasoning helpful in an argument in which you try to prove the truth of a general conclusion:

> Woody Allen's *Take the Money and Run* was a good movie.
> Woody Allen's *Sleeper* was a good movie.
> Woody Allen's *Love and Death* was a good movie.
> Therefore, Woody Allen makes good movies.

In order to make this argument convincing, you would need to establish the truth of the first three statements, explaining what you mean by "good" and just why each movie meets this standard. Even if all three statements are true, however, your conclusion could still be false. What if one of Allen's other movies were bad? What if he made a bad movie tomorrow? When you reason inductively, then, be sure to examine enough particulars to justify your conclusion. If examining all the relevant particulars is impossible, consider making your generalization more cautious; perhaps it would be wiser to say that "Woody Allen has made many good movies." Look back at the essays about women's sports in the Introductory Readings. Where do these essays use inductive reasoning? Do the authors supply enough particulars to support their generalizations?

Whether you use deductive or inductive reasoning, you need to support your assertions with evidence. Before you begin to write your paper, list the ideas and facts you plan to use as evidence and then check your list to *make sure that your evidence is accurate, relevant, and sufficient.*

Good evidence obviously must be *accurate,* so be careful to get your facts straight. Also, be sure that your facts really *are* facts, and that you have done all that is necessary to make your readers accept them as facts. It is all too easy to "support" an assertion with another assertion disguised as a fact: "The husband should be the head of the household because men are more emotionally stable than women are." The statement about emotional stability is itself an assertion that needs to be supported, so it is not adequate proof that men should be the heads of households.

A related problem is the fallacy of *begging the question* or making a *circular argument.* When we beg the question, we disguise a conclusion as a fact. Instead of supporting a conclusion, we might simply reword it and link the two statements with a convenient word such as *because:* "A liberal education makes you into a well-rounded person because it helps you to develop many different skills and interests." Begging the question can also involve using loaded words or phrases without proving that they are being used accurately: "It is ridiculous that students have to be shackled by all these worthless required courses." Unless we have proven that the courses are "worthless" and that they do indeed "shackle" students, we have not proven that the requirements are "ridiculous."

In addition to being accurate, evidence must also be *relevant.* Does your evidence really apply to and support your assertions? If it does not, you may have fallen into the fallacy of *evading the issue:* "People who think that hunting animals for sport is cruel and indecent forget that, long before the days of supermarkets, all people had to go into the woods and become hunters. A man cannot be condemned for trying to survive." The author begins by talking about hunting for sport but shifts to talking about hunting for survival. Few people would argue that a person does not have the right to hunt if the only alternative is starvation; that is not the issue. By evading the real issue and bringing in irrelevant considerations, the author has not said anything to defend people who could easily obtain food in some other way but choose to hunt because they enjoy it.

Several other logical fallacies also involve irrelevant evidence. Instead of discussing the issue, we might be tempted to make a *personal attack* on our opponent (called an argument *ad hominem* —"to the man"): "How can you support that proposal? Don't you know that the senator who authored it was once a member of the Socialist party?" It would, of course, be just as irrelevant to argue that the proposal should be supported because its author is a veteran and a former Eagle Scout. Admittedly, it is sometimes legitimate to consider a person's character. If you are trying to persuade someone not to vote for one of the candidates for student government treasurer, it would be completely relevant to argue that the candidate had been suspended for cheating on an exam and fined for stealing from the bookstore and therefore could not be trusted to handle funds honestly. Be sure, however, that a consideration of character really is relevant to the issue you're discussing —even a bad person can make a good suggestion.

It is also a fallacy to argue that something is good because it's popular or bad because it's unpopular: "This book sold over two million copies, so it must be good" or "That book sold only two thousand copies, so it must be bad." Such *appeals to the masses* (or arguments *ad populum*) are irrelevant to discussions of whether something is good or bad, excellent or awful. The majority is not an infallible judge of morality or quality. At one time, most of the people in the world thought that slavery was morally right, but we would not be likely to accept this fact as an argument in favor of slavery. In some kinds of arguments, a reference to public opinion may be relevant: "This plan is impractical. Its success depends upon the wholehearted cooperation of the citizens, but a survey shows that 83 percent of the citizens are opposed to it." Even in this example, however, we have shown only that the plan may be impractical, not that it is wrong.

*False analogies* can also be a way of evading the real issue. An analogy compares two things that are similar in at least one respect, often with the aim of explaining or clarifying the less familiar thing. For example, a biologist might explain how the body uses up various carbohydrates by saying that eating fatty foods is like throwing a large log on the fire, while eating sugar is like throwing paper scraps on the fire: it will take the fire a long time to consume the log, but the paper will be consumed quickly. An analogy is not, however, an argument. No two things are exactly alike in every respect, so we cannot say that everything that is true of one is true of the other. It is illogical to argue that "Just as a mother bird will provide worms for her young until they have learned to fly, so human parents must support their children until they graduate from college." A college student isn't a baby bird, going to college isn't learning to fly, and college tuition isn't worms.

Finally, evidence must be *sufficient.* Particularly when we are using inductive reasoning, it is tempting to come to a *hasty generalization,* a general conclusion based on only a few particulars. "My roommate never spends more than a few hours studying for a test, the woman who lives across the hall refuses to get a job to help with college expenses, and the woman next door never cleans her room. College students are just plain lazy." This generalization is unconvincing because the author has failed to consider the many students who work hard at their studies, devote many hours to jobs, and keep their rooms neat. The author would have to find many more examples before drawing a generalization and even so would be wise to make the generalization less sweeping: "*Many* college students are lazy." Hasty generalizations are most dangerous when they concern members of a racial, religious, or ethnic group. We meet a few Blacks, whites, Germans, or Canadians who seem to share the same flaw or virtue and start generalizing about all Blacks, all whites, all Germans, and all Canadians. At its worst, hasty generalization contributes to the creation and perpetuation of stereotypes.

Generalizations often seem more persuasive when they are supported by statistical evidence: What could be more objective and factual than numbers? Statistics by themselves prove nothing, however. Their value depends on the care and honesty with which they are gathered and interpreted. An author might argue, for example, that 85 percent of the students responding to a survey favored changing from a semester system to a quarter system. "Eighty-five percent" looks very impressive, but we have to ask ourselves just what it means. If only twenty students were surveyed, "85 percent" doesn't tell us much about the opinions of the hundreds or perhaps thousands of students attending the school. Were the people who administered the survey careful to make their sample representative? How many students who received copies of the survey responded? Could it be that students who favor a change are more likely to respond than those who are satisfied with the way things are? We have to examine a statistic very carefully before we accept it as evidence.

We also provide insufficient evidence when we commit the error of *false cause* (also called *post hoc, ergo propter hoc* —"after this, therefore because of this"). We assume that because two events followed each other in time, the first event must have caused the second. Sequence, however, does not prove causality. We might be tempted to argue, "In 1977, the college completed its new physical education center, and ever since then enrollments have climbed steadily. The new center clearly attracted many new students." In fact, the center may have had nothing to do with the increased enrollment. Has the author considered other changes that might have affected enrollment—a new admissions director, a more generous financial aid program, the creation of a dance department? Has the author interviewed new students and discovered that the physical education center actually did draw many of them to the college? We need to provide a great deal of evidence before we can prove that one event caused another (see Chapter 7, pp. 150–2).

## Acknowledging the Opposition

When you plan your argument, *list some opposing arguments*. If you plan to argue that your college's judicial system is ineffective, talk to the people who devised and administer the system. Acknowledge their views in your essay, and show why you believe these views to be mistaken. It is always possible, of course, that you will find that you cannot refute all the opposing arguments. If you find that your opponents have a few good points, concede these points graciously: "It is true that the judicial board has a good record of punishing offenders for minor offenses such as taking open containers of beer outdoors. However, . . ." If you find that your opponents have many good points, you may be honestly convinced to change your thesis statement: "Our college's judicial system is fair and effective."

Whether or not you concede any points, always try to acknowledge opposing views fairly and fully. It is dangerously tempting to distort the opposition's views so that they will be easier to refute. For example, a student arguing in favor of fraternities might write, "Those who dislike fraternities think that students should spend all their time studying. They believe that students have no right to a social life. I think, however, that a social life is important because students who work hard all week need to relax on the weekends." I doubt that even the stodgiest professor would argue that students should never take a break from studying and therefore have no need of any social life. Opponents of fraternities are more likely to argue that the particular kind of social life provided by fraternities is objectionable or that fraternities may interfere with studying even during the week. By distorting the views of those who oppose fraternities, the author has created a *straw man* — an imaginary, ridiculously weak opponent that is created only to be knocked down.

We create another kind of straw man when we present only part of our opponent's arguments, and probably not the strongest or most representative part. For example, you might be opposed to a tuition increase at your college and interview the college president to find out the reasons for it. The president might respond to your questions by saying, "We had to increase the tuition in order to keep up with rising expenses. The faculty has demanded and received a large across-the-board raise, it costs almost twice as much to heat the dormitories as it did a few years ago, it's more expensive to maintain buildings, and the cost of food for the cafeteria has also gone up. Why, it even costs more to print the college catalogue." You would be creating a straw man if you said in your essay, "When I asked President Walters why the tuition is going up so much, she said that printing the college catalogue is more expensive now than it used to be. Is this petty reason enough to justify an increase of almost $500 per student per year?" Straw-man arguments are seldom convincing, for most intelligent readers will suspect that you are not telling the whole truth. More important, people who make such arguments are being dishonest to their readers and unfair to their opponents.

## Organizing Your Essay

To some extent, the type of reasoning that is dominant in your essay will determine your method of organization. If you are using deductive reasoning, you will probably first try to establish the truth of your major premise, then support your minor premise, and then present your conclusion. If you are using inductive reasoning, you will probably present your specific evidence before drawing your general conclusion, although it is probably best to indicate your conclusion briefly in your thesis statement. When you are deciding how to order the paragraphs that present your evidence, remember that the *order of importance* is often a good choice. Save your strongest argument for last, so that the reader will be left with the impression that you have made some very convincing points. You may want to modify the order of importance somewhat, however, since you may lose your reader's interest and sympathy if you begin with your weakest argument. Donald Hall offers some good advice in *Writing Well:*

A relay team in track has four runners. Usually the fastest one runs last. The second fastest runs first, slowest is second, and third is third: 2, 4, 3, 1. It is a good arrangement for arguments, also.

Of course, none of your arguments should be extremely weak: a feeble, trivial point should be left out altogether, or your opponents may pounce on it and make a straw man out of you.

At what point should you acknowledge your opposition? Generally, present opposing views near the beginning of your essay. You don't want your readers to be objecting, "But what about . . ." throughout most of your essay; dispense with objections as soon as you can so that you and your reader can concentrate on the evidence that supports your own opinion. If you are going to have to concede points to your opponents, be especially sure to make your concessions early so that you don't have to end your essay by pointing out a weakness in your own argument. On the other hand, if you are confident that you can utterly destroy your opponent's best argument, you might decide that an attack is the most powerful way to conclude. In the Introductory Readings, at what point does the author of "Women's Sports at Edson: Unsupported and Neglected" acknowledge opposing views? Would this acknowledgment have been more effective elsewhere?

## Maintaining a Reasonable Tone

Since an argument is an appeal to your reader's reason, it is important that you remain reasonable yourself. Even if your arguments are logical and your evidence solid, you can alienate your readers if you let your tone become overly emotional or sarcastic. Your readers may suspect that you are out of control if you indulge in passionate pleas, accusations, or complaints; and although an occasional touch of irony may be amusing, heavy-handed sarcasm is nasty but not convincing. Your tone need not be dry and detached—show your concern, by all means, but don't overdo it. Your own good judgment should help you to detect passages that need to be toned down.

Writing an argumentative essay demands a great deal of thinking from you: thinking about just what your position will be, about the evidence that will best support your opinions, about the logical validity of your arguments, about the objections your readers might raise, about organization and tone. Building a sound argument may well seem an overwhelming task, and you may at times suspect that it is a futile one as well. No matter how strong your argument is, can you really hope to change anyone's mind? I think you can, for I can honestly say that some student essays have made me change my mind about several issues. Think about how your own opinions were formed, about how often a book or article or oral argument changed the way you think about an issue. To write convincing argumentative essays, you must first be convinced of the possibility of reasonable persuasion. The best argumentative essays are written by authors who have strong beliefs and a strong basis for those beliefs, and who see the people who disagree with them as reasonable creatures who may be moved by a reasonable argument.

## APPLICATION

**A.** All the following statements contain logical fallacies; some may contain more than one. Identify the fallacies and explain why each statement is illogical.

1. Last year I took two education courses, History and Methods of Education and Teaching Music in the Elementary School. Both courses were boring, and neither one prepared me for the challenges I encountered when I did my practice teaching. Education courses just don't teach you anything really useful about the art of teaching.
2. The tax cuts being debated in Congress should be passed. A Gallup Poll recently proved that most citizens favor tax cuts.
3. Just as soldiers never question their officers' orders, so students should never question their teachers' advice.
4. We need to have a longer spring vacation because a longer spring vacation is very necessary.
5. In 1978, the faculty voted to establish a new foreign language requirement. In 1979, we had the smallest freshman class we have had in five years. We must abolish the foreign language requirement before it scares off still more prospective students.
6. Our prisons are a national disgrace. Prisoners suffer because of inadequate rehabilitation programs and poor recreation facilities. This is a serious problem, for many of our citizens are hurt and embittered by these shocking conditions. In New Jersey alone, over two million people were arrested for drunkenness last year.
7. Last year, a proposal to give academic credit for participation in varsity sports was voted down by the faculty. The professor who led the opposition to this proposal is an admitted homosexual.
8. Language is very important because it makes communication possible. Without language, we would not be able to communicate with other people.
9. Writing is a skill, just as driving a car is a skill. To learn to drive well, all you have to do is memorize a few simple rules

and always follow them exactly. It should be just as easy to learn how to write.

10. When our house caught fire, my father and brother remained calm, but my mother and sisters got hysterical. Women are overly emotional and can't handle crises as well as men can.

11. In April, I dyed my hair blonde; by August, I was engaged. I guess it really is true that blondes have more fun!

12. This book deserves to be a literary classic. It was written by a man who spent most of his life helping underprivileged children.

13. I know four guys who are on the swim team, and they're all A students; most of the football players I know are constantly on academic probation. Swimmers are much more intelligent than football players.

14. I walked under a ladder on my way to work Thursday, and when I got to the office my boss told me I had been demoted. If only I hadn't walked under that ladder!

15. The semester system should be voted down. All the guys on my hall prefer the quarter system.

**B.** Evaluate the following thesis statements from argumentative essays. Have the authors selected workable topics? If not, how might they be improved? Do the thesis statements clearly identify the authors' topics and purposes? Suggest ways of improving any thesis statements that seem weak.

1. All forms of censorship are violations of freedom of the press and should not be allowed in a democratic country.

2. The housing system on this campus is unfair and poorly organized.

3. This college's attempts to recruit more Black students have been halfhearted and inadequate.

4. The Lion's Club, an organization that sponsors many programs to help the blind, is a worthwhile organization that deserves our support.

5. The plan to build a new mall in the suburbs should be defeated because it would lead to the deterioration of our downtown shopping district.

**C.** Following is a thesis statement for an argumentative essay on the draft, several arguments the author plans to make, and some counterarguments the author plans to refute.

*Thesis statement:* The military draft should be reinstituted because it is necessary for our country's defense.

*Arguments*
1. will deter Soviet aggression and thus prevent war
2. volunteer army hasn't attracted enough people
3. must be prepared for war, other emergencies
4. draft is justified: we benefit from the protection, education the country provides and should be willing to serve

*Counterarguments*
1. volunteer army is good enough
2. draft takes away individual rights
3. many people oppose the draft

1. Has the author chosen an appropriate topic? If not, how could the topic be improved?
2. Is the thesis statement clear and unambiguous?
3. Is the support the author provides accurate, relevant, and sufficient? Would further support be needed?
4. Has the author anticipated enough counterarguments? How could these counterarguments be refuted?
5. What would be the best plan of organization for this paper?

**D.** Write a thesis statement, a list of arguments, and a list of counterarguments for the argumentative essay you plan to write. Working in pairs or small groups, apply the questions in exercise 3 to your plans.

**E.** This exercise will require the cooperation of the entire class.
1. Find an issue about which the members of your class disagree. It might be best to pick a campus issue: for example, should the student paper be subject to any kind of censorship? Is racism a serious problem on the campus? Should a math or science course be required for graduation? Write a thesis statement taking a definite stand on the issue: for example, "The student newspaper should be free of all forms of censorship."
2. Divide into two groups, those who agree with the thesis statement and those who disagree with it. The groups should meet separately for about twenty minutes, and each group should make lists of all the arguments it can think of in favor of its position and all the counterarguments it suspects the other group will make.
3. Both groups then present their arguments to the full class.
4. Ask the members of the other group which of your arguments they found most convincing, which they found least convincing, and why.

5. Check your group's list of counterarguments. Did you anticipate all the arguments that the other group made?

**F.** After you have chosen a topic for an argumentative essay, interview at least four people to get their opinions about the topic. Try to find some who disagree with the stand you plan to take. How will you refute their views? Will you have to concede any points?

**G.** The following student essay argues against school prayer. Write one or two paragraphs analyzing the essay and suggesting possible improvements. Does the author make strong, well-supported arguments? Does the essay contain any logical fallacies? Does it do a good job of acknowledging and refuting opposing views? Are the paragraphs arranged in a logical order? Is the tone reasonable? What changes should the author make when revising? You might write your comments in the form of a note to the author.

### No School Prayer

Prayer in the public schools has been a controversial issue for many years. Even though the Supreme Court has proven that school prayer is unconstitutional, there are still many people who have the biased opinion that prayer should be permitted and even required in school. They do not realize that school prayer is unfair, unconstitutional, and impractical.

School prayer is unfair to atheists and to people who don't believe in praying in public places. The children of such people would be in a real dilemma if school prayer were permitted. If they prayed, they would be going against their own beliefs and might get in trouble with their parents. If these children refused to pray, however, they would feel like outcasts: their teachers would discriminate against them, and their classmates would make fun of them or refuse to have anything to do with them. It would be unfair to put any children in this position.

School prayer is unconstitutional because it violates the First Amendment, which forbids any establishment of religion. If we had school prayer, we would in effect have an established church, and that would be the end of freedom of religion. The next step would probably be that various religious groups would start asking for government funds for their own parochial schools, since there would now be no difference between public schools and parochial ones. Since the government can't afford to fund all religions, it would have to pick just one or two to fund, and that would be unfair to the other groups. Since Protestants are the majority in this country, they would probably get most or all of the money and be our established church—a clear violation of the First Amendment.

Finally, school prayer is too impractical because it just wouldn't work. Various groups would fight over what prayers should be said, when they should be said, and how they should be said. Will prayers be said in English, in Latin, or in Hebrew? We could never find a prayer that would please everyone. Our public schools have enough troubles without getting into this mess.

Most people realize that prayer should not be permitted in public schools, so we should not let a handful of right-wingers force us into having it. If those people are too cheap to send their children to parochial schools, they should just have their children pray in their own homes, churches, and temples. They should not expect the government to pay for their children's religious education.

# 10.
# Summaries

## INTRODUCTORY READINGS

On the following pages you will find a chapter from Richard Wright's autobiography, *Black Boy,* and four student essays summarizing that chapter. As you read the chapter, try to identify its main ideas: What is Wright's purpose or central point? As you read each summary, think about whether or not it clearly identifies and explains those main ideas. When you finish reading the summaries, you will be asked to comment briefly on each one's strengths and weaknesses.

### Black Boy

#### *Chapter Thirteen*

One morning I arrived early at work and went into the bank lobby where the Negro porter was mopping. I stood at a counter and picked up the Memphis *Commercial Appeal* and began my free reading of the press. I came finally to the editorial page and saw an article dealing with one H. L. Mencken. I knew by hearsay that he was the editor of the *American Mercury,* but aside from that I knew nothing about him. The article was a furious denunciation of Mencken, concluding with one, hot, short sentence: Mencken is a fool.

I wondered what on earth this Mencken had done to call down upon him the scorn of the South. The only people I had ever heard denounced in the South were Negroes, and this man was not a Negro. Then what ideas did Mencken hold that made a newspaper like the *Commercial Appeal* castigate him publicly? Undoubtedly he must be advocating ideas that the South did not like. Were there, then, people other than Negroes who criticized the South? I knew that during the Civil War the South had hated northern whites, but I had not encountered such hate during my life. Knowing no more of Mencken than I did at that moment, I felt a vague sympathy for him. Had not the South, which had assigned me the role of a non-man, cast at him its hardest words?

Now, how could I find out about this Mencken? There was a huge library near the riverfront, but I knew that Negroes were not allowed to patronize its shelves any more than they were the parks and playgrounds of the city. I had gone into the library several times to get books for the white men on the job. Which of them would now help me to get books? And how could I read them without causing concern to the white men with whom I worked? I had so far been successful in hiding my thoughts and feelings from them, but I knew that I would create hostility if I went about this business of reading in a clumsy way.

I weighed the personalities of the men on the job. There was Don, a Jew; but I distrusted him. His position was not much better than mine and I knew that he was uneasy and insecure; he had always treated me in an offhand, bantering way that barely concealed his contempt. I was afraid to ask him to help me to get books; his frantic desire to demonstrate a racial solidarity with the whites against Negroes might make him betray me.

Then how about the boss? No, he was a Baptist and I had the suspicion that he would not be quite able to comprehend why a black boy would want to read Mencken. There were other white men on the job whose attitudes showed clearly that they were Kluxers or sympathizers, and they were out of the question.

There remained only one man whose attitude did not fit into an anti-Negro category, for I had heard the white men refer to him as a "Pope lover." He was an Irish Catholic and was hated by the white Southerners. I knew that he read books, because I had got him volumes from the library several times. Since he, too, was an object of hatred, I felt that he might refuse me but would hardly betray me. I hesitated, weighing and balancing the imponderable realities.

One morning I paused before the Catholic fellow's desk.

"I want to ask you a favor," I whispered to him.

"What is it?"

"I want to read. I can't get books from the library. I wonder if you'd let me use your card?"

He looked at me suspiciously.

"My card is full most of the time," he said.

"I see," I said and waited, posing my question silently.

"You're not trying to get me into trouble, are you, boy?" he asked, staring at me.

"Oh, no, sir."

"What book do you want?"

"A book by H. L. Mencken."

"Which one?"

"I don't know. Has he written more than one?"

"He has written several."

"I didn't know that."

"What makes you want to read Mencken?"

"Oh, I just saw his name in the newspaper," I said.

"It's good of you to want to read," he said. "But you ought to read the right things."

I said nothing. Would he want to supervise my reading?

"Let me think," he said. "I'll figure out something."

I turned from him and he called me back. He stared at me quizzically.

"Richard, don't mention this to the other white men," he said.

"I understand," I said. "I won't say a word."

A few days later he called me to him.

"I've got a card in my wife's name," he said. "Here's mine."

"Thank you, sir."

"Do you think you can manage it?"

"I'll manage fine," I said.

"If they suspect you, you'll get in trouble," he said.

"I'll write the same kind of notes to the library that you wrote when you sent me for books," I told him. "I'll sign your name."

He laughed.

"Go ahead. Let me see what you get," he said.

That afternoon I addressed myself to forging a note. Now, what were the names of books written by H. L. Mencken? I did not know any of them. I finally wrote what I thought would be a foolproof note: *Dear Madam: Will you please let this nigger boy*—I used the word "nigger" to make the librarian feel that I could not possibly be the author of the note—*have some books by H. L. Mencken?* I forged the white man's name.

I entered the library as I had always done when on errands for whites, but I felt that I would somehow slip up and betray myself. I doffed my hat, stood a respectful distance from the desk, looked as unbookish as possible, and waited for the white patrons to be taken care of. When the desk was clear of people, I still waited. The white librarian looked at me.

"What do you want, boy?"

As though I did not possess the power of speech, I stepped forward and simply handed her the forged note, not parting my lips.

"What books by Mencken does he want?" she asked.

"I don't know, ma'am," I said, avoiding her eyes.

"Who gave you this card?"

"Mr. Falk," I said.

"Where is he?"

"He's at work, at the M—— Optical Company," I said. "I've been in here for him before."

"I remember," the woman said. "But he never wrote notes like this."

Oh, God, she's suspicious. Perhaps she would not let me have the books? If she had turned her back at that moment, I would have ducked out the door and never gone back. Then I thought of a bold idea.

"You can call him up, ma'am," I said, my heart pounding.

"You're not using these books, are you?" she asked pointedly.

"Oh, no, ma'am. I can't read."

"I don't know what he wants by Mencken," she said under her breath.

I knew now that I had won; she was thinking of other things and the race question had gone out of her mind. She went to the shelves. Once or twice she looked over her shoulder at me, as though she was still doubtful. Finally she came forward with two books in her hand.

"I'm sending him two books," she said. "But tell Mr. Falk to come in next time, or send me the names of the books he wants. I don't know what he wants to read."

I said nothing. She stamped the card and handed me the books. Not daring to glance at them, I went out of the library, fearing that the woman would call me back for further questioning. A block away from the library I opened one of the books and read a title: *A Book of Prefaces*. I was nearing my nineteenth birthday and I did not know how to pronounce the word "preface." I thumbed the pages and saw strange words and strange names. I shook my head, disappointed. I looked at the other book; it was called *Prejudices*. I knew what that word meant; I had heard it all my life. And right off I was on guard against Mencken's books. Why would a man want to call a book *Prejudices?* The word was so stained with all my memories of racial hate that I could not conceive of anybody using it for a title. Perhaps I had made a mistake about Mencken? A man who had prejudices must be wrong.

When I showed the books to Mr. Falk, he looked at me and frowned.

"That librarian might telephone you," I warned him.

"That's all right," he said. "But when you're through reading those books, I want you to tell me what you get out of them."

That night in my rented room, while letting the hot water run over my can of pork and beans in the sink, I opened *A Book of Prefaces* and began to read. I was jarred and shocked by the style, the clear, clean, sweeping sentences. Why did he write like that?

And how did one write like that? I pictured the man as a raging
demon, slashing with his pen, consumed with hate, denouncing
everything American, extolling everything European or German,
laughing at the weaknesses of people, mocking God, authority.
What was this? I stood up, trying to realize what reality lay behind the meaning of the words . . . Yes, this man was fighting,
fighting with words. He was using words as a weapon, using them
as one would use a club. Could words be weapons? Well, yes, for
here they were. Then, maybe, perhaps, I could use them as a
weapon? No. It frightened me. I read on and what amazed me was
not what he said, but how on earth anybody had the courage to
say it.

Occasionally I glanced up to reassure myself that I was alone
in the room. Who were these men about whom Mencken was talk-
ing so passionately? Who was Anatole France? Joseph Conrad?
Sinclair Lewis, Sherwood Anderson, Dostoevski, George Moore,
Gustave Flaubert, Maupassant, Tolstoy, Frank Harris, Mark
Twain, Thomas Hardy, Arnold Bennett, Stephen Crane, Zola,
Norris, Gorky, Bergson, Ibsen, Balzac, Bernard Shaw, Dumas,
Poe, Thomas Mann, O. Henry, Dreiser, H. G. Wells, Gogol, T. S.
Eliot, Gide, Baudelaire, Edgar Lee Masters, Stendhal, Turgenev,
Huneker, Nietzsche, and scores of others? Were these men real?
Did they exist or had they existed? And how did one pronounce
their names?

I ran across many words whose meanings I did not know, and I
either looked them up in a dictionary or, before I had a chance to
do that, encountered the word in a context that made its meaning
clear. But what strange world was this? I concluded the book with
the conviction that I had somehow overlooked something terribly
important in life. I had once tried to write, had once reveled in
feeling, had let my crude imagination roam, but the impulse to
dream had been slowly beaten out of me by experience. Now it
surged up again and I hungered for books, new ways of looking
and seeing. It was not a matter of believing or disbelieving what I
read, but of feeling something new, of being affected by something
that made the look of the world different.

As dawn broke I ate my pork and beans, feeling dopey, sleepy.
I went to work, but the mood of the book would not die; it lingered, coloring everything I saw, heard, did. I now felt that I
knew what the white men were feeling. Merely because I had
read a book that had spoken of how they lived and thought, I
identified myself with that book. I felt vaguely guilty. Would I,
filled with bookish notions, act in a manner that would make the
whites dislike me?

I forged more notes and my trips to the library became frequent. Reading grew into a passion. My first serious novel was

Sinclair Lewis's *Main Street.* It made me see my boss, Mr. Gerald, and identify him as an American type. I would smile when I saw him lugging his golf bags into the office. I had always felt a vast distance separating me from the boss, and now I felt closer to him, though still distant. I felt now that I knew him, that I could feel the very limits of his narrow life. And this had happened because I had read a novel about a mythical man called George F. Babbitt.

The plots and stories in the novels did not interest me so much as the point of view revealed. I gave myself over to each novel without reserve, without trying to criticize it; it was enough for me to see and feel something different. And for me, everything was something different. Reading was like a drug, a dope. The novels created moods in which I lived for days. But I could not conquer my sense of guilt, my feeling that the white men around me knew that I was changing, that I had begun to regard them differently.

Whenever I brought a book to the job, I wrapped it in newspaper—a habit that was to persist for years in other cities and under other circumstances. But some of the white men pried into my packages when I was absent and they questioned me.

"Boy, what are you reading those books for?"

"Oh, I don't know, sir."

"That's deep stuff you're reading, boy."

"I'm just killing time, sir."

"You'll addle your brains if you don't watch out."

I read Dreiser's *Jennie Gehardt* and *Sister Carrie* and they revived in me a vivid sense of my mother's suffering; I was overwhelmed. I grew silent, wondering about the life around me. It would have been impossible for me to have told anyone what I derived from these novels, for it was nothing less than a sense of life itself. All my life had shaped me for the realism, the naturalism of the modern novel, and I could not read enough of them.

Steeped in new moods and ideas, I bought a ream of paper and tried to write; but nothing would come, or what did come was flat beyond telling. I discovered that more than desire and feeling were necessary to write and I dropped the idea. Yet I still wondered how it was possible to know people sufficiently to write about them? Could I ever learn about life and people? To me, with my vast ignorance, my Jim Crow station in life, it seemed a task impossible of achievement. I now knew what being a Negro meant. I could endure the hunger. I had learned to live with hate. But to feel that there were feelings denied me, that the very breath of life itself was beyond my reach, that more than anything else hurt, wounded me. I had a new hunger.

In buoying me up, reading also cast me down, made me see

what was possible, what I had missed. My tension returned, new, terrible, bitter, surging, almost too great to be contained. I no longer *felt* that the world about me was hostile, killing; I *knew* it. A million times I asked myself what I could do to save myself, and there were no answers. I seemed forever condemned, ringed by walls.

I did not discuss my reading with Mr. Falk, who had lent me his library card; it would have meant talking about myself and that would have been too painful. I smiled each day, fighting desperately to maintain my old behavior, to keep my disposition seemingly sunny. But some of the white men discerned that I had begun to brood.

"Wake up there, boy!" Mr. Olin said one day.

"Sir!" I answered for the lack of a better word.

"You act like you've stolen something," he said.

I laughed in the way I knew he expected me to laugh, but I resolved to be more conscious of myself, to watch my every act, to guard and hide the new knowledge that was dawning within me.

If I went north, would it be possible for me to build a new life then? But how could a man build a life upon vague, unformed yearnings? I wanted to write and I did not even know the English language. I bought English grammars and found them dull. I felt that I was getting a better sense of the language from novels than from grammars. I read hard, discarding a writer as soon as I felt that I had grasped his point of view. At night the printed page stood before my eyes in sleep.

Mrs. Moss, my landlady, asked me one Sunday morning:

"Son, what is this you keep on reading?"

"Oh, nothing. Just novels."

"What you get out of 'em?"

"I'm just killing time," I said.

"I hope you know your own mind," she said in a tone which implied that she doubted if I had a mind.

I knew of no Negroes who read the books I liked and I wondered if any Negroes ever thought of them. I knew that there were Negro doctors, lawyers, newspapermen, but I never saw any of them. When I read a Negro newspaper I never caught the faintest echo of my preoccupation in its pages. I felt trapped and occasionally, for a few days, I would stop reading. But a vague hunger would come over me for books, books that opened up new avenues of feeling and seeing, and again I would forge another note to the white librarian. Again I would read and wonder as only the naïve and unlettered can read and wonder, feeling that I carried a secret, criminal burden about with me each day.

That winter my mother and brother came and we set up housekeeping, buying furniture on the installment plan, being cheated

and yet knowing no way to avoid it. I began to eat warm food and
to my surprise found that regular meals enabled me to read
faster. I may have lived through many illnesses and survived
them, never suspecting that I was ill. My brother obtained a job
and we began to save toward the trip north, plotting our time,
setting tentative dates for departure. I told none of the white men
on the job that I was planning to go north; I knew that the moment they felt I was thinking of the North they would change
toward me. It would have made them feel that I did not like the
life I was living, and because my life was completely conditioned
by what they said or did, it would have been tantamount to challenging them.

I could calculate my chances for life in the South as a Negro
fairly clearly now.

I could fight the southern whites by organizing with other Negroes, as my grandfather had done. But I knew that I could never
win that way; there were many whites and there were but few
blacks. They were strong and we were weak. Outright black re-
bellion could never win. If I fought openly I would die and I did
not want to die. News of lynchings were frequent.

I could submit and live the life of a genial slave, but that was
impossible. All of my life had shaped me to live by my own feelings and thoughts. I could make up to Bess and marry her and in-
herit the house. But that, too, would be the life of a slave; if I did
that, I would crush to death something within me, and I would
hate myself as much as I knew the whites already hated those
who had submitted. Neither could I ever willingly present myself
to be kicked, as Shorty had done. I would rather have died than
do that.

I could drain off my restlessness by fighting with Shorty and
Harrison. I had seen many Negroes solve the problem of being
black by transferring their hatred of themselves to others with a
black skin and fighting them. I would have to be cold to do that,
and I was not cold and I could never be.

I could, of course, forget what I had read, thrust the whites out
of my mind, forget them; and find release from anxiety and long-
ing in sex and alcohol. But the memory of how my father had conducted himself made that course repugnant. If I did not want
others to violate my life, how could I voluntarily violate it myself?

I had no hope whatever of being a professional man. Not only
had I been so conditioned that I did not desire it, but the fulfill-
ment of such an ambition was beyond my capabilities. Well-to-do
Negroes lived in a world that was almost as alien to me as the
world inhabited by whites.

What, then, was there? I held my life in my mind, in my consciousness each day, feeling at times that I would stumble and

drop it, spill it forever. My reading had created a vast sense of
distance between me and the world in which I lived and tried to
make a living, and that sense of distance was increasing each
day. My days and nights were one long, quiet, continuously contained dream of terror, tension, and anxiety. I wondered how long
I could bear it.

### *Summary 1*

"Reading was like a drug, a dope," says Richard Wright in
Chapter Thirteen of *Black Boy*. In this chapter, Wright describes
the time when reading was the object of learning for him. He discovers how words are used as weapons sometimes. He also tells of
how his opinions of others and of himself changed as a result of
his reading, and of how reading materials altered his life.

One of the first things that shocks Wright is when he begins to
realize that words are often used as weapons. The character
thinks to himself, "Yes, this man was fighting, fighting with
words." He says that it frightens him, yet he is amazed at how
much courage it takes to write what one feels.

Throughout the chapter, Richard Wright slowly shows how
reading helps him learn about the white men around him. After
reading a book, Wright tries to identify with the book. For example, when he finishes reading Sinclair Lewis's novel *Main Street*,
he sees the similarities between his boss, Mr. Gerald, and the
"American type." Wright discovers that he can relate to his boss
better through reading: he feels closer to him because he under-
stands him more, so he continues to have a drive to read.

Through his reading, Wright begins to realize that there is
more to life than what is offered to him. He starts to resent the
white Southerners for conditioning him to live in a certain way.
"But to feel that there were feelings denied me, that the very
breath of life itself was beyond my reach, that more than anything else hurt, wounded me." To carry these feelings inside him
became almost unbearable.

Richard Wright knew exactly what the white people thought of
him, and where they placed him in society. He therefore could estimate what kind of life to expect. Because Wright wants more
than what society offers, he dreams of moving to the North with
his brother. There he could create and shape his own feelings and
thoughts.

The main point that is stressed in the chapter is the point that
reading books, newspapers, and magazines can open up a whole
new world for an individual. No matter what race or religion a
person is, he has the right to shape his own life. One way to gain
knowledge about people and the rest of the world is through
reading.

### Summary 2

Richard Wright was born in 1908 and died in 1960. In his autobiography, *Black Boy,* he describes many important and interesting events in his life. Chapter Thirteen describes a time when he
was working at an optical company and decided to start reading
some books by H. L. Mencken.

After Wright arrived early at work one morning, he began
reading the newspaper. When he came to the editorial page, he
saw an article written about H. L. Mencken, who was the editor
of the *American Mercury.* He soon realized that the article was "a
furious denunciation of Mencken, concluding with one hot, short
sentence: Mencken is a fool." This made Wright feel sympathetic
toward Mencken and curious to find out what he had done to
cause the South to oppose him.

Wright wanted to read some of Mencken's books, but the library at that time was not for Negroes to use. Negroes were only
allowed to use the library if they were picking up books for
whites. So he decided he would ask one of his white coworkers
for the use of his library card. Wright weighed the possibilities of
which one of his coworkers would lend him the card. He considered Don, who was Jewish, and his boss, who was a Baptist, but
he didn't trust them enough. Most of the other men at work were
Kluxers or sympathized with the Klan, so they were obviously not
good people to ask. Wright finally decided to ask Mr. Falk, who
was Catholic. He had sometimes picked up books at the library
for this man, so he thought Mr. Falk would probably lend him a
card.

Wright decided to ask Mr. Falk for the use of his library card,
so that he could read books by H. L. Mencken. Falk wasn't sure
at first, but he took out a library card in his wife's name and decided to let Wright use it. He also said that he wanted Wright to
tell him about the books he was reading. Wright now faced another problem: How was he to get the books for himself without
seeming suspicious? He chose to forge the necessary notes. He
tried to make the first note sound more realistic by using the
term "nigger boy" in it so that the librarian wouldn't suspect that
he had written the note himself.

Finally, Wright was able to get two books, *A Book of Prefaces*
and *Prejudices.* Wright was almost nineteen years old, but he did
not know how to pronounce the word "preface." He was very disappointed, after thumbing through the pages and seeing a lot of
strange words and names which were unfamiliar to him. He knew
what "prejudices" meant: "I had heard it all my life. And right off
I was on guard against Mencken's books. Why would a man want
to call his book *Prejudices?* The word was so stained with all my
memories of racial hate that I could not conceive of anyone using

it for a title. Perhaps I had made a mistake about Mencken? A man who had prejudices must be wrong."

When Wright began reading *A Book of Prefaces,* he said, "I was jarred and shocked by the style, the clear, clean, sweeping sentences. Why did he write like that? And how did one write like that? I pictured the man as a raging demon, slashing with his pen, consumed with hate, denouncing everything American, extolling everything European or German, laughing at the weaknesses of people, mocking God, authority. What was this? I stood up, trying to realize what reality lay behind the meaning of the words." Wright was amazed, not because of what Mencken said, but at "how on earth anybody had the courage to say these things."

Wright states that "I had somehow overlooked something terribly important in life. I had once tried to write, had once reveled in feeling, had let my crude imagination roam, but the impulse to dream had slowly been beaten out of me by experience. Now it surged up again and I hungered for books, for new ways of looking and seeing. It was not a matter of believing or disbelieving what I read, but of feeling something that made the look of the world different."

I really enjoyed reading this chapter, written by Richard Wright, because it encouraged me to think about my own outlook on life.

### *Summary 3*

How can a poor Black man trapped deep in the South change his life? Sometimes the change may start with no more than a library card. In Chapter Thirteen of *Black Boy,* Richard Wright describes a time when reading became an obsession for him and changed his life forever. Wright had to work hard to find ways around the obstacles that the South had erected to keep a Black from reading: he persuaded a white man to lend him a library card, forged notes to the librarian, and hid his books when he went to work. The insights that Wright gained from reading made all his trouble and risks worthwhile, and may also explain why the South tried so hard to keep books away from Blacks. Books helped Wright to reject the submissive, inferior role that the South tried to impose upon him: he gained new insights into his world, he became deeply dissatisfied with his own life, and he became determined to write and to shape a new life in the North.

As soon as he started reading, Wright began to understand more about the people in his life. H. L. Mencken's *A Book of Prefaces* made him feel that he knew "what the white men were feeling," for he had "read a book that had spoken of how they lived and thought." When Wright started to read novels, his insights into other people increased. For example, Sinclair Lewis's *Main Street* helped him to understand his boss, Mr. Gerald, who resembled one of the characters in the novel. Understanding Mr. Gerald gave Wright almost a sense of power, of overcoming the distance between his boss's world and his own: "I felt closer to him, though still very distant. I felt now that I knew him, that I could feel the very limits of his narrow life."

Although Wright's reading brought him new knowledge, it also brought him new frustrations, for he now realized that there was a broader world that he had never been allowed to experience. When he first began to read, Wright was overwhelmed by the many strange words he encountered and realized that he had never even heard of many important writers and ideas. Reading thus made him realize "what was possible . . . what I had missed." By denying him education and experience, racial prejudice had kept Wright from living a full life. Realizing this was very painful: "to feel that there were feelings denied me, that the very breath of life itself was beyond my reach, that more than anything else hurt, wounded me. I had a new hunger."

To try to satisfy that hunger, Wright began thinking about ways to start a new life. He saw that writers such as Mencken were "fighting with words . . . using words as weapons" and wondered if he too could learn to fight with words. His first efforts to write were frustrating, but he was determined now to change his life. His reading had made him more dissatisfied than ever with the South, so he began to plan a move north. Wright had come to a real crisis in his life: "My reading had created a vast sense of distance between me and the world in which I lived and tried to make a living, and that sense of distance was increasing each day . . . I wondered how long I could bear it."

Chapter Thirteen of *Black Boy* thus shows us how hard Wright had to struggle to educate himself: society tried hard to keep him from reading at all, and there was no one to guide and encourage a young Black who wanted to learn more. This chapter also shows how important reading can be. Reading taught Wright a lot about people and the world, especially by making him realize just how limiting his own life in the South had always been. Reading gave Wright the awareness and determination he needed to change his life.

### Summary 4

The library card has three effects on Richard Wright's life. Using the library card helped him to see the problems of racism, to understand the white men he worked with and around, and to become dissatisfied with his own life.

Racism or prejudice was one thing that Wright really didn't

understand up to this point in his life when he was nineteen. One
morning when he was reading through the Memphis *Commercial
Appeal,* he saw an article about H. L. Mencken, which ended with
"Mencken is a fool," so Wright decided that he wanted to read
more about Mencken. Because of this he knew that he would have
to use someone else in order to get the books that he wanted. He
knew this because blacks weren't really allowed to use the library
unless they were there to pick up books for somebody else, so he
would have to get someone's library card to use in order to get the
books. After Wright finally decided on who he was going to use,
he went about getting the card without someone getting suspicious. A Catholic fellow let Wright use his wife's card because his
was filled up with books that were already taken out. Although
Wright hadn't read much, he began to pick up on Mencken's language about prejudices: this made Wright feel that in some way
he felt those things when he was younger, but he never really
knew why. And this pushed him to read and learn more about
whites.

Then Wright began reading novels, and they opened up new
doors in his brain. He read a book by Sinclair Lewis and after
reading it he know the complete movements of his boss. His boss
was the type of person who played golf every day, left the office
when he felt like leaving, and didn't have to return until he was
ready because he had people working for him. So this proved to
Wright that by reading these novels and books, he could actually
describe someone he had never known before.

After reading these books, Wright began to feel dissatisfied
with his life because there weren't many things he could do to get
away from it. Wright stated that "I felt trapped and occasionally,
for a few days, I would stop reading." I think Wright was getting
so fed up by the way things were going that he just needed to get
away from everyone and everything. He even began to calculate
his chances for life in the South as a Negro now.

In my opinion, Wright was the type of man that wanted to
make changes in the South, but he knew that one man couldn't
do something about it alone. Then he started thinking about moving to the North where he could really make something of his life
and talents. This chapter was very self-explanatory in many cases
and told about a black individual living in the South at that time.
I found this chapter quite easy to understand and grasp. I really
enjoyed reading this chapter, as I enjoyed reading all of *Black
Boy.*

## DISCUSSION QUESTIONS

1.  Comment briefly on the strengths and weaknesses of each summary. In your comments, you might want to consider such points as

- the author's identification and explanation of the most important ideas in the chapter
- the organization of the summary
- the use of quotations
- the introductory and concluding paragraphs

SUMMARY 1

*STRENGTHS:*

*WEAKNESSES:*

SUMMARY 2

*STRENGTHS:*

*WEAKNESSES:*

SUMMARY 3

*STRENGTHS:*

*WEAKNESSES:*

SUMMARY 4

*STRENGTHS:*

*WEAKNESSES:*

**2.** On the whole, which summary seemed best to you? Why?

**3.** On the whole, which summary seemed weakest to you? Why?

### GENERAL CONCLUSIONS

Draw together all the observations and comments you have made about the Introductory Readings in this chapter. List some of the characteristics of a strong summary, or summarize your conclusions in a paragraph that would be helpful to beginning composition students. What advice would you give to a student writing a summary?

## ADVICE

Summarizing is a central and continuous part of most college students' lives; it would be difficult to think of a skill more crucial to effective studying, reading, thinking, and writing. If you take careful notes in lecture classes, you are essentially summarizing what your professor says. Instead of trying to copy down every word, you watch for major points and conclusions. As a reader, you search for an author's main ideas and may try to capture these ideas as you underline or make notes in the margins. In order to think clearly and logically, you must be able to see through a mass of details and irrelevancies to identify the most important issues in a discussion, the major advantages and disadvantages of a plan, or the major strengths and weaknesses of an opponent's argument.

As a writer, too, you will frequently be asked to summarize. Since summarizing tests your ability to understand and explain what someone else has said or written, your professors may ask you to write summaries of assigned books, articles, or films. Moreover, summarizing is often the first step in many other kinds of papers: to contrast two authors' views, you must first be able to grasp each one's main ideas; to evaluate a book or article, you must first understand it. A research paper may require you to summarize the works of dozens of authors: What does each have to say about the problem you are investigating? You will even have to summarize your own writing from time to time, in an abstract for a research paper or in the introductory or concluding paragraph of a long essay. When you have a job, you may have to write summaries of reports, meetings, or even telephone conversations. The skills involved in writing a summary, then, are essential to doing well in college and after college; it makes sense to study and master them.

## Planning a Summary

A summary is a condensation of a longer work. When you write a summary, you try to capture a work's essence, its main argument or conclusion. A summary is not necessarily stripped of all detail, for you may want to include some significant details to illustrate major ideas. You will leave out most details and examples, however, as you concentrate on finding and explaining the central thesis that ties all the smaller points together.

When you write a summary, make sure that you understand all the requirements of the assignment. Summaries are often combined with other sorts of papers, so watch for such phrases as "summarize and interpret," "summarize and evaluate," or "summarize and compare"; if any such phrases are used, you know that a "straight" summary will not fulfill all the requirements of the assignment. Also, check to see whether you are being asked to summarize the whole work or only a part of it. The professor may want you to summarize only certain chapters of a book or only those sections that discuss a particular topic. Finally, make sure that you know how long your summary should be. A summary is almost never more than one-fourth the length of the original work, but it may be much shorter. If you are in doubt, ask your professor.

As always, it helps to consider your audience's needs and expectations before you start to write. In general, do not assume that your readers are familiar with the work you are summarizing. One of your purposes in writing a summary is to give your readers a quick over- view of the work, so that they can decide whether or not they want to read the entire work for themselves. Even if you are summarizing only part of a work, then, you should usually give your readers some indication of the scope and purpose of the whole. If you are summarizing the entire work, you should make your summary comprehensive, so that your readers will see the full range of topics covered; you should also try to make your summary balanced, so that your reader can judge approximately how much time the author devotes to each topic. Smooth transitions between paragraphs are especially important in a summary, for you have to help your reader see how the various ideas in the original work are related to each other. Above all, make sure your summary is so clear that even a reader who has not read the original work can follow your essay easily. Look back at the four summaries in the Introductory Readings. Would any be confusing to someone who had not read the chapter from *Black Boy?*

## Finding Main Ideas

There is no quick, foolproof way to identify the main ideas in a book or essay. Ultimately, no tricks or techniques can substitute for being a careful reader who can distinguish between more and less important ideas, see the pattern in a group of details, and generalize accurately and intelligently. Still, a few bits of advice may be helpful.

Start by paying especially close attention to a work's title and to its opening and closing sections. Admittedly, these can be misleading: titles may be playful; introductions may be devoted to anecdotes or to arguments the author intends to refute; and conclusions may make proposals or suggest parallels only indirectly connected to the work's main point. Clearly, studying a work's title, introduction, and conclusion cannot take the place of reading the entire work closely. Still, since careful authors usually devote special attention to choosing their titles and writing their introductions and conclusions, these parts of a work may give us valuable hints about the author's purpose, directing us as we read.

Try converting a work's title into a question that can guide you as you read: before reading George Orwell's "Politics and the English Language," for example, frame a question such as "What is the relationship between politics and language?" You might be able to devise further questions by examining a work's introductory paragraph closely: look for terms the author promises to define, concepts the author promises to explain, or any listing of points to be covered. Before you go on to read the rest of the work, study the concluding paragraph. If the author mentions some similar ideas in the introduction and the conclusion, you can be fairly sure that these ideas are important to the work as a whole. If you can at least frame some questions or identify some issues to focus on as you read, you are not as likely to feel baffled when you finish reading a work and have to identify its main ideas.

As you read, underline and make notes in the margins to keep yourself alert and to remind yourself of the need to look for main ideas and significant details. Especially when you are reading a long or complex work, your attention may falter from time to time; you may miss some important points, or you may finish the work and discover that you have only a vague idea of what you have read. Underlining and writing as you read can help. I often find it very helpful to write quick marginal notes summarizing the main idea of each paragraph. If I were taking marginal notes on the Advice section of this chapter, for example, my notes for the first three paragraphs might be "importance of summarizing," "types of written summaries," and "definition of summary." Taking such notes requires very little extra time, and it forces you to keep your attention focused sharply on what you are reading. Moreover, your margins will contain a helpful outline of the points the work covers.

A few other techniques may also help you identify main ideas. Notice how much time the author devotes to discussing various topics. If the author spends ten pages on one topic and only two on another, the first idea is probably more important than the second. Also, watch for ideas that keep showing up throughout a book or essay. An idea that is mentioned in almost every paragraph or chapter is probably more important than one that is mentioned only once or twice. Studying the work's organization carefully also helps. Do not make the common mistake of assuming that the first idea discussed is the most important: authors sometimes begin by stating their central ideas, but they often build up to these ideas gradually, presenting their evidence before drawing a conclusion or saving their most convincing arguments for last. Understanding the author's strategy can help you identify the work's central ideas and purposes.

## Organizing a Summary

Your summary's organization will depend to some extent on the nature and organization of the work you are summarizing. If the work is an argumentative essay that moves carefully from premises to conclusions, you should probably follow the author's organization. Often, however, you may find it best to organize your summary differently. The author may build up to the thesis or main idea gradually, but you will usually want to identify the main ideas right away: books and essays often keep readers in suspense, but summaries seldom should. You might also notice that an author discusses a particular topic at several points in a work and decide that your summary will be clearer if you consolidate everything the author has to say about that topic into one paragraph. In general, start by identifying the work's main ideas, and then organize your summary around them.

In your introduction, clearly identify the work you are summarizing by title and author. Think about what sorts of background information the reader might find helpful. Should you say anything about the author's life or other works? Would it be helpful for the readers to know when the work was written? Such information is sometimes crucial and sometimes irrelevant: you will have to base your decisions on the particular work and author you are discussing. If you are summarizing an article, you may want to name the periodical in which the article originally appeared. And, as previously mentioned, the introductory paragraph in a summary should usually identify the main idea of the original work.

You may decide to restate this idea in your conclusion, especially if your summary is more than a few pages long. It is tempting to evaluate a work in the last paragraph of a summary, but you should probably resist this temptation unless your professor has asked you for a comment. Summaries should be as objective as possible: your job is to report the author's views, not your own. In particular, do not end a summary by saying how much you enjoyed a work, how much it changed your life, or how much everyone would profit by reading it. Such statements may have been acceptable in elementary-school book reports, but they are usually so insincere and conventional that they make most college professors recoil.

## Using Quotations

You will probably use some direct quotations in your summary. Quotations give the reader a taste of the original work's tone or flavor, and they may help you to emphasize a particularly important point. Furthermore, you may want to discuss the author's use of a particular word or phrase. Do not, however, rely heavily on direct quotations. After all, one of your purposes in writing a summary is to demonstrate your understanding of an author's ideas, and you can best do this by stating those ideas in your own words. Filling your summary with long direct quotations proves only that you are an accurate copier, not that you are an intelligent reader. Use only a few quotations, then, and keep them short—often, an important phrase will do just as well as an entire sentence. Show that you understand the quotations by introducing them carefully and explaining them if necessary: for example, "Wright says that these books profoundly affected his view of life and 'made the look of the world different.'" By using quotations in this way, you will show that you truly understand the passage you are quoting.

## Using One Tense

Use the same tense throughout your summary. Your choice of a tense may depend on the type of work you are summarizing. Most people prefer to use the present tense in summaries of literary works: "Hamlet *dies* in Horatio's arms." Since Hamlet is a fictional character, he is as much alive now as he ever was—it seems odd to talk about his death as though it occurred at some point in the past. If you are summarizing a biographical or historical work, the past tense may seem a more logical choice: "Lincoln *was* shot in 1865." In summarizing other sorts of works—argumentative or expository essays, for example—the choice of a tense is largely up to you. Some authorities prefer using the present tense in all summaries, but you do not have to consider this preference binding. Once you have chosen a tense, however, keep to it throughout your summary. If you shift from one tense to another, you may confuse your readers: "Wright *is* afraid of whites, but he *overcame* this fear when he *approaches* Mr. Falk." Concern for your readers, which makes you careful about such major matters as identifying ideas accurately and organizing your summary coherently, should also make you pay close attention to such details as keeping to one tense.

## APPLICATION

**A.** Write a one-page summary of the Advice section in this chapter. Be sure to follow the advice you are summarizing.

**B.** If you are using an anthology of essays in class, look at the titles and the first and last paragraphs of several essays you have already read. How many of them are helpful in identifying the main ideas of the essays? Are some of them misleading? In what ways? How could you guard against being misled?

**C.** Following is the text of the acceptance speech William Faulkner gave when he received the Nobel Prize for Literature in 1949. As you read, underline and make marginal notes to help you identify the most important ideas in the speech.

### On Receiving the Nobel Prize

I feel that this award was not made to me as a man, but to my work—a life's work in the agony and sweat of the human spirit,

not for glory and least of all for profit, but to create out of the materials of the human spirit something which did not exist before.
So this award is only mine in trust. It will not be difficult to find
a dedication for the money part of it commensurate with the purpose and significance of its origin. But I would like to do the same
with the acclaim too, by using this moment as a pinnacle from
which I might be listened to by the young men and women already dedicated to the same anguish and travail, among whom is
already that one who will some day stand here where I am standing.

Our tragedy today is a general and universal physical fear so
long sustained by now that we can even bear it. There are no
longer problems of the spirit. There is only the question: When
will I be blown up? Because of this, the young man or woman
writing today has forgotten the problems of the human heart in
conflict with itself which alone can make good writing because
only that is worth writing about, worth the agony and the sweat.

He must learn them again. He must teach himself that the
basest of all things is to be afraid: and, teaching himself that,
forget it forever, leaving no room in his workshop for anything
but the old verities and truths of the heart, the old universal
truths lacking which any story is ephemeral and doomed—love
and honor and pity and pride and compassion and sacrifice. Until
he does so, he labors under a curse. He writes not of love but of
lust, of defeats in which nobody loses anything of value, of vic-
tories without hope, and, worst of all, without pity or compassion.
His griefs grieve on no universal bones. He writes not of the heart
but of the glands.

Until he relearns these things, he will write as though he stood
among and watched the end of man. I decline to accept the end of
man. It is easy enough to say that man is immortal simply because he will endure: that when the last ding-dong of doom has
clanged and faded from the last worthless rock hanging tideless
in the last red and dying evening, that even then there will still
be one more sound: that of his puny inexhaustible voice, still talking. I refuse to accept this. I believe that man will not merely endure: he will prevail. He is immortal, not because he alone among
creatures has an inexhaustible voice, but because he has a soul, a
spirit capable of compassion and sacrifice and endurance. The
poet's, the writer's duty is to write about these things. It is his
privilege to help man endure by lifting his heart, by reminding
him of the courage and honor and hope and pride and compassion
and pity and sacrifice which have been the glory of his past. The
poet's voice need not merely be the record of man, it can be one of
the props, the pillars to help him endure and prevail.

Plan a summary of this speech. Consider these questions:

1. What are the most important ideas in Faulkner's speech? Sum up these ideas in a sentence that could serve as the thesis statement for a summary.
2. How might you organize a summary of this speech? Make a quick outline.
3. What sorts of background information should you give the reader—about Faulkner, about his career, or about the occasion for the speech?
4. What passages from the speech might you quote directly? How would you introduce and explain these quotations?
5. In summarizing this speech, would you use the present tense or the past tense? Why?

**D.** Following are a short passage by John Holt and four student summaries of that passage. Evaluate the summaries, using the criteria suggested in your class discussion and in the Advice section of this chapter. Which summaries are strongest? Why? If all the summaries seem inadequate, write one of your own.

### The Bright Child and the Dull Child

Years of watching and comparing bright children and the not-bright, or less bright, have shown that they are very different kinds of people. The bright child is curious about life and reality, eager to get in touch with it, embrace it, unite himself with it. There is no wall, no barrier between him and life. The dull child is far less curious, far less interested in what goes on and what is real, more inclined to live in worlds of fantasy. The bright child likes to experiment, to try things out. He lives by the maxim that there is more than one way to skin a cat. If he can't do something one way, he'll try another. The dull child is usually afraid to try at all. It takes a good deal of urging to get him to try even once; if that fails, he is through.

The bright child is patient. He can tolerate uncertainty and failure, and will keep trying until he gets an answer. When all his experiments fail, he can even admit to himself and others that for the time being he is not going to get an answer. This may annoy him, but he can wait. Very often, he does not want to be told how to do the problem or solve the puzzle he has struggled with, because he does not want to be cheated out of the chance to figure it out for himself in the future. Not so the dull child. He cannot stand uncertainty or failure. To him, an unanswered question is not a challenge or an opportunity, but a threat. If he can't find the answer quickly, it must be given to him, and quickly; and he must have answers for everything. Such are the children of whom a second-grade teacher once said, "But my children *like* to have questions for which there is only one answer." They did, and by a mysterious coincidence, so did she.

The bright child is willing to go ahead on the basis of incomplete understanding and information. He will take risks, sail uncharted seas, explore when the landscape is dim, the landmarks few, the light poor. To give only one example, he will often read books he does not understand in the hope that after a while enough understanding will emerge to make it worth while to go on. In this spirit some of my fifth graders tried to read *Moby Dick*. But the dull child will go ahead only when he thinks he knows exactly where he stands and exactly what is ahead of him. If he does not feel he knows exactly what an experience will be like, and if it will not be exactly like other experiences he already knows, he wants no part of it. For while the bright child feels that the universe is, on the whole, a sensible, reasonable, and trustworthy place, the dull child feels that it is senseless, unpredictable, and treacherous. He feels that he can never tell what may happen, particularly in a new situation, except that it will probably be bad.

### Student Summaries

A. In John Holt's essay, "The Bright Child and the Dull Child," he compares the different ways that the two types of children have of viewing the world.

Holt characterizes the bright child as being interested and completely involved with living, "no barrier between him and life." The bright child is patient and enjoys experimenting and learns from his mistakes and failures. As Holt says, "He lives by the maxim that there is more than one way to skin a cat" and will "sail uncharted seas, explore when the landscape is dim, the landmarks few, the light poor."

The dull child, on the other hand, "will go ahead only when he thinks he knows exactly where he stands and exactly what is ahead of him." The dull child is characterized by being sort of out of touch; he "live(s) in worlds of fantasy." He is often afraid of trying something new and cannot tolerate failure. His life is spent doing what is certain, and he is constantly apprehensive.

Holt sums up the contradictions by saying that the bright child views the universe as "sensible . . . and trustworthy," while the dull child views it as "senseless . . . and treacherous."

B. Some children seek adventure, are curious, and live life to its fullest. However, other children are uncertain and afraid of experimenting with different aspects of life. There are really two types of children: the bright and the dull child.

C. John Holt, in "The Bright Child and the Dull Child," contrasts these two "very different kinds of people." The basic difference is that while the bright child sees the world as "sensible, reasonable, and trustworthy," the dull child thinks of the world as "senseless, unpredictable, and treacherous." As a result, the bright child is curious about the world—eager to explore and experiment, patient in his investigations, and willing to tolerate uncertainty, ambiguity, and failure. The dull child, however, is incurious, impatient, and eager to find quick, simple answers.

D. In this essay, the author explained the differences between a bright child and a dull child. He says that the bright child is a very inquisitive child who is always willing to experiment with something. He is persistent and never gives up, even when he failed previously. The dull child could not care less about what is going on. If he failed at something once, he would just give up trying. The dull child will not attempt to do things that might be a rather big challenge and often doubts his own ability.

# 11.
# Interpretation

## INTRODUCTORY READINGS

**A.**  Following is the opening paragraph of Donald Barthelme's short story "The School," followed by a summary of the paragraph and then by an interpretation of it. Compare the summary and the interpretation carefully.

> Well, we had all these children out planting trees, see, because we figured that . . . that was part of their education, to see how, you know, the root systems . . . and also the sense of responsibility, taking care of things, being individually responsible. You know what I mean. And the trees all died. They were orange trees. I don't know why they died, they just died. Something wrong with the soil possibly or maybe the stuff we got from the nursery wasn't the best. We complained about it. So we've got thirty kids out there, each kid has his or her own little tree to plant, and we've got these thirty dead trees. All these kids looking at these little brown sticks, it was depressing.

> —DONALD BARTHELME, *"The School"*

### Summary
The speaker in this paragraph says that he had all the children in his class plant orange trees to learn about root systems and individual responsibility. However, all the trees died. The speaker isn't sure why they died, but speculates that the soil may have been poor or the plants themselves may have been defective.

### Interpretation
The first paragraph of "The School" gives us some tentative insights into the speaker's character. His speech is halting and dis-

organized: he constantly interrupts himself to try to clarify his
ideas ("and also the sense of responsibility, taking care of things,
being individually responsible") and to throw in details that
should have been mentioned earlier or not at all ("They were orange trees"). He tries to find a rational explanation for the trees'
death, but his attempts are feeble and halfhearted. The paragraph also suggests what kind of teacher he is. His concern for
his students is evident in the last line: he clearly sympathizes
with their disappointment. Still, he does not seem to have
thought carefully about the objectives of the tree-planting project:
he stumbles through his explanation, finally collapsing with a
helpless "You know what I mean." The first paragraph leaves us
wondering whether the speaker is by nature a confused and foggy
thinker, or whether the mysterious death of the trees has shaken
him so deeply that he is no longer able to express himself coherently.

## DISCUSSION QUESTIONS

1.  What are some of the differences between the summary and the in-
    terpretation? List as many differences as you can think of: consider
    purpose, approach, and the kinds of statements made.
2.  In the summary, does the author assume that the readers have al-
    ready read the paragraph from "The School"? Does the author
    make the same assumption in the interpretation?
3.  How would you define *interpretation?* What do we do when we in-
    terpret something?

**B.**   Following are Theodore Roethke's "Elegy for Jane" and three student essays offering interpretations of that poem. Read the essays and
compare them carefully.

### Elegy for Jane
### My Student, Thrown by a Horse
### —THEODORE ROETHKE

*I remember the neckcurls, limp and damp as tendrils;*
*And her quick look, a sidelong pickerel smile;*
*And how, once startled into talk, the light syllables leaped for*
    *her,*
*And she balanced in the delight of her thought,*
*A wren, happy, tail into the wind,*                                          5
*Her song trembling the twigs and small branches.*
*The shade sang with her;*
*The leaves, their whispers turned to kissing;*
*And the mold sang in the bleached valleys under the rose.*

*Oh, when she was sad, she cast herself down into such a pure
    depth,*                                                                    10
*Even a father could not find her:*
*Scraping her cheek against straw;*
*Stirring the clearest water.*

*My sparrow, you are not here,*
*Waiting like a fern, making a spiny shadow,*                                  15
*The sides of wet stones cannot console me,*
*Nor the moss, wound with the last light.*

*If only I could nudge you from this sleep,*
*My maimed darling, my skittery pigeon.*
*Over this damp grave I speak the words of my love:*                           20
*I, with no rights in this matter,*
*Neither father nor lover.*

## Nature in "Elegy for Jane"

In the poem "Elegy for Jane" by Theodore Roethke, we can see irony expressed through nature. Jane was a part of nature, yet it was nature that ended her life.

In Jane's life, nature played an important part. Nature was not only important to Jane herself, but also to how people viewed her. People had always looked at Jane and associated her with nature. Even from the way her teacher described her physical characteristics, we could see her belonging to nature. He describes her curls as like tendrils, and her smile as like a pickerel's.

Not only her physical characteristics, but Jane's emotions also revolved around nature. Jane shared her happiness and joys with nature, as well as her sorrows. Animal and plant imagery is used to describe her emotions and feelings. When she was happy, she was described as a wren, whose song trembles the twigs and branches. Although Jane could be a very happy person, her emotions also went strongly the other way. While nature has extremes in it, so did Jane's emotions and feelings.

So while nature was Jane's way of life, a place where she lived and played and felt happiness and sorrow, nature was also what put an end to Jane's life. One day when she was riding her horse, she was thrown and killed. Her whole life she had been in control of nature by controlling her horse. She would ride and have the horse behave as she wished it to. While she once had control over nature, it finally got control over her by killing her.

After Jane had died, however, she was still thought about in terms of nature. Her teacher when thinking about her described her as his sparrow. His description of how he felt about Jane's death even used nature imagery.

While the whole poem has to do with nature, nature is shown

in two different ways. Nature ironically is both good and evil. Nature had been such an important part of Jane's life and something so beneficial to her. As it turned out, however, nature was what ended up killing Jane.

## An Interpretation of "Elegy for Jane"

Theodore Roethke's "Elegy for Jane" describes a teacher's grief over the loss of one of his students, who was thrown by a horse. As he stands by her grave, he remembers what she was like: her happy moods and her sad ones. Often, he compares her to nature. However, he feels he has no right to his emotions of grief, for he was neither her father nor her lover.

This student meant a great deal to him. She was young and usually very happy; he compares her to "A wren, happy, tail into the wind." She also must have been talkative, for he says that "the light syllables leaped for her." Just being around her must have made him feel happy, too. He might even have been in love with her, despite the differences in their ages.

At times, however, Jane got very depressed, so depressed that "even her father could not find her." At such times, the teacher probably wanted to reach out to her and comfort her, but he didn't because he was unsure of what his feelings for her were. He may also have felt guilty about loving someone so much younger than he was.

He uses nature to describe her—a wren, a sparrow, her pickerel smile. The setting is also full of nature imagery, such as "The shade sang with her" and "the mold sang in the bleached valleys under the rose." Whenever I think of nature, the first words that come into my mind are "feminine" and "pretty." Because Jane is compared to nature, I imagine her as a feminine girl, cute and tiny. Like all things in nature, Jane had to die eventually, and her teacher was left alone to express his great love for her.

## Imagery in "Elegy for Jane"

Theodore Roethke remembers a student he once loved and describes her affectionately in the poem "Elegy for Jane." Nature imagery used throughout the poem paints a vivid picture of the young girl and parallels the speaker's feelings for her.

The images used in the poem make it clear that the speaker's love for his student is not like that of a lover; rather, his love is more of an admiration for her harmonious existence with nature. This is illustrated by his extensive use of a particular type of nature imagery. Throughout the poem, he describes the young girl by using images of plants, birds, and fish that would not ordinarily be used to describe someone that a man is deeply in love with. For example, he compares her smile to a pickerel's, not to some more delicate natural image such as a rose. This type of imagery is significant in two ways. First, it enables the reader to understand that the speaker's feelings of love toward his student are feelings of "neither father nor lover." Second, the nature imagery creates in the reader's mind a picture of Jane as a person who is in harmony with nature: "The shade sang with her."

There is a significant difference in the type of images used to describe the two moods presented in the poem. In the first stanza the living imagery of both the birds and the trees represents a type of carefree innocence suggesting the young girl's happiness. These images are clarified by lively action words such as "skittery" and "leaped"—"skittery pigeon," "the light syllables leaped for her." By contrast, in the second stanza images of nonliving things in nature, such as water and straw, suggest her low depths of sadness.

Although there are two different types of nature images in the poem, the tone of these images is constant throughout. There is a specific toned-down effect of the dull, colorless, and shady images described. For example, all the birds mentioned—wrens, pigeons, and sparrows—are colored with muted earth tones; the straw and the water are colorless; and all the plants mentioned—mold, moss, and ferns—are shade-loving plants. This connection between the dull and shaded images is parallel to the speaker's subdued, unexpressed feelings for his student.

The natural imagery in the poem clearly and explicitly describes the young girl, and indirectly expresses the type of feelings the speaker had for her. The reader becomes aware of these feelings, however, only after focusing on the nature imagery.

## DISCUSSION QUESTIONS

1. Does each essay contain a thesis statement? In each essay, what is the central assertion the author tries to support? Do you consider this assertion clear and interesting?
2. How much summary does each essay contain? Do any of the essays contain more summary than you needed as a reader?
3. All three essays discuss Roethke's use of nature imagery. For example, compare paragraph 3 of "Nature in 'Elegy for Jane,'" paragraph 4 of "An Interpretation of 'Elegy for Jane,'" and paragraph 2 of "Imagery in 'Elegy for Jane.'"
   a. What assertions does each author make about Roethke's use of nature imagery? Comment on these assertions: Do they seem plausible? Do they go beyond the obvious?
   b. How do the authors support their assertions? Where do they

find their evidence? In each paragraph, is the support solid
and convincing?

4. The authors of "An Interpretation of 'Elegy for Jane'" and "Imagery in 'Elegy for Jane'" both discuss the speaker's feelings for
Jane. What assertions does each author make about these feelings? How does each author support her assertions? Which discussion of the speaker's feelings for Jane do you find more interesting
and convincing? Why?

5. Examine paragraph 4 of "Imagery in 'Elegy for Jane.'" Again,
identify the assertions the author makes and comment on the way
she supports them. Speculate about how the author formed the
ideas she discusses in this paragraph; what questions must she
have asked herself as she read the poem?

6. Comment on the organization of each essay. You might find it
helpful to draw up quick outlines by identifying the main point discussed in each paragraph. Are the paragraphs in each essay unified and adequately developed? In each essay, are the paragraphs
arranged in a logical order?

## GENERAL CONCLUSIONS

Draw together all the observations and comments you have made
about the Introductory Readings in this chapter. List some of the characteristics of a strong interpretive essay, or summarize your conclusions in a paragraph that would be helpful to beginning composition
students. What advice would you give to a student writing an interpretive essay?

## ADVICE

Many composition courses end with an assignment involving the interpretation of a literary work. It makes sense to end a writing course by
taking a close look at some really excellent writing. Furthermore, interpreting a literary work invites you to draw together many of the
skills and insights you have developed in writing other sorts of essays.
Your own experience in writing narrative and descriptive essays, for
example, should help you to understand some of the techniques poets
and fiction writers use. Interpretation also combines exposition and argumentation: your goal is to explain the literary work, but in the
course of doing so you must argue for your interpretation by finding
evidence to support any assertions you make. To write some sorts of
interpretive essays, you would need to consult biographies, histories,
and literary criticism; to write the sort of interpretive essay discussed
in this chapter, you can find all the evidence you need in the literary
work itself.

Although this chapter is limited to interpreting literary works, interpretation is an integral part of our day-to-day lives and a frequent element in papers assigned in many college courses. We constantly try to interpret politicians' speeches, newspaper editorials, and the professor's hints about what will be covered in the final examination. A psychology professor might ask you to interpret the results of an experiment; a political science professor might ask you to interpret a party's platform. In other courses, you might write an interpretation of a painting, a musical composition, a historical document, or an economic trend.

Many students are intimidated by the prospect of having to write about literature because it seems that literary criticism is the preserve of mystics gifted with special inspiration. In fact, mystics often make poor critics. It used to puzzle me that many of the best interpretive essays I receive in literature courses are written by science majors who have taken few if any English courses. Eventually, I realized that the abilities developed by a good science student are similar to those required for literary analysis: the abilities to pay close attention to details, to spot a pattern and anything that diverges from it, to ask intelligent questions about things that seem odd or confusing, to speculate about possible answers to those questions, and to decide whether or not the evidence really supports those answers. The science student develops these abilities in the laboratory; you can develop them through analyzing and writing about literature. And just as the science student can later use these abilities in a literature course, you can use them in a laboratory or in countless other situations in college or after college.

## Summary and Interpretation

One of the most frequent weaknesses in interpretive essays is a tendency to summarize too much or to let summary take the place of analysis. The first step toward writing a strong interpretive essay, then, is to understand the difference between summary and interpretation and to decide how much summary belongs in your paper.

Suppose that you have a friend named Joe who started a new job three months ago. You run into him and ask him how he likes his job, and this is his reply:

> Well, the pay is all right, and there are some good health benefits. And I get two weeks' paid vacation every year. And the office is comfortable, and most of the people are pleasant.

If you were asked to summarize Joe's remarks, you might say, "Joe pointed out several good features of his new job." If you were asked to interpret his remarks, however, you would probably take a different approach. You would consider Joe's halting, unenthusiastic tone: he begins with "well," not with "wow," and he strings together several short clauses with "and's" as though he is trying to think of good things to say about his job but can't get enthusiastic about any of them. You would also pay attention to his word choice and notice that most of his expressions are muted or qualified—"all right," "some good health benefits," "comfortable." You would speculate about the implications of "Most of the people I work with are pleasant"; does this mean that some are unpleasant and none are exciting? You would notice what Joe doesn't say, as well as what he does. He mentions his pay, benefits, vacation, office, and coworkers, but he says nothing about the work itself; perhaps he finds his work dull or unsatisfying. After you've done all this analysis, your interpretation will probably be very different from your summary. You might well conclude that, although he is unwilling to admit it, Joe is unhappy with his job.

Interpretation is thus more probing than summary. In a summary, your task is to condense what a work says. You usually assume that your readers have not read the work you are summarizing. In an interpretive essay, your task is not to repeat what the work says but to help your readers understand the work at a more profound level. To use a hackneyed phrase, we can say that you try to get "beyond the surface" of the text, to point out things that a casual reader might have missed. You can assume that your readers have already read the work you are discussing, so you shouldn't attempt to retell the plot or to give a great deal of background information about characters. You may have to remind your readers of some incidents in the plot, but keep such reminders as brief as possible: *refer* to incidents, but don't retell them.

## Getting Started: Reading the Work and Asking Questions

Your first task in writing an interpretive essay is reading the literary work well. Interpretation can be a frustrating and agonizing process if you rush to consider your "response" or your "approach" or the "hidden meaning" without devoting enough time to studying the work itself. Concentrate on understanding the work before you even begin to worry about your paper.

As your first step, *read the work slowly and carefully;* if it's at all possible, *read the work more than once.* Literature should not be read at the same speed as a newspaper or magazine, so read slowly, noticing all you can as you go along. It would be unrealistic to advise you to read every work more than once; although we would be wise to do so, few of us have the time or the self-discipline to read *Moby-Dick* three times before beginning to write a five-page essay about it. If you are writing about a fairly short work, however, you should certainly plan on reading it at least twice. It's also a good idea to read a poem aloud at least once to get a sense of its sound and rhythm.

Your first reading of a poem or story may be devoted to trying to get a general sense of what is going on or what is being said. During later readings, pause to *look up unfamiliar words in the dictionary* and to *jot down any ideas that occur to you.* Also look up any unfamiliar allusions to literature, history, geography, biography, or nature. You can't go beyond a superficial understanding of "Elegy for Jane" unless you know what a pickerel is or how a wren differs from a cardinal. Pay attention to connotations, the emotional associations of words and images, as well as to their literal meanings. Literature can't be read passively; by the time you finish reading, the margins should be filled with definitions, explanations, and observations.

As you read, *ask yourself questions about the work.* Make sure you have the facts of the work straight before you move on to drawing inferences; otherwise, you may go off in the wrong direction and get hopelessly lost. If you were analyzing a short poem, for example, basic questions such as these would help you get started:

- *Who is the speaker?* Don't be too quick to answer "the poet," even if the poem is written in the first person. Many poets use "I" in poems when it is clear that they are not the speakers. Robert Browning, for example, uses "I" in his dramatic monologues, but the speaker may be anyone from a duke to a monk to a madman. Search the poem for clues about the speaker's age, sex, and situation. In "Elegy for Jane," for example, what can we infer about the speaker? Can we be sure that it is Roethke?
- *Who is the speaker addressing?* In some poems, the speaker talks directly to the reader; in others, the speaker talks to some other person we can identify. Who does the speaker address in "Elegy for Jane"? Does he address the same person throughout the poem?
- *What is the setting?* Some poems have no definite setting, but in others we can gather some information about where the speaker is. Where is the speaker in "Elegy for Jane"?
- *What is happening or has happened?* Ask yourself whether the speaker is responding to or commenting on some event that is taking place or one that took place before the poem began. What is the dramatic context in "Elegy for Jane"? What has happened?
- *What is the poem's structure? Can the poem be divided into parts?* A poem will often seem more comprehensible if you can divide it into parts, analyze each part separately, and then see how the parts are related to each other. You don't need technical terms such as quatrain, terset, and couplet to talk intelligently about a poem's structure. You should pay attention to rhyme scheme and stanza breaks, of course, but you can also learn a great deal about a poem's structure by looking for shifts in the speaker's tone or mood, for changes in subject or in the kind of imagery used, and even for punctuation marks—sometimes the end of a

sentence indicates the end of a section. How could you divide "Elegy for Jane" into parts?

- *What kinds of images are used in the poem?* How does the poet appeal to all our senses—not just sight but hearing, taste, smell, and touch? What sorts of objects are mentioned in the poem? The more specific your observations about the imagery, the more insight you will gain into the poem. In the Introductory Essays, all three authors discuss nature imagery. Do they discuss specific images, or are they content with making general observations? Which discussion of nature imagery did you find most probing and enlightening?

- *What is the tone of the poem? Is it constant throughout?* In conversations, we pay close attention to tone of voice in order to understand what a statement really means. "You're a really clever person, aren't you?" can suggest either admiration or sarcastic disapproval, depending on the speaker's tone. In poetry, too, we have to pay close attention to tone in order to determine the speaker's attitude toward the subject, the people and situations mentioned, and the reader. Is the tone humorous or serious, happy or sad, passionate or detached, lofty or conversational? How would you describe the tone of "Elegy for Jane"? How is that tone conveyed?

Answering questions such as these is a necessary first step toward understanding a poem. What questions would you ask yourself when beginning an analysis of a play, a short story, or a novel?

After you have read the work carefully and answered some preliminary questions about it, you are ready to start thinking about what you will say in your paper. What sorts of assertions will you make about the work, and how will you support them?

## Making and Supporting Assertions About Literature

"But this is my interpretation of the poem; this is what the poem means *to me*. Why is your interpretation better than mine?" At some point, we have probably all been tempted to make such protests when a teacher or colleague criticizes our interpretation of a literary work. Clearly, interpretation is by nature controversial. Long after we have explored every planet in the solar system, we will still be arguing about *Hamlet* and *Paradise Lost*. It is certainly possible for two people to offer excellent but conflicting interpretations of the same work, and many questions about a literary work can never be answered with absolute certainty. Still, although more than one interpretation of a work is possible, not *every* interpretation of a work is possible. One of my students who wrote about "Elegy for Jane" thought that the horse had died, not the student; the text simply will not support this interpretation. Assertions made in interpretive essays, like the assertions made in argumentative essays, must be supported by evidence. The best source of such evidence is the work itself.

The sorts of assertions you make in an interpretive essay will of course depend on the work you are discussing, on your reading of it, and on the approach you decide to take. Still, we can establish some general guidelines.

*Your assertions should be both interesting and plausible*—not so obvious that your essay is dull and timid, but not so farfetched that your essay is unsubstantial and unbelievable. Try to tell your readers something they may not have discovered for themselves, but don't be so eager to startle and impress that you make assertions wildly. Interpretation requires some caution. You don't have to convince every reader that your interpretation is the best one possible, but your assertions should be reasonable enough so that all open-minded readers will at least consider them.

How do you make your assertions reasonable? One principle to keep in mind is that *your assertions should grow out of the text; they should not be imposed upon it.* Some writers are so determined to find "symbolic meanings" for every work that they seem to arrive at their interpretations before they have really studied the text. Their next step is to try to "fit" the text to their interpretation of it. It is often possible to impose any number of symbolic interpretations upon a work—poems seem especially vulnerable to this type of abuse. We could, I suppose, find some evidence to support the notions that "Elegy for Jane" is not really about the death of a student but about humanity's exploitation of nature or about the end of youth or about the failure of a literary effort. But why would we want to leap to such symbolic interpretations when the text offers no solid reason for doing so? Be a little cautious about looking for symbolic meanings. Before you assume that "X symbolizes Y," consider the possibility that X is simply X. If the poet seems to be talking about the death of a student, maybe he really is talking about the death of a student.

If they are to be truly reasonable and plausible, *your assertions should be supported by evidence from the text.* You may also decide to consult some outside sources, but it's a good idea to start by taking a very close look at the work itself. If you made an assertion about a friend—"Nancy is a warm, loving person"—you could support it by referring to specific things she has said or done. Take a similar approach in supporting the assertions you make about a literary work.

Consider, for example, the following passage from the first chapter of Jane Austen's novel *Emma*. Emma and her father, Mr. Woodhouse, are talking. Emma is twenty; we don't know her father's exact age, but we do know that he "had not married young." They are talking about Miss Taylor, who had been Emma's governess and companion for sixteen years and who had just that morning married Mr. Weston, who lives half a mile away at a house called Randalls. Since Emma's mother is dead and there are no other children living at home, Emma and Mr. Woodhouse will now be living alone with their servants. Mr. Woodhouse opens the conversation:

"Poor Miss Taylor!—I wish she were here again. What a pity it is that Mr. Weston ever thought of her."

"I cannot agree with you there, papa; you know I cannot. Mr. Weston is such a good-humored, pleasant, excellent man that he thoroughly deserves a good wife;—and you would not have had Miss Taylor live with us forever and bear all my odd humors, when she might have had a house of her own?"

"A house of her own! But where is the advantage of a house of her own? This is three times as large.—And you have never any odd humors, my dear."

"How often we shall be going to see them and they coming to see us!—We shall be always meeting! *We* must begin, we must go and pay our wedding-visit very soon."

"My dear, how am I to get so far? Randalls is such a distance. I could not walk half so far."

"No, papa, nobody thought of your walking. We must go in the carriage to be sure."

"The carriage! But James will not like to put the horses to for such a little way!—and where are the poor horses to be while we are paying our visit?"

"They are to be put into Mr. Weston's stable, papa. You know we have settled all that already. We talked it all over with Mr. Weston last night. And as for James, you may be very sure he will always like going to Randalls, because of his daughter's being housemaid there. I only doubt whether he will ever take us anywhere else. That was your doing, papa. You got Hannah that good place. Nobody thought of Hannah till you mentioned her— James is so obliged to you!"

"I am very glad I did think of her. It was very lucky, for I would not have had poor James think himself slighted upon any account; and I am sure she will make a very good servant; she is a civil, pretty-spoken girl; I have a great opinion of her. Whenever I see her, she always curtseys and asks me how I do, in a very pretty manner; and when you have had her here to do nee-dlework, I observe she always turns the lock of the door the right way and never bangs it. I am sure she will be an excellent servant; and it will be a great comfort to poor Miss Taylor to have somebody about her that she is used to see. Whenever James goes over to see his daughter, you know, she will be hearing of us. He will be able to tell her how we all are."

In order to make any definite assertions we would, of course, have to read the entire novel, but this conversation gives us enough evidence to make a number of tentative assertions about Mr. Woodhouse and Emma:

- Mr. Woodhouse is fussy and hard to please:
    —doesn't want to walk half a mile
    —objects to taking the horses to Randalls
    —remark about housemaid: notices such trivia as whether lock is turned the right way
- Mr. Woodhouse is rather stupid
    —has to have things explained repeatedly—details about visit were settled the night before
    —can't solve simplest problems for himself
    —conversation is about petty concerns—traveling half a mile, right way to turn locks
    —can't understand why Miss Taylor would want to marry, have her own house
- Emma is patient and loving to her father
    —has explained plan about carriage more than once
    —puts up with her father's silliness—doesn't lose temper
    —tries to cheer him up by distracting him from his worries, reminding him of good deed he did for Hannah

We could also make a tentative prediction based on this conversation: if Emma is an intelligent young woman, living alone with her father is going to be difficult for her. All the previous statements can be supported by solid literary evidence, by specific references to the text. They are thus legitimate interpretation. Again, more than one interpretation is possible. For example, instead of stressing Mr. Woodhouse's fussiness, we could stress his concern for others:

- affectionate toward Emma—denies she has any "odd humors"
- sympathy (although misplaced) for "poor Miss Taylor"
- concern for James, even horses
- found a good job for Hannah

Not *all* interpretations are possible, however; we couldn't find any support in this passage for the assertions that Mr. Woodhouse is a brilliant man or a witty conversationalist.

It's also important to be cautious about going very far beyond the text. Sometimes, we assume that characters will respond to situations in the same way we would and are tempted to impose our personalities and emotions on them. Reading this passage, we might think, "If I had a father like that, he would drive me crazy. Emma must hate her father." This seems a reasonable assumption, but there's nothing in the text to support it. In fact, as we find out as we read the novel, Emma loves her father very much and is always kind, patient, and tolerant with him. We would also be going too far beyond the text if we read this passage and concluded that Emma is always a kind, patient, and tolerant person; as the novel reveals, she always treats her father well but is often unkind, impatient, and intolerant with other people.

Of course, you should never do in your papers what we have just done here—make assertions about a text after reading only part of it. You can't avoid drawing some tentative conclusions as you read, but try to keep your mind open to new evidence, and be willing to change your conclusions if necessary. When you are writing your essay, keep the whole text in mind and consider any evidence that conflicts with your assertions; if you can, refute this evidence in your paper.

## Writing Your Essay

When you begin to write your interpretive essay, you may decide to use one of the patterns of organization discussed earlier in this book. For example, you may want to compare and contrast two types of imagery, explore the causes of a change in a character, or argue that a seemingly minor incident is in fact crucially important to understanding a work. It is therefore difficult to generalize about the form or organization of an interpretive essay, but we can set down a few general principles.

In an interpretive essay, as in any other type of essay, it is essential to *narrow your topic*. It may seem that if your assignment tells you to write a five-page paper about a fourteen-line poem, your topic has already been narrowed more than enough. Still, you will need to find a focus for your essay, a central idea that you can express in your thesis statement. You may decide, for example, to write about just one character; but will you need to narrow your topic further? An essay entitled "Emma's Personality" would almost certainly be too general to be interesting; an essay entitled "Emma's Relationship with her Father" would be more manageable. If you can't think of a focus for your essay, look back to the questions you asked as you were reading the work: Could you focus on the speaker, on the person the speaker is addressing, on imagery or tone? If you are writing about a longer work, consider taking one short section—a scene, a conversation, a descriptive passage—and showing how it relates to the whole.

It is usually wise to *organize your paragraphs around ideas, not around incidents*. If you are explicating a short poem, you may want to comment on it line by line. In most cases, however, organizing your essay around a work's plot makes it far too easy for you to lapse into summary. Draw up an outline of some sort before you begin to write. Does each topic sentence express an idea, or does it simply identify a stage in the action? Are your paragraphs arranged in a logical order—comparison and contrast, cause to effect, least important to most important point—or do they follow the sequence of events in the plot? If it looks like you may end up rehashing the plot rather than offering an interpretation of the work, consider revising your outline.

Many students, when they reach the last paragraph of an interpretive essay, offer some sort of evaluation of the work they are discussing. Sometimes a closing comment on the quality of the work is appropriate, but generally it is better to *resist the temptation to shift from interpretation to evaluation.* If your essay really did lead you to a new discovery about a specific excellence or weakness in a work, fine. But avoid ending with general praise that is not really related to or supported by the issues you have discussed in your paper: "Harriet is only one of the many characters who make *Emma* such a complex and exciting novel, undoubtedly one of Austen's best. Austen is a genius at creating memorable characters, and her novels give us many valuable insights into what life was really like in the England of her time." Such a conclusion will make your readers suspect that you simply ran out of ideas and were desperate for a way to end your paper.

Your day-to-day life has already done a good job of preparing you for the task of literary interpretation. You already have years of practice in listening to conversations and drawing conclusions about the speakers, in trying to understand situations, in paying attention to the way people use language. Your own experience will guide your interpretation of literature. And you may well find that the practice and discipline you gain from interpreting literature will make you a more careful and perceptive observer of people and events in your day-to-day life.

## APPLICATION

**A.** Following is Shakespeare's twenty-ninth sonnet. Read it carefully several times and then answer the questions that follow. You may find it helpful to work in a group with several other students.

### Sonnet 29

*When in disgrace with Fortune and men's eyes,*
*I all alone beweep my outcast state,*
*And trouble deaf heaven with my bootless cries,*
*And look upon myself and curse my fate,*
*Wishing me like to one more rich in hope,*    5
*Featur'd like him, like him with friends possess'd,*
*Desiring this man's art, and that man's scope,*
*With what I most enjoy contented least;*
*Yet in these thoughts myself almost despising,*
*Haply I think on thee, and then my state,*    10

*Like to the lark at break of dawn arising*
*From sullen earth, sings hymns at heaven's gate.*
 *For thy sweet love remembered such wealth brings*
 *That then I scorn to change my state with kings.*

1. Does the sonnet contain any unfamiliar words or any familiar words that seem to be used in unfamiliar ways? If so, look them up in the dictionary and explain how they are used in this poem. You might find it helpful to go to the library and consult the *Oxford English Dictionary*, which will tell you what the words meant in Shakespeare's time, as well as what they mean today.
2. Write a short summary of the poem. Limit yourself to two or three sentences; concentrate on paraphrasing the ideas the speaker is expressing.
3. Who is the speaker? Write a brief description of the speaker and make it as detailed as possible, supporting all your assertions with specific evidence from the poem.
4. Who is the speaker addressing? Again, write a brief description and make it as detailed as possible.
5. Does the poem have a definite setting?
6. What is the poem's structure? Can the poem be divided into parts?
7. List the images used in the poem and comment briefly, in writing, on their significance.
8. Write a brief description of the poem's tone. Is the tone consistent throughout?
9. What is the poem's subject? Does the poem seem to be making a point, conveying feelings, or doing both things? Express your ideas in a few sentences.
10. If you were going to write an interpretive essay about this poem, what might your topic be?

**B.** Following are another Shakespearean sonnet and a short essay a student wrote about it. Read the sonnet and the paper, and then answer the questions that follow.

### Sonnet 73

*That time of year thou mayst in me behold,*
*When yellow leaves, or none, or few, do hang*
*Upon those boughs which shake against the cold,*
*Bare ruined choirs, where late the sweet birds sang.*
*In me thou see'st the twilight of such day,*     5
*As after sunset fadeth in the west,*
*Which by and by black night doth take away,*

*Death's second self, that seals up all in rest.*
*In me thou see'st the glowing of such fire,*
*That on the ashes of his youth doth lie,* 10
*As the deathbed, whereon it must expire,*
*Consumed with that which it was nourished by.*
  *This thou perceiv'st, which makes thy love more strong.*
  *To love that well, which thou must leave ere long.*

### Student Essay

Death has always been one of man's greatest phobias. His mortality expands his vulnerability, and it causes him to become sensitive to issues he would otherwise never see. Shakespeare's seventy-third sonnet expresses how the fear of death initiates man's appreciation for the things he loves.

Man goes through his youth and adolescence being ignorant of his own mortality. He is carefree about his life and is dominated by his conceit and self-concern. In middle age, man begins to think about death and mortality, but he can still find ways to avoid the issue. Old age finally confronts the issue, causing him to review his life and accomplishments.

When man finds himself in his "twilight" days, he suddenly looks out "after the sunset fadeth in the west" and wonders where all the beauty and time in his life went so quickly. All those days he wished would hurry past and cared nothing for can never be replaced; they will always contain and remind him of the opportunities he had—or could have had—and instill within him a sense of appreciation for them and life itself.

Shakespeare concludes his poem by expressing that man should appreciate life while he can, before he becomes old, being on the edge of mortality. "To love that well which thou must leave ere long"—to care for the small things in life before death removes them beyond your senses.

Man will never be able to overcome the reality of his own mortality. He can, however, save himself from being defeated by death. By appreciating the small things in his life and by absorbing the beauty surrounding him, he will fully experience the love of those things that he "must leave ere long."

1. Does this paper seem to be based on a careful reading of the poem? Has the author asked himself the sorts of questions you asked yourself about the twenty-ninth sonnet?
2. Does the author support all his assertions with specific references to the text? Could he find support for all his assertions if he looked harder?
3. The author occasionally quotes lines from the poem. Does he use these quotations well and interpret them carefully?

**C.**   Following is a short story by Katharine Brush. Read it carefully and answer the questions that follow.

### Birthday Party

They were a couple in their late thirties, and they looked unmistakably married. They sat on the banquette opposite us in a little narrow restaurant, having dinner. The man had a round, self-satisfied face, with glasses on it; the woman was fadingly pretty, in a big hat. There was nothing conspicuous about them, nothing particularly noticeable, until the end of the meal, when it suddenly became obvious that this was an Occasion—in fact, the husband's birthday, and the wife had planned a little surprise for him.

It arrived, in the form of a small but glossy birthday cake, with one pink candle burning in the center. The headwaiter brought it and placed it before the husband, and meanwhile the violin-and-piano orchestra played "Happy Birthday to You" and the wife beamed with shy pride over her little surprise, and such few people as there were in the restaurant tried to help out with a pattering of applause. It became clear at once that help was needed, because the husband was not pleased. Instead, he was hotly embarrassed, and indignant at his wife for embarrassing him.

You looked at him and you saw this and you thought, "Oh, now, don't *be* like that!" But he was like that, and as soon as the little cake had been deposited on the table, and the orchestra had finished the birthday piece, and the general attention had shifted from the man and the woman, I saw him say something to her under his breath—some punishing thing, quick and curt and unkind. I couldn't bear to look at the woman then, so I stared at my plate and waited for quite a long time. Not long enough, though. She was still crying when I finally glanced over there again. Crying quietly and heartbrokenly and hopelessly, all to herself, under the gay, big brim of her best hat.

1.  The narrator herself draws some conclusions about the couple she observes. She says that the couple "looked unmistakably married"; on what sort of evidence might she be basing this assertion? She can't overhear their conversation, so how does she know that the husband said "some punishing thing, quick and curt and unkind"?
2.  If you were asked to analyze this short story, what sorts of questions would you ask yourself about it? How would you adapt the questions in the first exercise to suit a short story?
3.  What sorts of assertions can you make about the narrator, the

husband, and the wife? What specific support can you find for
these assertions?

4.  If you wanted to write an interpretive essay about this story,
    what sort of approach might you take? What would your topic
    be? How might you organize your essay?

D.   Following is a poem by W. H. Auden. Read it carefully, asking
yourself the questions listed in the first exercise. If you were asked
to write an interpretive essay about this poem, how might you proceed? List some topics that might serve as a focus for your essay.
Pick the most promising topic and draw up a brief outline for an
essay. What pattern of organization would you use? What precau-
tions would you take to make sure that your essay doesn't summarize too much?

### The Unknown Citizen
### (To JS/07/M/ 378
### This Marble Monument
### Is Erected by the State)

*He was found by the Bureau of Statistics to be*
*One against whom there was no official complaint,*
*And all the reports on his conduct agree*
*That, in the modern sense of an old-fashioned word, he*
    *was a saint.*
*For in everything he did he served the Greater Community.*    5
*Except for the War till the day he retired*
*He worked in a factory and never got fired,*
*But satisfied his employers, Fudge Motors, Inc.*
*Yet he wasn't a scab or odd in his views,*
*For his Union reports that he paid his dues,*    10
*(Our report on his Union shows it was sound)*
*And our Social Psychology workers found*
*That he was popular with his mates and liked a drink.*
*The Press are convinced that he bought a paper every day*
*And that his reactions to advertisements were normal in*
    *every way.*    15
*Policies taken out in his name prove that he was fully in-*
    *sured,*
*And his Health-card shows that he was once in hospital*
    *but left it cured.*
*Both Producers Research and High-Grade Living declare*
*He was fully sensible to the advantages of the Installment*
    *Plan*
*And had everything necessary to the Modern Man,*    20
*A phonograph, a radio, a car and a frigidaire.*

*Our researchers into Public Opinion are content*
*That he held the proper opinions for the time of year;*
*When there was peace, he was for peace; when there was*
*    war, he went.*
*He was married and added five children to the population,*        25
*Which our Eugenist says was the right number for a parent*
*    of his generation,*
*And our teachers report that he never interfered with their*
*    education.*
*Was he free? Was he happy? The question is absurd.*
*Had anything been wrong, we should certainly have heard.*

**E.**  Following are a short poem by Robert Frost and two versions of a
student essay about it. Analyze the poem carefully, compare the two
versions of the essay, and then answer the questions that follow.

### Spring Pools

*These pools that, though in forests, still reflect*
*The total sky almost without defect,*
*And like the flowers beside them, chill and shiver,*
*Will like the flowers beside them soon be gone,*
*And yet not out by any brook or river,*
*But up by roots to bring dark foliage on.*

*The trees that have it in their pent-up buds*
*To darken nature and be summer woods—*
*Let them think twice before they use their powers*
*To blot out and drink up and sweep away*
*These flowery waters and these watery flowers*
*From snow that melted only yesterday.*

### *Original*

Robert Frost uses the changes in Nature's seasons to show the
changes from a youth to an adult in his poem "Spring Pools." The
setting is the woods, making the changes from winter to spring.

The poem is divided into two paragraphs, each broken down
into a couplet and a quatrain. The couplet in the first paragraph
speaks of small puddles or pools that reflect the clear blue sky—a
symbol of perfection. Even though the puddles are surrounded by
trees, the sky still peeks through. This represents someone in his
youth, perhaps a baby. It is someone who hasn't fully experienced
the outside world, and who is surrounded by others who aren't as
perfect as he seems to be.

The first quatrain says the beauty of the spring flowers will
soon be gone, as will the pools. The roots of the trees will soak up

the water in order to produce leaves and blossoms. The pools are,
in a sense, dying. They will no longer be there. The perfection
they possessed will be gone. These words show the youth getting
older and experiencing things in life. The perfection he seemed to
have is slowly dying like the flowers and the pools. This person is
soaking up knowledge and finding out more about living every
day. To put it simply, he is maturing. In order for this person to
mature, he has to leave behind the things that made him seem so
perfect and beautiful while he was a small child.

The second paragraph begins by stating that the buds on the
trees are ready to bloom. They're tired of waiting. The trees will
darken the woods by keeping all sunlight out with their splendid
leaves and blossoms. This is a sign of spring, or rebirth, as some
think of spring. This image relates to the youth getting older, exploring adulthood. He's ready to explore, and he will not let anyone interfere with his life. In a way, he will be reborn because it
will seem like a whole new life for him. His view of life, however,
will get darker as he discovers more about the negative things in
the world.

As shown in the quatrain, the speaker is telling the trees not
to hurry. They want to bloom again before their time is ready.
They shouldn't drink all the water before the spring is actually
here. The puddles are from melted snow; winter has just ended.
The speaker is telling the youth not to rush into things; he should
enjoy his life while he is still young. The speaker is telling this
person there is plenty of time before he has to do the things
adults do. He's telling him not to forget the past, and to take
things slow because he is just beginning.

The images in "Spring Pools" are very vivid. Robert Frost does
a good job of making his point clear. It is very interesting how the
changing of seasons can reflect the changes in a person. A person
is a part of Nature, so it is very fitting.

### Revision

Robert Frost paints a vivid picture of what actually happens
during the time of winter changing to spring in his poem "Spring
Pools." The poem has a feeling of sadness that we don't usually
feel while thinking of spring. To most people, springtime means
beautiful flowers, blooming trees, and new life beginning. The
images Frost uses, however, make us stop and think about what
is actually happening. Something has to die to give another life.

The first stanza establishes the poem's setting. The first two
lines speak of spring pools that form from the melted snows of
winter. We know that it is still very early in the spring, for although the pools are in a forest, the sky still shows through. This
shows us that even though there are many trees, which would

usually be reflected in the water, they don't have any leaves on them yet. They still have bare branches from the winter. The pools are surrounded by flowers that thrive on the water in the pools and on the sunlight that still shines freely through the bare branches.

Frost has described a lovely natural scene, but he tells us that all this beauty will "soon be gone." The roots from the surrounding trees will soon soak up the water in the pools, so the pools are, in a sense, dying: they will have to disappear so that the trees may blossom and get many leaves. The flowers will also die when the trees soak up the pools that support them and block out the sunlight they need. The words "chill" and "shiver" suggest not only the time of year but also the coming deaths of both the pools and the flowers.

In the second stanza, the speaker shifts his attention from the pools and the flowers to the trees. The buds on the trees are ready to bloom; they're tired of waiting. We usually think of blossoming trees as a sign of rebirth, but Frost reminds us that this rebirth will require the deaths of the pools and the flowers. He says the trees will "darken nature," making them sound threatening and destructive. The trees will have splendid leaves and blossoms, but their beauty will destroy other beautiful parts of nature.

The speaker tells the trees not to hurry and implies a warning that their time, too, is limited. The snow melted "only yesterday," and yet the trees are already eager to "blot out and drink up and sweep away" both the pools and the flowers. If spring is a sign of rebirth, then the flowers and the pools mentioned in the first stanza have also just been reborn, and yet the trees are already starting to destroy them. The trees are so eager to be reborn themselves that they aren't giving the pools and the flowers a chance to live. By mentioning "snow" in the last line, Frost reminds the trees that before very long winter will come again, the trees will lose their leaves, the snows will melt, and the whole cycle will begin again.

The images in "Spring Pools" are vivid and make Robert Frost's point clear. The minute the snows melt, the trees are ready to begin the next cycle in the changing seasons. They are going to "kill" the pools and the flowers in order to come alive themselves. Spring may mean rebirth, but it also means death. Nature feeds on itself, and one beautiful thing must die so that another may live.

## DISCUSSION QUESTIONS

1.  What are the major differences between the original and the revision? Why do you think the author and her professor were dissatisfied with the original version of the essay?

2. In the revision, the author organizes her essay around the structure of the poem—the first two paragraphs are about the first stanza, and the next two paragraphs are about the second stanza. Is this a good method of organization, or could the author have found a better one? Does the essay contain too much summary?
3. Compare the concluding paragraphs of the two versions of the essay. How are they different? Why is the revision's conclusion stronger?
4. How could the author further improve the revision?

# PART 3

# SOME PRINCIPLES OF STYLE

**S** tyle can be defined as the way we choose to express our ideas. It would be a mistake, however, to think of *style* and *ideas* as completely separate, to imagine that we can make a neat and absolute division between form and content. Good style is dependent upon solid content, and to a large extent, upon correct grammar as well. A vague idea cannot be expressed precisely, and grammatical errors seldom make for good style.

What *is* good style? We have rules to tell us whether a word is correctly spelled or whether a sentence is grammatically complete, but it is more difficult to agree about what rules should govern style. Still, if we were all asked to list the characteristics of good style, most of us would probably agree on at least a few fundamental points. We don't like writing that wastes our time with unnecessary words, so we appreciate an economical style. We want to understand exactly what is being said, so we like style to be precise. We like writers to keep us in mind as they write, to write in a style that is appropriate to their readers. And a fresh and varied style makes for more interesting reading. Some of us might demand much more, but almost all of us would demand at least this much.

We can say, then, that economy, precision, appropriateness, freshness, and variety are among the characteristics of good style. These characteristics frequently overlap; in order to be truly fresh, for example, writing must be precise. Still, we can attempt to study these characteristics of good style separately, always remembering that they are in fact related to and dependent upon each other.

# 12.
# Economy, Precision, and Appropriateness

## ECONOMY

Economy is perhaps the most important characteristic of good writing style. Needless words rob your style of emphasis and clarity, annoying your readers by wasting their time and distracting them from your real purpose; and since many wordy expressions are widely used, they can also make your style trite. Wordiness should not, however, be confused with length: your goal is not to make your sentences as short as possible. For example, you might describe a dress as "pale blue in color." Since *blue* implies color, the phrase *in color* is unnecessary and should be cut; the word *pale,* on the other hand, adds information and therefore should be kept.

When you try to make your style more economical, ask yourself whether a phrase or sentence can be shortened or omitted without detracting from your meaning. Most of the changes you make will not be dramatic, but there is no reason to keep even one word if it does not add any detail or interest. If you can make a number of small cuts, the pace and emphasis of your style may improve considerably.

It also helps to become familiar with some of the more common wordy expressions and constructions. In the groups of sentences below, the wordy sentences on the left appeared in student papers; the sentences on the right have been revised for conciseness. Study each group of sentences, identify the common problem that makes the unrevised sentences wordy, and then write a brief general description of the problem. Watch your own style for these wordy expressions and constructions, and eliminate them whenever you can.

GROUP A

Housman states the fact that the athlete is a hero in his town.

Housman states that the athlete is a hero in his town.

In spite of the fact that Emma has many faults, the reader finds her irresistible.

Although Emma has many faults, the reader finds her irresistible.

Then I walked to the other side of the hole to make sure of the fact that the putt would break one inch to the right.

Then I walked to the other side of the hole to make sure the putt would break one inch to the right.

He claimed that he could not hire me due to the fact that I had never been a waitress before.

He claimed he could not hire me because I had never been a waitress before.

## WORDY EXPRESSION OR CONSTRUCTION:

### GROUP B

At the present time, we are both freshmen.

Now we are both freshmen.

I felt depressed at that point in time.

I felt depressed then.

I told him to call me again at a later point in time.

I told him to call me again later.

I had not expected to receive a letter at such an early point in time.

I had not expected to receive a letter so early.

## WORDY EXPRESSION OR CONSTRUCTION:

### GROUP C

This saying could be used in reference to the way the woman judged people.

This saying could refer to the way the woman judged people.

In the poem there is a contrast between the power of a conceited king and the power of death.

The poem contrasts the power of a conceited king and the power of death.

Jerome mentions that there is a lack of flair in Sandburg's passage.

Jerome mentions that Sandburg's passage lacks flair.

After reading Mencken, Wright feels a hunger for

After reading Mencken, Wright hungers for more

more books and becomes affected in viewing the world differently.

books and views the world differently.

*WORDY EXPRESSION OR CONSTRUCTION:*

## GROUP D

Austen has created a character who is arrogant.

Austen has created an arrogant character.

The ride home was a peaceful one.

The ride home was peaceful.

The question is an intriguing one.

The question is intriguing.

She entered the room in an unobtrusive manner.

She entered the room unobtrusively.

In a scornful manner, Pope dismisses his critics.

Scornfully, Pope dismisses his critics.

Drug abuse is a problem which is serious.

Drug abuse is a serious problem.

*WORDY EXPRESSION OR CONSTRUCTION:*

## GROUP E

The reason why I decided to major in biology is because I want to be a doctor.

I decided to major in biology because I want to be a doctor.

The characters in the story are not typical characters.

The characters in the story are not typical.

The presence of love is always present.

Love is always present.

He had a clear understanding of the direction of the economy and where it was headed.

He had a clear understanding of the direction of the economy.

*WORDY EXPRESSION OR CONSTRUCTION:*

## GROUP F

I stayed at the university for a week. During this time I practiced with the wrestling team.

I stayed at the university for a week and practiced with the wrestling team.

| | |
|---|---|
| I started to study my putt. What I could see was that the ball was going to curve to the right. | I started to study my putt and could see that the ball was going to curve to the right. |
| This statement is delivered with great force. It is said by his father. | His father delivers this statement with great force. |
| They all said they prefer small colleges. However, they couldn't explain why they felt this preference. | They all said they preferred small colleges, but they couldn't explain why. |

*WORDY EXPRESSION OR CONSTRUCTION:*

GROUP G

| | |
|---|---|
| The size of classes at Edson College is smaller than at State University. | Classes are smaller at Edson College than at State University. |
| We must be aware of the discrimination that is occurring on campus. | We must be aware of the discrimination on campus. |
| Cheating is a common phenomenon that is present on most campuses today. | Cheating is common on most campuses today. |
| Conrad was born in the country of Poland. | Conrad was born in Poland. |
| I first met Mr. Dixon in the month of August. | I first met Mr. Dixon in August. |

*WORDY EXPRESSION OR CONSTRUCTION:*

## APPLICATION

**A.** Improve these sentences—most of which are taken from student papers—by eliminating wordy expressions and constructions.

1. In this final statement, a great amount of passion is shown.
2. At the present time, a student may drop out of school at the age of sixteen years old.
3. Inflation is one of the major problems that exist in the country today.

4. He is a man who is not afraid of criticism.
5. Few people are aware of the fact that alcoholism can be just as dangerous as drug abuse.
6. Richard is physically deformed. His deformity makes it hard for him to win Lady Anne's love.
7. We soon see that there is a disagreement between the two authors about this issue.
8. A widespread consensus of opinion that prevails among a majority of individuals is that interpersonal communication is an important aspect of relationships among intimate acquaintances.
9. In today's modern world, society's social conventions are very powerful.
10. The reason for young people being unstable about making a decision is because they are not firm in their beliefs or values.
11. In *Joseph Andrews,* the narrator interrupts continuously and repeatedly throughout the entire novel.
12. Adolescents who want to rebel will often read pornographical material because of the shocking effect they hope it will have on their parents.
13. In the play *Hamlet,* Shakespeare explores many problems that are perplexing.
14. The idea that professional people, sociologists in particular, implement the use of doubletalk is mentioned constantly as the overriding theme in Cowley's essay.
15. When first entering into the college situation, I experienced a degree of apprehension. The reason for the apprehension was my uncertainty as to whether or not I was sufficiently familiarized with the compositional skills and abilities typically required of students in institutions of higher learning.

**B.** The following contains over 250 words. Without changing the meaning, replace all wordy constructions and expressions with concise ones. You should be able to eliminate at least half the words in the paragraph fairly easily; if you are very economical, you can express all the ideas in the paragraph in under 100 words.

In my opinion, I think it would be a good idea if people who are guilty of committing acts of vandalism against property were given harsh punishments for their actions. In the last few months since April, a number of various buildings that are located on this campus have been defaced by the destructive actions of people who are vandals. Graffiti that has been written on the walls of many classrooms and hallways has had the effect of spoiling their physical appearance, the windows in dormitory buildings have been broken when rocks and beer bottles have been thrown

through them, and in the month of June a vase that was valuable
and was being displayed at the art center was stolen and then
was also smashed. In spite of the fact that the people in the administration have learned the identities of many of the guilty cul-
prits, the administration has not done a great deal to put a stop
to this destructive activity. Some of the people who are known to
be vandals have not been punished at all in any way; others have
merely been punished by having to pay an amount of money as a
fine. I myself am in opposition to penalties that are so lenient in
nature and am of the opinion that people who are guilty of committing acts of destructive vandalism should be suspended temporarily from the college for a period of time or should be expelled
permanently from the college and not be allowed to return to it.

## PRECISION

"Use the right word, not its second cousin," Mark Twain declares in an
essay criticizing an author he considers sloppy and careless. Finding
the right word—the one that will most precisely express your meaning—requires knowledge, sensitivity, diligence, and honesty. Sometimes writers miss the right word simply because they lack information: they confuse *perspective* with *prospective* or *proceed* with *precede*.
English is so full of words with similar or identical sounds but very different meanings that it is easy to make such mistakes. Some of these
mistakes are amusing for the reader but embarrassing for the writer: a
student analyzing "The Secret Sharer" wrote that "The captain of the
*Sephora* says goodbye with much adieu." To avoid such errors, consult
a dictionary whenever you're uncertain of a word's precise meaning.
You may also find it helpful to use a guide such as Adrian Room's *Dictionary of Confusibles*.

Although a dictionary should keep you from choosing a disastrously
wrong word, it may not always guide you to the precisely right one.
Should you describe an overweight person as *obese* or *portly*? Should
you describe a person who works with you as a *colleague*, a *co-worker*,
or a *cohort*? A dictionary will give you some guidance in distinguishing
among such words, but it cannot list all the emotional associations that
a word has. You will have to become sensitive to what words suggest,
as well as to what they say outright, and to pick the words that will
best contribute to the tone you want to maintain in your essay.

Imprecise words may also reflect imprecise ideas. A writer who is
dissatisfied with a course but isn't sure exactly why may be tempted to
write, "I was uncomfortable with various negative aspects of the
course." Vague, ready-made phrases such as "various negative aspects" are always available to us, and it is often easier to fall back on
such phrases than it is to define our ideas precisely and to search for

the words that will express them well. Some writers may use imprecise language to slant the facts, to soften unpleasant or unwelcome facts, or to disguise the fact that they don't know what they are talking about. Such uses of language are dishonest as well as imprecise: writers may hide behind imprecise language, hoping that readers who might object to specific statements will be fooled by cloudy, general ones they can't fully understand. Writers may also use imprecise language in an attempt to be impressive: a politician who says, "I will give due consideration to all relevant factors before rendering a decision" may, at first, seem more statesmanlike than one who says, "I have to figure out how much this will cost before I decide whether or not to vote for it." Intelligent readers, however, will recognize vagueness for what it is—an indication that the writer either does not understand an idea, has not taken the trouble to be clear, or does not have the courage to say something explicitly. If you think your ideas are worth defending, you will want to take the trouble to find the right words, the words that will express your meaning accurately, honestly, and precisely.

## GROUP A

We frequently confuse some words that have very different meanings. In the following pairs of sentences, decide which italicized words are being used incorrectly. Using a dictionary, explain how the italicized words differ in meaning.

1. His comments *inferred* that he thought I was lying.
   His comments *implied* that he thought I was lying.

   *DIFFERENCE BETWEEN* INFER *AND* IMPLY:

2. We went out to inspect the *site* for the new building.
   We went out to inspect the *cite* for the new building.

   *DIFFERENCE BETWEEN* SITE *AND* CITE:

3. His decision will have no *effect* on our plans.
   His decision will have no *affect* on our plans.

   *DIFFERENCE BETWEEN* EFFECT *AND* AFFECT:

4. They were eager to *except* my offer.
   They were eager to *accept* my offer.

   *DIFFERENCE BETWEEN* EXCEPT *AND* ACCEPT:

5. My sophomore year was more difficult *than* my freshman year.
   My sophomore year was more difficult *then* my freshman year.

   *DIFFERENCE BETWEEN* THEN *AND* THAN:

## GROUP B

We use a number of words so often that we seem to have forgotten their precise meanings. Most of the following sentences were taken from student papers. Look up the italicized words in a dictionary and decide in which sentences, if any, they are being used correctly. If none of the sentences is correct, how *should* the words be used? How could the sentences be made more precise?

1. I feel that one of the most important *aspects* that a private school can offer a student is excellent preparation for college work.

   When I tried to look at things from John's point of view, I saw a different *aspect* of the problem.

   I feel that one of television's most detrimental *aspects* is that it takes away the desire to learn to play an instrument.

   *COMMENTS ON* ASPECT:

2. Borg's playing style is rather *unique*.

   My prep school provided me with a truly *unique* education.

   Ever since I first met him, I have known that he was a *unique* individual.

   *COMMENTS ON* UNIQUE:

3. Financial aid was an important *factor* in my final decision.

   Although I am no longer as obsessed with grades as I used to be, I have to admit that they are still a *factor*.

   His change in attitude was a *factor* in his success.

   *COMMENTS ON* FACTOR:

4. Eveline is unhappy because her father is not *nice* to her.

   Everyone had a *nice* time at the dance.

   Writing well requires making *nice* distinctions among words.

   *COMMENTS ON* NICE:

5. We had to do a lot of advance preparations—packing, getting the car checked, making reservations, *etc.*

   In order to understand a poem, one has to know a lot about the poet: biography, time period, background, *etc.*

   Dairy products—milk, cheese, butter, *etc.*—are essential to a balanced diet.

   *COMMENTS ON* ETC.:

GROUP C

The italicized words in the following sentences have similar *denotations* but different *connotations*. Explain the differences between the italicized words in each set of sentences and then try to generalize about the distinction between denotation and connotation.

1. Sally is very *proud* of her father's accomplishments.
   Sally is very *arrogant* about her father's accomplishments.
2. After six weeks of dieting, Rick looks *slim*.
   After six weeks of dieting, Rick looks *thin*.
   After six weeks of dieting, Rick looks *skinny*.
3. Don is a *drunkard*.
   Don is an *alcoholic*.
   Don is a *problem drinker*.
4. The union leader was *firm* throughout the negotiations.
   The union leader was *stubborn* throughout the negotiations.
5. Elise *claimed* that she was innocent.
   Elise *said* that she was innocent.

What is the difference between *denotation* and *connotation*?

How is understanding both denotation and connotation essential to writing with precision?

## GROUP D

While writing with precision means making sure that individual words are used correctly and appropriately, it also means replacing vague phrases or sentences with more direct, informative ones. The sentences on the left were taken from student papers; the sentences on the right have been revised for precision. Try to identify the common problem that makes all the unrevised sentences imprecise.

| | |
|---|---|
| For the first time, she sees the unpleasantness of urban life. | For the first time, she sees the city's drunkards, prostitutes, and rats. |
| Richard doesn't realize the possible negative outcomes of his actions. | Richard doesn't realize that he may be whipped for playing with fire. |
| He suffers from an acute lack of proper nourishment. | He eats only two meals a day: a breakfast of mush and a supper of greens and lard. |
| The game was very exciting. | The two teams were within a few points of each other during the entire game, and the winning basket wasn't made until the last seconds of overtime. |
| The patient's clothing had an unpleasant smell. | The patient's clothing smelled of dried urine. |

What is the common problem that makes all the unrevised sentences imprecise?

How can writers avoid this problem?

## GROUP E

Writers sometimes use imprecise language intentionally. Most of the sentences on the left were taken from student papers; all of them contain euphemisms. Compare the sentences on the left with those on the right and work out a definition of *euphemism*.

| | |
|---|---|
| Near the end of the story, she tells her father that her physiological state has changed. | Near the end of the story, she tells her father that she has had her first menstrual period. |
| During my first quarter at college, I did not work up to my potential, and my grades were not as high as I had hoped. | During my first quarter at college, I cut classes continually, and I got two C's and a D. |
| Ultimately, this means an increase in financial resources dedicated to this end. | Ultimately, this will cost more. |
| We asked where the powder room was because the tennis match had made us perspire and we wanted to freshen up. | We asked where the bathroom was because the tennis match had made us sweat and we wanted to wash. |
| The mortician urged his clients to buy a deluxe slumber chamber for the departed. | The undertaker urged his customers to buy an expensive coffin for the corpse. |

What is a *euphemism*? When is a euphemism imprecise?
Why do you think writers are tempted to use euphemisms?
Do you think using euphemisms is ever justified?

## GROUP F

Politicians and other public figures are often accused of using a particular kind of euphemism, sometimes called *doublespeak*. Compare the sentences on the left with those on the right and see what conclusions you can draw about the nature of doublespeak.

| | |
|---|---|
| "I misspoke myself," said the senator. | "I lied," said the senator. |

The head of the agency said
that some of the operatives
had engaged in covert intelli-
gence-gathering activities.

The head of the agency said
that some of the agents had
spied.

A member of the group said
they had utilized explosive devices in an attempt to create a
climate conducive to dialogue.

A member of the group said
they had set off bombs in an
attempt to force people to
grant their demands.

The general said that the initiation of a strategic with-
drawal had followed a reas-
sessment of the situation.

The general said that he had
decided to retreat after realizing that his soldiers were
losing the battle.

While freely conceding that
the Soviet regime exhibits certain features which the hu-
manitarian may be inclined to
deplore, we must, I think,
agree that a certain curtail-
ment of the right to political
opposition is an unavoidable
concommitant of transitional
periods, and that the rigors
which the Russian people
have been called upon to un-
dergo have been amply justified in the sphere of concrete
achievement.

I believe in killing off your opponents when you can get
good results by doing so.

—GEORGE ORWELL, "Politics
    and the English Language"

—GEORGE ORWELL, "Politics
    and the English Language"

What is *doublespeak?*
Why do you think people are tempted to use it?
Do you think using doublespeak is ever justified?

## APPLICATION

**A.**  Some of the words in the following sentences are used incorrectly
or imprecisely. Make any necessary changes, and be ready to defend
the changes you make. Use a dictionary to check on the precise meanings of words.

1. Many students find it hard to adopt to college.
2. The lecturer sighted a passage from Freud.

3. He suffered from the allusion that little green chipmunks were constantly pursing him.
4. The congresswoman's speech inferred that she would not run for reelection.
5. I have always tried to hold firmly to my principals.
6. The economy was the most important aspect of his campaign, but defense was also a factor.
7. The doctor pointed out that soybeans are a very healthy food.
8. They often helped me out by lending me money, etc.
9. The director of admissions is always happy to talk with per-spective students.
10. Extracurricular activities should compliment a college's academic program.

**B.**  The following paragraph gives an unflattering description of a person. Without changing the content of the paragraph, change its tone by replacing some of the words with ones that have similar denotations but different connotations.

In college, he had always been a bookworm and had picked up some bizarre notions. When I saw him again almost thirty years after graduation, I realized that he was as opinionated as ever. His prejudices had been frozen years before: he still held stubbornly to his religious dogmas, and his politics were as radical as ever. He was a domineering husband to his wife, a harsh disciplinarian to his children. Although he had become rich, he had never outgrown his stingy habits and was sloppily dressed in old slacks and a sweatshirt. His body was still as puny as it had always been, and he still had the same absentminded air that he had had in college.

**C.**  Some of the following sentences were taken from student papers. Evaluate them, decode them (you will have to use some ingenuity), and then revise them to make them more precise and straightforward.

1. When he heard about her decision, he reacted with violent activity.
2. My father's attempts to improve his financial status did not meet with success.
3. Some nonmilitary personnel were unfortunately among the casualties resulting from our attempts to provide adequate air support for our troops.
4. The senator's lecture was interesting and relevant.
5. Underprivileged senior citizens living in the inner city often encounter difficulty in attempting to meet their financial obligations.

6. The Lamaze instructor told the women that they could expect to experience some discomfort during labor and delivery.
7. His hair was a nice shade of brown.
8. The movie was very sexist and offensive.
9. The governor explained that recent events had necessitated some modifications in some of the planks in his election platform.
10. Having worked as a freelance writer for the past three years, I would like to return to an active, gregarious employment environment which would permit the utilization of my various skills in a secure working situation.

*—from a letter of application for a teaching position*

## APPROPRIATENESS

Truly flexible writers have mastered more than one sort of style so that they can communicate with more than one sort of reader. They might use one style when writing letters to close friends, another when writing a letter to the editor of a newspaper, and a third when writing a letter or memorandum to professional colleagues. Good writers are not being dishonest or artificial when they adapt their style to suit a particular audience; they are simply looking for the style that their readers will find clearest and easiest to understand.

You undoubtedly make some changes in your own style when you talk to various listeners. For example, if you were describing your duties as a student government representative, you would not use exactly the same language when talking to your roommate, to your seven-year-old cousin, and to your grandmother; for one thing, some listeners would need more background information and more explanation of terms than other listeners would. You might have some words that you use only when talking to members of your own racial, ethnic, or age group, or only when talking to people from your own area of the country. Even a college often develops its own special vocabulary, one that people from other colleges would not be able to understand. If I were talking to a friend at my college, I might say, "It was a busy weekend on campus. EPC had a three-hour meeting on Friday afternoon, three sections had parties on Saturday night, and on Sunday afternoon there was a pitstop on criteria for tenure." If I were talking to a friend who wasn't associated with the College of Wooster, I would have to explain that EPC is the Educational Policy Committee, that fraternities at Wooster are called sections, and that lectures or discussions held in a large sunken section of the student center are called pitstops; if I were talking to someone who was not connected with any college, I might also have to explain what tenure is.

When we aren't careful enough about deciding what sort of style is most appropriate for a particular audience, communication becomes difficult and misunderstandings are common. There is a story—probably, unfortunately, an untrue one—about a young English woman who came to live in the United States. Several months after her arrival, she went to a party where an elderly American woman asked her how she liked this country. The English woman replied, "Oh, I love it here—everyone's so friendly! My landlord knocks me up every morning, and at work my boss gives me a really good screw." The American woman fainted away before the puzzled younger woman could explain that in English slang *knocks me up* means "knocks on my door to wake me up" and *screw* means salary: and of course, the English woman had no idea of what these expressions mean in American slang. If you are not careful about suiting your language to your audience, the misunderstandings you create may not be so spectacular, but you will not be communicating as clearly and smoothly as you might be.

## Colloquial, Informal, and Formal Styles

As an experiment, the students in a freshman composition class were asked to write paragraphs complaining about the social life on campus. One-third of the class pretended they were writing letters to their best friends back home, one-third pretended they were describing the problem in a paper for their composition course, and one-third pretended they were writing letters to the college's Board of Trustees. Compare these three sample paragraphs and then answer the questions that follow.

A. After spending two quarters at this college, I've made a deci-sion about the social life here. I am disappointed by the oppor-tunities offered to students. The social activities on campus are few and often boring. If you don't belong to a fraternity or sorority and you don't like to dance or watch movies, there is really nothing left to do but to stay in your room and study. For the first time, I am finding that by the time Saturday night rolls around, I am actually finished with my work.

B. You wouldn't believe what the social life here is like. The most excitement we get here is when we get meatloaf for din-ner instead of spaghetti and meatballs. Every Saturday I look forward to that delicious meatloaf. Just makes my weekend. Weekends here are dead, boring, nothing. Everyone either studies or sleeps. The dudes are into themselves and their books, and the girls all think they're the hottest property on campus. The only way to survive around here is to road trip, so every chance I get I go to Ohio State where they really party.

C. As a student at this college, I am truly distressed by the poor quality of the social life on campus. Admittedly, the college does have a fine academic standing and compares favorably with other colleges in the area, and its facilities are excellent. However, there is more to experience than academics at any given college or university. If students are to be able to prepare themselves to enter society, they must be provided with programs and opportunities that will allow them to become truly well rounded, socially as well as academically. It is the consensus among the students that the college should try to improve the quality and variety of social activities on campus.

## QUESTIONS

1. How would you describe the style of paragraph A? List as many of its characteristics as you can. Consider types and lengths of sentences as well as vocabulary.
2. Do a similar analysis of paragraph B.
3. Do a similar analysis of paragraph C.
4. Which of these paragraphs seems to have been written for a letter to a friend? For a class paper? For a letter to the Board of Trustees? Do you agree that each paragraph is appropriate for its intended audience? Would you suggest any changes in any of the paragraphs?

## An Example of Technical Language

The members of a profession often have a special vocabulary that they use for communicating with each other. Carol White, a student at the University of Akron Law School, offers these examples of explaining a legal problem to two different readers. She made up a hypothetical case about a woman named Alice Tremble, who was struck and severely injured by a carelessly driven horse van. Because Tremble's injuries kept her from working for two months, she lost her job; she was therefore unable to keep up her mortgage payments, and the bank that gave her the mortgage is now threatening to foreclose.

There are some complications in the case. The van driver, Dudly Beat, is currently in prison on a drunk-driving charge. The Friendly Loan Agency has a judgment against Beat's van for a past debt. When Tremble's accident occurred, Beat had been driving his van to transport horses for the prosperous Shadowy Farm Inc.

Tremble wants to know whether she can sue either Beat or Shadowy Farm Inc. Here are two ways a lawyer might describe Tremble's case— first to another lawyer and then to Tremble herself.

### Interoffice Legal Memorandum

Tremble's recovery hinges on whether Shadowy Inc. is vicariously liable for Beat under the respondeat superior doctrine since Beat himself is likely to be judgment-proof. Shadowy will probably try to escape liability by claiming that Beat is an independent contractor rather than an employee. Even if Beat is deemed an independent contractor, he should fall within an exception to nonliability. The facts hint that Shadowy was negligent in its hiring of Beat even though Beat's DWI conviction is ex post facto. If we can hurdle the independent contractor obstacle and present the case to a jury, there is no doubt that Tremble will recover past and present pecuniary and nonpecuniary damage.

I recommend that we proceed by establishing a figure for which we would be willing to settle, then negotiate with Shadowy who should be quite willing to avoid a court action. We should take the case on a one-third contingency fee.

### Memorandum for Alice Tremble

Alice, in order to explain the legal concerns of your case, some background information is necessary. It is unlikely that you will be able to receive any money from Beat since he is currently not working and has legal judgments against him. Therefore, our concern is the possibility of recovering damages from Shadowy.

A small branch of tort law holds people liable for damages even though they did not cause any damages themselves. This is a doctrine of vicarious liability that is based upon the rationale that the party who can best suffer the loss should pay for it. Traditionally, vicarious liability arose under the respondeat superior doctrine, a doctrine holding that masters or employers are responsible for the conduct of their servants or employees. In this case, Shadowy is liable for Beat's conduct under the vicarious liability and respondeat superior doctrines providing that Beat is indeed an employee. Probably Shadowy will argue that Beat is an independent contractor rather than an employee, and thus they will attempt to escape liability. However, even if Beat is considered an independent contractor, he probably falls within an exception to the employer's nonliability for independent contractors. The particular exception concerns an employer's duty to hire people who will do their work safely and not endanger others. Should this case go to court, we would need to find evidence showing that Beat is an unreasonably careless driver and that Shadowy was aware of this when they hired him. If we can find such evidence, there is no legal argument a judge could raise to prevent this case from going to a jury, and a jury's sympathies would certainly be with you. The money award would include both out-of-pocket expenses—a pecuniary award—and intangibles—a nonpecuniary award—for your emotional and physical pain and suffering.

If you would like our office to proceed with your case, this is what we suggest. First, we need to establish your out-of-pocket expenses based on salary statements and any medical expenses such as prescriptions or office calls not covered by your health insurance company. Then we need to estimate future out-of-pocket expenses and intangible damages. Based on these figures, we would try to negotiate a settlement with Shadowy. If that fails, we would proceed to court.

Our offices would be willing to handle your case on a one-third contingency basis; that is, we would keep one-third of the settlement. If the case proceeds to court, however, you would have to pay filing fees and expert medical witness fees.

If further information would be helpful, feel free to contact us. Please advise us if you would like us to proceed with your case.

## QUESTIONS

1. What are some of the differences between the language used in the interoffice memorandum and the language used in the memorandum to Alice Tremble? List as many differences as you can.
2. Why do you suppose lawyers and other professional people use a special vocabulary when speaking or writing to each other? What advantages does such a vocabulary offer?
3. What are the disadvantages of the kind of language used in the interoffice memorandum? When would it be inappropriate to use such language?

## One Writer—Three Styles

C. S. Lewis (died 1963) was an unusually prolific British author who wrote on a variety of topics for a variety of audiences. His works include children's literature, science fiction, literary criticism, and theological books and essays. Here are brief passages from three of his works:

### Mere Christianity

I have been asked to tell you what Christians believe, and I am going to begin by telling you one thing that Christians do not need to believe. If you are Christian, you do not have to believe that all other religions are simply wrong all through. If you are an atheist, you do have to believe that the main point in all the religions of the whole world is simply one huge mistake. If you are a Christian, you are free to think that all these religions, even the queerest ones, contain at least some hint of the truth. When I was an atheist, I had to try to persuade myself that most of the human race have always been wrong about the question that mattered to them most; when I became a Christian, I was able to take a more liberal view. But, of course, being a Christian does mean thinking that where Christianity differs from other religions, Christianity is right and they are wrong. As in arithmetic —there is only one right answer to a sum, and all other answers are wrong; but some of the wrong answers are much nearer being right than others.

1. How would you describe Lewis's style in this passage? List as many of its characteristics as you can.
2. What sort of audience do you think Lewis had in mind when he wrote *Mere Christianity?* How is his style suited to that audience?

### The Abolition of Man

In order to understand fully what Man's power over Nature, and therefore the power of some men over other men, really means, we must picture the race extended in time from the date of its emergence to that of its extinction. Each generation exercises power over its successors: and each, in so far as it modifies the environment bequeathed to it and rebels against tradition, resists and limits the power of its predecessors. This modifies the picture which is sometimes painted of a progressive emancipation from tradition and a progressive control of natural processes resulting in a continual increase of human power. In reality, of course, if any one age really attains, by eugenics and scientific education, the power to make its descendents what it pleases, all men who live after it are the patients of that power. They are weaker, not stronger: for though we may have put wonderful machines in their hands, we have preordained how they are to use them.

1. How would you describe Lewis's style in this passage? List as many of its characteristics as you can. How is it different from his style in the passage from *Mere Christianity?*
2. What sort of audience do you think Lewis had in mind when he wrote *The Abolition of Man?* For example, does he seem to make any assumptions about the amount of education his readers have had? How is his style suited to his audience?

## The Allegory of Love

The characteristics of this sentiment, and its systematic coherence throughout the love poetry of the Troubadours as a whole, are so striking that they easily lead to a fatal misunderstanding. We are tempted to treat "courtly love" as a mere episode in literary history—an episode that we have finished with as we have finished with the peculiarities of Skaldic verse or Euphuistic prose. In fact, however, an unmistakable continuity connects the Provençal love song with the love poetry of the later Middle Ages, and thence, through Petrarch and many others, with that of the present day. If the thing at first escapes our notice, this is because we are so familiar with the erotic tradition of modern Europe that we mistake it for something natural and universal and therefore do not inquire into its origins.

1. How would you describe Lewis's style in this passage? List as many of its characteristics as you can. How is it different from his styles in the passages from *Mere Christianity* and *The Abolition of Man?*
2. What sort of audience do you think Lewis had in mind when he wrote *The Allegory of Love?* For example, does he seem to make any assumptions about the amount or kind of education his readers have had? How is his style suited to his audience?

## APPLICATION: WRITING FOR YOUR AUDIENCES

1. Describe possible audiences for the following writing assignments. What assumptions can you make about your audience in each case?
    a. an essay comparing and contrasting two movies, written for your composition class
    b. an essay arguing for changes in your college's freshman orientation program, written for your composition course
    c. a report arguing for changes in your college's freshman orientation program, written for the committee that planned last year's program
    d. a lab report for a biology class
    e. a summary of a book on the causes of inflation, written for an economics course
    f. an interpretation of a poem, written for an advanced poetry seminar; papers are read aloud in class
2. What sort of style would be most appropriate for each of the audiences you have identified in question 1?

3. In general, what considerations should guide you in deciding what sort of style is most appropriate for a particular audience?
4. If you do not have much information about your audience, or if your audience will include a wide variety of people—for example, if you are writing a letter or article for a newspaper—what sort of style should you adopt?

# 13.
# Freshness and Variety

## FRESHNESS: USING FIGURATIVE LANGUAGE

I have a friend who mixes up her figures of speech delightfully and quite unintentionally. "Oh, I don't care—it's six of one, a dozen of the other," she'll say, or "I'll just burn that bridge when I come to it." These scrambled clichés certainly do help to make her conversation fresh, sparkling, and even startling. In our writing, however, we have to be considerably more careful about the figures of speech we use and the contexts in which we use them. When used well, figures of speech can indeed make our writing styles fresher and more original; when used carelessly or inappropriately, they can make our styles trite and even ludicrous.

The exercises that follow give examples of similes and metaphors, the two figures of speech most often used in student writing. A *simile* makes an explicit comparison between two essentially different things, using *like* or *as*. For example, you might use similes to describe a country club you consider artificial: "The country club was like a theater: the members were like actors and actresses who had rehearsed their parts well, and the conversation was as proper and as predictable as the dialogue in a genteel but conventional comedy." A *metaphor* also compares two unlike things, but it does so without using *like* or *as*: "The country club was a theater." We often use metaphors without realizing it, for many are embedded in the language. "The salesman oozed apologies," "She has a fiery temper," "The runner flew past third base"—all these sentences contain metaphors. We sometimes think that only poets use similes and metaphors, but in fact we all use them every day. The trick is to use them well.

GROUP A
The following sentences were taken from student papers. Comment on the students' use of figurative language. What do their figures of

speech have in common? Do you think these students have used figures of speech well?

1. Ignoring the food on her plate, my sister concentrated on savoring and digesting my father's words.
2. The living room looked like a newspaper stand after it had been hit by a tornado. Old newspapers carpeted the floor. As I examined them more closely, I found that the more recent ones were nearest to the couch. But as I ventured from the couch, the past returned.
3. The washing machine shakes convulsively as it vomits the excess soap out of its mouth and onto the floor.
4. My grandmother's wake seemed unreal to me. They took her from the black station wagon and placed her on what would become her stage for three days. Every day the spectators came and went in silence.
5. The old woman's skin was like faded crepe paper—pale, fragile, and crisscrossed with a thousand tiny lines.

Do you find these figures of speech appropriate and effective? Why or why not? List any characteristics these figures of speech share.

GROUP B

The following sentences were taken from student papers. Comment on the students' use of figurative language. What is the common stylistic problem all these sentences share?

1. Hoping that the professor would not call on me, I sat in my seat, quiet as a mouse.
2. But, as experience has shown us, life is not a bowl of cherries.
3. His friends and relatives, not realizing that Richard was a budding genius, did not appreciate his first story.
4. Quick as a flash, the runner had stolen the base before I could stop him.
5. Wordsworth talks about our inability to commune with Mother Nature.

What stylistic problem do these sentences share? Why is it a problem; that is, how does it weaken these sentences?

GROUP C

The following sentences were taken from student papers. Comment on the students' use of figurative language. What stylistic problem do all these sentences share?

1. (from a paper on *David Copperfield*): This short period of bliss became diseased with the infection of the Murdstones. The sickness spread and became so strong that it killed Mrs. Copperfield and corroded the umbilical cord that had tied David to his old way of life.
2. As tempers began to boil, the argument became heated.
3. Bewilderment, as to the handling of the situation, meanders into her conscious state.
4. Our eyes and ears are our primary passageways to the outer world. As our minds travel down these paths, our other senses provide us with bridges to other phenomena.
5. Jennifer was so sensitive that it was as though her pores had sprung a thousand feelers reaching out to grasp all the emotions in our home.

What stylistic problem do these sentences share? How are these figures of speech different from those in Group A?

GROUP D

The following sentences were taken from student papers. Comment on the students' use of figurative language. What stylistic problem do all these sentences share?

1. Our coach wasn't afraid to put his foot down when we players got out of hand.
2. Ed was always hungry for praise and drowning in self-pity.
3. She remained blind to the nagging voice of conscience.
4. Love is the key that helps us heal the wounds of failure and disappointment.
5. (from a paper on *Joseph Andrews*): For Wilson, a lone black cloud in search of the rain, the lines of failure converge to stand as obstacles as he stumbles through the confusions of his own character in urban life.

What stylistic problem do these sentences share? Is it related to the problems you identified in Groups B and C?

## APPLICATION

**A.** Many of the following sentences were taken from student papers. Do these sentences use figures of speech well? Why or why not? Identify the precise problems with the sentences you consider uneffective. If the sentences are worth saving, revise them.

1. I had a mountain of homework to do but plowed into it bravely.

2. The snow fell quickly, as though someone had overturned a giant box of soapflakes.
3. As the man leaped from the window, a hush fell over the crowd.
4. The first pricks of suspicion were like the first hints of pain in a tooth when the novocaine starts to wear off.
5. The first time I saw her, Jean looked pretty as a picture.
6. Athlete's foot can be a pain in the neck.
7. The hungry stadium crowd converged upon the refreshment stand like ants swarming over a lump of sugar.
8. As the salesman snaked toward me, I realized I had been caught in his web.

**B.** Either devise fresh figures of speech for these clichés or state them in plain English.

1. brave as a lion
2. cold as ice
3. as flat as a pancake
4. red as a rose
5. black as night
6. add insult to injury
7. strike while the iron is hot
8. sick as a dog

## VARIETY

Writing good sentences involves much more than making sure your subjects and predicates agree; sentences can be perfectly correct and still be perfectly flat, lifeless, and dull. Consider, for example, the sentences in the following paragraph. The student is describing the ways in which his life will differ from his parents' lives:

> My life will be very different from my parents' lives. My father is a musician. I have very little musical talent. I also don't have a desire to be a musician. I see nothing in my future in this field. My mother runs a small florist's shop. She never went to college. I am going to college now. My parents live in a small suburb of Detroit. They are forced to live there because of their occupations. I do not want to live near a big city. I intend to live in a small town in the country. I want my job to be more flexible. This is another difference between my life and my parents' lives.

Clearly, this paragraph is an extreme example: few college students have such a choppy style. It is also clear that the paragraph's problems are not simply stylistic. The paragraph has no real central idea beyond the vague assertion that "My life will be very different from my parents' lives." The author simply lists a number of facts, rather than attempting to develop his ideas or to show how one idea is related to another.

It may be, however, that these problems with the paragraph's content are related to the problems with its style. The author seems to see each sentence as an island. We can guess that he has given little thought to the connections—or lack of connections—among his sentences. His failure to think about how one sentence is related to another may help to explain his failure to develop his ideas; his failure to subordinate one sentence to another may help to explain why his paragraph seems to have no central point. If the author worked on improving the sentences in his paragraph, he would have to do more than add a series of *and*'s and *however*'s. To make the sentences in the paragraph truly interesting and intelligent, he would also have to think more carefully about the relationships among his ideas and about the way his ideas develop or do not develop.

Finding ways to vary your sentences, then, is anything but a mechanical process of simply stringing sentences together to make them longer. You will need to examine your sentences carefully and to make deliberate decisions about which sentences should be combined, which methods of combination will be best, and which conjunctions will be most appropriate and precise. All these decisions will affect meaning as well as style. You may well find that making your style smoother and more varied will give you new insights into ways of developing your ideas.

## Five Ways of Combining

**1. Using coordinate conjunctions** (*and, but, for, nor, or, so, yet*)

SAMPLE SENTENCES

| | |
|---|---|
| *Without Coordination* | *With Coordination* |
| *Pride and Prejudice* is Jane Austen's most popular novel. *Emma* is her best. | *Pride and Prejudice* is Jane Austen's most popular novel, but *Emma* is her best. |
| My brother decided to attend the University of Minnesota. He was offered a large scholarship. | My brother decided to attend the University of Minnesota, for he was offered a large scholarship. |
| Our car is small. Our car is economical. | Our car is small but economical. |

| | |
|---|---|
| Charles might go to New York this weekend. Alternatively, he might visit his mother in Cleveland this weekend. | Charles might go to New York or visit his mother in Cleveland this weekend. |
| The professor walked to the front of the class. He shuffled through his papers for a few moments. Then he began his lecture. | The professor walked to the front of the class, shuffled through his papers for a few moments, and then began his lecture. |

## QUESTIONS

1. List the various uses of coordination illustrated in the sample sentences. What sorts of sentence elements can coordinate conjunctions combine?
2. Why are the sentences that use coordination generally better than those that do not? List more than one reason.
3. Observe the punctuation in the sample sentences. When should you use a comma with a coordinate conjunction?
4. Compare these four sentences:
   a. My father loves to spend quiet evenings at home, and my mother loves to go to parties.
   b. My father loves to spend quiet evenings at home, but my mother loves to go to parties.
   c. My father loves to spend quiet evenings at home, so my mother loves to go to parties.
   d. My father loves to spend quiet evenings at home, for my mother loves to go to parties.

   How does the choice of a conjunction affect the sentence's meaning?

2. **Using subordinate conjunctions** (some of the most common subordinate conjunctions are *after, although, as, because, before, if, since, unless, until, when, where,* and *while*)

## SAMPLE SENTENCES

| | |
|---|---|
| *Without Subordination* Charles Dickens enjoys enduring popularity. His novels are full of fascinating characters. | *With Subordination* Charles Dickens enjoys enduring popularity because his novels are full of fascinating characters. |

Linda is an intelligent student. She has not done well in most of her courses.

Although Linda is an intelligent student, she has not done well in most of her courses.

Tiny crabs frantically scurried about. Sandpipers searched for their breakfasts.

While tiny crabs frantically scurried about, sandpipers searched for their breakfasts.

My brother decided to attend the University of Minnesota. He was offered a large scholarship.

My brother decided to attend the University of Minnesota because he was offered a large scholarship.

## QUESTIONS

1. Describe the uses of subordinate conjunctions illustrated in the sample sentences. What sorts of sentence elements do subordinate conjunctions combine?
2. Observe the punctuation in the sample sentences. When should you use a comma in a sentence containing a subordinate conjunction?
3. Compare these two versions of the second sample sentence:
   Although Linda is an intelligent student, she has not done well in most of her courses.
   Although Linda has not done well in most of her courses, she is an intelligent student.
   How do these two versions of the sentence differ in meaning?
4. Compare these two sentences:
   John is stubborn, so he will never admit he is wrong.
   Because John is stubborn, he will never admit he is wrong.
   Does the choice of a method of combining affect the sentence's meaning? Can you generalize about when it's most appropriate to use coordinate conjunctions and when it's most appropriate to use subordinate conjunctions?

3. **Using relative pronouns** (the most common relative pronouns are *that, which,* and *who*)

## SAMPLE SENTENCES

*Without Relative Pronouns*
Robert hates fish. He was unhappy when his aunt served flounder for Thanksgiving dinner.

*With Relative Pronouns*
Robert, who hates fish, was unhappy when his aunt served flounder for Thanksgiving dinner.

A young girl was injured in the accident. She was taken to the hospital for treatment.

A young girl who was injured in the accident was taken to the hospital for treatment.

*Lyrical Ballads* was published in 1798. It contained such poems as "Tintern Abbey" and "The Rime of the Ancient Mariner."

*Lyrical Ballads,* which was published in 1798, contained such poems as "Tintern Abbey" and "The Rime of the Ancient Mariner."

My father picked up the book and put it on the table. The book had been on the floor.

My father picked up the book that had been on the floor and put it on the table.

## QUESTIONS

1. Describe the uses of relative pronouns illustrated in the sample sentences.
2. Observe the punctuation in the sample sentences. When should you use commas to set off clauses beginning with relative pronouns?
3. Compare these three sentences:
    John is stubborn, so he will never admit he is wrong.
    Because he is stubborn, John will never admit he is wrong.
    John, who is stubborn, will never admit he is wrong.
   How does the choice of a method of combining affect the sentence's meaning?

4. **Using conjunctive adverbs and connective phrases** (some common conjunctive adverbs are *also, afterwards, consequently, furthermore, hence, however, moreover, nonetheless,* and *therefore;* some common connective phrases are *as a result, because of this, despite this, in addition,* and *on the other hand*)

## SAMPLE SENTENCES

*Without Conjunctive Adverbs and Connective Phrases*
My doctor told me I had to lose twenty pounds. I went on a strict diet.

*With Conjunctive Adverbs and Connective Phrases*
My doctor told me I had to lose twenty pounds; therefore, I went on a strict diet.

Julia likes her new job. She thinks she is underpaid.

Julia likes her new job; nevertheless, she thinks she is underpaid.

The politician promised to lower taxes. He promised to fight corruption.

The politician promised to lower taxes; in addition, he promised to fight corruption.

The judges did not accept Carol's essay. They urged her to revise it and resubmit it for the next issue.

The judges did not accept Carol's essay; they urged her to revise it and resubmit it for the next issue, however.

## QUESTIONS

1. Describe the uses of conjunctive adverbs and connective phrases illustrated in the sample sentences.
2. Observe the punctuation in the sample sentences. How is it different from that used when joining clauses with coordinate conjunctions?
3. Compare these three versions of the last sample sentence:
    The judges did not accept Carol's essay; however, they urged her to revise it and resubmit it for the next issue.
    The judges did not accept Carol's essay; they urged her to revise it, however, and to resubmit it for the next issue.
    The judges did not accept Carol's essay; they urged her to revise it and resubmit it for the next issue, however.
    All three versions of the sentence are correct.
    a. How do the punctuation patterns in these three versions differ?
    b. Is one version of the sentence stronger than the others? Explain.
4. Compare these four sentences:
    John is stubborn, so he will never admit he is wrong.
    Because he is stubborn, John will never admit he is wrong.
    John, who is stubborn, will never admit he is wrong.
    John is stubborn; therefore, he will never admit he is wrong.
    How does the choice of a method of combining affect the sentence's meaning? Are some versions of the sentence preferable to others? Why?

5. **Using reduction** (reducing a clause to a phrase)

## SAMPLE SENTENCES

*Without Reduction*
Matt looked through the window. He saw Louise burning the letters.

*With Reduction*
Looking through the window, Matt saw Louise burning the letters.

| | |
|---|---|
| I review my notes carefully every day. This helps me to prepare for exams. | Reviewing my notes carefully every day helps me to prepare for exams. |
| The soldier stumbled into camp. His uniform was torn. His boots were worn to shreds. | The soldier stumbled into camp, his uniform torn, his boots worn to shreds. |
| Pamela set high goals for herself. She refused to become discouraged. Both of these things helped Pamela to succeed. | Setting high goals for herself and refusing to become discouraged helped Pamela to succeed. |

## QUESTIONS

1. Describe the uses of reduction illustrated in the sample sentences. How is reduction different from the other methods of combining?
2. Observe the punctuation in the sample sentences. When are commas used? Why don't the second and fourth sentences contain commas?
3. Compare these five sentences:
   John is stubborn, so he will never admit he is wrong.
   Because he is stubborn, John will never admit he is wrong.
   John, who is stubborn, will never admit he is wrong.
   John is stubborn; therefore, he will never admit he is wrong.
   Being stubborn, John will never admit he is wrong.
   How does the choice of a method of combining affect the sentence's meaning? Are some versions of the sentence preferable to others? Why?

## Varying Sentences

**A.** The students in a freshman composition class were given a paragraph and asked to improve its style. Compare the original paragrah and the two student revisions that follow.

### *Original Paragraph:*

I did not like my summer job. I had to work long hours. I typed memos and letters most of the day. I tried to get to know the other workers in the office. They didn't respond to my attempts. My boss seemed to dislike me. He constantly criticized my work. I felt bored and pressured. I also felt alone.

### *Student A*

I did not like my summer job, for I had to work long hours, and I typed memos and letters most of the day. I tried to get to know the other workers in the office, but they didn't respond to my attempts. My boss seemed to dislike me, so he constantly criticized my work. I felt bored and pressured, and I also felt alone.

### Student B

I did not like my summer job. I had to work long hours, typing memos and letters most of the day. Although I tried to get to know the other workers in the office, they didn't respond to my attempts. My boss, who seemed to dislike me, constantly criticized my work. I felt bored, pressured, and alone.

## QUESTIONS

1. What was wrong with the original paragraph? List several problems.
2. What methods of combining does Student A use?
3. What methods of combining does Student B use?
4. Which revision of the paragraph do you prefer? Give several reasons for your choice.

**B.** Following are two versions of a paragraph about the Santa Ana, a powerful wind that passes through Los Angeles occasionally and seems to have strange effects on people's emotions. One paragraph is from Joan Didion's *Slouching Toward Bethlehem;* the other has been purposely mangled. Compare the two versions carefully.

### Version A

For a few days now we will see smoke back in the canyons, and hear sirens in the night. I have neither heard nor read that a Santa Ana is due, but I know it, and almost everyone I have seen today knows it too. We know it because we feel it. The baby frets. The maid sulks. I rekindle a waning argument with the telephone company, then cut my losses and lie down, given over to whatever it is in the air. To live with the Santa Ana is to accept, consciously or unconsciously, a deeply mechanistic view of human behavior.

### Version B

We will see smoke back in the canyons and hear sirens in the night for a few days now. Although I have not heard or read that a Santa Ana is due, I know it, and almost everyone I have met today knows it too because we feel it. The baby frets, the maid sulks, and I rekindle a waning argument with the telephone company. Then I cut my losses and lie down because I am given over to whatever it is in the air. Living with the Santa Ana is accepting a deeply mechanistic view of human nature consciously or unconsciously.

# QUESTIONS

1. Assuming that Joan Didion is a good writer, decide which version of the paragraph is the one she wrote. Why do you prefer this version? Give several reasons for your choice.

2. What methods of combining sentences are used in each version of the paragraph? Comment on the appropriateness and effectiveness of these methods.

3. Take a closer look at Didion's version of the paragraph. Besides using several methods of combining sentences, what has she done to make the paragraph varied and smooth?

4. Compare the second and third sentences in Didion's version with the second sentence in the other version. Why are Didion's sentences clearer and more emphatic? Make a similar comparison of the fourth, fifth, and sixth sentences in Didion's version and the third and fourth sentences in the other version.

# APPLICATION

**A.** Combine these groups of sentences, using any of the methods of combining discussed in this chapter.

1. Carl was smiling happily.
   Carl was humming his favorite song.
   Carl walked quickly to Shirley's house.

2. Political Science 34 required a great deal of studying.
   The lectures were sometimes difficult to understand.
   Political Science 34 was one of the best courses I have ever had.
   Political Science 34 helped me to understand modern political philosophy.

3. Irving really shocked me.
   He dropped out of school.
   He gave all his belongings to the Salvation Army.
   He went to Canada to search for the Northwest Passage.

4. Karen might want to become a doctor.
   She might want to become an actress instead.
   She plans to take Organic Chemistry this quarter.
   She plans to take Introduction to Theater this quarter.

5. I insisted that I did not want any birthday presents this year.
   My father gave me a bedspread.
   My mother gave me a watch.
   My brother gave me a puppy.
   The puppy promptly chewed up my bedspread.
   The puppy promptly swallowed my watch.
   The puppy promptly died of indigestion.

**B.** Combine these sentences in as many ways as you can. If one of your versions of a sentence seems better than the others, underline it and explain why you prefer it.

1. Charlotte entered the room.
   She gasped in surprise.
2. We thought the politician was sincere.
   We suspected that he would not be able to keep all his promises.
3. The beach was calm and quiet.
   I could not help feeling at ease.
4. Mary wrote letters of protest to her senator.
   This helped her feel involved in national politics.
5. (Pick two sentences from your last essay.)

**C.** The following sentences are based on passages written by well-known authors. The sentences have been broken up, however, and needless repetition has been introduced. Improve the sentences by using various methods of combining. Don't worry about whether or not you are duplicating the authors' original sentences exactly; just try to make the sentences as effective as possible.

1. Marriage has many pains. Celibacy has no pleasures.

   —SAMUEL JOHNSON (one sentence)

2. The fifth wave of demonstrators were carefully selected and screened. The first wave of demonstrators conducted themselves exactly as they had been trained to do.

   —MARTIN LUTHER KING, JR. (one sentence)

3. There was a vague manginess about his appearance. There was an unpleasant manginess about his appearance. He somehow seemed dirty. A close glance showed him as carefully shaven as an actor. A close glance showed him clad in immaculate linen.

   —H. L. MENCKEN (one sentence)

4. The girl had a certain nobleness of imagination. This nobleness of imagination rendered her a good many services. It played her a great many tricks.

   —HENRY JAMES (one sentence)

5. Most of us are not compelled to linger with the knowledge of our aloneness. It is a knowledge that can paralyze all action

in this world. There are, forever, swamps to be drained. There are cities to be created. There are mines to be exploited. There are children to be fed.

—JAMES BALDWIN (two sentences)

6. We caught two bass. We hauled them in briskly as though they were mackerel. We pulled them over the side of the boat in a businesslike manner without any landing net. We stunned them with a blow on the back of the head.

—E. B. WHITE (one sentence)

7. The plain was rich with crops. There were many orchards of fruit trees. Beyond the plain the mountains were brown and bare. There was fighting in the mountains. At night we could see the flashes from the artillery. In the dark it was like summer lightning. The nights were cool. There was not the feeling of a storm coming.

—ERNEST HEMINGWAY (three sentences)

8. My family had been prominent, well-to-do people in this Middle Western city for three generations. The Carraways were something of a clan. We have a tradition that we're descended from the Dukes of Buccleuch. The actual founder of the line was my grandfather's brother. He came here in fifty-one. He sent a substitute to the Civil War. He started the wholesale business. My father carries on this wholesale business today.

—F. SCOTT FITZGERALD (two sentences)

9. They hastened up. They perceived that his face wore an expression. This expression told that he had at last found the place for which he had struggled.

—STEPHEN CRANE (one sentence)

10. The bearers carried the coffin along the narrow boards. The undertaker ran ahead with the coffin-rests. They bore it into a large room. They bore it into an unheated room. The room smelled of dampness. The room smelled of disuse. The room smelled of furniture polish. They set it down under a hanging lamp. The lamp was ornamented with jingling glass prisms. They set it down before a "Rogers group" of John Auden and Priscilla. The "Rogers group" was wreathed with smilax.

—WILLA CATHER (two sentences)

**D.** For this exercise, select a fairly long paragraph from one of your corrected essays or from the rough draft of your next essay.

1. Analyze the sentences in this paragraph. What techniques have you used to combine and vary your sentences? Do you consider your sentences sufficiently varied? If not, what could you do to introduce greater variety?

2. Play around with two or three of your sentences. Revise them in as many ways as you can, using any techniques you like. Comment on your revisions: Which do you prefer, and why? Do you think that any of your revisions are clearer or more emphatic than your original sentences? Do any of the changes you have made affect the sentences' meanings?

# PART 4

# DISCOVERING PRINCIPLES OF GRAMMAR AND MECHANICS

**T**he word "grammar" has unpleasant connotations for most of us: we think of grammar as unfamiliar and forbidding, a mysterious and senseless mass of rules that serves only to confuse us and lead us into errors. This attitude is hardly surprising, for the only time most of us think about grammar at all is when someone corrects us for making a mistake. We may make a few grammatical errors in the course of a five-page paper and conclude that we "don't know anything about grammar," forgetting that the same paper contains hundreds of sentences that are perfectly correct.

In fact, we all know a great deal about grammar, and we depend on our knowledge of it every day. If you have ever studied a foreign language, you know that studying vocabulary is not enough; even if you had memorized every word in a French dictionary, a paragraph written in French would make no sense to you unless you had also mastered French grammar. You already know almost everything there is to know about English grammar; if you didn't, you wouldn't be able to carry on a conversation, write a letter to a friend, or understand this book. Your knowledge of English grammar is already so extensive that it can help you to understand a sentence even if it contains unfamiliar vocabulary. Consider this sentence, for example:

The freeber splatnuck gormed the nardak's klotcher glotly.

Even though the words are nonsense words, grammar can tell you a great deal about what is going on in this sentence. *Inflections*—changes made in the forms of words—help you to identify the parts of speech of several words in the sentence: the *-er* in *freeber* tells you that this word is probably a comparative adjective; the *-ed* tells you that *gormed* is a past-tense verb; the *-'s* tells you that *nardak's* is a possessive singular noun; and the *-ly* tells you that *glotly* is probably an adverb. *Word order,* another element in grammar, also tells you a great deal. For example, you can tell that *freeber* modifies *splatnuck* and that the *klotcher* belongs to the *nardak*. Finally, the function word *the* helps you to identify both *splatnuck* and *klotcher* as nouns. *Function words*—such as articles, prepositions, and conjunctions—have little meaning in themselves, but they tell us a great deal about the relationships among the other words in the sentence.

Far from being useless, then, grammar is an essential part of communication; far from being unfamiliar, it is one of the things we all know best. Still, almost all writers—even English teachers— have occasional problems with grammar and mechanics when they write academic papers or articles. The conventions that govern academic writing differ in some ways from the conventions that govern other sorts of writing and also differ from the conventions that govern speech. The following chapters should help you to discover and understand some of the conventions of grammar and mechanics that most often trouble students doing academic writing.

Some of these conventions may seem trivial. Sometimes, however, even a slight change in grammar or mechanics can make a significant change in meaning:

the student's books
the students' books

The placement of the apostrophe tells us whether there is one student or more than one.

I have played basketball for years.
I had played basketball for years.

The tense tells us whether or not the speaker still plays basketball.

In some cases, then, a grammatical or mechanical error could obscure your meaning. At other times, an error might not obscure your meaning, but it could still interfere with smooth, efficient communication: if you write *its* when you should write *it's,* your readers will know what you mean, but the error might annoy them or distract them from the idea you wish to express.

Some of these conventions may strike you as illogical or arbitrary. In some ways, many conventions are arbitrary—but they may still be binding. For that matter, it's just as "logical" to call a piece of furniture a *splatnuck* as it is to call it a *chair;* the only problem is that people won't know what you're talking about if you call it a *splatnuck*. Grammar and mechanics, like vocabulary, are governed by convention, not by logic. The people who do academic writing agree to follow certain conventions so that they can understand each other easily; when they're in doubt about a convention, they consult a book such as this one to find answers to their questions.

# 14.
# Sentence Vocabulary, Structure, and Form

The first step in mastering the conventions of grammar and mechanics is understanding the sentence; the first step in understanding the sentence is learning sentence vocabulary—such terms as *subject, predicate, phrase,* and *clause.* Knowing these terms will make it much easier for you to understand the problems you may be having in your papers and to discuss ways to solve them. Also, knowing these terms will help you to see the grammatical patterns in sentences—a crucial step in learning about matters such as punctuation.

You may well have memorized definitions for these terms years ago. As you do the exercises, you may want to draw on what you know as well as on what you observe. Be ready, however, to test the definitions you have learned, to see whether or not they are completely clear and accurate. You may also find that you will understand a concept more fully and remember it longer if you try to arrive at your own definitions expressed in your own words.

The second half of this chapter is designed to help you recognize and avoid some of the most common errors in sentence structure and form.

## SENTENCE VOCABULARY
### Subjects and Predicates

In the following sentences, the simple subjects are underlined once and the simple predicates are underlined twice.

The professor lectured for half an hour.

She lectured for half an hour.

Golfing is an enjoyable sport.

Woody Allen and Diane Keaton <u>starred</u> in the movie.

Woody Allen <u>wrote and directed</u> the movie.

<u>Lincoln</u> <u>was shot</u> in a theater.

There <u>are</u> three <u>people</u> on the committee.

## SUBJECTS

1. What parts of speech can be simple subjects?
2. How would you describe the subject's function in a sentence?
3. Where is the subject of a sentence usually found?
4. Write a definition of *subject*.

## PREDICATES

1. What parts of speech can be simple predicates?
2. How would you describe the predicate's function in a sentence?
3. Where is the predicate of a sentence usually found?
4. Write a definition of *predicate*.

## Phrases and Clauses

| *Phrases* | *Clauses* |
|---|---|
| the old pine table | he bought the table |
| was afraid to speak | George was afraid to speak |
| running past the house | she ran past the house |
| behind the door | because it was behind the door |

1. What are the similarities between phrases and clauses?
2. What are the differences between phrases and clauses?
3. Write a definition of *phrase*.
4. Write a definition of *clause*.

## Independent and Dependent Clauses

| *Independent Clauses* | *Dependent Clauses* |
|---|---|
| he was only seven years old | because he was only seven years old |
| she visited our class | the woman *who visited our class* |

| | |
|---|---|
| we realized what had happened | when we realized what had happened |
| the room was empty | although the room was empty |
| the stairway was unsafe | the stairway *that was unsafe* |

1. What do independent and dependent clauses have in common?
2. How do independent and dependent clauses differ?
3. Write a definition of *independent clause.*
4. Write a definition of *dependent clause.*

## Sentences

Study the sentences below and then answer the questions that follow.

Are you familiar with the works of Jane Austen?
Jane Austen was a great English novelist.
She was born in 1775.
Her first novel, *Sense and Sensibility,* was published in 1811.
What an impressive first novel it is!
Elinor, the main character in this novel, strikes many readers as wooden and unsympathetic.
Marianne is a less admirable character, but she seems more human and likable.
By the end of the novel, the reader learns to appreciate Elinor's self-control.
Marianne also matures during the course of the novel because of the disappointments she experiences.
Although it is not one of Austen's greatest novels, *Sense and Sensibility* reveals her wit and her ironic insight into human nature.
Read *Sense and Sensibility* and compare it with Austen's later works if you want to understand her development as a novelist.

1. What are the essential components of a sentence? What do all these sentences have in common?
2. List some types of sentences. Consider the various purposes these sample sentences serve and the various ways in which they combine clauses.
3. Write a definition of *sentence.*

## ERRORS IN SENTENCE STRUCTURE AND FORM

### Sentence Fragments

A sentence fragment is an incomplete sentence. Several types of sentence fragments are found frequently in student papers. Study each group of sentences that follows and identify the common problem that makes the "sentences" in each group fragments. How can this problem be solved to make these fragments into sentences?

## GROUP A

*EXAMPLES:*

*Barchester Towers,* a novel about clergymen in an English cathedral city.

Scanning, the ability to locate specific facts or information quickly.

Peter studied the menu carefully for almost half an hour. *And then ordered a cheeseburger and a Coke.*

A forest full of tall, stately pine trees by the side of a rapid stream.

The meeting scheduled for later this month.

*PROBLEM:*

*SOLUTIONS:*

## GROUP B

*EXAMPLES:*

Rachel hoping to find a job in Washington, D.C.

Dan gone to Cape Cod for the rest of the summer.

Students planning to take the Graduate Record Examination this spring.

Fred to help with the scenery and props.

A fatal accident occurring during rush hour yesterday.

*PROBLEM:*

*SOLUTIONS:*

## GROUP C

*EXAMPLES:*

Although he made a sincere effort to understand his children.

Because they wished to contribute to the senator's reelection campaign.

When they realized how serious the damage had been.

Until you accept responsibility for last week's fiasco.

If the trustees will agree to these changes in the college's charter.

*PROBLEM:*

*SOLUTIONS:*

## GROUP D

*EXAMPLES:*
The pioneers who first settled in western Pennsylvania.
Three books that were ordered for next fall's seminar.
A problem that will only grow worse if we ignore it.
An experiment that indicated that certain food additives might cause cancer.
The man who came to dinner.

*PROBLEM:*

*SOLUTIONS:*

## Comma Splices and Run-on Sentences

Comma splices and run-on sentences are errors that result from join-ing clauses incorrectly. The first two columns contain comma splices and run-on sentences; the third column shows some of the many ways of correcting these errors. How would you define a *comma splice* and a *run-on sentence?* What are some correct ways of joining clauses?

| *Comma Splices* | *Run-on Sentences* | *Correct Sentences* |
|---|---|---|
| Wanda is a thoroughly un-pleasant little girl, she likes to steal toys from other children. | Wanda is a thoroughly un-pleasant little girl she likes to steal toys from other children. | Wanda is a thoroughly un-pleasant little girl. She likes to steal toys from other children. |
| She is insulting and sadistic, other children run when they see her coming. | She is insulting and sadistic other children run when they see her coming. | Because she is in-sulting and sadis-tic, other children run when they see her coming. |
| Dogs and cats also hide from her, they know she likes to pull their tails and ears. | Dogs and cats also hide from her they know she likes to pull their tails and ears. | Dogs and cats also hide from her, for they know she likes to pull their tails and ears. |

| | | |
|---|---|---|
| Wanda does not have any friends, she does not seem to mind, she enjoys being regarded as the neighborhood terror. | Wanda does not have any friends she does not seem to mind she enjoys being regarded as the neighborhood terror. | Wanda does not have any friends, but she does not seem to mind; she enjoys being regarded as the neighborhood terror. |
| My grades in history have been fairly good this year, however I want to do better. | My grades in history have been fairly good this year however I want to do better. | My grades in history have been fairly good this year; however, I want to do better. |
| Writing requires a great deal of practice, therefore students must work hard. | Writing requires a great deal of practice therefore students must work hard. | Writing requires a great deal of practice; therefore, students must work hard. |
| After completing four years of college, I have one regret, I wish I had studied more. | After completing four years of college, I have one regret I wish I had studied more. | After completing four years of college, I have one regret: I wish I had studied more. |
| Paul was disappointed by his first year at Edson College, he decided to transfer. | Paul was disappointed by his first year at Edson College he decided to transfer. | Disappointed by his first year at Edson College, Paul decided to transfer. |

Write a definition of *comma splice*.
Write a definition of *run-on sentence*.
List some correct ways of joining clauses.

## Problems with Modifiers

Sentences may become unclear or illogical if modifying clauses, phrases, or words are used carelessly. In the three groups that follow, contrast the sentences on the left with those on the right. Explain why the sentences on the left are incorrect, and then explain how the problem you have just described can be avoided or corrected.

## GROUP A

| | |
|---|---|
| Joe Brown was found guilty of selling drugs in the county courtroom. | In the county courtroom, Joe Brown was found guilty of selling drugs. |
| While Diane gripped my arm, I saw policemen on top of the roof with rifles. | While Diane gripped my arm, I saw policemen with rifles on top of the roof. |
| Have you ever felt the happiness of having a friend growing in your stomach? | Have you ever felt in your stomach the growing happiness of having a friend? |
| At the end of my junior year, I had almost taken all the courses required for my major. | At the end of my junior year, I had taken almost all the courses required for my major. |

*PROBLEM:*

*WAYS TO AVOID OR CORRECT:*

## GROUP B

| | |
|---|---|
| Our teacher told us constantly to watch for other drivers. | Our teacher constantly told us to watch for other drivers. *or* Our teacher told us to watch for other drivers constantly. |
| The teacher said after class she would return the papers. | The teacher said she would return the papers after class. *or* After class, the teacher said she would return the papers. |
| I decided when I had saved up more money to invest in a car. | I decided to invest in a car when I had saved up more money. *or* When I had saved up more money, I decided to invest in a car. |
| The student who had been writing happily looked up from his notes. | The student who had been happily writing looked up from his notes. *or* |

The student who had been
writing looked up from his
notes happily.

*PROBLEM:*

*WAYS TO AVOID OR CORRECT:*

GROUP C

| | |
|---|---|
| After hiking through the woods for half an hour, the tree stump was a welcome place for me to rest. | After hiking through the woods for half an hour, I found the tree stump a welcome place to rest. |
| While fearing for our lives, police cars streaked down Union Street. | While fearing for our lives, we saw police cars streak down Union Street. |
| After reading "Politics and the English Language," my thoughts agree with Orwell. | After reading "Politics and the English Language," I agree with Orwell. |
| To lose weight, calories must be counted carefully. | To lose weight, one must count calories carefully. |

*PROBLEM:*

*WAYS TO AVOID OR CORRECT:*

## Inconsistent Sentences

Sentences can become awkward or illogical if we fail to complete a grammatical pattern we have started or shift from one grammatical pattern to another. In the three groups below, contrast the sentences on the left with those on the right. Explain why the sentences on the left are incorrect, and then explain how the problem you have just described can be avoided or corrected.

GROUP A

| | |
|---|---|
| Jean's car is more expensive than Miriam. | Jean's car is more expensive than Miriam's. |
| His voice is like a professional singer. | His voice is like a professional singer's. |

Classes here are smaller than the University of Michigan.

Classes here are smaller than those at the University of Michigan.

Franklin Roosevelt was in office longer than any American president.

Franklin Roosevelt was in office longer than any other American president.

*PROBLEM:*

*WAYS TO AVOID OR CORRECT:*

GROUP B

In the third chapter of this book contains an intriguing conversation between the two main characters.

The third chapter of this book contains an intriguing conversation between the two main characters.
*or*
In the third chapter of this book, there is an intriguing conversation between the two main characters.

By discrediting Duncan's sons cleared Macbeth's path to the throne.

By discrediting Duncan's sons, Macbeth cleared his path to the throne.
*or*
Discrediting Duncan's sons cleared Macbeth's path to the throne.

Whenever you need information about dates or locations of the LSAT can be obtained from the Career Planning Office.

Whenever you need information about dates or locations of the LSAT, you can obtain it from the Career Planning Office.
*or*
Information about the dates or locations of the LSAT can be obtained from the Career Planning Office.

Because he had misunderstood the directions explains his confusion.

The fact that he had misunderstood the directions explains his confusion.
*or*
Because he had misunderstood the directions, he was confused.

*PROBLEM:*

*WAYS TO AVOID OR CORRECT:*

GROUP C

| | |
|---|---|
| I looked forward to my vacation as a time for being by myself, taking long walks, and to think through some of the questions that had been troubling me. | I looked forward to my vacation as a time for being by myself, taking long walks, and thinking through some of the questions that had been troubling me. |

*or*

I looked forward to my vacation as a time to be by myself, to take long walks, and to think through some of the questions that had been troubling me.

| | |
|---|---|
| Students transfer for many reasons: the school is too far from home, the social life isn't appealing, or can't handle the course load. | Students transfer for many reasons: the school is too far from home, the social life isn't appealing, or the course load is too much to handle. |
| The essay attempts to reach the student rather than to the literary critic. | The essay attempts to reach the student rather than the literary critic. |
| Sports should teach children to respect rules, a sense of fair play, and the subordination of personal interests to those of the group. | Sports should teach children to respect rules, to develop a sense of fair play, and to subordinate personal interests to those of the group. |

*PROBLEM:*

*WAYS TO AVOID OR CORRECT:*

## APPLICATION

### SENTENCE VOCABULARY

In the following sentences, identify all phrases, independent clauses, and dependent clauses. In each clause, identify the subject and the predicate.

1. In 1813, *Pride and Prejudice* was published; this novel is undoubtedly one of Jane Austen's greatest.
2. Like *Sense and Sensibility, Pride and Prejudice* centers on courtship and marriage.
3. Elizabeth Bennet, the heroine, is both beautiful and intelligent, but she is still capable of making serious errors in judgment.
4. Because of her tendency to judge people too quickly, Elizabeth admires a man who is in fact a scoundrel and scorns the man who truly loves her.
5. Although blinded by these prejudices through most of the novel, Elizabeth eventually realizes her mistakes.
6. Her older sister, Jane, is in some ways similar to Elinor of *Sense and Sensibility,* for both characters are remarkable for their self-restraint.
7. In *Pride and Prejudice,* however, such complete self-control seems problematic: because she keeps her emotions under such strict control, Jane almost loses the man she loves.
8. Elizabeth's younger sisters are amusing: Mary is a studious prig, Kitty is weak-willed, and Lydia is completely impetuous.
9. The plot of *Pride and Prejudice* is full of twists and surprises.
10. Those who enjoy *Sense and Sensibility* and *Pride and Prejudice* should also consider reading some of Austen's later novels.

## ERRORS IN SENTENCE STRUCTURE AND FORM

**A.**   Explain why the incomplete sentences below are fragments. Then correct each fragment in as many different ways as you can.

1. Because your sentences are too wordy.
2. The class that was cancelled last summer.
3. Cathy encouraging her brother to enter the contest.
4. A 1975 Ford with power brakes and power steering.
5. Congress to recess on Tuesday.

**B.**   Find at least four different ways to correct each of these comma splices and run-on sentences.

1. I am fascinated by Cervantes, I want to master Spanish thoroughly.
2. We wanted to see the ballet's annual performance of *The Nutcracker Suite* all the tickets had been sold weeks in advance.
3. The tall man yawned impolitely the speaker was upset by his rudeness.
4. Maria and Joan have completely different personalities and habits they have been roommates for three years.

5. Priscilla refused to marry John, she was disgusted by his table manners.

**C.** The following paragraph contains some correct sentences, but it also contains fragments, comma splices, and run-on sentences. Make all necessary corrections.

When *Adventures of Huckleberry Finn* was published in 1885, the Concord Library Committee called it "trash" and refused to make it available to their readers. This novel, which has since been recognized as a classic of American literature. Some people were shocked by Twain's language many others objected to his portrayal of the friendship between a white boy and a runaway slave. Many of these criticisms being simply the result of prejudice. *Huckleberry Finn* has triumphed over these criticisms, it has become perhaps the best-loved novel ever published in this country. Although there are still some groups which would like to see *Huckleberry Finn* banned from the public schools.

**D.** Most of the following sentences were taken from student papers; all contain errors in sentence structure or form. Correct the sentences, and be prepared to explain all your changes.

1. Walking into the waiting room, the nurse's smile reassured us all.
2. The play lacked originality, dragged out some scenes to the point of boredom, and some acting needed polishing.
3. By reviewing all the lecture notes was her approach to preparing for the final examination.
4. The man who was laughing loudly told us that we could come in.
5. Students might not like the dormitories because stereos are always being played, the inconvenient locations of the buildings, and maybe the people are not friendly.
6. The album cover pictured a wise, old man high atop a mountain with outstretched arms.
7. In spite of our arguments were unable to convince him he was wrong.
8. Looking out the window, the sky was growing dark.
9. The nurses here are more highly trained than most other hospitals.
10. I don't like most evening television programs because there is too much violence, too much sex, many of the plots are unrealistic, and commercials that insult your intelligence.
11. The sweet odors that were filling the room quickly reminded her of her childhood.

12. In the editorial reminded us of the importance of voting.
13. To attend these concerts, tickets must be bought months in advance.
14. I believe prospective students should thoroughly examine a college—the people, dormitories, classes, the social life—before making a decision.
15. When leaving the facility, the smell of perspiration filled the air from the hard-working athletes.

# 15.
# Sentence Punctuation

Many people underrate the importance of punctuation and take too casual an attitude toward it. The effective communication of ideas, however, depends in part upon correct punctuation. In speech we have gestures, tone of voice, volume, facial expressions, and dozens of other tools to help others understand our words; in writing, we have punctuation. Correct punctuation makes the reader's job smoother and easier; incorrect punctuation causes the reader needless confusion and delay.

Consider, for example, the following sentence from a student's paper on B. F. Skinner's *Walden Two:*

Money is not used for all goods and services are free at Walden Two.

Since this sentence has no comma to tell the reader where to pause, the reader might very well go too far and become confused:

Money is not used for all goods and services. . . .

If the reader takes all of this as one clause, the rest of the sentence— "are free at Walden Two"—makes no sense. So the reader is delayed and forced to go back and read the sentence over again. Even now, the reader could interpret the sentence in two different ways:

Money is not used, for all goods and services are free at Walden Two.
Money is not used for all goods, and services are free at Walden Two.

Because of an error in punctuation, the writer has not communicated clearly and smoothly. When a paper contains many such errors, confusions and delays multiply, becoming both a barrier to communication and an annoyance. Punctuation, then, is an important tool in conveying meaning. Furthermore, the rules governing punctuation are relatively simple, and they *do* make sense. If you devote some time and concentration to learning about punctuation, you can realistically hope to understand—not just memorize—the principles involved.

Most textbooks begin their discussions of punctuation by giving you rules to memorize and apply correctly. Here, the method is reversed. You will find no rules in this chapter; instead, you will find several groups of correctly punctuated sentences. The sentences in each group illustrate a particular rule about commas, semicolons, colons, or dashes. Study the sentences in each group, identify the common principle governing the punctuation, and then formulate a rule expressing the principle you see at work. In many cases, the main group of sentences is followed by a shorter group illustrating an exception to the rule; for these groups, write out the exception as well.

## COMMAS

RULE A

*SENTENCES:*
1. I had a hard time finding a job, for almost all the positions advertised required previous experience.
2. Everyone speculated about the reasons for her strange behavior, but no one could offer a satisfactory explanation.
3. I had lived in Cleveland for sixteen years, so adjusting to life in a small town was difficult at first.
4. I may go to graduate school right after college, or I may work for my uncle for a year or so.
5. Scribbling is a child's first discovery of art, and it is also the first step toward learning to draw.
6. Scribbling is a child's first discovery of art and also the first step toward learning to draw.
7. Ed wanted to fly to Boston this weekend, but all the flights were already fully booked.
8. Ed wanted to fly to Boston this weekend but couldn't get a ticket.

If you have trouble seeing the principle involved here, study the last four sentences carefully and ask yourself why there are commas in sentences 5 and 7 but none in sentences 6 and 8.

*RULE A:*

EXCEPTION TO RULE A:

*SENTENCES:*
1. He liked it but I did not.
2. Sam played the piano and we all danced.
3. Joe was late so I helped.
4. She persisted but I refused.

What is the most striking difference between the sentences listed under Rule A and those listed under Exception to Rule A?

*EXCEPTION TO RULE A:*

RULE B

*SENTENCES:*
1. Although the Republicans now have a majority in the Senate, the Democrats still control the House.
2. The Democrats still control the House although the Republicans now have a majority in the Senate.
3. Because Maxwell wasted so much time last week, he will have to work late tonight.
4. Maxwell will have to work late tonight because he wasted so much time last week.
5. If you hope to become a good tennis player, you will have to devote many hours to practicing.
6. You will have to devote many hours to practicing if you hope to become a good tennis player.
7. Everyone in the class began to cheer when the professor announced that the test had been postponed.
8. When the professor announced that the test had been postponed, everyone in the class began to cheer.

Again, ask yourself why there are commas in sentences 1, 3, 5, and 8 but not in sentences 2, 4, 6, and 7.

*RULE B:*

EXCEPTION TO RULE B:

*SENTENCES:*
1. Most of the participants found the seminar on the changing political situation in the South informative and intellectually challenging, although a few thought that the discussion leader often avoided the most complex issues involved.

2. We had to cancel the concert and refund all the money we had already raised, because we had sold only 300 tickets rather than the 500 we needed to cover our expenses.

What is the most striking difference between the sentences listed under Rule B and those listed under Exception to Rule B?

*EXCEPTION TO RULE B:*

RULE C

*SENTENCES:*
1. Blushing with embarrassment, Grace tried to explain her mistake.
2. Speaking very quickly, the officer told us what we should do.
3. Ignoring all the protests, the mayor went ahead with his plan.
4. Before starting out, we checked to make sure we all understood the directions. .
5. At least two hours before dawn, we started out for the campgrounds.
6. On a dark and rainy Tuesday evening, he came to visit me.
7. Of course, his father did not know anything about the arrest.
8. In fact, the dean agrees with me.
9. Furthermore, I think his suggestions are impractical.
10. Consequently, she decided to return to Detroit at once.

*RULE C:*

EXCEPTION TO RULE C:
1. Before dawn we started out for the campgrounds.
2. On Tuesday he came to visit me.

What is the main difference between these sentences and sentences 5 and 6 listed under Rule C?

*EXCEPTION TO RULE C:*

RULE D

*SENTENCES:*
1. My only sister, who lives in New York, works for the county.
2. My sister-in-law who lives in Seattle is older than my sister-in-law who lives in Cincinnati.
3. Sandra O'Connor, who was appointed to the Supreme Court, is from Arizona.

4. The woman who was appointed to the Supreme Court is from Arizona.
5. Ed Conrad, who eats too much at every meal, often gets indigestion.
6. A person who eats too much at every meal often gets indigestion.
7. Emily Brontë's only completed novel, *Wuthering Heights,* tells of the romance between Catherine Earnshaw and the mysterious Heathcliff.
8. Shakespeare's play *King Lear* is a perpetual challenge to actors and directors.
9. She decided, despite several serious reservations, to let her son move into his own apartment.
10. His briefcase, stuffed full of books and papers, sat in the middle of the floor.

Ask yourself why there are commas in sentences 1, 3, 5, and 7 but not in sentences 2, 4, 6, and 8.

*RULE D:*

RULE E

*SENTENCES:*
1. She wore a red and white dress.
2. She wore a red, white, and blue dress.
3. He entered the room and sat down.
4. He entered the room, sat down, and began reading a newspaper.
5. We had steak and potatoes for dinner.
6. We had steak, potatoes, salad, green beans, bread, and cake for dinner.

Why are there commas in sentences 2, 4, and 6 but not in sentences 1, 3, and 5?

*RULE E:*

EXCEPTION TO RULE E:

*SENTENCES:*
1. We get calcium and vitamin D and phosphorus from milk.
2. Go or stay or drop dead—it's all the same to me.

*EXCEPTION TO RULE E:*

## RULE F

*SENTENCES:*
1. Ellen wore a long, blue gown.
2. Ellen wore a pale blue gown.
3. They gave him a small, delicate violet plant.
4. They gave him a small African violet plant.
5. Jimmy ate a huge, nutritious omelet for breakfast.
6. Jimmy ate a huge cheese omelet for breakfast.

Why are there commas in sentences 1, 3, and 5 but not in sentences 2, 4, and 6?

*RULE F:*

## RULE G

*SENTENCES:*
1. John Milton published his *Aeropagitica* on November 23, 1644.
2. We completed our project by February 15, 1980, without any difficulty.
3. They moved to 11 Hatherly Road, Brighton, Massachusetts 02135.
4. The package should have gone to London, Ontario, but was sent to London, England.
5. Herman Tarnower, M.D., created the well-known Scarsdale Diet.
6. Maureen Scarlett, Ph.D., taught at the college for many years.

*RULE G:*

### COMMAS: FIVE GENERAL PRINCIPLES

1. Look at rules A and B and complete this general statement about one of the main uses of commas: "Commas are often used to help separate _____."
2. Look back at rules B and C and complete this general statement about one of the main uses of commas: "Commas are often used to separate _____."
3. Look back at rule D and complete this general statement about one of the main uses of commas: "Commas are often used to set off _____."
4. Look back at rules E, F, and G and complete this general statement about one of the main uses of commas: "Commas are often used to separate _____."
5. Look back at the exceptions to rules A, B, and C and complete this

general statement about exceptions to rules about commas: "Exceptions to rules about commas often involve _____."

## APPLICATION: COMMAS

**A.** Insert commas where necessary in the following sentences. In the space to the left of each sentence, indicate the rule or rules that apply to that sentence.

_____ 1. I like swimming and golfing more than football baseball and hockey.

_____ 2. Although he failed the quiz Steve did well on the final exam.

_____ 3. This article as I told you yesterday needs further revision.

_____ 4. George arrived on a hot summer day.

_____ 5. George arrived on a hot stuffy day.

_____ 6. Dickens's novel *Great Expectations* is about a boy named Pip.

_____ 7. Wendy hurried into the house and answered the telephone.

_____ 8. Wendy hurried into the house tripped over the dog and answered the telephone.

_____ 9. Wendy hurried into the house and then she answered the telephone.

_____ 10. Simple carelessness not malice caused all the trouble.

_____ 11. Alan got the job because he had more experience than Carl did.

_____ 12. My youngest brother who was in Hollywood last week saw Paul Newman at a grocery store.

_____ 13. The woman who tried to hijack a plane to Cuba was arrested.

_____ 14. I wanted to take Biology 204 this semester but my advisor told me I should take a chemistry course first.

_____ 15. In addition she must consider Rita's opinion.

_____ 16. Elaine always does careful intelligent research.

_____ 17. The witness infuriated by the lawyer's accusation sprang to her feet.

_____ 18. After reading the article on public housing Cindy wrote a letter to the editor.

_____ 19. Jeff became nervous when he noticed a tall heavy man walk into the room.

_____ 20. To encourage student interest in Black literature our committee invited Michael Perrin Ph.D. to give a public lecture on the works of James Baldwin.

_____ 21. Margie who loves rock music plans to come to the concert but Sue who hates large crowds has decided to stay home and do some reading.

_____ 22. When he noticed that we were running low on office supplies Phil ordered more pencils typing paper staples and tape.

_____ 23. Despite our efforts to encourage her Carol depressed by her low grades decided to withdraw from college.

_____ 24. Although I had hoped to leave for home on Monday May 19 my selfish inconsiderate roommate refused to give me a ride to the airport so I will have to wait until Wednesday May 21.

**B.** Insert commas where necessary in the following paragraphs.

The police the courts and the citizens of the United States seem unable to stop violent crime and the sociologists and psychologists seem unable to explain why crime is so prevalent in our society. Although many experts have offered theories explaining why the crime rate continues to increase every year these experts do not agree about what the most important causes of crime are.

Some sociologists point to our high unemployment rate and argue that people who are out of work commit crimes both because they need money and because they have too much time on their hands and become restless. Other sociologists however think that the violent atmosphere of our society is a far more important cause of crime for it affects all people and not just the unemployed. Television movies books and newspapers all glamorize crime and make it look appealing. Some studies have shown that children are more likely to behave violently after they have watched violent television shows so it seems reasonable to conclude that at least to some extent violence in the media contributes to the increase in crime.

One psychologist who has done extensive research over the last ten years thinks that the tensions of modern life are the most important causes of crime. The fast pace of modern life especially in the cities creates tremendous pressure and some people resort to violence to escape from this pressure. People who commit crimes for "kicks" this psychologist says are probably suffering from such pressure. Also as the pressures of modern life drive more and more people to abuse drugs we can expect an increase in drug-related crimes.

Some experts rejecting all these theories argue that the main cause of the increase in crime is our failure to capture prosecute and convict criminals. Since many police departments are understaffed officers have a hard time protecting neighborhoods and investigating crimes. Harried overworked prosecutors may encourage criminals to escape harsh punishment through plea bargaining and judges concerned about the overcrowding in prisons may hesitate to hand down long sentences.

Although the number of theories may suggest that we know a great deal about the causes of crime we still do not know what the primary cause is. Furthermore some of these theories might be incorrect and might mislead us into wasting our efforts. We might for example concentrate on eliminating violence in the media and then discover that there is no significant connection between media violence and violent crime after all. Unless we can identify the primary causes of violent crime we cannot hope to start an intelligent effective campaign to solve the problem.

## SEMICOLONS

RULE A

*SENTENCES:*
1. Some students consider Professor Blake an excellent teacher; others complain that his lectures are too dry.
2. She asked the committee to investigate the admission office's recruiting policies; she also suggested that they consider the effect a tuition increase might have on enrollment.
3. Last year I spent my vacation in Maine; this year I plan to visit Oregon.
4. Kathy soon found a summer job; her sister, however, was not so fortunate.
5. He thought that television contributed to passivity and conformity; therefore, he allowed his children to watch only two programs each week.

*RULE A:*

RULE B

*SENTENCES:*
1. To gather the information for this paper, I spoke to Paul Martin, the director of admissions; Diane Andrews, the assistant dean of students; and Ted Jennings, the chair of the Academic Standards committee.
2. In her lecture on T. S. Eliot, the speaker referred to a play, *Murder in the Cathedral;* an essay, "Tradition and the Individual Talent"; and two poems, "The Lovesong of J. Alfred Prufrock" and "The Journey of the Magi."

3. During the freshman year, the student must develop independence, the ability to make plans and decisions for oneself; discipline, the ability to keep working despite distractions, temptations, and exhaustion; and flexibility, the ability to adapt to the constant changes and surprises that are an inevitable part of college life.
4. Hawthorne explores the nature of the unpardonable sin in "Ethan Brand," a story about a man who relentlessly probes and examines the human heart for the advancement of "science"; "Young Goodman Brown," a story about a man who is unable to view his neighbors charitably after discovering their secret sins; and *The Scarlet Letter,* a novel that tells of Roger Chillingworth's attempt to destroy another man's soul by pitilessly searching out its innermost secrets.
5. At my high school, the students devoted too much energy to complaining about course requirements and too little energy to doing their studies; the teachers devoted too much energy to complaining about their course loads and too little energy to preparing for their classes; and the administrators devoted too much energy to complaining about the students and the teachers and too little energy to running the school.

Be sure your rule provides for sentence 5 as well as for sentences 1–4.

*RULE B:*

## COLONS

RULE C

*SENTENCES:*
1. Four people have volunteered to help out at registration: Grace Gartland, Peter Martin, Rick Morgan, and Lori Taylor.
2. Sam made a serious mistake: he forgot that the library closes at nine o'clock on Saturdays.
3. The answer was clear: our programs would never succeed unless we could interest more students.
4. The jury finally reached a verdict: guilty.
5. Ben Jonson said that those who wish to write well must do three things: read the best authors, observe the best speakers, and continually practice writing.
6. Ben Jonson said that those who wish to write well must read the best authors, observe the best speakers, and continually practice writing.

Why is there a colon in sentence 5 but not in sentence 6? Also, compare sentences 2 and 3 with the sentences listed under Rule A. How do the sentences using colons differ from those using semicolons?

*RULE C:*

## DASHES

RULE D

*SENTENCES:*
1. Four people—Grace Gartland, Peter Martin, Rick Morgan, and Lori Taylor—have agreed to help out at registration.
2. The subjects I am studying this quarter—political science, English, and philosophy—have helped me to see that many of my beliefs are unfounded.
3. You have to realize that Oliver—despite all his good intentions—seldom keeps his promises.
4. None of the city council members—not even those with small children of their own—came out in support of the increase in school taxes.
5. Only one state—Alaska—had decriminalized the possession of marijuana.
6. Only one state, Alaska, has decriminalized the possession of marijuana.
7. Only one state (Alaska) has decriminalized the possession of marijuana.

Sentences 5–7 are all punctuated correctly. Does the choice of punctuation marks affect the sentence's style and meaning?

*RULE D:*

RULE E

*SENTENCES:*
1. The jury finally reached a verdict—guilty.
2. After considering the question for five minutes, Rob decided which painting was the best—his own.
3. The lecturer spoke about the quality she most admires in writing—clarity.
4. Ultimately, just one person has to accept responsibility for the fiasco—the president.
5. Benjamin Franklin said that only two things are certain in this life—death and taxes.

Compare sentence 1 with the fourth sentence listed under Rule C. Does the choice of a punctuation mark affect the sentence's style or meaning?

*RULE E:*

## APPLICATION: SEMICOLONS, COLONS, AND DASHES

**A.** Insert all necessary semicolons, colons, and dashes in the following sentences. In the space to the left of each sentence, indicate the rule or rules that apply to that sentence.

_____ 1. I am doing very well in my history course I am having a lot of trouble in my math course.

_____ 2. You must remember three things measure the ingredients carefully, add them in the right order, and don't let the oven get too hot.

_____ 3. Krystin reasoned or at least, tried to reason with her little brother.

_____ 4. When we heard the news, Alice ran next door to tell Mrs. Williams I started calling some friends.

_____ 5. They finally admitted that there was only one solution to their problems bankruptcy.

_____ 6. I called my father, who was delighted to hear my good news my mother, who said little but was obviously pleased and my Aunt Dotty, who sniffed that some people certainly have all the luck.

_____ 7. Three of the students Roger, Tim, and Pat were unable to attend the banquet.

_____ 8. My father approved of my plans to go to graduate school my grandfather thought I would be wasting my time and money.

_____ 9. The success of this entire project depends upon one person you.

_____ 10. For his birthday, Jack received a book on the history of aviation from his mother a watch with an alarm and a radio attachment from his father a blue cotton suit with two pairs of pants from his uncle and a set of gold cufflinks inscribed with his initials from his girlfriend.

_____ 11. Adam did not expect to get the job he knew that the company was looking for someone with a better background in electronics.

_____ 12. Some people, who fear anything they don't understand, feel awkward when they meet a handicapped person others, who don't realize how much handicapped people can accomplish, are insultingly patronizing.

_____ 13. All people must have some force or principle the will to survive, a belief in a superior being, a devotion to work or family to keep them going from day to day.

_____ 14. When we realized that the house was on fire, most of the members of my family reacted irrationally my mother ran to save our financial records my father tried to gather together all his sports equipment I started to carry out my books and albums and only my little brother had the presence of mind to call the fire department.

_____ 15. King sees civil disobedience, properly guided by justice and reason, as a necessary, constructive force in our society indeed, at times a just person has no choice but to disobey the law.

**B.** Insert commas, colons, semicolons, and dashes where necessary in the following paragraphs. You will also have to insert some capital letters and periods to show where sentences begin and end.

Anthony Trollope who was one of the most popular novelists of the Victorian period wrote over fifty books Trollope attracted many loyal enthusiastic followers who devoured his books as quickly as he could write them his novels about the imaginary city of Barchester *The Warden Barchester Towers* and *Framley Parsonage* among others especially enchanted readers one of Trollope's books however seriously damaged his reputation his *Autobiography* which was not published until after his death in the *Autobiography* Trollope admits that he began writing novels to make extra money furthermore he says that even after he had become an established novelist making money remained one of his main motives for writing many readers who wanted to believe that novelists have far loftier motives were offended by Trollope's honesty Trollope also says in the *Autobiography* that he considers himself a simple craftsman not an inspired genius at one point he compares himself to a shoemaker readers who preferred to think of novelists as divinely inspired geniuses were shocked and began to think that Trollope must not be a good writer after all Trollope's popularity declined after the *Autobiography* was published many of his books went out of print and most critics refused to take him seriously.

In the last forty years Trollope has begun to regain his popularity modern readers who may be more cynical than Trollope's Victorian audience often find the *Autobiography*'s candor refreshing suspecting that few if any artists are divinely inspired modern readers are not shocked by Trollope's comparison of a novelist to a shoemaker many modern readers have long suspected that novelists even those who would never admit it write to make money therefore such readers are not upset by Trollope's confessions other readers do not care about the *Autobiography* one way or the other they simply enjoy Trollope's novels their common sense their humor and their memorable portraits of human types Trollope is again widely read many of his books are coming out in new editions are studied in college classrooms and are the subject of scholarly debates modern readers may admire Trollope's honesty or they may have forgotten all about it at any rate they are enjoying his novels.

# 16

# Agreement, Pronoun Reference, and Point of View

Agreement, pronoun reference, and point of view all involve maintaining clarity and consistency within a sentence by *matching* one part of a sentence with another part—a subject with a predicate, a pronoun with an antecedent, a verb with another verb, and so on.

## SUBJECT/PREDICATE AGREEMENT

The basic rule governing subject/predicate agreement is simple: subjects and their predicates must agree in number. That is, a singular subject (such as *man*) must be paired with a singular predicate (such as *is*) and a plural subject (*men*) must be paired with a plural predicate (*are*):

> The man is handsome.
> The men are handsome.

So far, there's no problem: few of us would be tempted to write "the man are" or "the men is." In more complicated sentences, however, making subjects and predicates agree can be more difficult:

> The committee, together with the dean and the vice president, (discuss/discusses) all matters relating to curriculum.

In such a sentence, we might have trouble identifying the true subject, we might not be sure about whether that subject is regarded as singular or plural, or we might become confused about singular and plural forms of the predicate. When we check subject/predicate agreement, then, we should follow three steps:

1. Find the subject and the predicate.
2. Determine the number of the subject.
3. Make the predicate agree with the subject.

## 1. Find the subject and the predicate.

In the following sentences, the simple subjects are underlined once and the simple predicates are underlined twice. Study the sentences carefully and then answer the questions that follow.

1. The dog barks at passing cars.
2. The dog barked at passing cars.
3. Elizabeth likes Irving very much.
4. Elizabeth liked Irving very much.
5. The causes of the argument are clear.
6. A complete listing of these programs is included with the proposal.
7. The members of the committee disagree constantly.
8. There is no logical reason for their disagreement.
9. There are no logical reasons for their disagreement.
10. With the fine weather come many new activities.

*QUESTIONS*

1. How can you identify the simple predicate of a sentence? (Pay special attention to sentences 1–4.)
2. How can you identify the simple subject of a sentence? Is the object of a preposition ever the simple subject of a sentence? (Pay special attention to sentences 5–7).
3. In most sentences, the subject precedes the predicate; in some sentences, however, the predicate comes first. How can you identify the subject and the predicate in such sentences? Is *there* ever the subject of a sentence? (Pay special attention to sentences 8–10.)

## 2. Determine the number of the subject.

In the following groups of sentences, the simple subjects are underlined once and the simple predicates are underlined twice. Study each group of sentences carefully, answer the questions that follow, and then formulate a rule to express the principle of agreement you see at work.

## GROUP A—Subjects Joined by *And*

*SENTENCES:*
1. <u>Lettuce and cottage cheese</u> <u>were</u> the staples of his diet.
2. <u>Dieting and exercising</u> <u>have become</u> obsessions for him.
3. <u>His roommate and his other friends</u> <u>share</u> these interests.
4. <u>My roommate and I</u> <u>pay</u> little attention to dieting.
5. <u>Spaghetti and meatballs</u> <u>is</u> our favorite meal.
6. <u>My roommate and eating companion</u> <u>is</u> gaining weight rapidly.

*QUESTIONS:*

1. Are subjects joined by *and* usually regarded as singular or plural?
2. When are subjects joined by *and* regarded as singular? (Consider sentences 5 and 6.)

*RULE FOR GROUP A:*

## GROUP B—Subjects Joined by *Or* or *Nor*

*SENTENCES:*
1. <u>Either Chris or Barb</u> <u>is</u> in charge of selling tickets for the dance recital.
2. <u>Neither the Bakers nor the Browns</u> <u>have visited</u> the campus before.
3. <u>Either the director or the actors</u> <u>were</u> responsible for the mistake.
4. <u>Either the actors or the director</u> <u>was</u> responsible for the mistake.
5. <u>Neither my parents nor my sister</u> <u>believes</u> my story.
6. <u>Neither my sister nor my parents</u> <u>believe</u> my story.

*QUESTIONS:*

1. When do subjects joined by *or* or *nor* take a singular predicate? (There will be two parts to your answer.)
2. When do subjects joined by *or* or *nor* take a plural predicate? (Again, there will be two parts to your answer.)

*RULE FOR GROUP B:*

GROUP C—Subjects Followed by Phrases

*SENTENCES:*
1. <u>Julia</u>, as well as her roommates, <u>is</u> planning to attend the lecture.
2. <u>The resident assistants</u>, together with the director, <u>are</u> in charge of discipline and programming.
3. <u>David</u>, accompanied by his nieces, <u>visits</u> the museum often.
4. <u>The nieces</u>, rather than their uncle, <u>plan</u> these excursions.

*QUESTIONS:*

1. When do subjects followed by phrases take singular predicates? Plural predicates?
2. Do phrases between the subject and the predicate affect agreement?

*RULE FOR GROUP C:*

GROUP D—Pronouns

*SENTENCES:*
1. <u>Everyone</u> <u>agrees</u> that our plan is the best.
2. <u>Nobody</u> in the class <u>was</u> able to offer an explanation.
3. <u>Everything</u> about that campus <u>is</u> delightful.
4. <u>Most</u> of the movie <u>was</u> exciting.
5. <u>Most</u> of the viewers <u>were</u> frightened.

*QUESTIONS:*

1. Are pronouns ending in *-one, -body,* and *-thing* singular or plural?
2. When does a pronoun such as *most* take a singular predicate, and when does it take a plural predicate? (The same rule applies to *all, any, more, none,* and *some.*)

*RULE FOR GROUP D:*

GROUP E—Collective Nouns

*SENTENCES:*
1. The <u>committee</u> <u>has reached</u> a decision.
2. Our football <u>team</u> <u>wins</u> almost all its games.
3. The <u>jury</u> <u>was deliberating</u> all last night.
4. Our <u>family</u> <u>is</u> close and united.
5. His <u>family</u> <u>were</u> scattered all over the country.

*QUESTIONS:*

1. What is a collective noun?
2. When are collective nouns regarded as singular subjects?
3. When are collective nouns regarded as plural subjects?

*RULE FOR GROUP E:*

GROUP F—Titles

*SENTENCES:*
1. <u>Sons and Lovers</u> <u>is</u> about the Morel family.
2. <u>Little Women</u> <u>is</u> my younger sister's favorite novel.
3. <u>Romeo and Juliet</u> <u>moves</u> inevitably to a tragic climax.
4. The <u>Brecksville Courier and Times</u> <u>covers</u> the news for several small communities.

*QUESTION:*

Are titles that are plural in form regarded as singular or plural?

*RULE FOR GROUP F:*

GROUP G—Nouns Ending in *s*

*SENTENCES:*
1. <u>Economics</u> <u>is</u> my most difficult subject this semester.
2. The <u>news</u> from the Middle East <u>was</u> very depressing.
3. <u>Athletics</u> <u>demands</u> strength and determination.
4. <u>Politics</u> <u>attracts</u> many talented young people.

*QUESTION:*

When are nouns ending in *s* regarded as singular?

*RULE FOR GROUP G:*

**3. Make the predicate agree with the subject.**

Confusion most often arises here because we are used to thinking of *s* as the sign of the plural. Most (but not all) nouns ending in *s* are indeed plural; does the same generalization hold true for verbs ending in *s*?

My <u>brother</u> <u>visits</u> me every Wednesday.
My <u>sisters</u> <u>visit</u> me on weekends.
<u>They</u> <u>visit</u> me often because <u>we</u> <u>enjoy</u> seeing each other.
My <u>brother</u> usually <u>drives</u> to my house, but sometimes <u>he</u> <u>takes</u>
the bus.

Are verbs ending in *s* singular or plural?

## PRONOUN/ANTECEDENT AGREEMENT

Pronouns should agree with their antecedents in number and in gender. Many of the principles governing pronoun/antecedent agreement are similar to those governing subject/predicate agreement, so a quick review of some of the most important rules should be sufficient. Again, study the following groups of sentences and then formulate rules to express the principles of agreement you see at work.

GROUP H—Antecedents Joined by *And*

*SENTENCES:*
1. <u>Andy and John</u> wrote <u>their</u> reports.
2. <u>The athletes and the coaches</u> discussed <u>their</u> strategy.
3. <u>My friends and I</u> pooled <u>our</u> money.

Compare these sentences with those in group A.

*RULE FOR GROUP H:*

GROUP I—Antecedents Joined by *Or* or *Nor*

*SENTENCES:*
1. Either Andy or John wrote his report.
2. Neither the doctor nor the nurses would reveal their salaries.
3. Neither the nurses nor the doctor would reveal her salary.

Compare these sentences with those in group B.

*RULE FOR GROUP I:*

GROUP J—Pronouns

*SENTENCES:*
1. Everyone must remember to bring his or her ticket.
2. Each of the students corrected his or her own quiz.
3. Nobody likes to admit to his or her own mistakes.
4. Nobody likes to admit to his own mistakes.
5. Nobody likes to admit to her own mistakes.

Compare these sentences with those in group D.

*RULE FOR GROUP J:*

After determining the basic rule at work in these sentences, discuss the advantages and disadvantages of the options represented in sentences 3, 4, and 5. Also consider these possibilities:

Nobody likes to admit to their own mistakes.
Nobody likes to admit to mistakes.
People do not like to admit to their own mistakes.

GROUP K—Collective Nouns

*SENTENCES:*
1. The committee reached its decision.
2. Our football team wins almost all of its games.
3. The family is delighted with its new house.
4. The family discussed their various plans for study and travel.

Compare these sentences with those in group E. When are collective nouns regarded as singular antecedents? When are they regarded as plural antecedents?

*RULE FOR GROUP K:*

## PRONOUN REFERENCE

Even when pronouns and their antecedents agree, confusion can result if a pronoun's antecedent is not absolutely clear. Do not rely on your reader to "figure out" what you mean: it's your job to make sure that pronoun reference is always obvious and unambiguous.

In the following groups, contrast the sentences in the left column with those in the right, decide why the sentences in the right column are clearer, and formulate an appropriate rule.

GROUP A

*SENTENCES*

| | |
|---|---|
| Becky tried to put the lid on the jar, but it was too big. | Becky tried to put the lid on the jar, but the lid was too big. *or* Becky tried to put the lid on the jar, but the jar was too big. |
| We left our cat with my sister when we went on vacation; when we returned, we learned she had run away. | We left our cat with my sister when we went on vacation; when we returned, we learned the cat had run away. |
| Don told his brother that he should look for a better job. | Don advised his brother to look for a better job. |
| Karl took all the coins out of his pockets and counted them. | Karl counted all the coins after taking them out of his pockets. |

*RULE FOR GROUP A:*

The sentences on the left in the next group are not as unclear as those in group A; still, they might cause problems. Why?

*SENTENCES*

| | |
|---|---|
| Rick studied the old journal for hours, hoping to find more details about his uncle's activities during the 1930's. Unfortunately, it contained no information. | Rick studied the old journal for hours, hoping to find more details about his uncle's activities during the 1930's. Unfortunately, the journal contained no information. |
| Pam explained the rules for chess, a game she had learned last fall when she was visiting her aunt in Michigan. They were very confusing. | Pam explained the rules for chess, a game she had learned last fall when she was visiting her aunt in Michigan. The rules were very confusing. |
| The rooms were dark, the paint was chipped, the windowpane was cracked, and the ceiling sagged; but at least they were spacious. | The paint was chipped, the windowpane was cracked, and the ceiling sagged; but at least the rooms, although dark, were spacious. |

*RULE FOR GROUP B:*

GROUP C:

*SENTENCES:*

| | |
|---|---|
| Carolyn spent hours at the library, checking all the available resources, conferring with the documents librarian, and taking careful notes. This proved to be profitable. | Carolyn spent hours at the library, checking all the available resources, conferring with the documents librarian, and taking careful notes. This research proved to be profitable. |
| He refused to attend the convention or to call on their clients in Indiana, which angered his employer. | His refusal to attend the convention or to call on their clients in Indiana angered his employer. |
| The driver neglected to have his brakes repaired before he left on his trip; that could have prevented the accident. | The driver neglected to have his brakes repaired before he left on his trip; the repairs could have prevented the accident. |

*RULE FOR GROUP C:*

## GROUP D

*SENTENCES:*

| | |
|---|---|
| She is an excellent ballerina because she studied it for years. | She is an excellent ballerina because she studied ballet for years. |
| A nursery school is located near the college, so students taking Child Development can observe them frequently. | A nursery school is located near the college, so students taking Child Development can observe the children frequently. |
| Even after spending two years in Italy, he could not speak it fluently. | Even after spending two years in Italy, he could not speak Italian fluently. |

*RULE FOR GROUP D:*

Another common misuse of pronouns is wordy and awkward rather than unclear.

## GROUP E

*SENTENCES*

| | |
|---|---|
| In C. S. Lewis's *The Abolition of Man,* he describes problems with modern education. | In *The Abolition of Man,* C. S. Lewis describes problems with modern education. |
| In the newspaper, it says that we can expect inflation to increase in the coming years. | The newspaper says that we can expect inflation to increase in the coming years. |
| In Rose's speech, she argued that coeducational dormitories offer many advantages. | In her speech, Rose argued that coeducational dormitories offer many advantages. |

*RULE FOR GROUP E:*

## POINT OF VIEW

Maintaining consistency in a sentence involves paying careful attention to point of view as well as to agreement and pronoun reference. An unnecessary shift in point of view can confuse your reader and make your sentence awkward.

The first exercise asks you to explain the differences between the active voice and the passive voice. In the other exercises, identify the inconsistencies in the sentences on the left and then formulate rules to explain the principles you see at work.

## GROUP A

The sentences on the left are in the active voice; those on the right are in the passive voice. Compare the sentences and then explain the differences between the active and passive voices.

| *Active* | *Passive* |
|---|---|
| The waiter dropped the tray. | The tray was dropped by the waiter. |
| The dean introduced the main speaker. | The main speaker was introduced by the dean. |
| Several musicians made serious mistakes. | Serious mistakes were made by several musicians. |
| I will make all the arrangements for the conference. | All the arrangements for the conference will be made by me. |
| A famous actress took these photographs. | These photographs were taken by a famous actress. |

Explain the differences between active and passive voices:

## GROUP B

*SENTENCES*

| After we investigated the problem, a solution was agreed upon. | After we investigated the problem, we agreed upon a solution. *or* After the problem was investigated, a solution was agreed upon. |
|---|---|
| First the batter was prepared carefully, and then Irving put the cake in the oven. | First Irving prepared the batter carefully, and then he put the cake in the oven. *or* |

First the batter was prepared carefully, and then the cake was put in the oven.

| | |
|---|---|
| Students enjoy that course even though high grades are seldom received. | Students enjoy that course even though they seldom receive high grades. |
| | *or* |
| | That course is enjoyed by students even though high grades are seldom received. |

*RULE FOR GROUP B:*

GROUP C

*SENTENCES:*

| | |
|---|---|
| First Joe listened to his friends' opinions, and then he expresses his own. | First Joe listened to his friends' opinions, and then he expressed his own. |
| | *or* |
| | First Joe listens to his friends' opinions, and then he expresses his own. |
| Every day, Joan comes to class and took careful notes. | Every day, Joan comes to class and takes careful notes. |
| | *or* |
| | Every day, Joan came to class and took careful notes. |
| Whenever I asked Paul to help, he refuses. | Whenever I asked Paul to help, he refused. |
| | *or* |
| | Whenever I ask Paul to help, he refuses. |

*RULE FOR GROUP C:*

GROUP D

*SENTENCES:*

| | |
|---|---|
| If one wants to succeed in tennis, you should get a good coach and practice every day. | If one wants to succeed in tennis, one should get a good coach and practice every day. |
| | *or* |

|  | If you want to succeed in tennis, you should get a good coach and practice every day. |
|---|---|
| When you are trying to improve your grades, one should start by examining one's study habits. | When one is trying to improve one's grades, one should start by examining one's study habits.<br>*or*<br>When you are trying to improve your grades, you should start by examining your study habits. |
| A person may have a great deal of difficulty when first studying Greek, but you should not give up. | A person may have a great deal of difficulty when first studying Greek, but one should not give up.<br>*or*<br>You may have a great deal of difficulty when first studying Greek, but you should not give up. |

*RULE FOR GROUP D:*

## *APPLICATION*

**A.**   Most of the following sentences were taken from student papers. Some are correct, but most contain errors in agreement, pronoun reference, or point of view. Correct the sentences where necessary and be prepared to explain all your changes.

1. The lack of national fraternities and sororities are another real problem.
2. In childhood, Coleridge was struck by rheumatic fever, which in some ways causes him physical pain for the rest of his life.
3. During the class discussion, everyone seemed to have their own ideas about the speech.
4. The detective, with the aid of Brent Carradine, uncover many startling facts about Richard III.
5. In my home town, they all love basketball.
6. The main part of the sailboat had now been finished, and we were ready to begin the various finishing touches. A brass strip was placed along the bottom center seam to protect the hull from rocks and abrasions.

7. The other rewards of being on the swim team were making friends and having fun.
8. A lot of people go to college and never used what they have learned.
9. After the gardener murdered the butler, he ran away.
10. Students have complained that there is not enough weekend activities on campus.
11. If one cuts class frequently, your grades will go down sooner or later.
12. Neither my father nor my brother would admit that they were responsible.
13. Our coach, as well as most of the other players, make the mistake of thinking that winning is everything.
14. She had a good education, a steady job, a husband who loved her, and two children, but this did not satisfy her.
15. On the left side of the hall were three doors.
16. I knew my father is proud of me, but he never tells me how he felt.
17. In Richard Wright's *Black Boy,* he tells the story of his own life.
18. Her opinion of the students were shocking.
19. The architecture on this campus combines inconvenience and ugliness; I don't know why they didn't plan more carefully.
20. Neither my adviser nor my other teachers realizes how difficult the freshman year really is.
21. *Crime and Punishment* was my downfall during my sophomore year.
22. Nobody was willing to take on their share of the cost.
23. The true facts about that crime were not revealed until long after the kidnapper had confessed and been sent to prison. They shocked many people.
24. On Wednesdays, the committee have to meet for two hours in order to finish their business.
25. Most of the money from the football games go to support the rest of the athletic programs.

**B.** In the following paragraphs, correct all errors in agreement, pronoun reference, and point of view. Be ready to explain all the changes you make.

Last week I went to a livestock auction in Kidron, Ohio, which is in the heart of Ohio's Amish country. When I first arrived in Amish country, I noticed that they resist the present in many ways. Perhaps the most striking difference between Amish people and most other Americans involve dress. The Amish look like people who just stepped out of a movie about the Old West. The men wear broad-brimmed hats, plain trousers, white shirts, and vests or loose-fitting coats; they all had beards but no mustaches. Little boys were similarly dressed. Even on hot summer days, all the women wear long dresses with long sleeves. The little girls wear long dresses, just as the women do, but their clothes are more brightly colored. All the women and girls wore bonnets or little white caps. When one is visiting Amish country, you are also sure to notice the horse-drawn buggies they drive. The Amish may ride in buses or in other people's cars, but owning cars is forbidden for them.

The Amish seem so removed from modern life that one might expect them to refuse to talk to strangers, but you soon find out that they are quiet but friendly. The Amish might have been shocked by the outfits worn by some of the non-Amish people at the auction, but they never show disgust or disapproval in any way. Whenever I approached an Amish person and asked a question, they politely explained their customs to me. During these conversations, I learned that the Amish, although their lives may seem rigidly controlled to us, are not unhappy and do not feel deprived. Their close-knit families and their faith in their religion gives them deep satisfaction and a sense of purpose. They work hard but also find time to relax and enjoy themselves at family and community gatherings. Those who are sick or in need are always cared for by the community, which allows the Amish to feel confident about the future. Some of the reasons for the Amish people's rejection of the conveniences of modern life is still mysterious to me, but I learned to respect and in some ways envy the security and dignity of the Amish way of life.

# 17.
# Word Punctuation

Just as such punctuation marks as commas and semicolons help us to understand sentences, the marks of word punctuation—apostrophes, hyphens, capitals, italics, and quotation marks—help us to identify words that have special status or grammatical functions within a sentence. Contrasting these two sentences makes clear the importance of correct word punctuation:

> when his new found friends told him that lord jim would be playing at the second run cinema on wednesday, george said, i wonder if the movie will be a successful recreation of conrads novel.

> When his new-found friends told him that *Lord Jim* would be playing at The Second-Run Cinema on Wednesday, George said, "I wonder if the movie will be a successful re-creation of Conrad's novel."

The format of this chapter is similar to that of Chapter 15. Study the groups of sentences, identify the common principles governing the word punctuation in each group, and then formulate rules to express the principles you see at work.

## APOSTROPHES

GROUP A

*SENTENCES:*
1. George's friends hated the movie.
2. Cordelia's answer was honest, but her two sisters' answers were deceitful.
3. The church's rummage sale was a success.

4. The truckers' strike was finally settled last week.
5. The children's progress in reading astonished their teachers.
6. Many readers consider *Great Expectations* Dickens's (or Dickens') greatest work.
7. Whose coat is this—yours or hers? I want to identify its owner.

Be sure your rule is detailed enough to explain all the ways in which apostrophes are used—and not used—in these sentences. Pay particular attention to the words in sentence 7.

*RULE A:*

## GROUP B

*SENTENCES:*
1. Elaine doesn't want to join us, and we can't persuade her to change her mind.
2. We agreed to meet at four o'clock.
3. The class of '58 decided to hold a joint reunion with the class of '59.
4. It's taken the committee three months to agree on a plan.
5. It's a shame that the committee didn't present its report sooner.

Pay particular attention to sentences 4 and 5. What is the difference between *its* and *it's?*

*RULE B:*

## GROUP C

*SENTENCES:*
1. My little brother can never remember how many *s*'s there are in *Mississippi*.
2. He also forgets to dot his *i*'s.
3. He can multiply by *2*'s but not by *3*'s.
4. I think there are too many *however*'s in my paper.

*RULE C:*

## HYPHENS

## GROUP D

*SENTENCES:*
1. Forty-seven students applied to the program, but only twenty-two were accepted.

2. We questioned one hundred seventy-five people for our survey.
3. Two-thirds of the parents offered to help with the project.
4. My brother-in-law has been unemployed for three months.

*RULE D:*

## GROUP E

*SENTENCES:*
1. His self-confidence helped him to succeed.
2. The defendants were accused of anti-Soviet activities.
3. Cynthia and her ex-husband still quarrel about the all-important question of custody.
4. President-elect Reagan considered declaring a state of economic emergency.

*RULE E:*

## GROUP F

*SENTENCES:*
1. My quick-thinking friend helped me to avoid embarrassment.
2. The cat's blue-green eyes were fascinating.
3. We rented a two-bedroom apartment in a rundown building.
4. We rented a small, damp apartment in an old brick building.
5. Sarah's well-written essay was published.
6. Sarah's essay was published because it was well written.

Why is there a hyphen in sentence 3 but not in sentence 4?
Why is there a hyphen in sentence 5 but not in sentence 6?

*RULE F:*

## CAPITALS

## GROUP G

*SENTENCES:*
1. In his lecture, Professor Noble discussed the theories of John Stuart Mill.
2. Professor Noble is an excellent professor.
3. She analyzed several Shakespearian sonnets in the paper she wrote on Wednesday.
4. We had a lovely vacation, crossing the Atlantic Ocean on the *Queen Elizabeth II.*

5. My grandmother was born in Odessa and spoke Russian, Yiddish, and English fluently.
6. Sharon is taking courses in mathematics, chemistry, and English this fall.
7. Sharon is taking Mathematics 113, Chemistry 318, and English 271 this September.
8. When asked whether he had decided what college or university he wanted to attend next year, Alvin replied that he still had not decided between Williams College and the University of Michigan.
9. Of all my aunts, Aunt Ruth is my favorite.
10. My family lived in the South for many years, but then we moved north.

Try to find an underlying principle that will explain all the ways capitals are used—and not used—in these sentences.

*RULE G:*

## GROUP H

*SENTENCES:*
1. In my course in Shakespearian comedies, we read such plays as *Love's Labor's Lost, The Taming of the Shrew, Measure for Measure,* and *Much Ado about Nothing.*
2. That issue of *The Kenyon Review* contains Barbara Myerhoff's short story "A Renewal of the Word" and a poem entitled "The Deodand" by Antony Hecht, author of the book *The Hard Hours.*
3. As James Baldwin has said, "One writes out of one thing only —one's own experience."
4. James Baldwin has said that "one's own experience" is the source of all one writes.
5. Your eyes on me were as eyes that rove
   Over tedious riddles of years ago;
   And some words played between us to and fro
      On which lost the more by our love.

                              —THOMAS HARDY, *"Neutral Tones"*

Again, look for the underlying principle that explains the capitalization in all these sentences.

*RULE H:*

## ITALICS

In handwritten or typed papers, indicate italics by underlining.

GROUP I

*SENTENCES:*
1. Before we began our study of Plato, the professor explained the concept of the *polis* to us.
2. The officer administered the *coup de grâce* to the unfortunate victim.
3. We all thought of Uncle Harry as a *shlmiel,* but he considered himself a *shlmozzel.*
4. I was nervous about introducing my fiancée to my family.

*RULE I:*

GROUP J

*SENTENCES:*
1. "Put down that vase and come over here *immediately,*" the harried babysitter ordered.
2. At first, the dean *seemed* to support our project.
3. We had a *truly delightful* trip because we *were* able to see *all* our cousins, including *many* we had *not* seen for *years.*
4. We had a truly delightful trip because we were able to see all our cousins, including many we had not seen for years.

Contrast sentences 3 and 4; which is better, and why?

*RULE J:*

GROUP K

*SENTENCES:*
1. My little brother often forgets to dot his *i*'s.
2. I think there are too many *however*'s in my paper.
3. I think there are too many "however's" in my paper.
4. The speaker's frequent uses of such words as *perhaps, maybe, possibly,* and *seems* indicated his lack of certainty.
5. The speaker's frequent use of such words as "perhaps," "maybe," "possibly," and "seems" indicated his lack of certainty.

Sentences 2–5 give two options for punctuating. Is there ever any reason for preferring one of these options?

*RULE K:*

## GROUP L

*SENTENCES:*
1. Wordsworth's first volume of poetry, *Lyrical Ballads,* contained the famous poem "Tintern Abbey."
2. Many readers consider Wordsworth's long poem *The Prelude* to be his greatest work.
3. I subscribe to the *New York Times* and *Newsweek.*
4. Arthur Miller's play *The Crucible* is set during the Salem witch trials.
5. *A Night to Remember* is a movie about the sinking of the *Titanic.*
6. *Gunsmoke* was one of the longest-running shows on television.
7. "It's Too Late," one of Carole King's greatest songs, is recorded on her album *Tapestry.*

*RULE L:*


## QUOTATION MARKS

## GROUP M

*SENTENCES:*
1. "A Modest Proposal" is a famous essay by Jonathan Swift.
2. The *Newsweek* article "Why Johnny Can't Write" created a great deal of controversy in 1975.
3. Before writing his masterpiece, *Paradise Lost,* Milton distinguished himself in such shorter works as "Lycidas," "L'Allegro," and "Il Penseroso."
4. "Where I Lived and What I Lived For" is the first chapter in Thoreau's *Walden.*
5. Of all the stories in Joyce's *Dubliners,* "Snow" and "Araby" are my favorites.
6. The church choir performed such traditional favorites as "Silent Night" and "The First Noel."

Compare these sentences with those in group L. Try to find a general principle which will explain the punctuation in all these sentences.

*RULE M:*

## GROUP N

*SENTENCES:*
1. In the oath of office, the president pledges to "preserve, protect, and defend" the United States Constitution.

2. The student said that he had decided to transfer because "this college doesn't offer enough opportunities for off-campus study."
3. Chris asked, "Will you be able to attend the meeting on Wednesday?"
4. Chris asked us if we would be able to attend the meeting on Wednesday.
5. "The orchestra's scheduled concert has been cancelled," the conductor announced.
6. The conductor announced that the orchestra's scheduled concert had been cancelled.
7. In *The Preface to Shakespeare,* Samuel Johnson describes Shakespeare as "the poet of nature, the poet that holds up to his readers a faithful mirror of manners and of life."
8. In *The Preface to Shakespeare,* Samuel Johnson describes what he sees as Shakespeare's greatest virtue as a poet:

   > Shakespeare is, above all writers, at least above all modern writers, the poet of nature, the poet that holds up to his readers a faithful mirror of manners and of life. His characters are not modified by the customs of particular places, unpractised by the rest of the world; by the peculiarities of studies or professions which can operate but upon small numbers; or by the accidents of transient fashions or temporary opinions: they are the genuine progeny of common humanity, such as the world will always supply, and observation will always find.

   Johnson goes on to discuss other characteristics of Shakespeare's plays.

Make your rule comprehensive enough to explain all the ways in which quotation marks are used—and not used—in these sentences. Be particularly careful to contrast sentences 3 and 4, sentences 5 and 6, and sentences 7 and 8.

*RULE N:*

GROUP O

*SENTENCES:*
1. "In the oath of office," the teacher explained, "the president pledges to 'preserve, protect, and defend' the United States Constitution."
2. "When I asked him why he had decided to transfer," the dean said, "he told me that the college 'doesn't provide enough opportunities for off-campus study.'"
3. Tony said, "Chris distinctly said that the meeting would be 'on Wednesday.'"

4. "Johnson praised Shakespeare by calling him the 'poet of nature,'" the lecturer said.

*RULE O:*

GROUP P

*SENTENCES:*
1. E. M. Forster explains the difference between a "plot" and a "story" in *Aspects of the Novel*.
2. The lawyer explained that contracts are not binding unless there is some "consideration."
3. We were very surprised when the student said she had "proficiencied out of" the writing requirement by taking a test.
4. E. B. White discourages the use of such words as "beauteous" and "discombobulate."
5. The Lamaze instructor explained the differences between "early-active labor," "active labor," and "transition."
6. The senator's answer was a "cop-out."
7. The senator's answer was a cop-out.
8. The senator's answer was evasive.

Compare sentences 6, 7, and 8—which is preferable?

*RULE P:*

## APPLICATION

**A.** Insert all necessary apostrophes, hyphens, capitals, italics, and quotation marks in the following sentences. In the space to the left of each sentence, indicate the rule or rules that apply.

_____ 1. The spoiled child demanded thirty four new toys for christmas.

_____ 2. He wouldnt explain his confusing remark.

_____ 3. Ivy day in the committee room, a short story in james joyces collection dubliners, is in some ways similar to a play.

_____ 4. A well known critic, whose reviews have often appeared in the new york times, spoke to our journalism class on tuesday.

_____ 5. At the press conference, ex president ford announced that he would not seek reelection.

_____ 6. The senator said, the responsibility for the disaster is yours, not ours.

_____ 7. Even before she had graduated from high school, eileen began taking courses at the university of buffalo.

_____ 8. She studied biology, history, and italian.

_____ 9. Even after a three year separation, the dog could still recognize its master.

_____ 10. I told her that my favorite poem is coleridges frost at midnight.

_____ 11. My favorite poem is keats to autumn she replied.

_____ 12. Jim graduated magna cum laude from a fine university in the midwest.

_____ 13. Pete wanted to see the colleges production of the merchant of venice, but doug wanted to stay home and watch threes company on television.

_____ 14. I decided to take sociology 250 because i heard its an excellent course.

_____ 15. Forty one students essays were submitted to the contest sponsored by the universitys newspaper.

_____ 16. what beckoning ghost, along the moonlight shade invites my steps, and points to yonder glade?

—alexander pope, elegy to the memory of an
unfortunate lady

_____ 17. When i asked uncle harvy to advise me, he said, youd better speak to your father, mary explained.

_____ 18. My cousin asked me how many ms there are in roommate.

_____ 19. The mens softball team won its fifth victory on thursday; its been a great spring for them.

_____ 20. Dieters should remember some advice benjamin franklin gives in poor richards almanack: eat to live, not live to eat.

**B.** Insert all necessary apostrophes, hyphens, capitals, and quotation marks in the following paragraphs. The last twenty words in the third paragraph are a direct quotation from an essay by Louie Crew.

i was reminded of many of my most humiliating high school experiences when i read an essay by louie crew titled the physical miseducation of a former fat boy. like crew, i wasnt at all athletic when i was younger, and neither my teachers nor the other students could understand how painful every gym class was for me. i can still remember how terrified i felt every time the gym teacher yelled, all right, line up and choose sides. trying to keep from blushing, i would stare down at my sneakers, pretending that i didnt care whether i was chosen or not. usually, i was one of the last to be chosen, not only because i couldnt play most games well but also because i wasnt a member of what we called the group, a clique of popular and athletic girls. i admired these girls and wished my athletic skills were equal to theirs, but my attempts to improve always failed. with every gym class, i lost a little more self confidence and self respect.

i needed help and encouragement from my gym teachers but didnt receive any. i think its a teachers job to help all the students, not just the most talented ones. i could never seem to get a gym teachers attention or sympathy, however. i remember one teacher who began every semester with a ten minute lecture on good sportsmanship, but even she ignored and sometimes insulted the physically inept students and concentrated on helping the most promising athletes.

crews essay criticizes physical education teachers for neglecting many of their students needs. crews own gym teachers never took a real interest in him, never showed him how participating in sports could help him to enjoy himself and lose weight. when crew was thirty two, he started jogging and in six months lost 105 pounds. its ironic that it wasnt until long after crew stopped taking physical education courses that he discovered the value of exercise. his teachers, crew says, never tempted me into the personal discoveries that i had to wait more than a decade to make for myself.

# GUIDE FOR CORRECTING ESSAYS: A CHECKLIST OF GRAMMAR AND MECHANICS

Your professor may use the numbers on this checklist to identify grammatical and mechanical errors in your essay. If your professor asks you to do a *correction sheet,* number the grammatical and mechanical errors in your paper and then, on a separate sheet of paper, write a two-part correction for each error:

1. *Explain* why the word, phrase, or sentence you have numbered is incorrect. Consult this checklist for help. Make sure that your explanations are clear, correct, and complete (for example, don't just say, "I need a comma here"; explain *why* you need the comma).
2. *Correct* the word, phrase, or sentence.

### Sample Paragraph and Correction Sheet

During my sophomore year of high school, I decided to visit my <u>sister a</u>

<u>freshman</u> at a college in New York. <u>Arriving at the campus, envy over-</u>

came me as I learned about her new life. <u>While I had been taking over</u>

<u>her dishwashing duties at home.</u> She had been taking exciting courses

and becoming close with new friends. By the end of my stay, I knew that

I <u>to</u> wanted to go to college.

1. *Explanation:* This is a parenthetical phrase, so I should set it off with a comma.
   *Correction:* my sister, a freshman . . .

2. *Explanation:* This is a dangling modifier; it sounds as though envy arrived at the college.
   *Correction:* Arriving at the campus, I was overcome by envy . . .

3. *Explanation:* This is a subordinate clause, not a sentence; *while* (a subordinate conjunction) makes it a fragment.
   *Correction:* While I had been taking over her dishwashing duties at home, she had been taking exciting courses and becoming close with new friends.

4. *Explanation:* I confused *to* and *too,* which sound the same but have different meanings and spellings.
   *Correction:* I too wanted to go to college.

## SENTENCE STRUCTURE

**1.** FRAGMENT (INCOMPLETE SENTENCE)

**1a.** *A complete sentence must have both a subject and a predicate.*
    *Examples:* The book on the table. (fragment—no predicate)
            Frank accepted the prize. *And then made a short speech thanking the judges.* (fragment—no subject)
In an imperative sentence, the subject (*you*) is implied:
Come over here this minute!

**1b.** *A complete sentence must have a finite verb.*
    *Examples:* Applicants *hoping* to be admitted to the college.
            Ed *gone* to Florida for the winter.
            The judges *to choose* the winners.
Some verb forms can be used without auxiliary (helping) verbs: "I go" (present); "I went" (past). Other verb forms, however, can never be used alone in a sentence: the present participle (the *-ing* form), the past participle, and the infinitive (the *to*— form). Notice that the sample sentences do not tell us *when* the action described happened because an incomplete verb has no tense. Thus, depending on the auxiliary you add, "Applicants hoping" can become "Applicants are hoping," "Applicants were hoping," "Applicants will be hoping," and so on.

**1c.** *A subordinate clause is not a complete sentence.*
    *Example:* Although many scholars attribute this play to Shakespeare.
A subordinate conjunction at the beginning of a clause makes the

clause dependent (or subordinate). The subordinate conjunction raises an expectation in the reader's mind: it tells the reader that this will be a two-clause sentence. You can correct fragments of this type in two ways:

1. Remove the subordinate conjunction. (Many scholars attribute this play to Shakespeare.)
2. Add an independent clause. (Although many scholars attribute this play to Shakespeare, we have no solid information about its authorship.)

**1d.**  *A fragment can be caused by a relative pronoun between the subject and the simple predicate* (verb).
   *Example:* The journalist who won the Pulitzer Prize.
In the example above, placing *who* between the subject (journalist) and the verb (*won*) raises a question in the reader's mind: what did the journalist who won the Pulitzer Prize *do*? The sentence does not contain an independent clause. You can correct fragments of this type in two ways:

1. Remove the relative pronoun. (The journalist won the Pulitzer Prize.)
2. Add a new verb. (The journalist who won the Pulitzer Prize *admitted* the article was a fraud.)

**1e.**  *Fragments can be caused by the incorrect use of a semicolon.*
   *Examples: While his roommate went to buy the lumber;* Andy worked on the plans for the platform.
   The teacher took the slingshot away from the child; *and put it in the desk drawer.*
A semicolon is used to separate two independent clauses. When we use a semicolon to separate an independent clause from any other sort of sentence element—for example, a dependent clause or a phrase—we create a fragment. Correct such fragments by removing the semicolon and, when necessary, replacing it with the correct punctuation mark.

**2.**  RUN-ON SENTENCE: *A run-on sentence is created when two independent clauses are joined without any punctuation mark or conjunction to separate them.*
   *Example:* Sex education should be studied in high school teachers can help students to understand their problems and emotions.
Since a sentence expresses a complete thought, it should be presented to the reader as an independent unit. If two sentences are run together, confusion can result. In the sample sentence, for example, the two independent clauses are not separated in any way, so the reader does not know when one idea ends and the next one begins. Not knowing when to stop, the reader might at first think you mean that "Sex education should be studied in high school teachers"—a provocative but confusing statement.
   You can use several different methods to correct a run-on sentence:
   *Sample Sentence:* The violinist was eager to impress the judges she performed her most difficult piece.

1. Make two sentences. (The violinist was eager to impress the judges. She performed her most difficult piece.)
2. Separate the clauses with a semicolon. (The violinist was eager to impress the judges; she performed her most difficult piece.)
3. Use a coordinate conjunction and a comma to separate the clauses. (The violinist was eager to impress the judges, so she played her most difficult piece.)
4. Use a subordinate conjunction to separate the clauses (with or without a comma, depending on the placement of the conjunction). (The violinist performed her most difficult piece because she was eager to impress the judges. Because she was eager to impress the judges, the violinist performed her most difficult piece.)
5. Reduce one of the clauses to a phrase. (Eager to impress the judges, the violinist performed her most difficult piece.)

Think carefully about which method will make your corrected sentence most graceful and effective.

**3.** COMMA SPLICE: *A comma splice is created when two independent clauses are separated by only a comma.*

> *Example:* Sex education should be studied in high school, teachers can help students to understand their problems and emotions.

A comma splice is similar to a run-on sentence except that in a comma splice, the writer uses a comma to separate the two independent clauses. A comma is not equal to this task, however. A comma indicates a slight pause within a clause—"The flag was red, white, and blue." It cannot, by itself, separate two independent clauses.

Correct a comma splice by using any of the methods above. Remember that you *cannot* correct a comma splice by removing the comma —you will simply be creating a run-on sentence.

Some professors will accept a comma splice as correct if both clauses are very short: "Heads I win, tails you lose."

## AGREEMENT AND REFERENCE

**4.** SUBJECT/PREDICATE AGREEMENT
**4a.** *The simple predicate (verb) must agree with the true subject of the sentence.*

> *Examples:* The books in that collection were donated by a wealthy alumnus.
>
> There is a simple explanation for the mystery.
>
> Professor Ashe, together with the other members of the department, plans to vote against the motion.

A prepositional phrase between a subject and a verb does not affect agreement. Make sure that the verb agrees with the subject, not with the object of the preposition. In the first sample sentence, *were* agrees with *books* (subject), not with *collection* (object of the preposition *in*). Remember that the object of a preposition cannot be the subject of a sentence.

In some sentences, the subject follows the verb. In the second sample sentence, *is* agrees with *explanation* (subject), not with *there* (expletive—can't be the subject of a sentence).

When a subject is followed by a phrase such as *as well as, together with,* or *in addition to,* the phrase does not affect agreement. In the third sample sentence, the subject is *Professor Ashe,* not *members,* so the verb is singular—*plans.*

**4b.** *Two or more subjects joined by* and *require a plural verb.*

 *Example: The subject and the verb* in this sentence *agree.*

Two or more subjects joined by *and* are considered a *compound subject* and require a plural verb unless both parts of the subject name the same person or thing:

 *Supply and demand is* a basic principle in economics.

 *A distinguished scientist and successful novelist was* given an honorary degree.

**4c.** *When two or more subjects are joined by* or *or* nor, *the verb agrees with the subject nearer to it.*

 *Examples: Neither the father nor the children were* aware of the accident.

    *Neither the children nor the father was* aware of the accident.

If the second sample sentence sounds hideous to you, just make sure that you always put the plural subject nearer to the verb in such sentences.

**4d.** *Singular pronouns require singular verbs.*

 *Example: Everyone* in the family *has* attended the same college.

Pronouns ending in *-one, -body,* and *-thing* are singular. Pronouns such as *most, all, any, more, none,* or *some* may take either a singular or a plural verb, depending on the context:

 *Most* of the paper *was* written by Thursday. (*most* refers to a part of something)

 *Most* of the tickets *were* sold. (*most* refers to many tickets)

**4e.** *A collective noun takes a singular verb when the group is acting as a unit and a plural verb when the members of the group are acting as individuals.*

 *Examples: The faculty has* decided to change to the semester system.

    The *faculty disagree* about whether the college should have a language requirement.

In the first sentence, the faculty is considered as a unit; in the second sentence, the members of the faculty are considered as individuals.

**4f.** *Titles of books, plays, newspapers, and so on take singular verbs even if the titles are plural in form.*

 *Example: Two Gentlemen of Verona was* performed at the college theater last spring.

**4g.** *Nouns that end in -s but are singular in meaning take singular verbs.*
*Example: Physics is* a difficult but fascinating subject for me.

## 5. PRONOUN/ANTECEDENT AGREEMENT

**5a.** *Two or more antecedents joined by* and *require a plural pronoun.*
*Example: Mary and Wendy* declared *their* majors.

**5b.** *When two or more antecedents are joined by* or *or* nor, *the pronoun agrees with the antecedent nearer to it.*
*Examples: Neither the actress nor the actors* could remember *their* lines.
*Neither the actors nor the actress* could remember *her* lines.
If the second sentence sounds hideous to you, be sure **you** always put the plural antecedent nearer to the pronoun in such sentences.

**5c.** *Singular antecedents such as* person, one, anyone, anybody, everyone, nobody, *and* someone *require singular pronouns.*
*Examples· Everyone* must register before *he or she* can vote.
*Everyone* must register before *he* can vote.
*Everyone* must register before *she* can vote.
In conversation, we often use a plural pronoun after antecedents such as the ("Everyone must register before *they* can vote"). In writing, however, the use of a singular pronoun is still widely preferred. Traditionally, *he* has been used in such situations, with the assumption that *he* is understood to include both men and women, but some readers now consider this use of *he* offensive. Some people have suggested using *he or she* or *he/she* in such sentences, but this construction can be awkward ("Everyone has to make up his or her mind and decide whether he or she is willing to commit himself or herself to this cause"). Other people have suggested alternating between *he* and *she,* but this solution can be confusing ("*Nobody* remembered to bring *his* money, but *everybody* remembered to bring *her* ticket"). Perhaps the best solutions are to cast sentences in the plural or to avoid using pronouns in **such** sentences:
*All* must register before *they* can vote.
Everyone must register before voting.

**5d.** *A collective noun takes a singular pronoun when the group is acting as a unit and a plural pronoun when the members of the group are acting as individuals.*
*Examples:* The *team* discussed *its* strategy for the next game.
The *team* discussed *their* plans for postseason vacations.

## 6. PRONOUN REFERENCE

**6a.** *A pronoun should have only one possible antecedent.*
*Example:* When Anne talked to Elaine, she became angry.
(Did Anne or Elaine become angry?)

In some sentences where there are two possible antecedents for a pronoun, you may simply have to repeat the antecedent: "When Anne talked to Elaine, Anne became angry." Sometimes you can avoid such repetition by recasting the sentence: "Anne became angry when she talked to Elaine."

**6b.** *A pronoun should not be too far away from the antecedent to which it refers.*

>   *Example:* The catalogue contains useful facts about over 1,000 colleges and universities, describing their programs of study, faculties, special services, and admissions requirements. You can find *it* at the public library.

Even though *catalogue* is the only antecedent to which *it* can refer, the pronoun is so far away from the antecedent that the reader may become confused and have to reread the sentence. Repeat the antecedent: "You can find *the catalogue* at the public library."

**6c.** *Using* this, that, *or* which *to refer to the general idea of a preceding clause or sentence can be confusing.*

>   *Example:* Cynthia received D's on her first three papers and a B on her fourth paper. *This* delighted her parents.

Generally, a pronoun should refer to a single word, not to the general idea of a clause or sentence. Broad reference with *this, that,* or *which* is acceptable if your meaning is absolutely clear ("She graduated at the top of her class, and *this* delighted her parents"). If there is any chance that your reader might become confused, however, revise the sentence: "Cynthia received D's on her first three papers and a B on her fourth paper. *This progress* delighted her parents."

**6d.** *Pronouns should refer to antecedents that are actually stated, not merely implied.*

>   *Example:* Alison decided to become a psychologist after majoring in *it* in college.

Although the readers can probably figure out that *it* means *psychology,* don't put them to this trouble. State the antecedent: "Alison decided to become a psychologist after majoring in psychology in college."

**6e.** *Reference to an antecedent in the possessive case is awkward.*

>   *Example:* In Trollope's *Autobiography, he* discusses his literary career.

It is clearer and more graceful to write, "In his *Autobiography,* Trollope discusses his literary career."

# POINT OF VIEW

**7.** TENSE: *Verb tenses should be consistent unless there is a reason for a shift.*

>   *Example:* He *packs* his suitcase and *rushed* out the door.

The tense shifts from present to past for no reason. Change the tense of either *packs* or *rushed* to make the sentence consistent.

> *Example:* Last year I *worked* at a department store, but now I *work* in an office.

Here, there is a reason for the change from past to present tense since the author is referring to two different times.

8. VOICE: *Voice (active or passive) should be consistent throughout a sentence.*

> *Example:* The judicial board listened to statements from all the students involved, and then a verdict was reached.

The sample sentence shifts from the active voice to the passive voice for no reason. Rewrite the sentence so that it is entirely in the active or entirely in the passive:

> *Active:* The judicial board listened to statements from all the students involved and then reached a verdict.

> *Passive:* Statements from all the students involved were listened to, and then a verdict was reached.

Although the passive voice is sometimes useful and appropriate, the active voice is often more informative and concise. Notice, for example, that the passive version of the sentence doesn't tell us who listened to the statements or reached a verdict. If we added this information and still kept to the passive voice, the sentence would become wordy: "Statements from all the students involved were listened to by the judicial board, and then a verdict was reached by the judicial board."

9. PERSON: *Person should be consistent throughout a sentence.*

> *Example:* If *one* wants to understand behaviorism, *you* should start by reading B. F. Skinner.

The sample sentence shifts unnecessarily from the third person (*one*) to the second person (*you*). The sentence could be revised in two ways:

> If *one* wants to understand behaviorism, *one* should start by reading B. F. Skinner.

> If *you* want to understand behaviorism, *you* should start by reading B. F. Skinner.

Using *one* is generally considered more formal than using *you*. In most papers you write for your composition class, either *one* or *you* should be acceptable—just be consistent.

## SENTENCE LOGIC

10. MISPLACED MODIFIER: *Modifying words, phrases, and clauses should be placed next to the words they modify.*

> *Examples:* I felt confident about the final examination because I had almost read all the books required for the course.

Since *almost* is next to *read,* it looks as though the writer had been on the verge of reading all these books but had not actually read any of them. Place *almost* closer to the word it actually should modify—"I had read almost all the books."

*Example:* David Hardy was accused of setting off a fire extinguisher
during the judicial board hearing.
Hardy must have been very bold if he set off a fire extinguisher during the
hearing. Move the modifying phrase closer to the word it actually should
modify: "During the judicial board hearing, David Hardy was accused of
setting off a fire extinguisher."
*Example:* He saw a stereo in the store that was very expensive.
Presumably, the stereo was expensive, not the store. Again, bring the
modifier and the word it modifies closer together: "In the store, he saw a
stereo that was very expensive.")

11. "SQUINTING" MODIFIER: *Modifiers should be placed so that there is no
doubt about which word they modify.*
    *Example:* The woman who had been speaking angrily left the room.
In this sentence, *angrily* is placed between *speaking* and *left*, so we can't
be sure about which word it is supposed to modify. Eliminate the ambiguity by moving the modifier:
The woman who had been angrily speaking left the room.
The woman who had been speaking left the room angrily.

12. DANGLING MODIFIER: *The word to which a modifier refers should be
clearly stated, not merely implied.*
    *Example:* Marching down the aisle, our diplomas were grasped firmly
in our hands.
Dangling modifiers most often occur in sentences that open with verbal
phrases (such as *marching down the aisle*). When you open with such a
phrase, make sure that the main clause of your sentence begins by identifying the person or thing that performed the action described in the verbal
phrase ("Marching down the aisle, *we* grasped our diplomas firmly in our
hands")—otherwise, the reader will picture a Walt Disney movie in
which diplomas march down an aisle. Simply moving the verbal phrase to
the end of the sentence will not solve the problem. ("Our diplomas were
grasped firmly in our hands marching down the aisle"—now the hands
are marching.)

13. INCOMPLETE AND MIXED CONSTRUCTIONS
    13a. *Comparisons should be stated clearly and logically.*
    *Examples:* The admission's office was disappointed because this
year's freshman class was smaller.
Beverly Sills is more famous than any opera singer.
A reader might well respond to the first sample question by asking,
"smaller than what?" Make the sentence clearer by completing the
comparison—"smaller than last year's class," "smaller than it had
hoped."
The second sentence says that Beverly Sills is more famous
"than any opera singer." But Beverly Sills *is* an opera singer—is
she more famous than herself? Clarify the comparison: "Beverly
Sills is more famous than any *other* opera singer."

**13b.** MIXED CONSTRUCTION: *A sentence's construction should be consistent throughout.*

> *Example:* In the short introductory chapter explains the authors' purpose.

The sample sentence "mixes up" two sentence patterns or constructions. The sentence begins with a prepositional phrase that should, logically, be followed by an independent clause. But the author has apparently lost track of the way the sentence began and has made the object of the preposition (*chapter*) do double duty as the subject of the clause. As a result, the prepositional phrase and the clause are tangled together. We can correct the sentence either by adding a subject for the clause or by dropping the preposition:

> In the short introductory chapter, the authors explain their purpose.

> The short introductory chapter explains the authors' purpose.

**14.** ILLOGICAL PREDICATES: *Predicates must combine logically with subjects and complements.*

> *Examples:* A comma splice *is* when you separate two independent clauses with only a comma.

> These facts finally *conclude* that Richard III was not guilty.

The verbs in the two sample sentences are illogical. A comma splice is not a time ("a comma splice is when . . ."); facts cannot draw a conclusion ("these facts finally conclude . . ."). Be sure the verbs you choose make sense in the contexts of your sentences:

> A comma splice *results* when you separate two independent clauses with only a comma.

> These facts finally *prove* that Richard III was not guilty.

**15.** PARALLELISM: *Parallel ideas should be expressed in parallel form.*

> *Examples:* His duties are keeping the discussion relevant and to make sure everyone participates.

> The paper was disorganized, redundant, and the logic was weak.

> Before making her decision, Patty inspected a Maverick, Datsun, and a Toyota.

The sample sentences contain parallel ideas or items: two duties, three weaknesses, three cars. These parallel elements should be expressed in parallel form:

> His duties are *to keep* the discussion relevant and *to make* sure everyone participates. (two infinitives; could also use two gerunds—*keeping* and *making*.)

> The paper was disorganized, redundant, and illogical. (three adjectives)

> Before making her decision, Patty inspected a Maverick, a Datsun, and a Toyota. (repeat the article before each item)

# PUNCTUATION

**16.  COMMAS**

**16a.**  *A comma precedes a coordinate conjunction joining two indepen-*
*dent clauses. (or: A comma precedes the conjunction in a compound*
*sentence.)*

> *Examples:* Jim decided to buy a vinyl wallet, *for* the leather ones
> were too expensive.
>
> The lawyer accused the witnesses of lying, *and* then
> she returned to her seat.

Notice that the comma is placed *before* the conjunction, not after it:

| independent clause | , | coordinate conjunction | independent clause |
|---|---|---|---|

Also, notice that a comma is generally *not* used when a coordinate
conjunction joins other kinds of sentence elements—two predicates
or two complements, for example:

> The lawyer accused the witnesses of lying and then returned to
> her seat.
>
> He was proud of his record in college and determined to get into
> a good graduate school.

*Exception:* You do not need a comma before a coordinating conjunction joining two very short independent clauses.

> *Example:* Laura stayed but Joan left.

A comma would not be incorrect in such a sentence, but it might
make your style choppy.

**16b.**  *When a subordinate clause is joined to an independent clause, a*
*comma should separate the clauses if the subordinate clause comes*
*first.*

> *Examples:* Although he is a famous poet, he is often lonely and
> unhappy.
>
> He is often lonely and unhappy although he is a fa-
> mous poet.

It might also help to think of the rule this way: in a complex sentence, you need *something* to separate the two clauses, to show the
reader where the first one ends and the second begins. If the subordinate conjunction comes between the two clauses, that makes the
separation; if there is no subordinate conjunction separating the
clauses, you need a comma to make the separation:

| independent clause | subordinate conjunction | subordinate clause |
|---|---|---|

| subordinate conjunction | subordinate clause | , | independent clause |
|---|---|---|---|

*Exception:* Use a comma before a subordinate conjunction in a complex sentence if the clauses are very long.

> *Example:* We must all look for ways to limit our expenses and
> increase our income, because otherwise we will
> never be able to overcome the severe financial prob-
> lems facing the family.

**16c.** *A comma is used to set off introductory phrases and transitional words.*

> *Examples:* Walking past the house, Joe could see several lights on inside.
>
> Nevertheless, you will have to complete the assignment.

As in 16a and 16b, use a comma to show the beginning of a clause. Even when a sentence has only one clause, we should use a comma to show the reader where the introductory material ends and the clause begins.

*Exception:* You don't need a comma after a very short introductory prepositional phrase.

> *Example:* At night we could see fireflies in the field.

You will have to use your judgment in applying this rule: when does a prepositional phrase become long enough to require a comma? Don't interrupt your reader unnecessarily, but use a comma whenever it will help to make your meaning clear.

**16d.** *Commas are used to set off words that add information but are not crucial to the meaning of the sentence.* (or: *Commas are used to set off* parenthetical *or* nonrestrictive elements.)

> *Examples:* Philander Chase, who founded Kenyon College, was a bishop.
>
> The man who founded Kenyon College was a bishop.

Thus, in the first sentence, the clause "who founded Kenyon College" is set off by commas: it adds information but is not absolutely crucial to the meaning of the sentence. The sentence would have essentially the same meaning if the "who" clause were omitted: "Philander Chase was a bishop." In the second sentence, however, the "who" clause *is* absolutely essential. If it were left out, the sentence's meaning would change: "The man was a bishop." The reader now has no idea who "the man" was—the sentence has changed its meaning.

**16e.** *Commas are used to separate three or more items in a series.*

> *Examples:* He studied French and geology.
>
> He studied French, geology, and history.

Some writers consider the comma immediately before the coordinate conjunction optional, but this comma can sometimes prevent confusion:

> *line on a college application form:* "State your name, age, address, sex, and housing preferences."

If the final comma were omitted, the applicant might think the college is unusually cooperative:

> "State your name, age, address, sex and housing preferences."

Since this final comma is sometimes necessary to prevent confusion, it's best to use it all the time for the sake of consistency.

*Exception:* If there is a coordinate conjunction after each item in the series, commas are not necessary.

> *Example:* Adam and Sarah and John came to class.

**16f.** *Commas separate adjectives in a series* (coordinate adjectives).
  *Examples:* Wilma wrote a clear, concise letter.
  Wilma wrote a concise business letter.
Place commas between adjectives that equally and independently modify the same noun. In the first sample sentence, both *clear* and *concise* modify *letter;* they should therefore be separated by a comma. In the second sentence, however, *concise* modifies *business letter: concise* and *business* therefore should not be separated by a comma.

You can use two simple tests to see whether or not you need a comma:

  1. *Can the order of the adjectives be reversed? If so, use a comma.*
      "clear, concise letter"; "concise, clear letter"—*yes:* use a comma
      "concise business letter"; "business concise letter"—*no:* don't use a comma
  2. *Can you insert* and *between the adjectives? If so, use a comma.*
      "clear, concise letter"; "clear and concise letter"—*yes:* use a comma
      "concise business letter"; "concise and business letter"—*no:* do not use a comma

**16g.** *Commas are used to set off items in dates, addresses, and titles.*
  *Examples:* She was born on December 4, 1947, in a town in Michigan.
  My friend lives at 52 Putnam Road, Reading, Massachusetts 01867.
  Elizabeth Johnson, M.D., performed the delicate surgery.

*Note:*
  1. If a date is used in the middle of the sentence, use a comma after the year.
  2. Do not use a comma between the name of the state and the zip code.
  3. Use commas when a title follows a name but not when it precedes a name: Elizabeth Johnson, M.D.; Dr. Elizabeth Johnson

### *Five General Principles*
You may find it easier to remember these rules if you keep five general principles in mind:
  1. As in 16a and 16b, commas are often used to help separate *clauses.*
  2. As in 16b and 16c, commas are often used to separate *introductory material* from an independent clause.
  3. As in 16d, commas are often used to set off *parenthetical material.*

4. As in 16e, 16f, and 16g, commas are often used to separate *items in a series,* whether these items are nouns, adjectives, phrases, or parts of a date, address, or title.

5. Exceptions to rules about commas often involve *length.*

**17. SEMICOLONS**

**17a.** *Semicolons are used to separate items in a series if the items themselves contain commas.*

> *Example:* The representatives were Elizabeth Sheriden, the dean of the faculty; Hal Brooks, the president of the alumni association; and Lisa Shea, president of the student government.

The semicolons in the sample sentence are absolutely necessary: if commas had been used to separate the items in the series, the reader might think that there are five people on the committee, not three. Some writers use semicolons for added clarity whenever the items in a series are very long.

**17b.** *Semicolons are used to separate independent clauses not connected by a coordinate conjunction.*

> *Examples:* A thesis statement indicates the purpose and scope of a paper; a topic sentence indicates the purpose and scope of a paragraph.
>
> Medicine has always fascinated me; therefore, I have decided to become a doctor.

Notice that a semicolon is used to separate two independent clauses joined by a conjunctive adverb such as *therefore.* Some writers also use semicolons to separate unusually long independent clauses that are connected by a coordinate conjunction. This is a matter for your judgment. You should *never,* however, use a semicolon after a clause beginning with a subordinate conjunction, no matter how long the clauses are (see 1e and 16b).

**18.** COLONS: *Colons are used after independent clauses followed by material that explains or clarifies: a list, another independent clause, or a single word.*

> *Examples:* In my freshman seminar, we studied various kinds of literary works: novels, short stories, plays, and poems.
>
> Marian made an important contribution to our meetings: she always cautioned us when we started to be unrealistic.

A colon makes a sharp break in a sentence, so don't use one unnecessarily:

> I studied such subjects as music, math, and French.

You don't need a colon here, for the phrase *such . . . as* lets the reader know that examples will follow. Also, notice that the part of the sentence *before* the colon must be grammatically complete:

> The topics mentioned included grammar, punctuation, and manuscript form. (no colon after *included*)

**19.** DASHES
  **19a.** *Dashes are used to set off interruptions that the writer wishes to emphasize.*
    *Example:* We studied various kinds of literary works—novels, short stories, plays, and poems—in my freshman seminar.
  Use dashes sparingly. Like colons, dashes make sharp breaks in sentences; if you use dashes often, your style may become choppy. In many sentences, you could use commas or parentheses to set off interruptions. Dashes tend to emphasize the interruption, parentheses tend to deemphasize it, and commas represent a "middle ground." In the sample sentence, either dashes or parentheses would do; commas would be confusing since the material being set off contains commas.

  **19b.** *Dashes are used to set off clarifying material at the end of a sentence.*
    *Example:* The lecturer spoke about the problem he considered most threatening to world peace—hunger.
  A colon would also be correct in this sentence. Some writers prefer to use dashes when the clarifying material is only a word or a short phrase; some think that dashes are more dramatic. It's up to you.

**20.** QUOTATION MARKS
  **20a.** *Short direct quotations are enclosed in quotation marks.*
    *Example:* "I think Dorothy Sayers's novels should be more highly regarded," the professor said.
  Indirect quotations, however, are *not* enclosed in quotation marks: The professor said he thought Dorothy Sayers should be recognized as a serious novelist.

  **20b.** *Longer direct quotations are indented from both right and left margins and are not enclosed in quotation marks.*
    *Example:* In *The Enlightenment and English Literature,* John L. Mahoney explains why many people regard eighteenth-century literature as less exciting than the literature of other periods:

      Because the Enlightenment follows an age dominated by figures like Spenser, Shakespeare, the Metaphysical poets, and Milton, there is the attitude that it represents a major falling-off in literary achievement. High art, some feel, precludes an undue concern with philosophy, critical theory, satire of all kinds, and the literature of the mundane.

    Mahoney goes on to argue that the eighteenth century nevertheless has its own fascinations and rewards for the student of literature. . . .

Generally, any quotation more than four lines long should be indented. Double-space indented quotations unless your professor tells you to single-space.

**20c.** *Quotations within quotations are enclosed in single quotation marks.*

> *Example:* "Mahoney says that many regard the eighteenth century as 'a major falling-off in literary achievement,'" the lecturer said.

**20d.** *Titles of essays, short stories, articles, short poems, songs, chapters, and any parts of a longer work are enclosed in quotation marks.*

> *Example:* "Politics and the English Language" may be George Orwell's greatest essay.

Titles of longer works are italicized (see 26a).

**20e.** *Words used in a special sense may be enclosed in quotation marks.*

> *Example:* The eighteenth century is sometimes referred to as "the Enlightenment," "the Neoclassical period," or "the Augustan Age."

Use quotation marks to set off words used as words, technical words your reader may not know (and which you will then define), and coined words. Some writers enclose slang words in quotation marks, but such a practice seems apologetic and also emphasizes the slang expression. If you use a slang expression, don't call attention to it by enclosing it in quotation marks; better yet, avoid the expression altogether.

> *not:* Listening to that album makes me feel "laid-back."
> *but:* Listening to that album makes me feel laid-back.
> *or:*   Listening to that album makes me feel relaxed.

**20f.** *Various rules govern the use of quotation marks with other punctuation marks.*

**1.** Commas and periods are always placed *inside* quotation marks, whether or not they are part of the quotation:

> *Examples:* Wordsworth said that poetry is "the spontaneous overflow of powerful feelings."
> Although Wordsworth said that poetry is "the spontaneous overflow of powerful feelings," he also stressed the need for thought and judgment.

**2.** Semicolons and colons are always placed *outside* quotation marks.

> *Example:* Wordsworth said that poetry is "the spontaneous overflow of powerful feelings"; however, he also stressed the need for thought and judgment.

**3.** Dashes, question marks, and exclamation points are placed *inside* quotation marks when they are part of the quotation and *outside* when they are not.

> *Examples:* A major section of Wordsworth's "Preface" to *Lyrical Ballads* is an answer to the question "What is a Poet?"
>
> What did Wordsworth mean when he called poetry "the spontaneous overflow of powerful feelings"?

**21.** QUESTION MARKS: *Question marks are used after direct questions.*
> *Examples:* Did you remember to make the reservations?
>> He asked me if I had remembered to make the reservations.
>> Ask her if she remembered to make the reservations.

The first sample sentence ends with a question mark because it actually asks a question. The other sentences imply questions but do not ask them, so they end with periods.

**22.** EXCLAMATION MARKS: *Exclamation marks are used after highly emotional or emphatic statements.*
> *Example:* The house is on fire!

Use exclamation marks sparingly, or your style may seem hysterical or insincere. There are other and better ways to make sentences emphatic.

## WORD PUNCTUATION

**23.** APOSTROPHES
> **23a.** *Apostrophes are used to make nouns and some pronouns possessive.*
>> *Examples:* John's friends gave him a farewell party.
>>> Someone's suitcase was left at the station.

When you want to make a singular noun possessive, add *'s.*
> the trucker's lunch the child's toy

Some writers add only an apostrophe to singular nouns ending in *s* (Keats' poetry), but most prefer adding an *s* as well as an apostrophe:
> Keats's poetry Charles's wedding

Also add *'s* to form possessives of plural nouns that do not end in *s.*
> the children's toys the people's choice

For a plural noun ending in *s,* add an apostrophe *after* the *s.*
> the truckers' strike her parents' vacation

Do *not* add an apostrophe to possessive pronouns; they are already possessive in form.
> The poster read, "Whose college is this—theirs or ours?" Its message was a clear challenge to the Board of Trustees.

Be especially careful not to confuse *its* (possessive pronoun) with *it's* (contraction for *it is*):
> It's a shame the team didn't win its first game.

> **23b.** *Apostrophes are used to show the omission of letters or numbers in contractions and other expressions.*
>> *Example:* The class of '67 couldn't decide whether it should meet at two o'clock or three o'clock.

Notice that in contractions, the apostrophe is placed where the omitted letter would be.

could + not = couldn't (*not* could'nt)

**23c.** *Apostrophes are used to form the plurals of letters, numbers, and words used as words.*

*Examples:* I got three A's last semester.

Multiply by 7's.

His style was monotonous—a series of short clauses strung together by *and*'s.

## 24. HYPHENS

**24a.** *Hyphens are used to form compound numbers, fractions, and words.*

*Examples:* thirty-two

three-fourths

father-in-law

**24b.** *Hyphens are used with the prefixes* self-, ex-, *and* all-, *and with the suffix* -elect.

*Examples:* self-esteem

ex-president

all-American

secretary-elect

**24c.** *Hyphens are used to join two or more words acting together as a single adjective before a noun (compound adjective).*

*Examples:* Act I was followed by a ten-minute intermission.

The professor praised her well-organized essay.

Notice that a compound adjective is *not* hyphenated if it follows the noun:

The professor praised her essay because it was well organized.

## 25. CAPITALS

**25a.** *Proper nouns and their derivatives are capitalized.*

*Examples:* Samuel Taylor Coleridge

Byronic hero

Wednesday

Notice that only the names of *particular* persons, places, or things are capitalized:

*Titles:* Professor Blane; my favorite professor

*Place names:* Pacific Ocean; cross the ocean

Kenmore West High School; a large high school

Kenyon College; an excellent college

*Courses:* Biology 350; a difficult biology course

(English, French, and the names of other languages are always capitalized.)

Capitalize words such as *uncle* and *father* only when they are used as names or parts of names:

My favorite uncle is Uncle Harry.

I'll ask Father what to do; he's a very wise father.

Generally, the names of seasons are not capitalized. Names of directions are capitalized only when they refer to specific places.

I plan to travel this summer.

Turn south when you get to the overpass.

Most of my relatives live in the South.

**25b.** *In titles, the first word and all words except articles and short prepositions (under five letters) are capitalized.*
Examples: *The Mill on the Floss; All About Eve*

**25c.** *In quotations, the first word is capitalized only if it begins a complete sentence.*
Examples: When the reporters asked Senator Ward to comment, he said, "The statement I made yesterday speaks for itself."

Senator Ward said the comment he made yesterday "speaks for itself."

**26.** *ITALICS* (in typed and handwritten papers, show italics by underlining)

**26a.** *The titles of books, plays, long poems, newspapers, magazines, movies, television series, record albums, and all works long enough to be published separately are italicized, as are the names of ships.*
Examples: *Jane Eyre*
*Hamlet*
*Paradise Lost*
*Wooster Daily Record*
*Star Wars*
*The Intrepid*

The titles of shorter works are placed in quotation marks (see 20d).

**26b.** *Foreign words and phrases are italicized unless they have become a part of the English language.*
Examples: We both graduated *cum laude*.
The candidates submitted their dossiers.

**26c.** *Words that need special emphasis are italicized.*
Examples: The registrar announced that he would *not* accept late requests for course changes.

If you use italics for emphasis frequently, your style can seem immature or hysterical. Whenever it is possible, find another way to draw attention to words or phrases you wish to emphasize.

*Tom Jones* was the most *exciting* book I read last year.

Of all the books I read last year, *Tom Jones* was the most exciting.

**26d.** *Words used as words and letters used as letters may be italicized.*
Examples: Don't forget the *c* in *acquire*.

His style was monotonous—a series of short clauses joined by *and*'s.

You may also use quotation marks to set off words used as words (see 20e). Italics sometimes look neater, especially if you are setting off a series of expressions.

Don't overuse qualifiers such as *rather, quite, very,* and *really.*

Don't overuse qualifiers such as "rather," "quite," "very," and "really."

## 27. SPELLING

English spelling is inconsistent, illogical, and generally frustrating. Some people have given up hope about improving their spelling, declaring "I'm just a bad speller, and there's nothing I can do about it." There are, however, at least a few things we can do about our spelling: there are a few rules worth learning, and there are a few techniques we can use to make correct spelling a reasonable goal.

The rules in this section are taken from Mina Shaughnessy's *Errors and Expectations.*

**27a.** *ie* and *ei*

If you have problems with words containing *ie* or *ei,* memorize this rule:

*i* before *e*

except after *c*

or when sounded like *ā*

as in *neighbor* and *weigh*

Some exceptions:

1. Does not apply to nouns that form their plurals by changing *y* to *i* and adding *es*—for example, *democracies.*
2. Does not apply to words in this sentence: "Neither counterfeit financier seized either species of weird leisure."

**27b.** *adding prefixes*

1. When you add a prefix to a root word, do not change the root word itself (for example, *dis*satisfied, *inter*racial, *mis*spelling—note the double letters).
2. Becoming more familiar with some common prefixes and their meanings should help you. For example, you are not as likely to confuse *intermural* and *intramural* if you remember that *inter-* means "between or among" and *intra-* means "within."

**27c.** *adding suffixes—the diacritic ("silent")* e

If you get confused about whether or not to drop a silent *e* at the end of a word when you add a suffix, memorize these rules:

1. Is there an unpronounced *e* at the end of the word?

   Does the suffix begin with a vowel?

   If "yes" to both questions, drop the *e* before adding the suffix. (achievable, advisable, exciting)

   *Exceptions:* If the silent *e* is preceded by a *c* or a *g* and the suffix begins with *a, o,* or *u,* the *e* remains (manageable, peaceable).
2. Is there an unpronounced *e* at the end of the word?

Does the suffix begin with a consonant?
If "yes" to both questions, keep the *e* when adding the suffix
(advisement, achievement, excitement)
*Common exceptions:* truly, argument, judgment

**27d.** *adding suffixes—changing "y" to "i"*
If you have problems adding suffixes to words ending in *y,* learn
this rule:
Does the word end in a consonant plus *y?*
Change the *y* to *i* and add the suffix (cities, worried, loveliest).
*Exception:* Keep the *y* when the suffix is *-ing* or the pos-
sessive *'s* (worrying, city's).

**27e.** *adding suffixes—doubling consonants*
If you get confused about whether or not to double a final consonant
when adding a suffix, remember this rule:
Does the word end in one vowel plus one consonant?
Is the word one syllable, or is its accent on the final syllable?
Does the suffix begin with a vowel?
If "yes" to all three questions, double the final consonant before
adding the suffix (conferred, beginning, hottest).

**27f.** *other ways to improve your spelling*
1. Keep a list of your spelling errors. Every time you misspell a
   word on an essay, add it to your list.
   a. You may prefer to use index cards for your list, rather
      than a sheet of paper, so that you can add new words and
      still keep your list in alphabetical order.
   b. If one particular part of a word gives you trouble, enlarge
      that part when you write the word on your list. For ex-
      ample, if you tend to leave out the *s* in *conscious,* enlarge
      it—*conScious.* Similarly, if you tend to write *a lot* as one
      word, exaggerate the space between the words on your
      list: *a      lot.* These techniques should make it easier for
      you to visualize the words when you have to write them.
   c. Go over your list as often as you can, reviewing the words
      whenever you have five minutes to spare.
2. Use memory tricks to help yourself learn troublesome words.
   Make up nonsense sentences and look for words within words.
   To remember the spelling of *arithmetic,* remember that "*a* r*at*
   *in* t*he* *h*ouse *m*ight *e*at *t*he *i*ce *c*ream." If you tend to misspell
   *their* as *thier,* remember that *the*ir, *the*re, and *the*y're all begin
   with the word *the.*
3. Use the dictionary. Often, the only difference between a "good
   speller" and a "bad speller" is that one has developed the habit
   of using the dictionary and the other has not. Looking up a
   word in the dictionary takes only a few seconds, and it is the
   surest way to improve your spelling. Get a small paperback
   dictionary and put it on your desk *before* you begin to write,
   *every* time you write.

4. Proofread carefully. "Spelling errors" are often simply typing errors. After you have typed your final draft, put your paper aside for a few hours (or a few days, if possible) and then proofread carefully for spelling errors—with your dictionary in hand. For more advice on proofreading, see Chapter 3, page 76.

# MANUSCRIPT FORM

**28.** Your professor may give you some special instructions about preparing your manuscript, but these general guidelines are widely accepted.

**28a.** *Paper:* Most professors prefer 8½ × 11″ bond paper. Erasable paper tends to smudge.

**28b.** *Typing:* Many professors require students to type their papers. Be sure to double-space. If your professor accepts handwritten essays, write neatly in blue or black ink, not pencil. Don't use paper torn out of a spiral notebook.

**28c.** *Margins:* Leave ample margins, at least one inch on all four sides. Some professors prefer wider margins at the top and on the left.

**28d.** *Title:* Do *not* underline your title or put it in quotation marks. Capitalize the first word in your title and all other words except articles and short prepositions (see 25b). Do not place a period at the end of your title even if it is a complete sentence. If your title asks a question, end it with a question mark; you may end a title with an exclamation mark, but think twice or three times before you decide to do so.

Unless your professor requires a separate title page, center your title about two inches from the top of the first page. Place your name, the date, and any other information your professor requires in the upper right-hand corner.

**28e.** *Binding:* Most professors find folders and other binders a nuisance and would prefer that you use a paper clip—not a staple—in the upper left-hand corner of your paper. Do not find clever ways to tear the corners of your paper and weave them together.

**28f.** *Conserving paper:* This is, I admit, an idiosyncrasy. I see no need to surround a short essay with a title page and blank sheets of paper before and after the essay. If all freshman composition students in the country stopped wasting paper in these ways, we could save dozens of trees every year.

# Acknowledgments

# INDEX

## Sentence Structure

1. Sentence fragments (Frag)
   - 1a. missing subject or predicate
   - 1b. incomplete (nonfinite) verb
   - 1c. dependent clause (subordinate conjunction)
   - 1d. dependent clause (relative pronoun)
   - 1e. incorrect use of semicolon
2. Run-on sentence (fused sentence) (R-O; FS)
3. Comma splice (CS)

## Agreement and Reference

4. Subject/verb agreement (S/V Agr)
   - 4a. verb doesn't agree with true subject
   - 4b. subjects joined by *and*
   - 4c. subjects joined by *or/nor*
   - 4d. singular pronoun
   - 4e. collective noun
   - 4f. title
   - 4g. singular noun ending in *s*
5. Pronoun/antecedent agreement (P/A Agr)
   - 5a. antecedents joined by *and*
   - 5b. antecedents joined by *or/nor*
   - 5c. *everyone, a person,* and so on as antecedent
   - 5d. collective noun as antecedent
6. Pronoun reference (Ref)
   - 6a. two possible antecedents
   - 6b. remote antecedent
   - 6c. broad reference
   - 6d. antecedent implied but not stated
   - 6e. antecedent in possessive case

## Shifts in Point of View

7. Unnecessary shift in tense (PV/T)
8. Unnecessary shift in voice (PV)
9. Unnecessary shift in person (PV)

## Sentence Logic

10. Misplaced modifier (MM)
11. "Squinting" modifier (SqM)
12. Dangling modifier (DM)
13. Incomplete and mixed constructions (COMP/MC)
14. Parallelism (//)
15. Illogical predication (Pred)